Authors
& Artists
for Young
Adults

ISSN 1040-5682

Authors & Artists for Young Adults

VOLUME 77

GALE
CENGAGE Learning

Detroit • New York • San Francisco • New Haven, Conn • Waterville, Maine • London

Authors and Artists for Young Adults, Volume 77

Project Editor: Lisa Kumar

Editorial: Dana Ferguson, Amy Elisabeth Fuller, Michelle Kazensky, Jennifer Mossman, Joseph Palmisano, Mary Ruby, Amanda D. Sams, Marie Toft

Rights and Permissions: Vernon English, Barb McNeil, Tracie Richardson, Robyn Young

Imaging and Multimedia: Lezlie Light

Composition and Electronic Capture: Amy Darga

Manufacturing: Cynde Bishop

Product Manager: Meggin Condino

For product information and technology assistance, contact us at **Gale Customer Support, 1-800-877-4253.**
For permission to use material from this text or product, submit all requests online at **www.cengage.com/permissions.**
Further permissions questions can be emailed to **permissionrequest@cengage.com**

While every effort has been made to ensure the reliability of the information presented in this publication, Gale, a part of Cengage Learning, does not guarantee the accuracy of the data contained herein. Gale accepts no payment for listing; and inclusion in the publication of any organization, agency, institution, publication, service, or individual does not imply endorsement of the editors or publisher. Errors brought to the attention of the publisher and verified to the satisfaction of the publisher will be corrected in future editions.

EDITORIAL DATA PRIVACY POLICY. Does this product contain information about you as an individual? If so, for more information about our editorial data privacy policies, please see our Privacy Statement at www.gale.cengage.com.

Gale
27500 Drake Rd.
Farmington Hills, MI, 48331-3535

LIBRARY OF CONGRESS CATALOG CARD NUMBER 89-641100

ISBN-13: 978-0-7876-7796-1
ISBN-10: 0-7876-7796-5

ISSN 1040-5682

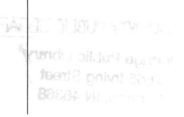

Printed in the United States of America
1 2 3 4 5 6 7 12 11 10 09 08

Contents

Introduction

Authors and Artists for Young Adults is a reference series designed to serve the needs of middle school, junior high, and high school students interested in creative artists. Originally inspired by the need to bridge the gap between Gale's *Something about the Author,* created for children, and *Contemporary Authors,* intended for older students and adults, *Authors and Artists for Young Adults* has been expanded to cover not only an international scope of authors, but also a wide variety of other artists.

Although the emphasis of the series remains on the writer for young adults, we recognize that these readers have diverse interests covering a wide range of reading levels. The series therefore contains not only those creative artists who are of high interest to young adults, including cartoonists, graphic novelists, photographers, music composers, bestselling authors of adult novels, media directors, producers, and performers, but also literary and artistic figures studied in academic curricula, such as influential novelists, playwrights, poets, and painters. The goal of *Authors and Artists for Young Adults* is to present this great diversity of creative artists in a format that is entertaining, informative, and understandable to the young adult reader.

Entry Format

Each volume of *Authors and Artists for Young Adults* will furnish in-depth coverage of approximately twenty-five authors and artists. The typical entry consists of:

—A detailed biographical section that includes date of birth, marriage, children, education, and addresses.

—A comprehensive bibliography or filmography including publishers, producers, and years.

—Adaptations into other media forms.

—A distinctive essay featuring comments on an artist's life, career, artistic intentions, world views, and controversies.

—References for further reading.

—Extensive illustrations, photographs, movie stills, cartoons, book covers, and other relevant visual material.

A cumulative index to featured authors and artists appears in each volume.

Compilation Methods

The editors of *Authors and Artists for Young Adults* make every effort to secure information directly from the authors and artists through personal correspondence and interviews. Sketches on living authors and artists are sent to the biographee for review prior to publication. Any sketches not personally reviewed by biographees or their representatives are marked with an asterisk (*).

Highlights of Forthcoming Volumes

Among the authors and artists planned for future volumes are:

Algernon Blackwood
Ed Brubaker
Countee Cullen
Walter De La Mare
Lynne Ewing
Terence Fisher
Andy Goldsworthy
Lisi Harrison
Kristen Heitzmann
Anna Hyatt Huntington
Buster Keaton
Elmer Kelton
M. Alice Legrow
Peter Lovesey
Jaclyn Moriarty
Paul Park
Dan Piraro
Kashmira Sheth
Charles Simic
Leander Watts

Contact the Editor

We encourage our readers to examine the entire *AAYA* series. Please write and tell us if we can make *AAYA* even more helpful to you. Give your comments and suggestions to the editor:

BY MAIL: The Editor, *Authors and Artists for Young Adults,* 27500 Drake Rd., Farmington Hills, MI 48331-3535.

BY TELEPHONE: (800) 347-GALE

Authors and Artists for Young Adults
Product Advisory Board

The editors of *Authors and Artists for Young Adults* are dedicated to maintaining a high standard of excellence by publishing comprehensive, accurate, and highly readable entries on writers, artists, and filmmakers of interest to middle and high school students. In addition to the quality of the entries, the editors take pride in the graphic design of the series, which is intended to be orderly yet appealing, allowing readers to utilize the pages of *AAYA* easily, enjoyably, and with efficiency. Despite the success of the *AAYA* print series, we are mindful that the vitality of a literary reference product is dependent on its ability to serve its readers over time. As critical attitudes about literature, art, and media constantly evolve, so do the reference needs of students and teachers. To be certain that we continue to keep pace with the expectations of our readers, the editors of *AAYA* listen carefully to their comments regarding the value, utility, and quality of the series. Librarians, who have firsthand knowledge of the needs of library users, are a valuable resource for us. The *Authors and Artists for Young Adults* Product Advisory Board, made up of school, public, and academic librarians, is a forum to promote focused feedback about *AAYA* on a regular basis, as well as to help steer our coverage of new authors and artists. The advisory board includes the following individuals, whom the editors wish to thank for sharing their expertise:

- **Eva M. Davis,** Youth Department Manager, Ann Arbor District Library, Ann Arbor, Michigan

- **Joan B. Eisenberg,** Lower School Librarian, Milton Academy, Milton, Massachusetts

- **Susan Dove Lempke,** Children's Services Supervisor, Niles Public Library District, Niles, Illinois

- **Robyn Lupa,** Head of Children's Services, Jefferson County Public Library, Lakewood, Colorado

- **Caryn Sipos,** Community Librarian, Three Creeks Community Library, Vancouver, Washington

- **Stephen Weiner,** Director, Maynard Public Library, Maynard, Massachusetts

Kingsley Amis

(AP Images.)

■ Personal

Born April 16, 1922, in London, England; died after suffering severe injuries in a fall, October 22, 1995, in London, England; son of William Robert (an office clerk) and Rosa Annie Amis; married Hilary Ann Bardwell, 1948 (divorced, 1965); married Elizabeth Jane Howard (a novelist), 1965 (divorced, 1983); children: (first marriage) Philip Nicol William, Martin Louis, Sally Myfanwy. *Education:* St. John's College, Oxford, B.A. (first class honors in English), 1947, M.A., 1948. *Hobbies and other interests:* Music (jazz, Mozart), thrillers, television, science fiction.

■ Career

University College of Swansea, Swansea, Glamorganshire, Wales, lecturer in English, 1949-61; Cambridge University, Peterhouse, Cambridge, England, fellow, 1961-63; full-time writer, 1963-95. Princeton University, Princeton, NJ, visiting fellow in creative writing, 1958-59; Vanderbilt University, Nashville, TN, visiting professor of English, 1967-68. *Military service:* British Army, Royal Signal Corps, 1942-45; became lieutenant.

■ Member

Authors' Club (London), Bristol Channel Yacht Club, Garrick Club.

■ Awards, Honors

Somerset Maugham Award, 1955, for *Lucky Jim;* Booker-McConnell Prize nomination, Great Britain's Book Trust, and *Yorkshire Post* Book of the Year Award, both 1974, for *Ending Up;* fellowship, St. John's College, Oxford, 1976; Commander of the Order of the British Empire, 1981; fellowship, University College of Swansea, 1985; Booker-McConnell Prize for Fiction, Great Britain's Book Trust, 1986, for *The Old Devils;* Cholmondeley Award, 1990; knighted, 1990.

■ Writings

NOVELS

Lucky Jim, Doubleday (New York, NY), 1954, edited and abridged edition by D.K. Swan, illustrations by William Burnard, Longmans (London, England), 1963, abridged edition with glossary and notes by R.M. Oldnall, Macmillan (New York, NY), 1967.

That Uncertain Feeling, Gollancz (London, England), 1955, Harcourt (New York, NY), 1956.

I Like It Here, Harcourt (New York, NY), 1958.

Take a Girl Like You, Gollancz (London, England), 1960, Harcourt (New York, NY), 1961.

One Fat Englishman, Gollancz (London, England), 1963, Harcourt (New York, NY), 1964.

(With Robert Conquest) *The Egyptologists,* J. Cape (London, England), 1965, Random House (New York, NY), 1966.

The Anti-Death League, Harcourt (New York, NY), 1966, Gollancz (London, England), 1978.

(Under pseudonym Robert Markham) *Colonel Sun: A James Bond Adventure,* Harper (New York, NY), 1968.

I Want It Now, J. Cape (London, England), 1968, collected edition, 1976, Harcourt (New York, NY), 1969.

The Green Man, J. Cape (London, England), 1969, Harcourt (New York, NY), 1970.

Girl, 20, J. Cape (London, England), 1971, Harcourt (New York, NY), 1972.

The Riverside Villas Murder, Harcourt (New York, NY), 1973.

Ending Up, Harcourt (New York, NY), 1974.

The Alteration, J. Cape (London, England), 1976, Viking (New York, NY), 1977.

Jake's Thing (also see below), Hutchinson (London, England), 1978, Viking (New York, NY), 1979.

Russian Hide-and-Seek: A Melodrama, Hutchinson (London, England), 1980, Penguin (New York, NY), 1981.

Stanley and the Women (also see below), Hutchinson (London, England), 1984, Summit Books (New York, NY), 1985.

The Old Devils (also see below), Hutchinson (London, England), 1986, Summit Books (New York, NY), 1987.

The Crime of the Century, Dent (New York, NY), 1987.

A Kingsley Amis Omnibus (includes *Jake's Thing, Stanley and the Women,* and *The Old Devils*), Hutchinson (London, England), 1987.

Difficulties with Girls, Summit Books (New York, NY), 1988.

The Folks That Live on the Hill, Hutchinson (London, England), 1990.

The Russian Girl, Viking (New York, NY), 1994.

You Can't Do Both, limited edition, Hutchinson (London, England), 1994.

The Biographer's Moustache, Flamingo (London, England), 1995.

POETRY

Bright November, Fortune Press (London, England), 1947.

A Frame of Mind: Eighteen Poems, School of Art, Reading University, 1953.

Poems, Oxford University Poetry Society (Oxford, England), 1954.

Kingsley Amis, Fantasy Press (Oxford, England), 1954.

A Case of Samples: Poems, 1946-1956, Gollancz (London, England), 1956, Harcourt (New York, NY), 1957.

(With Dom Moraes and Peter Porter) *Penguin Modern Poets 2,* Penguin (New York, NY), 1962.

The Evans Country, Fantasy Press (Oxford, England), 1962.

A Look Round the Estate: Poems, 1957-1967, J. Cape (London, England), 1967, Harcourt (New York, NY), 1968.

Collected Poems: 1944-1979, Hutchinson (London, England), 1979, Viking (New York, NY), 1980.

OTHER

Socialism and the Intellectuals, Fabian Society (London, England), 1957.

New Maps of Hell: A Survey of Science Fiction, Harcourt (New York, NY), 1960.

My Enemy's Enemy (short stories; also see below), Gollancz (London, England), 1962, Harcourt (New York, NY), 1963.

Reading His Own Poems (recording), Listen, 1962.

(With Thomas Blackburn) *Poems* (recording), Jupiter (London, England), 1962.

(Under pseudonym William Tanner) *The Book of Bond; or, Every Man His Own 007,* Viking (New York, NY), 1965.

The James Bond Dossier, New American Library (New York, NY), 1965.

Lucky Jim's Politics, Conservative Political Centre (London, England), 1968.

What Became of Jane Austen? and Other Questions (essays), J. Cape (London, England), 1970, Harcourt (New York, NY), 1971, published as *What Became of Jane Austen and Other Essays,* Penguin (New York, NY), 1981.

Dear Illusion (short stories; also see below), Covent Garden Press (London, England), 1972.

On Drink (also see below), illustrations by Nicolas Bentley, J. Cape (London, England), 1972, Harcourt (New York, NY), 1973.

First Aid for ABA Conventioneers (excerpt from *On Drink*), Harcourt (New York, NY), 1973.

Rudyard Kipling and His World, Scribner (New York, NY), 1975.

Interesting Things, edited by Michael Swan, Cambridge University Press (New York, NY), 1977.

Harold's Years: Impressions of the Harold Wilson Era, Charles River Books (Boston, MA), 1977.

The Darkwater Hall Mystery (also see below), illustrations by Elspeth Sojka, Tragara Press (Edinburgh, Scotland), 1978.

(Editor) *The New Oxford Book of English Light Verse,* Oxford University Press (New York, NY), 1978.

An Arts Policy?, Centre for Policy Studies, 1979.

(Editor) *The Faber Popular Reciter,* Faber & Faber (London, England), 1979.

Collected Short Stories (includes "My Enemy's Enemy," "Dear Illusion," and "The Darkwater Hall Mystery"), Hutchinson (London, England), 1980, Penguin (New York, NY), 1983, revised edition, 1987.

Every Day Drinking, illustrations by Merrily Harper, Hutchinson (London, England), 1983.

How's Your Glass? A Quizzical Look at Drinks and Drinking, Weidenfeld & Nicolson (London, England), 1984, with cartoons by Michael Heath, Arrow, 1986.

The Amis Anthology, Century Hutchinson (London, England), 1988.

The Amis Collection: Selected Non-Fiction, 1954-1990, Hutchinson (London, England), 1990.

The Pleasure of Poetry, Cassell (London, England), 1990.

Kingsley Amis, in Life and Letters, edited by Dale Salwak, Macmillan (Basingstoke, Hants), 1990, St. Martin's (New York, NY), 1991.

Memoirs, Summit Books (New York, NY), 1991.

We Are All Guilty (for children), Viking Children's Books (New York, NY), 1992.

Mr. Barrett's Secret and Other Stories, Hutchinson (London, England), 1993.

The Biographer's Mustache, HarperCollins (New York, NY), 1995.

The King's English: A Guide to Modern Usage, St. Martin's Press (New York, NY), 1998.

The Letters of Kinsley Amis, edited by Zachary Leader, HarperCollins (New York, NY), 2000.

Also author of a science fiction radio play, *Something Strange,* and of television plays *A Question about Hell,* 1964, *The Importance of Being Harry,* 1971, *Dr. Watson and the Darkwater Hall Mystery,* 1974, and *See What You've Done,* 1974. Also editor of *Spectrum: A Science Fiction Anthology,* Amereon. Author of column on beverages in *Penthouse.* Editor of and contributor to literary anthologies. Contributor to periodicals, including *Spectator, Encounter, New Statesman, Listener, Observer,* and *London Magazine.*

The Harry Ransom Humanities Research Center, University of Texas at Austin, possesses some of Amis's letters, working materials for many of his novels (notably the manuscript, typescript, and notes for *Lucky Jim*), and the typescript of *The James Bond Dossier.* Manuscripts of several of his early poems are in the Lockwood Memorial Library, State University of New York at Buffalo.

■ Adaptations

Lucky Jim was adapted as a motion picture, written by Jeffrey Dell and Patrick Campbell, directed by John Boulting, starring Sharon Acker and Ian Carmichael, British Lion, 1957; *That Uncertain Feeling* was adapted as a motion picture as *Only Two Can Play,* written by Bryan Forbes, directed by Sidney Gilliat, starring Peter Sellers, Mai Zetterling, Virginia Maskell, and Richard Attenborough, Columbia, 1962; *Take a Girl Like You* was adapted as a motion picture, written by George Melly, directed by Jonathan Miller, starring Hayley Mills and Oliver Reed, Columbia, 1970; *Jake's Thing* was recorded on audiocassette, Books on Tape, 1988; *The Old Devils* was adapted as a play, 1989; *The Green Man* was adapted for television, 1990; *Take a Girl Like You* was adapted as a television film by the BBC in 2000.

■ Sidelights

A prolific novelist, poet, story writer, essayist, and critic, Kingsley Amis was perhaps best known for his comic novel *Lucky Jim.* This 1954 novel, a satiric look at the modern university, gained Amis national attention in England. Along with such young English writers as John Osborne and John Wain, Amis was grouped as one of the Angry Young Men of the time. The term referred to the informal group's dissatisfaction with the way English life had changed following World War II. The collapse of the British Empire, the ascension of the Labour Party into power, and the rationing that continued in England for long after the war was over were all targets for the Angry Young Men, whose writings usually depicted the restricted lives of young people in the 1950s. Despite the similarities his work had with the other novelists, Amis rejected the Angry Young Man label. "Amis," stated *Los Angeles Times* writer William D. Montalbano, "rejected the label as 'a very boring journalistic phrase.'"

In the ensuing years, Amis would try his hand at many kinds of writing, from serious literature to science fiction, ghost stories, and even a James Bond novel. Clancy Sigal suggested in the *National Review* that Amis had "the virtue, rare in England, of refusing to accept an imposed definition of what a Seri-

The 1954 Amis novel *Lucky Jim* satirizes the English university system and brought Amis to national attention. (Penguin Books, 2002. Used by permission of Doubleday Books, a division of Random House, Inc.)

Old Devils, won the Booker Prize, Britain's highest literary award. In 1990, he was knighted by Queen Elizabeth II. According to Mathew David Fisher in the *Dictionary of Literary Biography,* Amis was "a writer able to illuminate great ideas using common people, situations, and language."

Amis was born in 1922 in south London, the only child of William Robert and Rosa Annie Amis. His father was senior export clerk for Colman's Mustard. Amis claimed that he got his love of literature from his mother. Writing in his *Memoirs,* Amis remembered that she "continued all her life as inveterate a reader as I was in my youth: a book was as much part of her accoutrements at home as handbag and knitting." Amis claimed that his frequent arguments with his father—"We quarrelled violently at least every week or two for years," he remembered—spurred him to develop his polemical skills for arguing and defending an intellectual position. At the age of twelve he was sent to the City of London School, where his father and two uncles had gone before him. He then went on to attend Saint John's College, Oxford, where he met his lifelong friend, the poet Philip Larkin. "While attending Oxford," Fisher recounted, "Amis edited the publication sponsored by the University Labour Club and professed strong liberal, even pro-Soviet, political convictions. These underwent drastic alteration when, after only a year at Oxford, Amis was drafted for military service. In 1942 he was commissioned in the Royal Corps of Signals, eventually rising to the rank of lieutenant, serving in France, Belgium, and Germany." After his military service, Amis earned his college degree in 1947. In 1949 he got a teaching position in the English department of the University College of Swansea, Wales. He was to remain there for the next twelve years.

Takes a Satiric Look at School

Amis won critical acclaim in 1954 with the publication of his first novel, *Lucky Jim.* The story tells of Jim Dixon, a junior lecturer at a provincial university. Jim has no desire to be an intellectual—or a "gentleman"—because of his profound, almost physical, hatred of the social and cultural affectations of university life. Writing in the *New Yorker,* Adam Gopnik explained that *Lucky Jim* "tells of a few weeks in the life of Jim Dixon, a young history don, from a background like Amis's, who is on probation at a provincial university, and who gets into various kinds of misunderstandings while carrying on with two girls, one cool and pretty, one needy and plain. Postwar, the university is already becoming for Amis's characters . . . a place where you go to make a career when you're too timid or

ous Writer ought to write about." His style of writing, as well as his subject matter, was also deceptively everyday. "For better or worse—mostly better—Amis loosened the collar of English prose," as James Wolcott described it in the *New Yorker.* "He loosened its tongue. . . . Amis's deceptively casual approach was more than a tactical ploy, a way of sneaking in punches; it expressed his conviction that language loses its responsive energy and observant value when it becomes overjewelled and forcibly sublime." Amis once wrote in *Contemporary Literature:* "I'm not exactly an entertainer pure and simple, not exactly an artist pure and simple, certainly not an incisive critic of society, and certainly not a political figure though I'm interested in politics. I think I'm just a combination of some of those things." His place in British literature was recognized in 1986, when his seventeenth novel, *The* ill equipped for any other." The story ends with Jim, a bit drunk, delivering a lecture that insults the whole school. Bruce Stovel in the *Dictionary of Literary Biography* wrote: "Jim Dixon, lower-middle-class, secretly and inventively in revolt against the 'cultivated' world in which he finds himself, quickly became a culture hero for a society which had suddenly lost most of its empire and world influence, where the old class system seemed discredited and a new social order was visibly in the making." Anthony Burgess in *The Novel Now* called Jim Dixon "the most popular anti-hero of our time." Writing in the *New Criterion,* David Yezzi stated: "*Lucky Jim* is simply one of the funniest (and best) books of the last hundred years."

Critics generally see the three novels that followed *Lucky Jim* as variations on this theme of appealing to common sense and denouncing affectation. Discussing *Lucky Jim, That Uncertain Feeling, I Like It Here,* and *Take a Girl Like You* in the *Hudson Review,* James P. Degnan stated: "In the comically outraged voice of his angry young heroes—e.g., Jim Dixon of *Lucky Jim* and John Lewis of *That Uncertain Feeling*—Amis [lampoons] what C.P. Snow . . . labeled the 'traditional culture,' the 'culture of the literary intellectuals,' of the 'gentleman's world.'" James Gindin noted in *Postwar British Fiction* that the similarity of purpose is reflected in a corresponding similarity of technique: "Each of the [four] novels is distinguished by a thick verbal texture that is essential comic. The novels are full of word play and verbal jokes. . . . All Amis's heroes are mimics: Jim Dixon parodies the accent of Professor Welch, his phony and genteel professor, in *Lucky Jim;* Patrick Standish, in *Take a Girl Like You,* deliberately echoes the Hollywood version of the Southern Negro's accent. John Lewis, the hero of *That Uncertain Feeling,* also mimics accents and satirically characterizes other people by the words and phrases they use."

The heroes in these four novels are in fact so much alike that Brigid Brophy charged Amis with "rewriting much the same novel under different titles and with different names for the characters," although Walter Allen in the *Modern Novel* insisted that the "young man recognizably akin to Lucky Jim, the Amis man as he might be called, . . . has been increasingly explored in depth." Consistent with her assessment of Jim Dixon in *Lucky Jim,* Brophy saw the other three Amis heroes also as "militant philistines,"a view that was not shared by Caplan, Burgess, or Degnan. Caplan explained that though the Amis hero in these novels is seemingly anti-intellectual, he is nonetheless "always cerebral," and Burgess pointed out that the hero "always earns his living by purveying culture as teacher, librarian, journalist, or publisher." Representing a common-sensical approach to life, the Amis protagonist, ac-

cording to Degnan, is an inversion of a major convention of the hero "as 'sensitive soul,' the convention of the 'alienated' young man of artistic or philosophical pretensions struggling pitifully and hopelessly against an insensitive, middle-class, materialistic world. . . . In place of the sensitive soul as hero, Amis creates in his early novels a hero radically new to serious contemporary fiction: a middle-class hero who is also an intellectual, an intellectual who is unabashedly middle-brow. He is a hero . . . whose chief virtues, as he expresses them, are: 'politeness, friendly interest, ordinary concern and a good natured willingness to be imposed upon. . . .' Suspicious of all pretentiousness, of all heroic posturing, the Amis hero . . . voices all that is best of the 'lower middle class, of the non-gentlemanly' conscience."

Degnan, however, did believe that Patrick Standish in *Take a Girl Like You* came dangerously close to "the kind of anti-hero—e.g., blasé, irresponsible, hedonistic—that Amis's first three novels attack," and that this weakened the satirical aspect of the novel. Echoing this observation in *The Reaction against Experiment in the English Novel, 1950-1960,* Rubin Rabinovitz detected an uncertainty as to what "vice and folly" really are and who possesses them: "In *Take a Girl Like You* Amis satirizes both Patrick's lechery and Jenny's persistence in preserving her virginity. . . . The satire in *Lucky Jim* is not divided this way: Jim Dixon mocks the hypocrisy of his colleagues in the university and refuses to be subverted

Amis at home in 1961 playing chess with his sons Martin and Philip. (Hulton-Deutsch Collection/Corbis.)

by it. [In *Lucky Jim*] the satire is more powerful because the things being satirized are more boldly defined."

Pens a James Bond Thriller

After *Take a Girl Like You,* Amis produced several other "straight" novels, as *Time's* Christopher Porterfield described them, as well as a James Bond spy thriller, written under the pseudonym of Robert Markham, called *Colonel Sun: A James Bond Adventure;* a work of science fiction, *The Anti-Death League;* and a ghost story, *The Green Man.* When Gildrose Productions, the firm to which the James Bond copyright was sold after Ian Fleming's death, awarded the first non-Fleming sequel to Amis, the literary world received the news with a mixture of apprehension and interest. Earlier, Amis had done an analysis of the nature of Fleming's hero, *The James Bond Dossier,* and he appeared to be a logical successor to Bond's creator. But the reactions to *Colonel Sun* were mixed. Though Clara Siggins stated in *Best Sellers* that Amis "produced an exciting narrative with the expertise and verve of Fleming himself," S.K. Oberbeck claimed in the *Washington Post Book World* that the changes Amis made "on Bond's essential character throw the formula askew. . . . In humanizing Bond, in netting him back into the channel of real contemporary events, Amis somehow deprives him of the very ingredients that made his barely believable adventures so rewarding." Similarly, David Lodge, discussing the book in *The Novelist at the Crossroads and Other Essays on Fiction and Criticism,* considered *Colonel Sun* "more realistic" yet "duller" than most of the Fleming novels, because "the whole enterprise, undertaken, apparently, in a spirit of pious imitation, required Amis to keep in check his natural talent for parody and deflating comic realism."

Amis's comic spirit, so prominent in his first four novels and muted in *Colonel Sun,* is noticeably absent from *The Anti-Death League,* which was published two years before the Bond adventure. Bernard Bergonzi commented in *The Situation of the Novel* that in *The Anti-Death League,* Amis "has written a more generalised kind of fiction, with more clearly symbolic implications, than in any of his earlier novels. There is still a trace of sardonic humor, and his ear remains alert to the placing details of individual speech; but Amis has here abandoned the incisive social mimicry, the memorable responses to the specificity of a person's appearance or the look of a room that have previously characterized his fiction."

The story concerns a British army officer who becomes convinced that a nonhuman force of unlimited malignancy, called God, is responsible for a pattern of seemingly undeserved deaths. Bergonzi viewed the work as a provocative, anti-theological novel of ideas and maintained that it "represents Amis's immersion in the nightmare that flickers at the edges of his earlier fiction." He did, however, find one shortcoming in the novel: "*The Anti-Death League* . . . is intensely concerned with the questions that lead to tragedy—death, cruelty, loss of every kind—while lacking the ontological supports—whether religious or humanistic—that can sustain the tragic view of life." A *Times Literary Supplement* reviewer admitted that the rebellion against the facts of pain and death "seems rather juvenile, like kicking God's ankle for doing such things to people," but asserted: "[Amis] takes the argument to more audacious and hopeful lengths. . . . We do care about his creatures; the agents intrigue us and the victims concern us. The handling is vastly less pompous than the theme: oracular, yes, but eloquent and earthly and even moving."

Amis followed *The Anti-Death League* with *The Green Man,* a comic horror novel, and *Girl, 20,* a comic novel with serious overtones. In *The Green Man,* boozy Maurice Allington runs The Green Man, a restaurant that was once a coaching inn. Although there is an old tale of the building being haunted, the skeptical Maurice does not believe the story, until he begins to see strange things himself. When his own father dies of a stroke while apparently witnessing a ghostly visit, Maurice becomes unhinged. Gradually Maurice becomes aware that Dr. Thomas Underhill, a lecherous 17th-century nobleman, is trying to use magical means to take over his body. "Amis made a significant contribution to every genre in which he worked," wrote an essayist for the *St. James Guide to Horror, Ghost & Gothic Writers.* "Although *The Green Man* is his sole book-length tale of the supernatural, its disquieting sophistication and the deepening of its darkness by contrasting veins of light comedy make it a major 20th-century horror story."

Paul Schleuter in *Saturday Review* viewed *Girl, 20* as a harmonious addition to Amis's body of work. He wrote: "[Amis's] talent for creating humorous situations, characters, and dialogue is as fresh as ever. . . . Amis also has a distinct undercurrent of pathos, darkness, and trauma. The result is not really a 'new' Amis so much as a more mature examination of human foibles and excesses than was the case in his earlier novels." But Amis's next novel, *The Riverside Villas Murder,* "offers no comfort to those who look for consistency in [his] work," according to a *Times Literary Supplement* reviewer.

Tells a Detective Tale

A departure from Amis's previous works, *The Riverside Villas Murder* is a detective story, though there was some debate among critics whether it is to be read "straight" or as a parody of the genre. Patrick Cosgrave, for example, claimed in *Saturday Review/World* that the book was "a straight detective story, with a murder, several puzzles, clues, a great detective, and an eminently satisfying and unexpected villain. So bald a statement is a necessary introduction in order to ensure that nobody will be tempted to pore over *The Riverside Villas Murder* in search of portentiousness, significance, ambiguity, or any of the more tiresome characteristics too often found in the work of a straight novelist who has turned aside from the main road of his work into the byways of such subgenres as crime and adventure. More, the book is straight detection because Amis intended it to be such: It is written out of a great love of the detective form and deliberately set in a period—the Thirties—when that form was . . . most popular." The *Times Literary Supplement* reviewer, however, considered the book "something more and less than a period detective story. Mr. Amis is not one to take any convention too seriously, and on one plane he is simply having fun." Patricia Coyne, writing in the *National Review,* and *Time*'s T.E. Kalem expressed similar opinions. Coyne described the story as "a boy discovers sex against a murder-mystery backdrop," and Kalem concluded that by making a fourteen-year-old boy the hero of the novel, "Amis cleverly combines, in mild parody, two ultra-British literary forms—the mystery thriller with the boyhood adventure yarn."

Almost as if to befuddle readers searching for consistency in his work, Amis followed his detective story *The Riverside Villas Murder* with a straight novel, *Ending Up,* before producing *The Alteration,* which *Time*'s Paul Gray said "flits quirkily between satire, science fiction, boy's adventure, and travelogue. The result is what *Nineteen Eighty-Four* might have been like if Lewis Carroll had written it: not a classic, certainly, but an oddity well worth an evening's attention." According to Bruce Cook in the *Saturday Review, The Alteration* belongs to a rare subgenre of science fiction: "the so-called counterfeit-or alternative-world novel." Though set in the twentieth century (1976), the book has as its premise that the Protestant Reformation never occurred and, as a result, that the world is essentially Catholic. The plot centers on the discovery of a brilliant boy soprano, the Church's plans to preserve his gift by "altering" his anatomy through castration, and the debate on the justice of this decision.

Thomas R. Edwards noted in the *New York Review of Books* that though "Amis isn't famous for his

Amis with his son, novelist Martin Amis, in London in the 1990s. (Dave Benett/Getty Images Entertainment/Getty Images.)

compassion," in *The Alteration* he "affectingly catches and respects a child's puzzlement about the threatened loss of something he knows about only from descriptions." John Carey insisted in the *New Statesman* that the book "has almost nothing expectable about it, except that it is a study of tyranny." What Carey referred to was the destructive power of the pontifical hierarchy to emasculate life and art, which he saw as the theme of the novel. Bruce Cook shared this interpretation. Calling *The Alteration* "the most overtly and specifically theological of all [Amis's] books," Cook argued: "Fundamentally, *The Alteration* is another of Kingsley Amis's angry screeds against the Catholic faith and the Catholic idea of God. And it is not just what Amis sees as the life-hating, sex-hating aspect of High Christianity—something that made possible such monstrous phenomena as the castrati—that concerns him here [but] . . . Christianity itself. At the end of *The Anti-Death League,* his oddest and most extreme book and in some ways his best, Amis allows some talk of reconciliation, of forgiving God the wrongs He has done humanity. But there is none of that in *The Alteration*. It is an almost bitter book by a man grown angry in middle age."

Another Comic Novel

From *The Alteration* to *Jake's Thing*, Amis again made the transition from science fiction to "comic diatribe," according to V.S. Pritchett in the *New York Review of Books*. Pritchett considered *Jake's Thing* "a very funny book, less for its action or its talk than its prose. . . . Mr. Amis is a master of laconic mimicry and of the vernacular drift." A reviewer wrote in *Choice* that this is "the Amis of *Lucky Jim*, an older and wiser comic writer who is making a serious statement about the human condition."

The story focuses on Jake Richardson, a sixty-year-old reader in early Mediterranean history at Oxford who in the past has been to bed with well over a hundred women but now suffers from a loss of libido. Referred to sex therapist Dr. Proinsias (Celtic, pronounced "Francis") Rosenberg, Jake, stated *Nation*'s Amy Wilentz, "is caught up in the supermarket of contemporary life. The novel is filled with encounter groups, free love, women's liberation, and such electronic contrivances as the 'nocturnal mensurator,' which measures the level of a man's arousal as he sleeps." Christopher Lehmann-Haupt of the *New York Times* noted that Amis "makes the most of all the comic possibilities here. Just imagine sensible, civilized Jake coming home from Dr. Rosenberg's office with . . . assignments to study 'pictorial pornographic material' and to 'write out a sexual fantasy in not less than six hundred words.' Consider Jake struggling to find seventy-three more words, or contemplating the nudes in *Mezzanine* magazine, which 'had an exotic appearance, like the inside of a giraffe's ear or a tropical fruit not much prized by the locals.'"

But for all the hilarity, there is an undercurrent of seriousness running through the novel. "It comes bubbling up," wrote Lehmann-Haupt, "when Jake finally grows fed up with Dr. Rosenberg and his experiments." Wilentz argued that the novel expresses "outrage at, and defeat at the hands of, modernity, whose graceless intrusion on one's privacy is embodied in Dr. Rosenberg's constantly repeated question, 'I take it you've no objection to exposing your genitals in public?'" Malcolm Bradbury shared this interpretation, writing in the *New Statesman*: "Amis, watching [history's] collectivising, behaviourist, depersonalizing progress, would like nice things to win and certain sense to prevail.

Indeed, a humanist common sense—along with attention to farts—is to his world view roughly what post-Heideggerian existentialism is to Jean-Paul Sartre's."

After the problems of libido in *Jake's Thing*, wrote Blake Morrison in the *Times Literary Supplement*, *Russian Hide-and-Seek* "signals the return of the young, uncomplicated, highly sexed Amis male; . . . the more important connection, however, is with Amis's earlier novel, *The Alteration*." Another example of the "alternative world" novel, *Russian Hide-and-Seek* depicts an England, fifty years hence, that has been overrun by the Soviet Union; oddly enough, though, the Soviets have abandoned Marxism and returned to the style of Russia under the czars. Paul Binding described the book in the *New Statesman* as "at once a pastiche of certain aspects of nineteenth-century Russian fiction and an exercise in cloak-and-dagger adventure. The two genres unite to form a work far more ambitious than those earlier *jeux*—a fictional expression of the author's obsessive conviction that, whatever its avatar, Russian culture is beastly, thriving on conscious exploitation, enamoured of brutality."

Provokes Outrage

Amis placed himself at the center of political controversy with his next novel, *Stanley and the Women*. Well received upon publication in England, the book was rejected by publishing houses in the United States twice because of objections to its main character's misogyny, said some sources. "When rumors that one of Britain's most prominent and popular postwar novelists was being censored Stateside by a feminist cabal hit print [in early 1985], the literary flap echoed on both sides of the Atlantic for weeks," reported *Time*'s Paul Gray. After the book found an American publisher a critical debate ensued, with some reviewers condemning its uniformly negative depiction of women, and others defending the book's value nonetheless.

In a *Washington Post Book World* review, Jonathan Yardley charged, "Amis has stacked the deck against women, reducing them to caricatures who reinforce the damning judgments made by Stanley and his chums." Though Yardley felt that "much else in the novel is exceedingly well done," he also felt that its "cranky misogynism" is too prominent to be ignored. Indeed, Stanley casts himself as the victim of a gang of female villains: a self-centered ex-wife; a current wife who stabs herself and accuses Stanley's emotionally unstable son; and a psychiatrist who deliberately mishandles the son's case and blames Stanley for the son's schizophrenia. On the other hand, "the men in the novel hardly fare any better," remarked Michiko Kakutani of the *New York Times.* In her view, shared by Susan Fromberg Schaeffer in the *New York Times Book Review, Stanley and the Women* proves Amis to be "not just a misogynist, but a misanthrope as well. Practically every character in the novel is either an idiot or a scheming hypocrite." Amis, who observed that British women take less offense from the book, claims it is not anti-female; *Time* presented his statement that "all comedy, . . . all humor is unfair. . . . There is a beady-eyed view of women in the book, certainly. . . . But a novel is not a report or a biographical statement or a confession. If it is a good novel, it dramatizes thoughts that some people, somewhere, have had."

Viewing the book from this perspective, some critics found it laudable. *Spectator* contributor Harriet Waugh argued, "It does have to be admitted . . . that Mr. Amis's portrayal of Stanley's wives as female monsters is funny and convincing. Most readers will recognise aspects of them in women they know. . . . [Amis] has written a true account of the intolerableness of women in relation to men." Such a tract, she felt, is comparable in many respects to novels by women that show women "downtrodden" by men. Wrote Gray, "Amis has excelled at rattling preconceptions ever since the appearance of his classically comic first novel, *Lucky Jim.* . . . Is this novel unfair to women? Probably. Is the question worth asking? No. . . . The females in the world of this book all commit 'offences' . . . at least in the eyes of Stanley, who is . . . nobody's idea of a deep thinker." In the *Times Literary Supplement,* J.K.L. Walker concluded, "*Stanley and the Women* reveals Kingsley Amis in the full flood of his talent and should survive its ritual burning in William IV Street unscathed."

Wins a Major Prize

The author's next novel, *The Old Devils,* "manifests little of the female bashing that made the satiric *Stanley and the Women* so scandalous. In fact, dissatisfied wives are given some tart remarks to make about their variously unsatisfactory husbands. . . . Even so, these concessions never denature Amis's characteristic bite," wrote Gray. In a London *Times* review, Victoria Glendinning concurred: "This is vintage Kingsley Amis, 50 percent alcohol, with splashes of savagery about getting old, and about the state of the sex-war in marriages of thirty or more years' standing." Reviewers admired most the book's major female character; Amis gives her a relationship with her daughter "so close, candid

and trusting that the most ardent feminist must applaud," noted Martin Champlin in the *Los Angeles Times Book Review.* Her husband, Alun, an aggressive womanizer, drew the most disfavor. In what Gray felt was the author's "wisest and most humane work," both sexes enjoy their best and worst moments. "This is one of Amis's strengths as a novelist, not noticeably to the fore in recent work but making a welcome return here: 'bad' characters are allowed their victories and 'good' characters their defeats. Yet Amis comes down against Alun in a firmly 'moral' conclusion," commented Morrison in the *Times Literary Supplement.*

Alun's funeral near the close of the book is balanced with "the reconciliation of two of the feuding older generation, and the marriage of two of the younger," such that the ending has "an almost Shakespearean symmetry," stated Morrison. But the mood, he warned, is not exactly one of celebration. He explained that the character Amis seems to most approve of "belongs in that tradition of the Amis hero who would like to believe but can't," whose "disappointed scepticism" keeps him from seeing a romantic encouragement behind a pleasant scene. "Finally," reflected Bryan Appleyard in the London *Times,* "it is this sense of an empty, somewhat vacuous age which seems to come close to the heart of all [Amis's] work. His novels are no-nonsense, well-made, good-humored products. They are about the struggle to get by in the gutter and their heroes seldom roll over to gaze at the stars. Like Larkin he is awestruck by the *idea* of religion but he cannot subscribe. Instead, his novels are happily committed to the obliteration of cant without thought of what to put in its place."

For *The Old Devils,* Amis received the Booker-McConnell Prize for Fiction (usually known as the Booker Prize), the most prestigious book award in England. Among critics who felt the prize was well deserved was Champlin, who referred to "its sheer storytelling expertise, and its qualities of wit, humanity, and observation." In the *New York Times Book Review,* William H. Pritchard recognized *The Old Devils* as Amis's "most ambitious and one of his longest books, . . . neither a sendup nor an exercise in some established genre. It sets forth, with full realistic detail, a large cast of characters at least six of whom are rendered in depth. . . . *The Old Devils* is also Mr. Amis's most inclusive novel, encompassing kinds of feeling and tone that move from sardonic gloom to lyric tenderness."

Critics celebrated Amis's return to the satiric comic-novel again in *Difficulties with Girls,* a sort of sequel to his 1960 work *Take a Girl Like You.* "In returning to the characters of . . . *Take a Girl Like You,*" wrote

New York magazine contributor Rhoda Koenig, "Amis has also . . . reverted to his style of that period, the sprightly, needling tone he had only six years after *Lucky Jim.*" Patrick Standish has not changed much from the "dedicated sexual predator" who married the girl he raped after getting her drunk at a party, declared Judith Grossman in the *New York Times Book Review*. He has left his job as a high school teacher and entered the world of publishing, which provides him with just as many opportunities for sexual conquests. When his wife, Jenny, discovers the latest of these, she leaves him; then, discovering she is pregnant, she returns. "Amis is one of the best chroniclers we have of the lost world [of 1950s-era male chauvinism]," stated Michael Wood in the *Times Literary Supplement*, "in large part because he knows it's not lost at all, but lies around us everywhere. . . . Amis is not a praiser of the old world, but he is very suspicious of the new one. Maybe it's not even there; maybe it's just a phantom bred of our lame trendiness, our cult of tolerance."

The Folks That Live on the Hill again looks at problems in modern life—alcoholism, prostate surgery, and divorce. "Formally," stated *New Statesman and Society* contributor Anthony Quinn, "it's another funny-sad comedy of social and sexual manners, cast in the old-farts-ensemble mould of *Ending Up* and *The Old Devils.*" It tells of the struggles of retired librarian Harry Caldecote to resolve the problems of different members of his extended family—his son's financial irresponsibility, his brother's suffering marriage, and the various problems of relatives of his ex-wives. "Mr. Amis is, however, less interested in exploring Harry's burden of obligation toward others than in focusing on the novel's different characters as they undergo their troubles," declared William H. Pritchard in the *New York Times Book Review*. Although critics recognized that *The Folks That Live on the Hill* covers ground that Amis had covered before, they agreed with Quinn that "Amis is still *funny*. The knack of capturing the false starts and dead ends of everyday chatter, the gift for mimicry, the elaborate expressions of outrage—time has withered none of these. You wince as he drives a coach and horses over the liberal consensus, but you find yourself cackling like a maniac."

Amis reviewed his own career in *Memoirs*, published four years before his death. "Television interviewers and others who expected him to be uniformly reactionary on every issue," wrote Merle Rubin in the *Christian Science Monitor*, "were often surprised to discover that he was not an advocate of capital punishment, a racist, or an America-basher, after all." However, many critics deplored the work, declaring that it lacked focus and personal insight. "The faint hope might have been that, in writing

directly about himself, the irascible old shag would come over as . . . cuddlier than his usual public image makes him seem," said *London Review of Books* critic Ian Hamilton. "To any such tender expectations, though, Amis offers here a close-to-gleeful 'In a pig's arse, friend'—i.e. you bastards will get nothing out of me, or not much and what you do get you won't like." "Amis," Craig Brown stated in the *Times Literary Supplement*, "has created his autobiographical persona along the lines of one of his most comically pitiless characters." Paul Fussell, writing in *The Anti-Egotist: Kingsley Amis, Man of Letters*, claimed that Amis's *Memoirs* "encountered severe criticism from some readers failing to recognize the moralist's and satirist's way he dealt with some of his now defunct relatives."

In his twenty-first novel, *The Russian Girl*, Amis returned to skewer one of his prime targets: the halls of academe. Richard Vaisey is an academic at a British university who specializes in Russian literature. Like other Amis protagonists, he is also oversexed and unhappily married—to Cordelia, whose good points are that she is good in bed and independently wealthy. Vaisey is approached by an expatriate Russian poet named Anna Danilova, who is circulating a petition to have her brother released from prison in Russia. "Anna Danilova is a terrible poet but sweet, gentle and deferential," explained Diane Roberts in the *Atlanta Journal-Constitution*. "Richard must choose between Cordelia (and money) and Anna (and true love)." "Amis, the old master, somehow orchestrates all these themes, and several more, into a wonderful new concert of plot and language," Gary Abrams declared in the *Los Angeles Times Book Review*, "that provokes both belly laughs and twinges of discomfort over the silly messes we humans make while blundering through life." "*The Russian Girl*," stated *New York Times Book Review* contributor Christopher Buckley, "is . . . vintage Amis: smooth, dry and not overpriced."

If you enjoy the works of Kingsley Amis, you may also want to check out the following books:

Evelyn Waugh, *Scoop*, 1938.
Richard Russo, *Straight Man*, 1998.
Martin Amis, *Night Train*, 1999.

Amis died unexpectedly late in 1995, while he was being treated in St. Pancras Hospital, London, after having crushed several vertebrae in his back in a severe fall. A posthumous publication, *The King's English* (1998), represented a last foray into nonfiction for an author who had written works of literary criticism, political commentary, and history dating back to *Socialism and the Intellectuals*, published by the Fabian Society in 1957. The publication gave occasion for a new round of obituaries-cum-reviews, many of them appreciative commentaries regarding Amis's vigorous stance with regard to proper English usage—the subject of the book itself. Several reviewers noted that by choosing the title he did—taken from that of a definitive 1906 volume by British lexicographer Henry Watson Fowler and his brother George Francis Fowler—Amis, perhaps in a final act of audacity, raised the stakes to an almost insurmountable height. For Roger Draper of the *New Leader*, the author's gambit failed: "In appropriating the title *The King's English . . .* for his posthumously published effort, the English comic novelist Kingsley Amis gives the impression of having aspired to a very high standard—and, perhaps inevitably, fell short of it. Amis' opus is largely a collection of crochets and jokes."

Those "crochets and jokes," however, are precisely what endeared the book to other reviewers, particularly in England. Several British critics, in fact, had known Amis, and they peppered their reviews with personal reminiscences. "Kingsley loved to present his prejudices outrageously," wrote James Michie in the *Spectator*. "I remember him clinching an argument with me about Milton by a simple mime, one hand pinching his nose, the other pulling a lavatory chain. There's plenty of gratuitous provocation here." Thus, as Michie went on to note, Amis lambasted the seemingly innocuous "continental crossed 7" as "gross affectation" or even "straightforward ignorance." The old anti-feminist issues were much in evidence as well, a fact noted both by Michie and E.S. Turner in the *Times Literary Supplement*. "Women will not expect to find much for their comfort in these pages," wrote Turner, "though Lady Thatcher is commended for saying 'There is no alternative' (and not 'no other alternative'). Women, it seems, know nothing about etymology, but 'can be trusted with revision and kindred tasks.'" Though some might have found Amis's social views objectionable, Sebastian Faulks suggested in the *New Statesman* that his knowledge of the language itself was above reproach: "Kingsley Amis wrote in a style that was as close to actual speech as one can get without talking, or without foregoing effects only written language can produce; yet it was based on a classical education and a lifelong exploration of grammar and etymology."

Amis's death prompted many retrospectives and assessments of his career. His first novel, *Lucky Jim*, is widely regarded as his masterpiece. "It estab-

lished him as a master of invective and a man well able to raise a guffaw from his readers, especially the male ones," stated a London *Times* obituary writer. "For the next 40 years Amis produced a regular flow of books which established him as the leading British comic novelist of his generation. The tone varied considerably, but Amis picked his targets carefully and his aim was deadly accurate. He wrote about what he knew well and made sure that he did not too much like what he saw around him." According to Paul Gray in *Time*: "He began and remained throughout his writing life a brilliant practitioner of English prose and a hilarious debunker of received opinions."

■ Biographical and Critical Sources

BOOKS

Allen, Walter, *The Modern Novel*, Dutton (New York, NY), 1984.

Allsop, Kenneth, *The Angry Decade*, P. Owen (London, England), 1958.

Amis, Martin, *Koba the Dread: Laughter and the Twenty Million*, Talk Miramax Books (New York, NY), 2002.

Bell, Robert H., editor, *Critical Essays on Kingsley Amis*, G.K. Hall, 1998.

Bergonzi, Bernard, *The Situation of the Novel*, University of Pittsburgh Press, 1970.

Bradford, Richard, *Lucky Him: The Life of Kingsley Amis*, Peter Owen, 2002.

Brophy, Brigid, *Don't Never Forget: Collected Views and Reviews*, Holt (New York, NY), 1967.

Burgess, Anthony, *The Novel Now: A Guide to Contemporary Fiction*, Norton (New York, NY), 1967.

Contemporary Literary Criticism, Gale (Detroit, MI), Volume 1, 1973, Volume 2, 1974, Volume 3, 1975, Volume 5, 1976, Volume 8, 1978, Volume 13, 1980, Volume 40, 1987, Volume 44, 1988.

Contemporary Novelists, 6th edition, St. James Press (Detroit, MI), 1996.

Contemporary Poets, 6th edition, St. James Press (Detroit, MI), 1996.

Dictionary of Literary Biography, Gale (Detroit, MI), Volume 15: *British Novelists, 1930-1959*, 1983, Volume 27: *Poets of Great Britain and Ireland, 1945-1960*, 1984, Volume 100: *Modern British Essayists, Second Series*, 1990, Volume 139: *British Short-Fiction Writers, 1945-1980*, 1994.

Feldman, Gene, and Max Gartenberg, editors, *The Beat Generation and the Angry Young Men*, Citadel (Kent, England), 1958.

Fussell, Paul, *The Anti-Egotist: Kingsley Amis, Man of Letters,* Oxford University Press (New York, NY), 1994.

Gardner, Philip, *Kingsley Amis,* Twayne (Boston, MA), 1981.

Gindin, James, *Postwar British Fiction: New Accents and Attitudes,* University of California Press (Berkeley, CA), 1962.

Gohn, Jack Benoit, *Kingsley Amis: A Checklist,* Kent State University Press, 1976.

Jacobs, Eric, *Kingsley Amis: A Biography,* Hodder and Stoughton (London, England), 1995.

Johnson, William, compiler, *Focus on the Science Fiction Film,* Prentice-Hall (Englewood Cliffs, NJ), 1972.

Karl, Frederick R., *The Contemporary English Novel,* Farrar, Straus (New York, NY), 1962.

Keulks, Gavin, *Father and Son: Kingsley Amis, Martin Amis, and the British Novel since 1950,* University of Wisconsin Press, 2005.

Laskowski, William E., *Kingsley Amis,* Twayne (Boston, MA), 1998.

Leader, Zachary, *The Letters of Kingsley Amis,* HarperCollins (New York, NY), 2000.

Leader, Zachary, *The Life of Kingsley Amis,* Pantheon (New York, NY), 2007.

Lodge, David, *Language of Fiction,* Columbia University Press (New York, NY), 1966.

Lodge, David, *The Novelist at the Crossroads and Other Essays on Fiction and Criticism,* Cornell University Press (Ithaca, NY), 1971.

McDermott, John, *Kingsley Amis: An English Moralist,* St. Martin's Press (New York, NY), 1988.

Morrison, Blake, *The Movement: English Poetry and Fiction of the 1950s,* Oxford University Press (New York, NY), 1980.

Moseley, Marritt, *Understanding Kingsley Amis,* University of South Carolina Press (Columbia, SC), 1993.

Nemerov, Howard, *Poetry and Fiction: Essays,* Rutgers University Press (New Brunswick, NJ), 1963.

O'Connor, William Van, *The New University Wits and the End of Modernism,* Southern Illinois University Press (Carbondale, IL), 1963.

Press, John, *Rule and Energy: British Poetry since the Second World War,* Oxford University Press (New York, NY), 1963.

Rabinovitz, Rubin, *The Reaction against Experiment in the English Novel, 1950-1960,* Columbia University Press (New York, NY), 1967.

St. James Guide to Horror, Ghost & Gothic Writers, St. James Press (Detroit, MI), 1998.

St. James Guide to Science Fiction Writers, 4th edition, St. James Press (Detroit, MI), 1996.

Salwak, Dale, *Kingsley Amis: A Reference Guide,* Macmillan (New York, NY), 1978.

Salwak, Dale, editor, *Kingsley Amis: In Life and Letters,* St. Martin's Press (New York, NY), 1990.

Salwak, Dale, *Kingsley Amis, Modern Novelist,* Barnes & Noble (Lanham, MA), 1992.

Shapiro, Charles, editor, *Contemporary British Novelists,* Southern Illinois University Press (Carbondale, IL), 1963.

Swinden, Patrick, *English Novel of History and Society, 1940-1980: Richard Hughes, Henry Green, Anthony Powell, Angus Wilson, Kingsley Amis, and V.S. Naipaul,* St. Martin's Press (New York, NY), 1984.

Thwaite, Anthony, *Contemporary British Poetry: An Introduction,* Heinemann (London, England), 1959.

Wilson, Edmund, *The Bit between My Teeth: A Literary Chronicle of 1950-1965,* Farrar, Straus (New York, NY), 1965.

PERIODICALS

America, May 7, 1977.

Atlanta Journal-Constitution, July 24, 1994, p. N10.

Atlantic Monthly, April, 1956; April, 1958; July, 1965; June, 1968; June, 1970; February, 1977; November, 1985; May, 2002, Christopher Hitchens, "The Man of Feeling: 'Lucky Jim,' Kingsley Amis's Comic Masterpiece, May Be the Funniest Book of the Past Half Century," pp. 103-108.

Best Sellers, May 15, 1968; April 4, 1969.

Bloomsbury Review, March, 1992, p. 2.

Booklist, June 1, 1998, p. 1691.

Books and Bookmen, December, 1965; July, 1968; January, 1969; September, 1969; October, 1978.

Bookseller, November 11, 1970.

Boston Globe, May 22, 1994, p. B18; September 7, 1994, p. 74.

British Book News, June, 1981.

Chicago Tribune, August 1, 1989.

Chicago Tribune Book World, October 13, 1985.

Choice, November, 1979.

Christian Science Monitor, January 16, 1958; September 24, 1970; September 11, 1985; March 10, 1987; October 7, 1991, p. 13.

Chronicle of Higher Education, June 22, 2007, Michael Dirda, "Kingsley Amis's Troublesome Fun."

Commonweal, March 21, 1958.

Contemporary Literature, winter, 1975, Dale Salwak, "An Interview with Kingsley Amis," pp. 1-18.

Critical Quarterly, summer, 1977.

Critique, spring-summer, 1966; Volume 9, number 1, 1968; summer, 1977.

Economist, March 9, 1991, p. 89; April 21, 2007, "Booze and Birds: Kingsley Amis," p. 96.

Encounter, November, 1974; January, 1979; September/October, 1984.

Essays in Criticism, January, 1980.

Harper's Bazaar, May, 1989, p. 76.

Hudson Review, summer, 1972; winter, 1973-74; winter, 1974-75; winter, 1980-81.

Library Journal, July, 1970; May 15, 1998, p. 84.

Life, May 3, 1968; March 14, 1969; August 28, 1970.

Listener, November 9, 1967; January 11, 1968; November 26, 1970; May 30, 1974; February 20, 1975, Melvyn Bragg, "Kingsley Amis Looks Back," pp. 240-241; October 7, 1976; May 22, 1980; October 23, 1980; May 24, 1984; October 16, 1986.

London Magazine, January, 1968; August, 1968; October, 1968; January, 1970; January, 1981; October, 1986.

London Review of Books, June 7-20, 1984; September 18, 1986; December 4, 1986; April 2, 1987; September 29, 1988, pp. 14, 16; March 22, 1990, p. 20; March 21, 1991, p. 3; November 16, 1995, p. 8.

Los Angeles Times, September 25, 1985; July 6, 1989.

Los Angeles Times Book Review, May 4, 1980; April 26, 1987; June 12, 1994, p. 3.

Manchester Guardian, February 2, 1954; August 23, 1955; November 30, 1956.

Nation, January 30, 1954; August 20, 1955; April 28, 1969; May 5, 1969; October 5, 1970; April 7, 1979.

National Observer, September 15, 1969; June 29, 1977.

National Review, June 18, 1968; June 3, 1969; August 25, 1970; October 27, 1973; February 1, 1974; March 14, 1975; October 27, 1983; February 22, 1985; May 8, 1987; August 1, 1994, p. 62; September 14, 1998, pp. 66-67.

New Criterion, April, 2007, David Yezzi, "The Amis Country," p. 32.

New Leader, September 21, 1970; December 6, 1976; June 29-July 13, 1998, pp. 3-4.

New Republic, March 24, 1958; September 19, 1970; October 12, 1974; May 28, 1977; November 26, 1977; February 25, 1985; May 30, 1987.

New Review, July, 1974, Clive James, "Kingsley Amis," pp. 21-28.

New Statesman, January 30, 1954; August 20, 1955; January 18, 1958; September 24, 1960; November 28, 1963; July 7, 1967; December 1, 1967; October 11, 1968; November 21, 1975; October 8, 1976; September 15, 1978; April 13, 1979; May 23, 1980; December 5, 1980; September 19, 1986; March 21, 1997, pp. 51-52.

New Statesman & Society, March 30, 1990, p. 38; October 5, 1990, p. 44; March 29, 1991, p. 38.

Newsweek, March 2, 1964; May 8, 1967; May 6, 1968; September 14, 1970; September 30, 1974; January 17, 1977; February 4, 1985.

New York, April 17, 1989, p. 73.

New Yorker, March 6, 1954; March 24, 1958; April 26, 1969; September 13, 1969; October 21, 1974; March 14, 1977; August 20, 1979; April 27, 1987; June 12, 1989, pp. 121-24; April 23, 2007, Adam Gopnik, "The Old Devil," p. 78.

New York Review of Books, October 6, 1966; August 1, 1968; March 9, 1972; March 20, 1975; April 15, 1976; March 3, 1977; May 17, 1979; March 26, 1987; June 9, 1994, p. 29.

New York Times, January 31, 1954; February 26, 1956; February 23, 1958; April 25, 1967; April 25, 1968; March 12, 1969; August 17, 1970; January 6, 1972; May 11, 1979; September 14, 1985; October 8, 1985; November 8, 1986; February 25, 1987; March 28, 1989.

New York Times Book Review, April 28, 1963; July 25, 1965; April 28, 1968; May 19, 1968; March 23, 1969; August 23, 1970; November 11, 1973; October 20, 1974; April 18, 1976; January 30, 1977; May 13, 1979; January 13, 1985; June 13, 1985; September 22, 1985; March 22, 1987; April 2, 1989, p. 11; July 1, 1990, p. 5; September 8, 1991, Joel Conarroe, "Nasty Boy," p. 7; May 15, 1994, p. 11.

Observer (London, England), January 14, 1962, John Silverlight, "Profile: Kingsley Amis," p. 13; October 10, 1976; December 12, 1976; February 12, 1978; July 23, 1978.

Observer Review, November 12, 1967; October 6, 1968.

Paris Review, winter, 1975, Michael Barber, "The Art of Fiction—LIX: Kingsley Amis," pp. 39-72.

Poetry, spring, 1968; July, 1969.

Publishers Weekly, October 28, 1974.

Punch, April 24, 1968; August 28, 1968; October 12, 1968; October 22, 1969; November 18, 1970; October 4, 1978.

Saturday Review, February 20, 1954; May 7, 1955; February 25, 1956; July 27, 1957; March 8, 1958; April 6, 1963; April 5, 1969; February 5, 1977; May/June, 1985.

Saturday Review/World, May 8, 1973.

Southern Review, autumn, 1996, Russell Fraser, "Lucky Jim as I Remember Him," p. 783.

Southwest Review, fall, 2002, David Galef, "The Importance of Being Amis, Revisited," p. 554.

Spectator, January 29, 1954; September 2, 1955; January 17, 1958; September 23, 1960; October 11, 1969; October 9, 1976; June 2, 1984; September 13, 1986; November 29, 1986; December 6, 1986; December 14, 1991, pp. 40-2; March 22, 1997, pp. 43-44.

Sunday Telegraph Magazine, September 17, 1978, Auberon Waugh, "Amis: A Singular Man," pp. 33-36.

Sunday Times (London, England), September 28, 1986.

Time, May 27, 1957; August 31, 1970; September 10, 1973; September 30, 1974; January 3, 1977; June 12, 1978; September 20, 1985; September 30, 1985; March 9, 1987; September 16, 1991, p. 74.

Times (London, England), May 15, 1980; December 31, 1980; May 17, 1984; May 24, 1984; December 15, 1984; September 4, 1986; September 11, 1986; October 23, 1986; December 12, 1987; March 26, 1988; March 31, 1990.

Times Educational Supplement, March 14, 1997, p. A9.

Times Literary Supplement, February 12, 1954; September 16, 1955; January 17, 1958; September 21, 1962; November 23, 1967; March 28, 1968; September 24, 1971; April 6, 1973; October 8, 1976; September 22, 1978; May 16, 1980; October 24, 1980; November 27, 1981; May 25, 1984; September 12, 1986; December 26, 1986; September 23-29, 1988, p. 1039; March 30-April 5, 1990, p. 339; October 5-11, 1990, pp. 1061-1062; March 8, 1991, p. 9; November 22, 1991, p. 24; May 30, 1997, p. 32.

Tribune Books (Chicago, IL), March 8, 1987.

Twentieth Century, July, 1961, Pat Williams, "My Kind of Comedy," pp. 46-50.

Vanity Fair, May, 1987.

Village Voice, October 25, 1973.

Washington Post, September 10, 1973; May 30, 1994, p. C2.

Washington Post Book World, May 5, 1968; August 8, 1968; October 20, 1968; September 1, 1985; March 1, 1987; March 26, 1989.

Wilson Library Bulletin, May, 1958; May, 1965.

World, May 8, 1973.

World Literature Today, summer, 1977; winter, 1977.

Yale Review, autumn, 1969; summer, 1975.

■ Obituaries

PERIODICALS

New Yorker, October 30, 1995, p. 52.

New York Times, October 23, 1995, p. B11.

Time, November 6, 1995, Paul Gray, obituary, p. 87.*

Fredric Brown

■ Personal

Born October 29, 1906, in Cincinnati, OH; died March 11 (some sources say March 12 or 13), 1972, in Tucson, AZ; son of Karl Lewis (a journalist) and Emma Amelia Brown; married Helen Ruth, 1929 (divorced, 1947); married Elizabeth Charlier, October 11, 1948; children: (first marriage) James Ross, Linn Lewis. *Education:* Attended Hanover College and University of Cincinnati. *Hobbies and other interests:* Chess, music, poker, reading.

■ Career

Office worker, 1924-36; *Milwaukee Journal,* Milwaukee, WI, proofreader and writer, beginning 1936; writer, 1947-72.

■ Member

Mystery Writers of America, Writers Guild of America.

■ Awards, Honors

Edgar Allan Poe Award for best first mystery novel from Mystery Writers of America, 1948, for *The Fabulous Clipjoint;* the Fredric Brown Society was founded in 1997.

■ Writings

Murder Can Be Fun (mystery), Dutton (New York, NY), 1948, published as *A Plot for Murder,* Bantam (New York, NY), 1949, reprinted, Blackmask.com, 2004.

The Screaming Mimi (mystery), 1949, reprinted, Blackmask.com, 2004.

What Mad Universe (science fiction), Dutton (New York, NY), 1949, reprinted, introduction by Phil Klass, Bantam (New York, NY), 1978.

Here Comes a Candle: A Novel, Dutton (New York, NY), 1950, reprinted, Millipede Press, 2006.

Night of the Jabberwock (mystery), Dutton (New York, NY), 1950, reprinted, Morrow (New York, NY), 1984.

The Case of the Dancing Sandwiches, Dell (New York, NY), 1951.

The Far Cry (detective novel), Dutton (New York, NY), 1951, reprinted, Vintage (New York, NY), 1991.

The Deep End (mystery), Dutton (New York, NY), 1952.

We All Killed Grandma (mystery), Dutton (New York, NY), 1952.

The Lights in the Sky Are Stars (science fiction), Dutton (New York, NY), 1953, published as *Project Jupiter,* Boardman (London, England), 1954.

Madball, Dell (New York, NY), 1953.

(Editor with Mack Reynolds, and author of introduction) *Science-Fiction Carnival: Fun in Science-Fiction,* Shasta Publishers (Chicago, IL), 1953.

His Name Was Death (mystery), Dutton (New York, NY), 1954.

Martians, Go Home (science fiction), Dutton (New York, NY), 1955.

The Wench Is Dead (mystery), Dutton (New York, NY), 1955.

The Lenient Beast (mystery), Dutton (New York, NY), 1956.

Rogue in Space, Dutton (New York, NY), 1957.

The Office (novel), Dutton (New York, NY), 1958.

One for the Road (mystery), Dutton (New York, NY), 1958.

Knock Three-One-Two (mystery), Dutton (New York, NY), 1959.

The Mind Thing (science fiction), Bantam (New York, NY), 1961.

The Murderers, Dutton (New York, NY), 1961.

The Five-Day Nightmare (mystery), Dutton (New York, NY), 1962.

Mitkey Astromouse (juvenile), illustrations by Heinz Edelmann, Harlin Quist (New York, NY), 1971.

Martians and Madness: The Complete SF Novels of Fredric Brown, NESFA (Framingham, MA), 2002.

Also author of scripts for the *Alfred Hitchcock* and *Boris Karloff's Thriller* television series. Also author of *Star Spangled Night* and *Madman's Holiday.*

STORY COLLECTIONS

Space on My Hands, Shasta (Chicago, IL), 1951, Corgi (London, England), 1953.

Mostly Murder: Eighteen Stories, Dutton (New York, NY), 1953.

Angels and Spaceships, Dutton (New York, NY), 1954, published as *Star Shine,* Bantam (New York, NY), 1956.

Honeymoon in Hell, Bantam (New York, NY), 1958.

Nightmares and Geezenstacks: 47 Stories, Bantam (New York, NY), 1961, reprinted, 1979.

The Shaggy Dog and Other Murders, Dutton (New York, NY), 1963.

Daymares, Lancer (New York, NY), 1968.

Paradox Lost and Twelve Other Great Science Fiction Stories, Random House (New York, NY), 1973.

The Best of Fredric Brown, edited by Robert Bloch, Ballantine (New York, NY), 1977.

The Best Short Stories of Fredric Brown, New English Library (London, England), 1982.

Homicide Sanitarium, [San Antonio, TX], 1984.

Carnival of Crime: The Best Mystery Stories of Frederic Brown, Southern Illinois University Press, 1985.

And the Gods Laughed: A Collection of Science Fiction and Fantasy, Phantasia Press (West Bloomfield, MI), 1987.

From These Ashes: The Complete Short SF of Fredric Brown, NESFA (Framingham, MA), 2001.

"AMBROSE AND ED HUNTER" DETECTIVE SERIES

The Fabulous Clipjoint (first published in a condensed version as "Dead Man's Indemnity" in *Mystery Book,* 1946), Dutton (New York, NY), 1947, reprinted with new introduction by Ron Goulart, Gregg (Boston, MA), 1979, reprinted, Blackmask. com, 2004.

The Dead Ringer, Dutton (New York, NY), 1948.

The Bloody Moonlight, Dutton (New York, NY), 1949, published as *Murder in the Moonlight,* Boardman (London, England), 1950, reprinted, Blackmask. com, 2004.

Compliments of a Fiend, Dutton (New York, NY), 1950, reprinted, Blackmask.com, 2004.

Death Has Many Doors, Dutton (New York, NY), 1951, reprinted, Blackmask.com, 2004.

The Late Lamented, Dutton (New York, NY), 1959.

Mrs. Murphy's Underpants, Dutton (New York, NY), 1963.

Hunter and Hunted: The Ed and Am Hunter Novels, Part One, Stewart Masters (Hermitage, PA), 2002.

"FREDRIC BROWN IN THE DETECTIVE PULPS" SERIES

Homicide Sanitarium, Dennis McMillan (Missoula, MT), 1984.

Before She Kills, Dennis McMillan (Missoula, MT), 1984.

The Freak Show Murders, Dennis McMillan (Belen, NM), 1985.

Thirty Corpses Every Thursday, Dennis McMillan (Belen, NM), 1986.

Pardon My Ghoulish Laughter, Dennis McMillan (Belen, NM), 1986.

Red Is the Hue of Hell, Dennis McMillan (Miami Beach, FL), 1986.

Sex Life on the Planet Mars, Dennis McMillan (Miami Beach, FL), 1986.

Brother Mouse, Dennis McMillan (Miami Beach, FL), 1987.

Nightmare in Darkness, Dennis McMillan (Miami Beach, FL), 1987.

Who Was That Blonde I Saw You Kill Last Night?, Dennis McMillan (Miami Beach, FL), 1988.

Selling Death Short, Dennis McMillan (Missoula, MT), 1988.

Three-Corpse Parlay, Dennis McMillan (Missoula, MT), 1988.

Whispering Death, Dennis McMillan (Missoula, MT), 1989.

Happy Ending, Dennis McMillan (Missoula, MT), 1990.

The Water-Walker, Dennis McMillan (Missoula, MT), 1990.

The Gibbering Night, Dennis McMillan (Hilo, Hawaii), 1991.

The Pickled Punks, Dennis McMillan (Hilo, Hawaii), 1991.

■ Adaptations

Short story "Madman's Holiday" was adapted as the film *Crack-Up,* RKO, 1946; *The Screaming Mimi* was released as a film by Columbia, 1958; the story "Arena" was adapted as an episode of the *Star Trek* television series, 1967; *Martians, Go Home* was adapted as a film in 1990; the story "Solipsist" was adapted as a film in 2005; the story "One Dead Man" is being adapted for film. Several of Brown's works have been filmed in France.

■ Sidelights

Fredric Brown was a prolific science fiction and mystery writer who wrote classic novels in both genres. Brown first appeared on the literary scene during the golden age of "pulp fiction." Distinguishing himself from his pulp peers, Brown—who won the Edgar Award for best first mystery novel and a place in the *Science Fiction Hall of Fame* anthology—became known as a writer of depth and perception; his novels often explored deep themes and challenged readers to think for themselves. "Using many of the conventions of science fiction, including bug-eyed monsters, time-travel, and alternate worlds, Brown created situations in which he could probe human foibles with a humorous or ironic twist," wrote Amelia A. Rutledge in the *Dictionary of Literary Biography;* in the best of his fiction "one finds intensity, psychological perception, and a true grasp of the fantastic mode."

Early Troubles

Brown was born in 1906 in Cincinnati, Ohio. His father, S. Karl Lewis, was a newspaperman and his mother, Emma Amelia, was a homemaker. Brown's early life was not pleasant. His mother passed away in 1920, when he was fourteen years old. His father died the following year. The boy was left to live

Cover of the 2002 collection *Martians and Madness: The Complete SF Novels of Fredric Brown,* which contains all of Fredric Brown's science fiction novels. (NESFA Press, 2002. Cover art copyright © 2002 by Bob Eggleton. Reproduced by permission.)

with friends and relatives through high school. After graduation, he got a job as an office boy with a small factory until the company closed in 1924. He then worked odd jobs and spent a year at Hanover College in Hanover, Indiana. In 1929, Brown married Helen Ruth Brown, a woman he had known only through a series of letters they had exchanged by mail. In 1930 the couple moved to Milwaukee, where jobs were more plentiful. Again, he worked a number of odd jobs, including as a dishwasher, a stock clerk, and a busboy.

Brown had been writing stories and poems since he was a teenager, but he only got serious about writing in the early 1930s. That is when he joined the Allied Authors, a group of budding writers in the Milwaukee area who met regularly to encourage each other and critique each others' work. Brown was soon writing and selling humorous stories to trade magazines of the time. These magazines, aimed at specific industries, were meant for those who worked within the industry. Brown began working as a proofreader for the *Milwaukee Journal* newspaper, while earning a significant amount of his income as a freelancer for such trade magazines as *American Printer*.

Turns to Mystery Fiction

In 1937 Brown sold his first mystery story. By 1940, he had dropped most of his writing for the trade magazines in favor of fiction for the "pulp" magazines of the time. The pulps were the cheapest magazines on the newsstand, printed on the least durable paper, and usually filled with wildly original stories. The paper was so cheap that small pieces of wood could sometimes be seen in the pages, thus the term pulp. Enormously popular in their time, the pulp magazines proved to be the training ground for a number of writers, including Brown, who wrote detective and science fiction stories for such magazines as *Detective Fiction Weekly, Unknown Worlds, Thrilling Detective, G-Men Detective, Phantom Detective, Masked Detective, Dime Mystery, Planet Stories,* and *Clues.* In 1942 alone, Brown published forty-one stories in the pulps.

After proving his hand at crime and science fiction short stories, Brown made an auspicious feature-length debut with *The Fabulous Clipjoint.* The 1947 mystery was the first in a series that featured the uncle-and-nephew detective team of Ambrose and Ed Hunter. The book seemed "refreshingly unhackneyed" to *Chicago Sun Book Week* reviewer James Sandoe. The story begins when Ed Hunter's father Wally is found murdered. Ed turns to his Uncle Ambrose, who works in a carnival, to help solve the crime. The pair investigate a number of leads, including a Chicago gangster who may have wanted Wally dead for having served as a juror against him. But ultimately, as Jack Seabrook remarked in *Martians and Misplaced Clues: The Life and Work of Fredric Brown, The Fabulous Clipjoint* "is a novel of an adolescent's growth from boy to man, played out among Chicago's gritty, working-class characters." Brown followed this novel with numerous short stories in the genre and other mystery novels—many unrelated to the Hunter series—demonstrating an ingenuity in plotting and a combination of violence and wry humor that became hallmarks of his work.

One of Brown's most acclaimed mystery novels is 1951's *Night of the Jabberwock.* Set in a small town and focusing on the town's newspaper publisher—

who also writes, edits, and sells the advertising—the story combines humor, horror, and mystery. Doc Stoeger is an *Alice in Wonderland* buff and, during an evening's conversation with Yehudi Smith, another buff, over a few drinks, the two begin getting reality a bit confused. Doc must put out his weekly newspaper that evening, but newsworthy things seem to be happening all over town. He keeps delaying the newspaper to get in the breaking stories, including bank robbers, missing friends, haunted houses, and a monster who may or may not be on the loose. One by one, all the exciting stories seem to fall apart. Then Doc becomes a prime murder suspect and the police are after him. Philip Higgins of the *New Mexican* recommended the novel to "readers with a sense of humor as well as a yen for mystery and fast action."

Darius Conn, the protagonist of *His Name Was Death,* is the owner of a print shop who has committed the perfect murder. He killed his wife and nobody in his small town realizes it. But now he faces a dilemma. His employee has used certain currency from the shop's safe to cash a check, and Darius cannot afford to let that money be found in circulation. Murder again seems his only way out. "There is a whopping climax, perfect, well-prepared, and joyfully unexpected," wrote Dorothy B. Hughes in the *Albuquerque Tribune.*

SF Writing

In addition to his mystery novels, Brown was also writing science fiction novels and short stories. Among these is the 1949 title *What Mad Universe,* "Brown's first science-fiction novel and one of his most popular works," according to Rutledge. "It is an extended parody of space opera. Keith Winton, editor of a pulp science-fiction magazine, is blasted into a parallel world that is the replica of one in a science-fiction tale conceived by one of the magazine's adolescent enthusiasts. The world is real, nevertheless, and he must eventually act out a heroic role before being returned to his own world."

The science fiction novel *The Lights in the Sky Are Stars* is considered among Brown's most penetrating psychological studies. In a characterization deemed exceptionally rich and mature for the science fiction of its time, the novel portrays a man obsessed by space travel yet denied it because he has been handicapped in an accident. Battling alcoholism and bureaucracy, he helps arrange an exploratory flight to Jupiter only to see the ship leave without him. According to Rutledge, the novel "best represents all of [Brown's] qualities as an

Pat O'Brien and Claire Trevor star in the 1946 film *Crack-Up,* based on Brown's story "Madman's Holiday." (RKO/The Kobal Collection/The Picture Desk, Inc.)

author: the probing of motivation, concealed hints of the true story, and the depiction of human love, determination, and belief in the stars as man's destiny." An essayist in the *St. James Guide to Science Fiction Writers* stated: "*The Lights in the Sky Are Stars* devotes its entire span to the repeated assertions that man can become, that there may or may not be a God, but that there assuredly will be one if and when man develops to his fullest."

The 2001 title, *From These Ashes: The Complete Short SF of Fredric Brown,* gathers over one hundred of Brown's stories, ranging in length from 200-word quickies to some of his longest works. Ray Olson of *Booklist* explained that "a Brown story typically takes an odd situation, develops it risibly, eerily, or suspensefully enough, and concludes with a surprise calculated to rouse chuckles, chills, or both." According to the reviewer for *Kirkus Reviews,* the collection's stories are "gimmicky, sardonic, and sharply twisted: short, snappy gifts to contemporary fantasy that are still worth reading." The critic for the *Library Journal* was moved to describe Brown as "one of the genre's most incisive satirists and outstanding innovators."

Steps Away from Genre Fiction

It was in 1958 that Brown produced his first "straight" (non-genre) novel. *The Office* presents the recollections of thirty-five years in the front office of

Conger & Way. The workplace is staffed by an array of character types: salesmen, bookkeepers, secretaries, and the office boy who matures into the story's narrator. Their interactions and changing relationships over the years propel the plot.

The Office garnered the author some of his best reviews. The *San Francisco Chronicle* reviewer, for example, noted that while the characters are intentionally portrayed as "dull," it is through Brown's skill that "drama is made of ordinary human beings' emotions. . . . What he has made of his remembered knowledge is a fine story, homely in its basic quality and filled with sympathetic perception." Further, the novel "is a new direction for Brown. It will not surprise anyone who knows his great ability in story-telling that he has made such a rich human document of *The Office*."

Armchair Detective writer Newton Baird gave an overall assessment of Brown, noting that in the author's best works he "fought the paradox that would seem to exist between naturalism and romanticism. He never conquered this dilemma, he was pulled on the one hand by determinism, on the other by human volition, and he never created a hero who was complete and confident in the real world." A common denominator in Brown stories, Baird continued, "is that the worst horrors are not those in reality (which are difficult enough to deal with), but those in the unreality of our delusions, in our fantasies and irrational imaginations—in our nightmares."

If you enjoy the works of Fredric Brown, you may also want to check out the following books:

Ray Bradbury, *The Martian Chronicles*, 1950.
A.E. Van Vogt, *Transfinite: The Essential A.E. Van Vogt*, 2003.
Otto Penzler, editor, *The Black Lizard Big Book of Pulps*, 2007.

Baird gave another assessment of Brown, this time in the *St. James Guide to Crime and Mystery Writers*. In this article Baird singled out the novel *The Far Cry* as Brown's "tour de force. It probes a love/hate perplex to one of mystery writing's most startling endings, but the horror almost spoils the achievement." At the same time, Baird remarked that "the

best expressions of his ingenuity and imagination are in some of his short stories, particularly the collection *Nightmares and Geezenstacks,* a delightful potpourri of innocent and ribald humor, expectation and surprise."

Brown's vast literary output sometimes diluted his inventiveness, Baird noted, with "everyday characters and conventional villainy [dominating] his lesser work, like *Murder Can Be Fun* or a failed experiment, *Here Comes a Candle*." But in the long run, Baird stated: "Brown is really one of a kind. . . . [He] portrayed a world that always betrayed and terrified idealists, making them yearn for a place that inspired rather than suppressed freedom and adventure. In his detective novels and mysteries his characters sometimes found that what they had hoped for proved more horrifying than what they had to begin with. In his fantasies, through 'loopholes in reality,' happiness is achieved. So this unique writer wrote from his own time and the future." As the essayist for the *St. James Guide to Science Fiction Writers* noted: "For the most part Brown's style was crisply journalistic. But he drew from his newspaper experience an even more valuable characteristic: each of his yarns had a 'hook' or 'gimmick' to give the work zest and interest. . . . Despite whatever limitations and shortcomings one may detect, Fredric Brown was a buoyant asset to the field of science fiction. The reading diet of all of us became poorer with his death."

■ Biographical and Critical Sources

BOOKS

Baird, Newton, *A Key to Fredric Brown's Wonderland: A Study and an Annotated Bibliographical Checklist*, Talisman (Georgetown, CA), 1981.
Dictionary of Literary Biography, Volume 8: *Twentieth-Century American Science Fiction Writers*, Gale (Detroit, MI), 1981.
St. James Guide to Crime and Mystery Writers, St. James Press (Detroit, MI), 1996.
St. James Guide to Science Fiction Writers, 4th edition, St. James Press (Detroit, MI), 1996.
Seabrook, Jack, *Martians and Misplaced Clues: The Life and Work of Fredric Brown*, Bowling Green State University Popular Press, 1993.

PERIODICALS

Albuquerque Tribune, June 4, 1954, Dorothy B. Hughes, review of *His Name Was Death*, p. 18.

Armchair Detective, July, 1977; winter, 1986, review of *Carnival of Crime: The Best Mystery Stories of Frederic Brown,* p. 79.

Bloomsbury Review, January, 1990, review of *Murder Can Be Fun,* p. 26.

Booklist, June 1, 1985, review of *Carnival of Crime,* p. 1368; March 1, 1986, review of *Homicide Sanitarium,* p. 947; April 15, 2001, Ray Olson, review of *From These Ashes: The Complete Short SF of Fredric Brown,* p. 1539; November 15, 2002, Bill Ott, review of *Hunter and Hunted: The Ed and Am Hunter Novels, Part One,* p. 579.

Book World, June 17, 1984, review of *Night of the Jabberwock,* p. 13.

Chicago Sun, April 2, 1948; December 2, 1949, p. 61; December 23, 1949, p. 40.

Chicago Sun Book Week, March 2, 1947, p. 9.

Kirkus Reviews, March 1, 1973, review of *Paradox Lost and Twelve Other Great Science Fiction Stories,* p. 276; April 15, 2001, review of *From These Ashes,* p. 548.

Library Journal, May 1, 1973, review of *Paradox Lost and Twelve Other Great Science Fiction Stories,* p. 1512; June 15, 2001, review of *From These Ashes,* p. 107.

Ms. Magazine, July, 1984, Michele Slung, review of *Night of the Jabberwock,* p. 24.

New Mexican, January 14, 1951, Philip Higgins, review of *Night of the Jabberwock,* p. 10; June 12, 1977, Alice Bullock, review of *The Best of Fredric Brown,* p. 73.

New Yorker, April 28, 1951, p. 27; January 12, 1952, p. 27.

New York Herald Tribune Book Review, April 6, 1947, p. 19; December 4, 1949, p. 42; May 21, 1950, p. 19; August 27, 1950, p. 11; September 23, 1951, p. 22; December 23, 1951, p. 9; December 6, 1953, p. 50; June 6, 1954, p. 12; February 22, 1959, p. 11.

New York Times, November 7, 1948, p. 40; November 27, 1949, review of *The Screaming Mimi;* April 16, 1950, p. 39; August 13, 1950, p. 22; December 30, 1951, p. 14; June 14, 1953, p. 19; October 24, 1954, p. 36; December 4, 1955, review of *Martians, Go Home,* p. 52; April 15, 1956, p. 20; February 22, 1959, p. 31.

New York Times Book Review, August 16, 1959, p. 24; May 15, 1977, review of *The Best of Fredric Brown,* p. 45; December 25, 1988, review of *The Screaming Mimi,* p. 24; December 24, 1989, review of *Murder Can Be Fun,* p. 22.

Publishers Weekly, March 12, 1973, review of *Paradox Lost and Twelve Other Great Science Fiction Stories,* p. 64; April 4, 1977, review of *The Best of Fredric Brown,* p. 87; April 12, 1985, Sybil Steinberg, review of *Carnival of Crime,* p. 90.

San Francisco Chronicle, January 7, 1951, p. 18; December 25, 1955, p. 15; April 24, 1958, p. 33; March 8, 1959, p. 23; September 20, 1959, p. 25.

Saturday Review of Literature, September 9, 1950, p. 33.

Village Voice, July 3, 1984, review of *Night of the Jabberwock,* p. 52.

Wilson Library Bulletin, September, 1984, review of *Night of the Jabberwock,* p. 55.

ONLINE

Paradox Lost: The Fredric Brown Home Page, http://devernay.free.fr/paradoxlost/html/paradox.html (October 12, 2007).

■ Obituaries

PERIODICALS

New York Times, March 14, 1972, p. 46.
Washington Post, March 14, 1972.*

(The Library of Congress.)

Thomas Cole

■ Personal

Born February 1, 1801, in Bolton-le-Moors, Lancashire, England; died February 8, 1848, near Catskill, New York; buried in the Thomson Street Cemetery, Catskill, NY; son of James (a woolen manufacturer) and Mary Cole; married Maria Bartow, 1836; children: Theodore Alexander. *Education:* Attended school in Chester, England.

■ Career

Painter. Apprenticed to an engraver, then became an engraver's assistant in Liverpool, England; emigrated to the United States, 1818; worked with his father in wallpaper business, Steubenville, OH, 1819; worked as a painter, 1821-48; worked in Philadelphia, 1823-25; settled in New York, 1825; one of the founders of the National Academy of Design, 1826. Paintings in art museum collections, including the National Gallery in Washington, DC, the Institute of History and Art in Albany, New York, and museums in Boston, Cleveland, Detroit, Fort Worth, Los Angeles, Minneapolis, New York City, Toledo, and Utica, New York.

■ Writings

Thomas Cole's Poetry: The Collected Poems of America's Foremost Painter of the Hudson River School, edited by Marshall Tymn, Liberty Cap Books (York, PA), 1972.

The Collected Essays and Prose Sketches, edited by Marshall Tymn, J. Colet Press, 1980.

The Correspondence of Cole and Daniel Wadsworth: Letters in the Watkinson Library, Trinity College, Hartford, and in the New York State Library, Albany, New York, edited by J. Bard McNulty, Connecticut Historical Society (Hartford, CT), 1983.

■ Sidelights

Founder of the Hudson River School of painting in 1825, Thomas Cole was one of the first American landscape painters. Cole believed that paintings done by Americans of the American landscape would result in a uniquely national art different from that of Europe. Cole believed, too, that European artists were at a disadvantage: the great vistas of their continent had already been painted hundreds of times. He wrote: "The painter of American scenery has, indeed, privileges superior to any other. All nature here is new to art." His work also reflected his strong religious, almost mystical, beliefs. Cole made his home on the Hudson River in New York and many of his paintings are depictions of the scenes in that area. According to Stephen Goode in *Insight on the News,* Cole "left

Cole's 1826 painting "Romantic Landscape" depicts a dramatic view of the the Hudson River region. (Copyright © North Carolina Museum of Art/Corbis.)

behind numerous enduring works—icons of 19th-century America that will last as long as landscape painting continues to be admired." An essayist for the *International Dictionary of Art and Artists* explained that Cole's "compositions of real or imaginary scenery, produced between the fall of 1825 and his untimely death early in 1848, helped to establish landscape as a viable alternative to portraiture or figure painting for professional artists in the United States." As Matthew Baigell wrote in his *Thomas Cole:* "Cole provided American painting with a religious profundity and a national relevance it had previously lacked, and because of these qualities, his work was then and still is central to the ongoing dialogue between American artists and their culture."

Life in England and the Midwest

Cole was born in England in 1801 to James and Mary Cole. By 1815 he was apprenticed to an engraver and, by 1817, had become an engraver's assistant. In 1818, when his family moved to Philadelphia, Cole stayed behind and worked as an engraver of book illustrations. In 1819 he sailed to the West Indies; by the summer he had joined his family in America. At first, Cole worked for his father in Steubenville, Ohio, in his wallpaper-manufacturing business. But by 1820, he began to try to make a living with his art. Unable to find art supplies in the frontier of his time, Cole made paint brushes out of hog bristles. He got colors from a local cabinetmaker and learned to mix oil and turpentine to make his own paints. He then toured the state of Ohio looking for work. To find customers in a new town, Cole would set up his easel in the local tavern and offer to paint portraits of the patrons. He also was commissioned to create some religious paintings and created scenery for a theatrical company. But the wandering life of an itinerant artist was not financially successful. In Zanesville, Ohio, Cole could not pay the rent on his apartment.

His landlord threatened to throw him in jail. Cole's offer of an unfinished historical painting in exchange for the unpaid rent was refused. Several friends managed to raise the thirty-five dollars owed, and Cole was obliged to leave town. In 1823 he moved to Philadelphia and began painting landscapes. By 1825 Cole had moved to New York and first visited the Hudson River Valley. In 1826 Cole, who enjoyed the great scenic wonders of the White Mountains and Niagara, made his home in the Hudson River Valley town of Catskill.

Cole's early paintings of the Hudson River region display his love for the natural beauty of the land. They also show Cole's "love for the big, dramatic scenes of America—today we would call them 'productions'—featuring mountains, forests, waterfalls, gorges, caverns, storms and atmospheric effects. His Catskill views are exuberant evocations of nature, painted in oil from sketches made on the spot," according to Miles A. Smith in the *Progress-Index*. Cole's "Romantic Landscape," painted in about 1826, is one of his earliest efforts to capture the natural beauty of the Hudson River region and the Catskill Mountains. Within the dramatic landscape, which is both peaceful and wild at the same time, American Indians can be seen in the distance, dwarfed by the majesty of the natural world. Cole's early works, often dramatically composed and depicting moments of emotional intensity, draw the viewer into the landscape. He makes the viewer feel man as a helpless creature overwhelmed by the all-powerful forces of nature. He frequently placed a highly detailed tree at the right or left foreground (an inheritance from baroque stage settings), and the landscape beyond unfolds as on a stage. Baigell found that these early paintings "mirror an odd union of refinement of feeling, based on artistic tradition and authority, with a relish of painting wild nature as experienced individually." Cole's 1829 painting, "The Subsiding of the Waters of the Deluge," draws on Biblical imagery. The landscape is set after the chaos of the Great Flood of the Old Testament, with an ark in the calm water in the distance symbolizing the new world to come.

Paints His Magnum Opus

In 1829 Cole sailed for England under the patronage of Robert Gilmore of Baltimore. He spent little time in European museums, preferring to sketch out of doors. After a brief visit to Paris, he went down the Rhone River and then to Italy. After nine weeks in Florence he went to Rome, accomplishing most of the journey on foot. Returning to New York in 1832, Cole was given a commission by an art patron to execute five large panels. Known as the "Course of Empire," these paintings were consider-

ably influenced by J.M.W. Turner's "Building of Carthage," which Cole had seen in London. Tom Mack, writing in the *Aiken Standard*, noted: "This is the painter's magnum opus; it is also the most ambitious summary of his political and social philosophy. . . . The five paintings trace the rise and fall of an archetypal civilization. The titles tell it all: 'The Savage State,' 'The Pastoral State,' 'The Consummation of Empire,' 'Destruction,' and 'Desolation.' Thomas Cole believed that history is a cyclical process in which civilizations have their youth, maturity, and old age. As a landscape painter, Cole further believed that historical cycles resemble natural cycles, and in 'The Course of Empire' the different stages of empire coincide with the seasons of the year and the times of the day." "This series," noted an essayist for the *International Dictionary of Art and Artists*, "was intended to cover the fireplace wall in the front room of a third-floor gallery in the new house owned by Luman Reed, a wealthy retired grocery wholesaler, at 13 Greenwich Street, near the Bowling Green at the tip of Manhattan Island."

In 1983, the "Course of Empire" series was displayed at the Munson-Williams-Proctor Institute Museum of Art in Syracuse, New York. At this exhibition, the series was finally displayed in the manner that Cole had originally intended: On the left, the first painting in the series was hung above the second; on the right, the fourth painting was hung above the fifth; and, in the middle, was hung the third painting of the series. "One is able to see how the works had been composed so that, hung in this manner, an overall harmony and balance is created," according to Thomas Piche in the *Syracuse Herald American*. "There is a great deal of interrelationships between the five paintings, in terms of color, atmosphere, and form. Such artistic control only adds to Cole's credit."

Paints "The Voyage of Life" Series

In November of 1836 Cole married Maria Barton, whose family home in Catskill became their permanent residence. In 1839, Cole was commissioned to create a four-painting series entitled "The Voyage of Life." The paintings depicted the stages of life: "Childhood," "Youth," "Manhood," and "Old Age." As an essayist for the *International Dictionary of Art and Artists* explained, the paintings show "the pleasures of Childhood, the worldly ambitions of Youth, the trials and temptations of Manhood, and the ultimate hope and promise of salvation in Old Age." These allegorical works were extremely popular with American art enthusiasts of the time, and Cole often had them on display. They were also made into engravings that sold throughout the country. In 1964, the series was displayed at the New York World's Fair. In 1841 Cole again visited Europe, this time travelling through England, France, Switzerland, Rome, and Sicily, where he painted studies of Mount Etna. He returned to America in 1842.

Cole died at his home in Catskill at the age of forty-seven. At the time of his death, he had been working on a series of religious paintings known as "The Cross and the World." This series includes "Hercules at the Crossroads," "Pilgrim's Progress," and "The Separation of the Blessed and the Damned at the Last Judgment."

Henry Adams, writing in the *Smithsonian*, explained that Cole "left a legacy of paintings in which landscape, for the first time, served as the expression of American destiny. America had a brief history, Cole had noted, and thus had no temples, cathedrals, castles or other monuments of the grandeur of the past. Instead, the 'most distinctive, and perhaps the most impressive characteristic of American scenery, is its wildness.' This did not mean, however, that American scenery lacked historical interest, since it served as an open playing field for the future march of progress. As Cole noted, in the somewhat purple language of the time: 'In looking over the yet uncultivated scene, the mind's eye may see far into futurity. Where the wolf roams, the plough shall glisten; on the gray crag shall rise temple and tower; mighty deeds shall be done in the now pathless wilderness; and poets yet unborn shall sanctify the soil.'" "As founder of our first indigenous art movement—the Hudson River School—he helped elevate American landscape painting from the category of topographical survey to an art form that was able to express philosophical, spiritual and political meaning," according to Piche.

The 1829 painting "The Subsiding of the Waters of the Deluge" is inspired by the Biblical story of Noah's Ark. (Smithsonian American Art Museum, Washington, DC/Art Resource, NY.)

If you enjoy the works of Thomas Cole, you may also want to check out the following:

The works of Hudson River School landscape painters Frederic Church, Sanford Robinson Gifford, and Albert Bierstadt.

Cole's wife, Maria Cole, according to an essayist for the *International Dictionary of Art and Artists*, "kept his house and studio as a kind of shrine to what a Romantic landscape painter, deeply imbued with a love of nature and a passionate desire to teach grand moral lessons, could achieve despite many obstacles in an abbreviated lifetime." The house, known as Cedar Grove, remained in the Cole family until the 1960s. In 1998, the Greene County Historical Society purchased the site for restoration and preservation. It is now named the Thomas Cole National Historic Site. It was officially opened to visitors in 2001, Cole's 200th birthday, and both the living quarters and Cole's art studio can now be toured.

■ Biographical and Critical Sources

BOOKS

Baigell, Matthew, *Thomas Cole*, Watson-Guptill Publications (New York, NY), 1981.

Bryant, William Cullen, *A Funeral Oration Occasioned by the Death of Thomas Cole*, Appleton (New York, NY), 1848.

Cooper, James F., *The Knights of the Brush: The Hudson River School and the Moral Landscape*, Hudson Hills (New York, NY), 2000.

Flexner, James Thomas, *That Wilder Image, the Native School from Thomas Cole to Winslow Homer*, Dover Publications (New York, NY), 1970.

Foshay, Ella M., and Barbara Novak, editors, *Intimate Friends: Thomas Cole, Asher B. Durand, William Cullen Bryant*, New York Historical Society (New York, NY), 2000.

International Dictionary of Art and Artists, St. James Press (Detroit, MI), 1990.

Kelly, Franklin, *Thomas Cole's Paintings of Eden*, Amon Carter Museum (Fort Worth, TX), 1994.

McNulty, J. Bard, *Correspondence of Thomas Cole and Daniel Wadsworth: Letters in the Watkinson Library, Trinity College, Hartford, and in the New York State Library, Albany, New York*, Connecticut Historical Society, 1983.

Merritt, Howard S., *To Walk with Nature: The Drawings of Thomas Cole*, Hudson River Museum, 1981.

Noble, Louis Legrand, *The Life and Works of Thomas Cole*, Harvard University Press (Cambridge, MA), 1964.

Parry, III, Elwood C., *The Art of Thomas Cole: Ambition and Imagination*, University of Delaware Press (Newark, DE), 1988.

Powell, Earl A., *Thomas Cole*, H.N. Abrams (New York, NY), 1990.

Seaver, Esther I., *Thomas Cole: One Hundred Years Later*, Wadsworth Atheneum (Hartford, CT), 1948.

Siegel, Nancy, *Along the Juanita: Thomas Cole and the Dissemination of American Landscape Imagery*, Juniata College Museum of Art/University of Washington Press (Huntington, PA), 2003.

Stilgoe, John R., *Thomas Cole: Drawn to Nature*, Albany Institute of History and Art (Albany, NY), 1993.

Sullivan, Mark W., *The Hudson River School: An Annotated Bibliography*, Scarecrow Press (Metuchen, NJ), 1991.

Sutermeister, Howard, *Studies on Thomas Cole, An American Romanticist*, Museum of Art (Baltimore, MD), 1967.

Truettner, William H., and Alan Wallach, editors, *Thomas Cole: Landscape into History*, Yale University Press/National Museum of American Art, Smithsonian Institution (New Haven, CT), 1994.

PERIODICALS

Aiken Standard (Aiken, SC), June 26, 1994, Tom Mack, "Landscapes Merge Nature and History," p. 8C.

American Artist, November, 2001, "Thomas Cole's House Opened," p. 60.

Art Bulletin, June, 2002, Alan Wallach, "Thomas Cole's River in the Catskills as Antipastoral," p. 334.

Art in America, May-June, 1967, Edward H. Dwight and Richard J. Boyle, "Rediscovery: Thomas Cole's 'Voyage of Life,'" pp. 60-63.

Art Journal, summer, 1993, Randall C. Griffin, "The Untrammeled Vision: Thomas Cole and the Dream of the Artist," p. 66.

Arts Magazine, April, 1978, Earl A. Powell, III, "Thomas Cole and the American Landscape Tradition: Associationism," pp. 113-117; January, 1980, John R. Clarke, "An Italian Landscape by Thomas Cole," pp. 116-120.

Insight on the News, June 27, 1994, Stephen Goode, "Politics Overshadow Art in Cole Exhibition," p. 26.

"Desolation," one of Cole's "Course of Empire" series of paintings, depicts the ruins of a civilization. (New York Historical Society, New York, USA/The Bridgeman Art Library.)

Magazine of Art, February, 1949, E. Parker Lesley, "Some Clues to Thomas Cole," pp. 42-48.

Progress-Index (Petersburg, VA), July 20, 1969, Miles A. Smith, "Whitney Exhibits Thomas Cole's Painting," p. 6.

Smithsonian, May, 1994, Henry Adams, "The American Land Inspired Cole's Prescient Visions," p. 98.

Syracuse Herald American, July 31, 1983, Thomas Piche, "Cole Series Makes First Visit Upstate," p. 9.

Times Recorder (Zanesville, OH), January 15, 1967, Norris F. Schneider, "Gallery of Animal Paintings," p. 5B.

ONLINE

Antiques & the Arts Online, http://antiquesandthe arts.com/ (August 28, 2001), "Thomas Cole's 'Cedar Grove' Lovingly Restored."

Cedar Grove, The Thomas Cole National Historic Site Web site, http://www.thomascole.org/ (September 26, 2007).*

Joan Druett

(Reproduced by permission.)

City & Sea, Friends of the Turnbull Library (New Zealand), Friends of Te Papa (National Museum of New Zealand), Friends of the International Arts Festival (New Zealand), Friends of the New Zealand Symphony Orchestra.

■ Personal

Born April 11, 1939, in Nelson, New Zealand; daughter of Ralph Totten Griffin and Colleen Butcher; married Ronald John Druett (a maritime artist), February 11, 1966; children: Lindsay John, Alastair Ronald. *Education:* Victoria University of Wellington, B.A., 1960.

■ Addresses

Home—Wellington, New Zealand. *Agent*—Laura J. Langlie, 275 President St., No. 3, Brooklyn, NY 11231. *E-mail*—druettjo@yahoo.com.au.

■ Career

Writer and educator. Teacher of biology and English literature until 1983; writer, 1983—.

■ Member

Authors Guild, Martha's Vineyard Historical Society (Edgartown, MA), Mystic Seaport Museum, New Bedford Whaling Museum, Wellington Museum of

■ Awards, Honors

Best first prose book, International PEN, 1984, for *Exotic Intruders: The Introduction of Plants and Animals to New Zealand;* Fulbright Writer's Cultural Award, 1986; John Lyman Award for best book of American maritime history, 1992, for *"She Was a Sister Sailor": The Whaling Journals of Mary Brewster, 1845-1851;* Oysterponds Historical Society Scholar-in-residence Award, 1993; New York Public Library Award, 1998, for *Hen Frigates: Wives of Merchant Captains under Sail;* L. Byrne Waterman Award for outstanding contributions to history and women's history, 1999; John David Stout Research Fellowship Award, University of Wellington, 2001.

■ Writings

NONFICTION

Exotic Intruders: The Introduction of Plants and Animals to New Zealand, Heinemann (Auckland, New Zealand), 1983.

Fulbright in New Zealand, New Zealand-U.S. Educational Foundation (Wellington, New Zealand), 1988.

Petticoat Whalers: Whaling Wives at Sea, 1820-1920, illustrated by husband, Ron Druett, HarperCollins (Auckland, New Zealand), 1991, HarperCollins (New York, NY), 1992.

(Editor) *"She Was a Sister Sailor": The Whaling Journals of Mary Brewster, 1845-1851,* Mystic Seaport Museum (Mystic, CT), 1991.

(With Mary Anne Wallace) *The Sailing Circle: Nineteenth-Century Seafaring Women from New York,* introduction by Lisa Norling, Three Village Historical Society (East Setauket, NY)/Cold Spring Harbor Whaling Museum (Cold Spring Harbor, NY), 1995.

Hen Frigates: Wives of Merchant Captains under Sail, Simon & Schuster (New York, NY), 1998.

Rough Medicine: Surgeons at Sea in the Age of Sail, Routledge (New York, NY), 2000.

She Captains: Heroines and Hellions of the Sea, Simon & Schuster (New York, NY), 2000.

In The Wake of Madness: The Murderous Voyage of the Whaleship Sharon, Algonquin Books (Chapel Hill, NC), 2003.

Island of the Lost: Shipwrecked at the Edge of the World, Algonquin Books of Chapel Hill (Chapel Hill, NC), 2007.

NOVELS

Abigail, Random House (New York, NY), 1988.

A Promise of Gold, Bantam (New York, NY), 1990.

Murder at the Brian Boru, HarperCollins (Auckland, New Zealand), 1992.

"WIKI COFFIN" MYSTERY SERIES

A Watery Grave, St. Martin's Minotaur (New York, NY), 2004.

Shark Island, St. Martin's Minotaur (New York, NY), 2005.

Run Afoul, St. Martin's Minotaur (New York, NY), 2006.

Deadly Shoals, St. Martin's Minotaur (New York, NY), 2007.

OTHER

Also author of *Captain's Daughter, Coasterman's Wife: Carrie Hubbard Davis of Orient,* 1994. Contributor to periodicals, including *Log of Mystic Seaport, Newport History, Sea History, Dukes County Intelligencer, Mains'l Haul, Seaport, Nautical Collector, Alfred Hitch-* cock's *Mystery Magazine,* and *No Quarter Given.* Author of science-fiction stories published under pseudonym Jo Friday in magazine *Worlds of If.*

■ Sidelights

A New Zealand writer of maritime history, Joan Druett has written extensively about the history of women at sea. In 1999 she was awarded the L. Byrne Waterman Award for outstanding contributions to history and women's history. Druett is also known for her "Wiki Coffin" mystery series, which chronicles the adventures of a 19th century ship's translator, Wiki Coffin, who solves murders around the world. The series combines criminal sleuthing with seafaring adventure. According to Cheryl Solimini in *Mystery Scene,* in these mysteries, Druett "not only offers you-are-there joyrides on authentic sailing ships of the early 1800s, but also presents one of the most engaging sleuths on land or sea— Wiki Coffin, a fictional 24-year-old half-Yankee, half-Maori." The Wiki Coffin mysteries include *A Watery Grave, Shark Island,* and *Deadly Shoals.* Among Druett's nonfiction titles are *The Sailing Circle: Nineteenth-Century Seafaring Women from New York, Hen Frigates: Wives of Merchant Captains under Sail, In the Wake of Madness: The Murderous Voyage of the Whaleship Sharon,* and *Island of the Lost: Shipwrecked at the Edge of the World.*

From Teaching to Writing

Druett was born in Nelson, New Zealand, but her family soon moved to the town of Palmerston North, where her father was a builder. "It was an extremely crimping place to grow up, a really small town," she told Heather Vogel Frederick in *Publishers Weekly.* "Perhaps because of that, Palmerston North produced a large number of writers. Everyone was a big reader." Druett studied at Victoria University of Wellington in New Zealand and went on to become a teacher of both biology and English literature. In 1983, however, she decided to concentrate on a writing career. That year she published her first book, *Exotic Intruders: The Introduction of Plants and Animals to New Zealand,* which won an award from International PEN. While visiting the Pacific island of Rarotonga with her maritime artist husband, Ron, Druett came across a graveyard where shipwrecked sailors had been buried. She, in fact, fell into an open hole that turned out to be the grave of a captain's wife. The fall made her curious. "I wanted to find out about her," she told Solimini.

Five years of research led to her first novel, *Abigail,* based on the real story of the woman whose grave she had found. Following that success, Druett began writing about seafaring women and their role in maritime history.

Petticoat Whalers: Whaling Wives at Sea, 1820-1920, Druett's first nonfiction book about maritime history, was inspired by her discovery of a buried headstone. "My engrossing interest in the history of women in whaling began in May, 1984, when I came across a young Maori scraping at a patch of waste ground on the tiny South Pacific island of Rarotonga," she once explained to *CA.* "I was told that he had a dream in which an ancestor came to him and told him to clear the land because it was a lost graveyard. Three days later the young man had gone, so I investigated the heaps of weeds and broken stones. . . . I found a coral rock grave with a headstone set into it like a door. The inscription was a memorial to a twenty-four-year-old American girl, Mary Ann Sherman, the wife of the captain of the American whaling ship *Harrison,* who had died January 5, 1850. A girl on a whaling ship? It seemed impossible! How had she lived . . . and died? This was the beginning of my quest." The book is illustrated with paintings by Druett's husband, maritime artist Ron Druett.

After producing *Petticoat Whalers,* Druett served as editor of *"She Was a Sister Sailor": The Whaling Journals of Mary Brewster, 1845-1851,* which provides what a *Publishers Weekly* contributor described as "detail concerning shipboard life and the whaling industry, as well as a portrait of missionary life on the island of Maui." She then wrote *Murder at the Brian Boru* and—three years later—*Captain's Daughter, Coasterman's Wife: Carrie Hubbard Davis of Orient,* released in 1994. In addition, she collaborated with Mary Anne Wallace in writing *The Sailing Circle.*

Maritime History of Women

Druett's 1998 book, *Hen Frigates,* relates the experiences of women on shipping expeditions. Among the notable women in this volume is a teenager who replaced her dead father as commander and subsequently repelled a sexually aggressive sailor, quashed a mutiny, and even convinced her crew to dump the ship's alcohol overboard. Other women in Druett's study bear children, combat illnesses such as malaria and plague, and endure dangerous storms.

Hen Frigates won praise for its exploration of a little-known topic. An *Atlantic* contributor wrote that the book "casts light on an odd corner of nineteenth-

Druett holds a copy of her 1991 title *"She Was a Sister Sailor": The Whaling Journals of Mary Brewster, 1845-1851,* an account of a 19th century woman's life. (Reproduced by permission.)

century life," and *Library Journal* contributor Roseanne Castellino called it "informative and entertaining reading." Another reviewer, Margaret Flanagan, declared in *Booklist* that Druett's volume constituted "an intimate glimpse" back in time and noted that *Hen Frigates* "provides the reader with an intriguing entrée into an exotic lifestyle." Holly Morris, meanwhile, wrote in the *New York Times Book Review* that Druett's work serves as "a valuable collective portrait of intrepid seafaring women."

Druett's other books include *Rough Medicine: Surgeons at Sea in the Age of Sail* and *She Captains: Heroines and Hellions of the Sea.* In *Rough Medicine* Druett describes the adventures of English physicians who put to sea in the early nineteenth century in the wake of John Woodall, considered "the father of sea surgery." Based on primary documents, Druett notes that the doctors were driven to dangerous positions on shipboard mainly for the sake of adventure. The latter volume relates the exploits of seafaring women from the time of ancient Egypt to the twentieth century. Among the various figures in the book are Tomyris, a Massegetae queen who triumphed in battle against Persian forces, and Lucy Brewer, who posed as a man and obtained assignment as a sailor aboard the U.S.S. *Constitution.*

Upon its publication in 2000, *She Captains* received recognition as a provocative chronicle. *Booklist* contributor Donna Seaman wrote: "Maritime lore has always been rich in romance and suffering; Druett's revelations increase its fascination tenfold." A *Publishers Weekly* contributor was likewise impressed, describing *She Captains* as an "entertaining work . . . filled with fascinating characters." *Library Journal* reviewer Roseanne Castellino remarked: "The stories are lively, the characters vivid and eccentric," while Louise Jarvis noted in the *New York Times Book Review* that *She Captains* presents "wild tales of women's bravery and bloodlust from antiquity to the twentieth century." Jarvis added: "Druett descends on the gory tidbits and operatic tableaus with a cheeky tone that seems to acknowledge our own perverse fascination—delight even—with atrocities and hardships that would make Melville's or Hemingway's sea dogs buckle."

Having exhausted research documentation on seafaring women in her previous books, Druett's next work, *In the Wake of Madness: The Murderous Voyage of the Whaleship Sharon,* concentrates on a specific incident in maritime lore. In 1841 the whaler *Sharon,* led by Captain Howes Norris, "a seagoing psychopath of the classic mold," according to Peter Nichols of the *New York Times Book Review,* left Fairhaven, Massachusetts, for the South Pacific. When the ship returned three years later, only four of the original twenty-nine crew members were aboard, and Captain Norris was not among them. He had been murdered in the South Pacific by Kanaka tribesmen taken aboard as crew members. Based on the journals of Benjamin Clough, the third mate who recaptured the ship from the Pacific islanders who killed Norris, and Andrew White, the ship's cooper, Druett's account analyzes Norris's behavior and shows it to have been instrumental in his demise.

According to the records Druett uncovered, Norris was a racist and a drunkard who repeatedly beat and tortured his crew members and eventually killed his steward. In return, many men deserted the ship, which forced Norris to hire locals to flesh out the crew during the long voyage. The Kanaka tribesmen had no reason to remain loyal to the captain, so when the rest of the crew was offboard searching for whales, three of them hacked Norris in half with a sharp spade used for cutting whale

blubber. For the remainder of their days, the surviving crew members largely skirted the truth about what happened during the voyage. Druett asserts they were ashamed by their lack of courage in standing up to a captain who did not have a firm grip on reality.

A reviewer for *Publishers Weekly* called *In the Wake of Madness* "a terrific account of an unusually eventful voyage," adding that it "manages a perfect balance between telling the story in an unfussy yet dramatic manner and honoring its complexity." *Library Journal* contributor Robert C. Jones characterized the book as "a murder investigation mixed with equal parts whaling lore, mystery, retribution, and history" that is "informative and vividly recreated." Nichols wrote that Druett "draws a fine picture of the floating community of whalers and deserters scattered across the Pacific." Other critics also appreciated Druett's ability to evoke a detailed portrait of a bygone era. *In the Wake of Madness* provides an "excellent insight into the whaling life and human nature," wrote *Kliatt* reviewer Sunnie Grant, and a writer for *Kirkus Reviews* called the book a "swift, absorbing saga of the sea [that] invokes malice, mayhem, murder, and, hovering over it all, Herman Melville."

Enter Wiki Coffin

Druett turned to mystery writing with *A Watery Grave,* published in 2004. The author introduces her hero and sleuth William "Wiki" Coffin, who is half Maori with an American father who is a sea captain. Raised in New England, Wiki never feels a part of the society around him. As soon as he is old enough, he joins the United States Exploring Expedition of 1838 as a "linguister," or translator. His knowledge of the Maori language seems invaluable to an expedition going to the South Pacific. The expedition is to travel from the United States, around the southern tip of South America, and into the Pacific Ocean. They will then sail throughout the South Seas, mapping and exploring the little-known region. Also on board are Wiki's friend Captain George Rochester, and Captain Charles Wilkes, leader of the expedition.

Before the expedition leaves Wiki is arrested for the murder of Mrs. Tristram T. Stanton, who is married to the expedition's civilian astronomer. When Wiki clears himself, the sheriff finds a connection between the murder and the expedition, asks Wiki to serve as investigator during the course of the expedition. A *Publishers Weekly* contributor called *A Watery Grave*

Druett with her American agent, Laura Langlie, in New York City in 1997. (Reproduced by permission.)

"a fine start to a series sure to appeal to lovers of historical mysteries and fans of sea adventures." Lesley Dunlap, writing on the *MysteryReader.com* Web site, noted that the author's "familiarity with naval matters is evident," adding: "The whodunit is satisfyingly complex, but the real pleasure in reading *A Watery Grave* is the glimpse into the past and the world it portrays." Rex E. Klett in the *Library Journal* believed that the novel "blends strong plotting and scads of authentic maritime detail in an impressive debut," A *Kirkus Reviews* contributor found the novel to be "the debut of a smart, appealing hero whose tale unfolds amid lots of interesting cross-cultural, historical, and nautical detail."

In *Shark Island*, Wiki is still part of the Exploring Expedition and investigating the foundering of the *Anawan* at Shark Island, off the coast of Brazil. When Wiki, Rochester, and their crewmates board the *Anawan*, they meet Captain Ezekiel Reed and his beautiful bride Annabelle, who previously had an affair with Wiki. When Captain Reed is murdered and the unlikable Captain Forsythe is accused of the crime, Wiki thinks someone else is guilty and

investigates. He soon believes that the murder may have to do with some missing cargo. A *Publishers Weekly* contributor noted that the author "should win plaudits from both mystery fans and aficionados of naval adventures." A critic for *Mystery Lovers Corner* concluded: "Druett's mysterious mind weaves yet another dark tale of intrigue and surprise on the high seas."

Wiki returns once again in *Run Afoul*, this time investigating the illness and, according to Dr. Olliver, the possible poisoning of the expedition's astronomer Grimes. When Grimes dies, the crew believes that the cook Festin killed him. Festin had been tried for poisoning on a previous voyage but found innocent. An inquest rules Grimes death accidental but Wiki suspects a villain, a suspicion supported when Dr. Olliver is killed. The novel also features Wiki's reunion with his adventuresome father, Captain William Coffin, who is later charged with murder. "Comic complications and unsettling racist views bubble up" during the course of the story, noted a *Kirkus Reviews* contributor. A *Publishers Weekly* reviewer commented that the author "makes the vanished world she depicts come alive."

If you enjoy the works of Joan Druett, you may also want to check out the following books:

Patrick O'Brian, *The Commodore*, 1995.
Bernard Cornwell, *Sharpe's Fury*, 2006.
Julian Stockwin, *The Admiral's Daughter*, 2007.

Deadly Shoals finds Wiki on the Brazilian coast. He is called in when Captain Stackpole claims to have been cheated. He paid Trader Caleb Adams for a schooner, but Adams is missing, and so is the money and the schooner. Wiki follows a trail that takes him upriver into rugged Patagonia. When he finds Adams, the man has been killed and the receipt for the schooner is gone. The critic for *Publishers Weekly* noted that "gauchos, Indians, revolutionaries and adventurers flock across the beautifully rendered landscape." Margaret Flanagan, writing in *Booklist*, found that "Druett continues to pepper her suspenseful plots with the same type of authentic seafaring facts and lore that so distinguished the novels of the late Patrick O'Brien." Mary Helen Becker in *Mystery Scene* concluded: "A fast-moving tale with plenty of crime and suspense, *Deadly Shoals* will delight readers."

In a statement posted on her Web site, Druett commented on the Wiki Coffin books: "The experiences of the brave 'kanakas'—Pacific Islanders—and adventurous Maori who so willingly signed up on Yankee ships just for the hell of it has always intrigued me, and the series has given me a wonderful opportunity to explore the topic, as well as express the dash and romance of life under sail at a time when the Pacific Ocean was both intriguingly exotic and largely uncharted. But most of all it has given me the chance to write marvellously swashbuckling seafaring yarns, so as well as having a rich fund of lore to draw upon, I am having a terrific time."

■ Biographical and Critical Sources

PERIODICALS

American History Illustrated, July-August, 1993, review of *"She Was a Sister Sailor": The Whaling Journals of Mary Brewster, 1845-1851*, p. 17.

Atlantic, August 1, 1998, review of *Hen Frigates: Wives of Merchant Captains under Sail*, p. 104.

Biography, fall, 2000, Louise Jarvis, review of *She Captains: Heroines and Hellions of the Sea*, p. 835.

Boating, April, 2001, Randy Steele, review of *She Captains*, p. 32.

Booklist, May 15, 1998, Margaret Flanagan, review of *Hen Frigates*, p. 1570; February 15, 2000, Donna Seaman, review of *She Captains*; September 15, 2000, William Beatty, review of *Rough Medicine: Surgeons at Sea in the Age of Sail*, p. 197; April 1, 2003, Gavin Quinn, review of *In the Wake of Madness: The Murderous Voyage of the Whaleship Sharon*, p. 1373; September 1, 2004, Barbara Bibel, review of *A Watery Grave*, p. 68; October 1, 2005, Margaret Flanagan, review of *Shark Island*, p. 37; November 1, 2006, Margaret Flanagan, review of *Run Afoul*, p. 32; February 1, 2007, George Cohen, review of *Island of the Lost*, p. 18; September 1, 2007, Margaret Flanagan, review of *Deadly Shoals*, p. 60.

Choice, April, 2001, review of *Rough Medicine*.

Entertainment Weekly, May 18, 2007, Wook Kim, review of *Island of the Lost*.

Historian, fall, 2001, B.R. Burg, review of *She Captains*, p. 202.

International Herald Tribune, July 13, 2007, Florence Williams, review of *Island of the Lost*.

JAMA: The Journal of the American Medical Association, April 11, 2001, Hans A. Brings, review of *Rough Medicine*, p. 1894.

Journal of the American Medical Association, April 11, 2000, Hans A. Brings, "Nautical Medicine," p. 1894.

Journal of the Early Republic, winter, 1993, Mary Zwiep, review of *"She Was a Sister Sailor,"* p. 582.

Kirkus Reviews, March 1, 2003, review of *In the Wake of Madness*, p. 359; August 1, 2004, review of *A Watery Grave*, p. 715; August 15, 2005, review of *Shark Island*, pp. 883-884; September 1, 2006, review of *Run Afoul*, pp. 876-877.

Kliatt, May, 2002, Mary T. Gerrity, *Petticoat Whalers: Whaling Wives at Sea, 1820-1920*, p. 40; September, 2003, Sunnie Grant, review of *In the Wake of Madness*, p. 60.

Lancet, October 27, 2001, Alexander Campbell, review of *Rough Medicine*, p. 1468.

Library Journal, July, 1998, Roseanne Castellino, review of *Hen Frigates*, p. 108; March 15, 2000, Roseanne Castellino, review of *She Captains*, p. 104; March 15, 2003, Robert C. Jones, review of *In the Wake of Madness*, p. 96; August 15, 2004, Rex E. Klett, review of *A Watery Grave*, p. 59.

Motorboating, September, 2003, review of *In the Wake of Madness*, p. 10.

Mystery Scene, Number 102, 2007, Mary Helen Becker, review of *Deadly Shoals*, pp. 75-76; Number 103, 2008, Cheryl Solimini, "Joan Druett: High Crimes on the High Seas," pp. 28-30.

New York Times Book Review, July 26, 1998, Holly Morris, "First Helpmates"; March 26, 2000, Louise Jarvis, "Dames at Sea," review of *She Captains*,

p. 15; May 4, 2003, Peter Nichols, "Psycho at Sea," review of *In the Wake of Madness*, p. 16; July 15, 2007, Florence Williams, review of *Island of the Lost*, p. 26.

Publishers Weekly, November 16, 1992, review of *"She Was a Sister Sailor,"* p. 55; January 31, 2000, review of *She Captains*; December 18, 2000, review of *Rough Medicine*, p. 70; April 28, 2003, review of *In the Wake of Madness*, p. 61; June 23, 2003, Heather Vogel Frederick, "Joan Druett: A Woman Happily at Sea," p. 41; July 26, 2004, review of *A Watery Grave*, p. 41; August 8, 2005, review of *Shark Island*, p. 216; September 18, 2006, review of *Run Afoul*, p. 39; March 12, 2007, review of *Island of the Lost*, p. 44; October 15, 2007, review of *Deadly Shoals*, p. 45.

ONLINE

Joan Druett Web site, http://members.authorsguild. net/druettjo (March 7, 2007).

Mystery Lovers Corner, http://www.sleuthedit.com/ (August 2, 2007), review of *Shark Island*.

MysteryReader.com, http://www.themysteryreader. com/ (March 6, 2007), Lesley Dunlap, review of *A Watery Grave*.

Paste Magazine Online, http://www.pastemagazine. com/ (July 3, 2007), H.M. Starkey, review of *Island of the Lost*.

Rambles, http://www.rambles.net/ (September 2, 2006), Tom Knapp, review of *She Captains*.*

Kathleen Ernst

■ Personal

Born May 7, 1959, in Scranton, PA; daughter of Henry (a Methodist minister) and Priscilla Johnston (a librarian) Ernst; married Scott C. Meeker; children: Meghan McGill Meeker. *Education:* West Virginia University, B.S., 1981; Antioch University, M.A., 1994. *Politics:* "Independent liberal." *Religion:* Unitarian Universalist. *Hobbies and other interests:* Travel, hiking, kayaking, baking, sewing, quilting.

■ Addresses

E-mail—k.ernst@distaff.net.

■ Career

Writer and writing instructor. Old World Wisconsin Historic Site, Eagle, WI, interpreter and curator of education and collections, 1982-93; Wisconsin Educational Communications Board, Madison,, senior educational specialist, 1994-2003; instructor, University of Wisconsin-Madison Division of Continuing Studies, 1998—. Instructor at Edgewood College, 1994, Carroll College, 1997-99, and Mount Mary College, 2005. Civil War interpreter at living-history presentations.

■ Member

Society of Children's Book Writers and Illustrators, Mystery Writers of America, Women Writing the West.

■ Awards, Honors

Award of Excellence, Central Education Network, 1996, for *Exploring Wisconsin Our Home;* Books for the Teen Age listing, New York Public Library, 1998, for *The Night Riders of Harpers Ferry;* Crystal Award, Association for Educational Communications and Technology, 2000, for *Investigating Wisconsin History;* Edgar Allan Poe Award nomination, Mystery Writers of America, 2001, for *Trouble at Fort La Pointe;* Arthur Tofte Juvenile Fiction Book Award, Council for Wisconsin Writers, 2001, for *Retreat from Gettysburg,* 2004, for *Ghosts of Vicksburg,* and 2005, for *Betrayal at Cross Creek;* Agatha Award nomination for best young adult mystery, 2002, for *Whistler in the Dark,* and 2004, for *Betrayal at Cross Creek;* Emmy for Outstanding Children's Programming—Children's Series, National Academy of Television Arts & Sciences, Midwest Chapter, 2002, for *Cultural Horizons of Wisconsin;* Aurora Award Gold Medal, Aurora Independent Film and Video Competition, for *Cultural Horizons of Wisconsin;* Wilbur Schramm Award for Excellence, National Educational Telecommunications Association, 2003, for *Cultural Horizons;* Flora MacDonald Award, Scottish Heritage Center, St. Andrews Presbyterian College, 2004, for *Betrayal at Cross Creek;* Judge's Award for Instructional Innovation, National Educational Telecommunications Association, and Aurora Award Platinum Medal for Best of Show, Aurora International Independent Film and Video Corporation, both 2004, both for *Cultural Horizons;* Flora MacDonald Award, 2006; Outstanding Achievement in Children's Literature Citation from the Wisconsin Library Association, Children's Literature Award from Society of Midland Authors, Arthur Tofte/ Betty Ren Wright Children's Literature Award from Council for Wisconsin Writers, Editors' Choice Selection from *Historical Novels Review*, Books for the Teen Age listing from the New York Public Library, all 2007, all for *Hearts of Stone*.

■ Writings

YOUNG-ADULT HISTORICAL NOVELS

The Night Riders of Harpers Ferry, White Mane (Shippensburg, PA), 1996.

The Bravest Girl in Sharpsburg, White Mane Kids (Shippensburg, PA), 1997.

Retreat from Gettysburg, White Mane Kids (Shippensburg, PA), 2000.

Ghosts of Vicksburg, White Mane Kids (Shippensburg, PA), 2003.

Hearts of Stone, Dutton Children's Books (New York, NY), 2006.

Highland Fling, Cricket Books (Chicago, IL), 2006.

"HISTORY MYSTERIES" SERIES

Trouble at Fort La Pointe, Pleasant Company (Middleton, WI), 2000.

Whistler in the Dark, Pleasant Company (Middleton, WI), 2002.

Betrayal at Cross Creek, Pleasant Company (Middleton, WI), 2004.

"AMERICAN GIRL MYSTERIES" SERIES

Danger at the Zoo: A Kit Mystery, Pleasant Company (Middleton, WI), 2005.

Secrets in the Hills: A Josefina Mystery, Pleasant Company (Middleton, WI), 2006.

Midnight in Lonesome Hollow: A Kit Mystery, American Girl (Middleton, WI), 2007.

The Runaway Friend: A Kirsten Mystery, American Girl (Middleton, WI), 2008.

FOR TELEVISION

(With others) *Exploring Wisconsin, Our Home*, Wisconsin Educational Communications Board/ Wisconsin Public Television, 1995.

New Dawn of Tradition: A Wisconsin Powwow, Wisconsin Educational Communications Board, 1998.

Investigating Wisconsin History, Wisconsin Educational Communications Board/ Wisconsin Public Television, 1998.

(And project director) *Cultural Horizons of Wisconsin* (series), Wisconsin Educational Communications Board/Wisconsin Public Television, 2002–03.

OTHER

Too Afraid to Cry: Maryland Civilians in the Antietam Campaign (nonfiction), Stackpole (Mechanicsburg, PA), 1999.

Contributor to periodicals, including *America's Civil War, Civil War Times Illustrated, Columbiad, Wilderness, Boundary Waters Journal, Wisconsin Trails,* and *Quilters' Newsletter Magazine.*

■ Sidelights

Kathleen A. Ernst is a writer of mysteries and historical novels for teenaged readers. Among her novels about the American Civil War are *The Night Riders of Harpers Ferry, The Bravest Girl in Sharpsburg, Retreat from Gettysburg,* and *Ghosts of Vicksburg.* Her mystery novel, *Trouble at Fort La Pointe,* received an Edgar Allan Poe Award nomination from the Mystery Writers of America. *Whistler in the Dark* and *Betrayal at Cross Creek* were nominated for the Agatha Award for best young adult mystery.

"I was born in Pennsylvania, but grew up in Maryland," Ernst recounted on her Web Site, "surrounded by books! My mother was a librarian and my father an avid reader. Before going on vacation, my mom would bring home historical fiction about whatever area or historic site we planned to visit. Obviously that really made an impression on me! We visited lots of historic sites and museums while I was growing up. I have two sisters, one older and one younger, and we all love to read. When I was a kid, I'd read with a flashlight under the covers when I was supposed to be asleep. Now I use one of those mini book lights—a truly great invention." Ernst earned a bachelor's degree from West Virginia University, majoring in environmental education, and a master's degree from Antioch University, where she majored in history education and writing.

From 1982 to 1994, Ernst worked as the curator of education at the Old World Wisconsin Historic Site. This outdoor historic site provides visitors with the opportunity to see the clothing, customs, and daily work activities of people who lived in the nineteenth century. "Old World Wisconsin has over fifty restored buildings," Ernst stated on her Web site. "It was the best training ground for an historical fiction writer imaginable!" She then became the senior educational specialist for the Wisconsin Educational Communications Board, where she wrote and produced educational television programs about Wisconsin history. "Writing for television is very different than writing novels or nonfiction books," Ernst explained at her Web site. "I had to learn what parts of a story were best told in words, and what parts best told with visual images. It was challenging at times, but I grew as a writer."

Writes Historical Fiction

Ernst's first book contract was for *The Night Riders of Harpers Ferry,* a novel of the U.S. Civil War. This first novel is based on a true incident. Young Union soldier Solomon is a map sketch artist for the New York Cavalry, currently bivouacked at Harpers Ferry, who meets Mahalia when he pulls her out of the Potomac River. After he gives Mahalia a ride home, her mother invites him in for supper though Mahalia says not a word of thanks. Solomon's commanding officer encourages him to visit her family, for Mahalia's twin is a member of the Confederate cavalry. Solomon enjoys the assignment because he is smitten with Mahalia. After a while, Solomon begins to wonder if there really is a twin brother: he feels certain he has seen Mahalia riding with the Confederate army. Carolyn Phelan, writing for *Booklist,* remarked that *The Night Riders of Harpers Ferry* "conveys the strain of divided families, misguided loyalties," and the difficulties of life during the Civil War.

The Bravest Girl in Sharpsburg, Ernst's second novel, also takes place during the U.S. Civil War. Teresa Kretzer and Savilla Miller, best friends who once shared the reputation for being the bravest girls in Sharpsburg, find themselves at political odds as civil war looms over Maryland. Their difficulties come to a head as both girls must face the Battle of Antietam. Ernst once commented about why she chose to write on historical topics: "Most of my work is historical fiction because that's what I grew up reading, and I still love to disappear into a good historical novel. Novelists know that history is about stories, not strings of dates and facts. When I'm settling in on a new project, I try to find themes and stories that haven't been covered already in fiction— stories that might otherwise be lost."

Having grown up in Maryland, Ernst spent many years visiting the Antietam Battlefield and the small towns nearby. As she once explained: "At that time there was little interest in social history," Ernst recalled, "but I always looked at the old houses near the battlefield and wondered what happened to the people living there when the armies came. That interest led to my lone adult nonfiction book, *Too Afraid to Cry: Maryland Civilians in the Antietam Campaign,* which took over a decade to research and write. The first three Civil War novels I had published stemmed from research I did for that project, too."

Too Afraid to Cry focuses on the changes civilians were forced to make when the Civil War landed on their doorsteps. The Battle of Antietam was the single bloodiest day in the history of the United States, and while there are numerous military studies of the event, very few books discuss the effect the battle had on the people living in the area, according to Theresa McDevitt of the *Library Journal,* who considered it a "fascinating topic." Sharon Sea-

Kathleen A. Ernst's *Too Afraid to Cry: Maryland Civilians in the Antietam Campaign* discusses the effects the historic Civil War battle had on local residents. (Stackpole Books, 1999. Reproduced by permission.)

ger, writing in *Civil War History*, praised Ernst's book, noting that "the writing is vivid, skillfully blending military and social history."

Ernst followed her adult nonfiction book with a third young-adult novel focusing on the same era in American history. In *Retreat from Gettysburg* young Chigger O'Malley's father and three brothers were killed while serving in the Union Army, and Chigger hopes that the Confederates suffer a sound defeat. However, when he and his mother are forced to take in a wounded Confederate soldier retreating from the disastrous battle of Gettysburg, Chigger begins to question his own faith in what is right and what is wrong. "The ethical issues that follow move beyond the battle lines and involve the growing up of a young man," wrote the critic for the *Wisconsin State Journal*. "It's an interesting and surprising story." "Meticulous attention to history is the strong point" of the novel, according to Carolyn Phelan in *Booklist*. Toniann Scime, writing in the *School Library Journal*, praised the novel as "an excellent example of how to teach history through fiction."

Jamie Carswell and his cousin Althea find themselves on opposite sides of the Civil War in *Ghosts of Vicksburg*. Though Jamie currently serves in the Fourteenth Wisconsin Infantry Regiment, he grew up summering in Mississippi with his cousins. As Jamie watches while he and the other soldiers cause civilians to suffer, he begins to wonder if the army is doing the right thing. Nancy P. Reeder wrote in her *School Library Journal* review that Ernst "does a commendable job of remaining neutral."

In *Hearts of Stone*, the author created Hannah Cameron, a girl whose father must leave home to join the Union army during the Civil War. After her father and mother are both killed, Hannah looks for refuge in Nashville, a city crowded with starving refugees. According to a *Kirkus Reviews* writer, the "memorable tale demonstrates in vivid detail how wars affect women and children." Although the historical foundation of the book is sound, its greatest value lies in its depiction of the human emotions and conflicts stirred up by war, according to Nancy P. Reeder in the *School Library Journal*. She suggested that the book provides good material for "discussions about authority, family bonds, and selflessness."

Speaking to Nancy Castaldo for the *Historically Speaking* Web site, Ernst explained: "I'm never short of ideas; I have so many story ideas swirling in my head that I'll never have time to write them all. But somehow, certain stories wriggle up to the top of my subconscious, nudging until I take the time to

write this particular story. Sometimes stories simmer for years before I feel compelled to write them. Other times it happens more quickly, and this was the case with *Hearts of Stone*. As soon as I started reading and thinking about homeless refugee children during the Civil War, Hannah appeared, wanting her story to be told."

In an interview for the *Favorite PASTimes* Web site, Ernst stated: "I hope *Hearts of Stone* will help readers understand that during the Civil War there were unknown thousands of children who found themselves homeless, perhaps orphaned, wandering the south looking desperately for some haven. Very few of them left any written record of their experiences, but they shouldn't be forgotten. And of course, this has modern parallels. Every war creates a refugee population. The tragedy is still going on."

The contemporary novel *Highland Fling* features Tanya, a fifteen-year-old who has to move from Wisconsin to North Carolina after her parents divorce. Tanya's mother and sister are enthusiastic about their Scottish heritage and enjoy taking part in cultural events, such as Highland Games and dances, but Tanya feels alienated. The book contains information about Scots culture and documentary filmmaking, while containing the deeper themes of the effects of divorce and the nature of history and culture. Bob Spear, writing for the *Heartland Reviews*, explained that the novel was "about coping, adapting, and coming out from one's shell to see life from more than one's own point of view." "There are a lot of strands here and Ernst balances them nicely for the most part," remarked a *Kirkus Reviews* writer.

Begins Writing Mystery Stories

In addition to penning historical fiction, Ernst has written several titles for Pleasant Company's American Girl imprint. As she once explained: "I came to mystery writing unexpectedly when an editor from American Girl invited me to submit a story for the new series being planned, 'History Mysteries.'" Ernst's first novel in the series is *Trouble at Fort La Pointe*, which takes place in the 1730s. Suzette Choudoir's mother is Ojibwe and her father is a French fur trapper who spends most of the year away from his family. If he wins a fur competition, he will be able to spend the winter with Suzette and her mother. But just as it seems he is about to win, Mr. Choudoir is framed for a crime of theft. Suzette knows her father is not guilty, and she sets out to prove his innocence. Ernst "does a commendable job of integrating setting and cultural details into the story," according to Kay Weisman in a *Booklist* article, while Maureen Griffin of *Kliatt* called the story "a delight."

Another of Ernst's "History Mysteries" is *Betrayal at Cross Creek,* which takes place during the American Revolution. Elspeth and her family are Scottish immigrants to the North Carolina territory; her grandfather fought in the war for Scottish independence years earlier and now wants nothing to do with a new war. When the patriots come to convince Elspeth's family to fight, the family is mysteriously put in danger, and Elspeth takes it upon herself to discover the identity of the person who would cause them harm. A *Kirkus Reviews* contributor considered *Betrayal at Cross Creek* to be "a grand read and an important addition" to the historical novels for young adults about the Revolutionary Era. Hazel Rochman, writing in *Booklist,* noted that Ernst's "characters are drawn with extraordinary depth," while Kristen Oravec of the *School Library Journal* commented that "this well told story has an intriguing plot. . . . The element of mystery keeps readers guessing."

In *Secrets in the Hills: A Josefina Mystery,* another historical mystery for the "American Girl" series, a mysterious stranger shows up at the home of Josefina, a young girl who lives on a ranch in New Mexico during the 1820s. He is injured, and the family cares for him. While washing the man's clothes, Josefina finds a treasure map. A subplot includes a mystery about a ghost, and readers also see Josefina trying to develop her skills as a *curandera,* or healer. Gillian Engberg, a reviewer for *Booklist,* felt that "readers will be easily drawn in" by the story, and will "see themselves" in Josefina's place.

If you enjoy the works of Kathleen Ernst, you may also want to check out the following books:

Edith Morris Hemingway and Jacqueline Cosgrove Shields, *Broken Drum,* 1996.
Lynda Durrant, *My Last Skirt: The Story of Jennie Hodgers, Union Soldier,* 2006.
Kathleen Benner Duble, *Hearts of Iron,* 2006.

In *Midnight in Lonesome Hollow: A Kit Mystery,* Ernst tells of Kit, a Depression-era girl who is sent to live with relatives in Kentucky. Professor Lucy Vanderpool asks Kit to help her research basket weaving in the Appalachian community, and Kit soon finds that someone wants to stop this research. Meanwhile,

her brother tries to earn a living in the poverty-stricken community and Kit's friend Fern has been sent to an orphanage. "The mystery element is solid," Ilene Cooper wrote in *Booklist,* "but this works best as an evocation of time and place."

Ernst once commented: "I love research. It's like a treasure hunt! Researching books has taken me from university libraries to the Cincinnati Zoo; from tiny museums in rural Scotland to the Smithsonian Institution; from Ojibwe reservations to hiking trails in Colorado; from Highland Games in North Carolina to ghost tours in New Mexico. What could be more fun than that?"

Ernst also offered the following advice to aspiring writers: "One: Take the time to learn your craft. Two: Get connected—join a professional writer's group, and hook up with other writers who can help critique your work. Three: Read a lot. Keep up with work being published in your genre. Read like a writer—take time to analyze what you like, and why."

■ Biographical and Critical Sources

PERIODICALS

Booklist, January 1, 1997, Carolyn Phelan, review of *The Night Riders of Harpers Ferry,* p. 842; September 15, 2000, Carolyn Phelan, review of *Retreat from Gettysburg,* p. 239; October 1, 2000, Kay Weisman, review of *Trouble at Fort La Pointe,* p. 339; September 15, 2003, Traci Todd, review of *Trouble at Fort La Pointe,* p. 254; March 1, 2004, Hazel Rochman, review of *Betrayal at Cross Creek,* p. 1203; April 15, 2006, Chris Sherman, review of *Highland Fling,* p. 40; May 15, 2006, Gillian Engberg, review of *Secrets in the Hills: A Josefina Mystery,* p. 45; November 1, 2006, Anne O'Malley, review of *Hearts of Stone,* p. 53; May 15, 2007, Ilene Cooper, review of *Midnight in Lonesome Hollow,* p. 47.

Capital Times (Madison, WI), February 19, 2001, "She's in the Run for Poe Award," p. 2A.

Civil War History, June, 2000, Sharon Seager, review of *Too Afraid to Cry: Maryland Civilians in the Antietam Campaign,* p. 171.

Kirkus Reviews, February 15, 2004, review of *Betrayal at Cross Creek,* p. 77; February 15, 2006, review of *Highland Fling,* p. 182; October 1, 2006, review of *Hearts of Stone,* p. 1013.

Kliatt, January, 2004, Maureen Griffin, review of *Trouble at Fort La Pointe,* p. 51; November 1, 2006, Claire Rosser, review of *Hearts of Stone,* p. 10.

Library Journal, June 15, 1999, Theresa McDevitt, review of *Too Afraid to Cry,* p. 89.

School Library Journal, December, 2000, Carrie Schadle, review of *Trouble at Fort La Pointe,* p. 144, Toniann Scime, review of *Retreat from Gettysburg,* p. 144; July, 2003, Katherine Devine, review of *Trouble at Fort La Pointe,* p. 71; December, 2003, Nancy P. Reeder, review of *Ghosts of Vicksburg,* p. 150; May, 2004, Kristen Oravec, review of *Betrayal at Cross Creek,* p. 146; April 1, 2006, *Secrets in the Hills,* p. 138; June 1, 2006, Catherine Ensley, review of *Highland Fling,* p. 154; December 1, 2006, Nancy P. Reeder, review of *Hearts of Stone,* p. 138.

Wisconsin State Journal (Madison, WI), July 2, 2000, review of *Retreat from Gettysburg,* p. 3F.

ONLINE

Favorite PASTimes Web site, http://favoritepastimes. blogspot.com/ (July 25, 2007), "Interview with Kathleen Ernst."

Heartland Reviews, http://www.heartlandreviews. com/ (March 11, 2008), Bob Spear, reviews of *Hearts of Stone* and *Highland Fling.*

Historically Speaking Web site, http://nancycastaldo. blogspot.com/ (October 9, 2007), Nancy Castaldo, "An Interview with Author Kathleen Ernst."

Kathleen Ernst Home Page, http://www.distaff.net/ (March 11, 2008).*

(Copyright © Bettmann/Corbis.)

■ Personal

Born July 27, 1889, in Malden, MA; died March 11, 1970, in Temecula, CA; son of Charles Walter (a mining engineer) and Grace Adelma Gardner; married Natalie Talbert, April 9, 1912 (separated, 1935; died, February, 1968); married Agnes Jean Bethell, August 7, 1968; children: (first marriage) Natalie Grace. *Education:* Attended high school.

■ Career

Writer. Admitted to California Bar, 1911; attorney, Oxnard, CA, 1911-16; Consolidated Sales Co., president, 1918-21; Sheridan, Orr, Drapeau, and Gardner, Ventura, CA, attorney, 1921-33; founder and member, Court of Last Resort, 1948-60; founder, Paisano Productions, 1957; consultant and editor, *Perry Mason* television show, 1957-66.

■ Member

American Bar Association, American Judicature Society, Academy of Scientific Interrogation, American Academy of Forensic Sciences, Law Science

Erle Stanley Gardner

Academy of America, American Society of Criminology, California Bar Association, American Polygraph Association (honorary life member), Harvard Association of Political Science, New Hampshire Medico Society, Kansas Peace Officers Association, Elks, Adventurers (Chicago and New York).

■ Awards, Honors

Mystery Writers of America, Edgar Allan Poe Award, 1953, for *The Court of Last Resort,* and Grand Master Award, 1961; honorary alumnus, Kansas City University, 1955; Doctor of Law, McGeorge College of Law, 1956, and New Mexico University.

■ Writings

"PERRY MASON" MYSTERY SERIES

The Case of the Velvet Claws, Morrow (New York, NY), 1933, reprinted, Im-Press, 2002.
The Case of the Sulky Girl, Morrow (New York, NY), 1933, reprinted, Fawcett (New York, NY), 1992.
The Case of the Lucky Legs, Morrow (New York, NY), 1934, reprinted, Ballantine (New York, NY), 1990.
The Case of the Howling Dog, Morrow (New York, NY), 1934, reprinted, Fawcett (New York, NY), 1987.

The Case of the Curious Bride, Morrow (New York, NY), 1934, reprinted, Aeonian Press, 1976.

The Case of the Counterfeit Eye, Morrow (New York, NY), 1935, reprinted, Amereon, 1976.

The Case of the Caretaker's Cat, Morrow (New York, NY), 1935, reprinted, Aeonian Press, 1976.

The Case of the Sleepwalker's Niece, Morrow (New York, NY), 1936, reprinted, Ballantine (New York, NY), 1991.

The Case of the Stuttering Bishop, Morrow (New York, NY), 1936, reprinted, Fawcett (New York, NY), 1988.

The Case of the Dangerous Dowager, Morrow (New York, NY), 1937, reprinted, Ballantine (New York, NY), 1998.

The Case of the Lame Canary, Morrow (New York, NY), 1937, reprinted, Fawcett (New York, NY), 1987.

The Case of the Substitute Face, Morrow (New York, NY), 1938, reprinted, Amereon, 1988.

The Case of the Shoplifter's Shoe, Morrow (New York, NY), 1938, reprinted, Chivers, 2002.

The Case of the Perjured Parrot, Morrow (New York, NY), 1939, reprinted, Ballantine (New York, NY), 1982.

The Case of the Rolling Bones, Morrow (New York, NY), 1939, reprinted, Ballantine (New York, NY), 1985.

The Case of the Baited Hook, Morrow (New York, NY), 1940, reprinted, Amereon (New York, NY), 1983.

The Case of the Silent Partner, Morrow (New York, NY), 1940, reprinted, Ballantine (New York, NY), 1986.

The Case of the Haunted Husband, Morrow (New York, NY), 1941, reprinted, Fawcett (New York, NY), 1985.

The Case of the Empty Tin, Morrow (New York, NY), 1941, limited edition, Aeonian Press, 1993.

The Case of the Drowning Duck, Morrow (New York, NY), 1942.

The Case of the Careless Kitten, Morrow (New York, NY), 1942, reprinted, Fawcett (New York, NY), 1989.

The Case of the Buried Clock, Morrow (New York, NY), 1943.

The Case of the Drowsy Mosquito, Morrow (New York, NY), 1943, reprinted, Fawcett (New York, NY), 1994.

The Case of the Crooked Candle, Morrow (New York, NY), 1944, reprinted, Ballantine (New York, NY), 1987.

The Case of the Black-Eyed Blonde, Morrow (New York, NY), 1944, reprinted, Pocket Books (New York, NY), 1968.

The Case of the Golddigger's Purse, Morrow (New York, NY), 1945.

The Case of the Half-Wakened Wife, Morrow (New York, NY), 1945.

The Case of the Borrowed Brunette, Morrow (New York, NY), 1946.

The Case of the Fan Dancer's Horse, Morrow (New York, NY), 1947.

The Case of the Lazy Lover, Morrow (New York, NY), 1947.

The Case of the Lonely Heiress, Morrow (New York, NY), 1948, reprinted, Fawcett (New York, NY), 1986.

The Case of the Vagabond Virgin, Morrow (New York, NY), 1948, reprinted, Ballantine (New York, NY), 1982.

The Case of the Dubious Bridegroom, Morrow (New York, NY), 1949.

The Case of the Cautious Coquette, Morrow (New York, NY), 1949.

The Case of the Negligent Nymph, Morrow (New York, NY), 1950, reprinted, Ballantine (New York, NY), 1982.

The Case of the One-Eyed Witness, Morrow (New York, NY), 1950, reprinted, Fawcett (New York, NY), 1995.

The Case of the Fiery Fingers, Morrow (New York, NY), 1951, reprinted, Ballantine (New York, NY), 1981.

The Case of the Angry Mourners, Morrow (New York, NY), 1951.

The Case of the Moth-Eaten Mink, Morrow (New York, NY), 1952.

The Case of the Grinning Gorilla, Morrow (New York, NY), 1952, reprinted, Ballantine (New York, NY), 1982.

The Case of the Hesitant Hostess, Morrow (New York, NY), 1953, reprinted, Fawcett (New York, NY), 1993.

The Case of the Green-Eyed Sister, Morrow (New York, NY), 1953, reprinted, Fawcett (New York, NY), 1993.

The Case of the Fugitive Nurse, Morrow (New York, NY), 1954, reprinted, Fawcett (New York, NY), 1993.

The Case of the Runaway Corpse, Morrow (New York, NY), 1954.

The Case of the Restless Redhead, Morrow (New York, NY), 1954, reprinted, Ballantine (New York, NY), 1982.

The Case of the Glamorous Ghost (also see below), Morrow (New York, NY), 1955, reprinted, Ballantine (New York, NY), 2000.

The Case of the Sun Bather's Diary, Morrow (New York, NY), 1955, Fawcett Books (New York, NY),. 2000.

The Case of the Nervous Accomplice, Morrow (New York, NY), 1955.

The Case of the Terrified Typist (also see below), Morrow (New York, NY), 1956, reprinted, Ballantine (New York, NY), 1987.

The Case of the Demure Defendant, Morrow (New York, NY), 1956, reprinted, Pocket Books (New York, NY), 1970.

The Case of the Gilded Lily, Morrow (New York, NY), 1956, reprinted, Robert Bentley, 1981.

The Case of the Lucky Loser (also see below), Morrow (New York, NY), 1957, reprinted, Fawcett (New York, NY), 1990.

The Case of the Screaming Woman (also see below), Morrow (New York, NY), 1957.

The Case of the Daring Decoy, Morrow (New York, NY), 1957, reprinted, Fawcett (New York, NY), 1989.

The Case of the Long-Legged Models (also see below), Morrow (New York, NY), 1958.

The Case of the Foot-Loose Doll (also see below), Morrow (New York, NY), 1958, reprinted, Ballantine (New York, NY), 1986.

The Case of the Calendar Girl, Morrow (New York, NY), 1958.

The Case of the Deadly Toy, Morrow (New York, NY), 1959, reprinted, Fawcett (New York, NY), 2000.

The Case of the Mythical Monkeys, Morrow (New York, NY), 1959, reprinted, Fawcett (New York, NY), 2000.

The Case of the Singing Skirt, Morrow (New York, NY), 1959, reprinted, Fawcett (New York, NY), 1992.

The Case of the Waylaid Wolf (also see below), Morrow (New York, NY), 1960.

The Case of the Duplicate Daughter, Morrow (New York, NY), 1960.

The Case of the Shapely Shadow, Morrow (New York, NY), 1960, reprinted, Ballantine (New York, NY), 1991.

The Case of the Spurious Spinster, Morrow (New York, NY), 1961, reprinted, G.K. Hall (Boston, MA), 1982.

The Case of the Bigamous Spouse, Morrow (New York, NY), 1961.

The Case of the Reluctant Model, Morrow (New York, NY), 1962.

The Case of the Blonde Bonanza, Morrow (New York, NY), 1962.

The Case of the Ice-Cold Hands, Morrow (New York, NY), 1962, reprinted, Ballantine (New York, NY), 1989.

The Case of the Mischievous Doll, Morrow (New York, NY), 1963, reprinted, Ballantine (New York, NY), 1990.

The Case of the Step-daughter's Secret, Morrow (New York, NY), 1963.

The Case of the Amorous Aunt, Morrow (New York, NY), 1963.

The Case of the Daring Divorcee, Morrow (New York, NY), 1964.

The Case of the Phantom Fortune, Morrow (New York, NY), 1964.

The Case of the Horrified Heirs, Morrow (New York, NY), 1964, reprinted, Ballantine (New York, NY), 1995.

The Case of the Troubled Trustee, Morrow (New York, NY), 1965, reprinted, Fawcett (New York, NY), 1995.

The Case of the Beautiful Beggar, Morrow (New York, NY), 1965.

The Case of the Worried Waitress, Morrow (New York, NY), 1966.

The Case of the Queenly Contestant, Morrow (New York, NY), 1967, reprinted, Fawcett (New York, NY), 1993.

The Case of the Careless Cupid, Morrow (New York, NY), 1968.

The Case of the Fabulous Fake, Morrow (New York, NY), 1969, Fawcett (New York, NY), 2000.

The Case of the Fenced-in Woman, Morrow (New York, NY), 1972, Fawcett (New York, NY), 1994.

The Case of the Postponed Murder, Morrow (New York, NY), 1973, reprinted, House of Stratus, 2002.

"DOUG SELBY" SERIES

The D.A. Calls It Murder, Morrow (New York, NY), 1937.

The D.A. Holds a Candle, Morrow (New York, NY), 1938.

The D.A. Draws a Circle, Morrow (New York, NY), 1939.

The D.A. Goes to Trial, Morrow (New York, NY), 1940.

The D.A. Cooks a Goose, Morrow (New York, NY), 1942.

The D.A. Calls a Turn, Morrow (New York, NY), 1944.

The D.A. Breaks a Seal, Morrow (New York, NY), 1946.

The D.A. Takes a Chance, Morrow (New York, NY), 1948.

The D.A. Breaks an Egg, Morrow (New York, NY), 1949.

"TERRY CLANE" SERIES

Murder Up My Sleeve, Morrow (New York, NY), 1938.

The Case of the Backward Mule, Morrow (New York, NY), 1946.

"GRAMPA WIGGINS" SERIES

The Case of the Turning Tide, Morrow (New York, NY), 1941.

The Case of the Smoking Chimney, Morrow (New York, NY), 1943.

STORY COLLECTIONS

The Case of the Murderer's Bride, and Other Stories, edited by Ellery Queen, Davis Publications, 1969.

The Case of the Crimson Kiss, Morrow (New York, NY), 1971.

The Case of the Crying Swallow, and Other Stories, Morrow (New York, NY), 1971.

The Case of the Irate Witness, Morrow (New York, NY), 1972.

The Amazing Adventures of Lester Leith, Dial, 1981.

The Human Zero: The Science Fiction Stories of Erle Stanley Gardner, edited by Martin H. Greenberg and Charles G. Waugh, Morrow (New York, NY), 1981.

Whispering Sands: Stories of Gold Fever and the Western Desert, edited by Charles G. Waugh and Martin H. Greenberg, Morrow (New York, NY), 1981.

Pay Dirt and Other Whispering Sands Stories, edited by Charles G. Waugh and Martin H. Greenberg, J. Curley (South Yarmouth, MA), 1983.

Honest Money: And Other Short Novels, Carroll & Graf (New York, NY), 1991.

The Danger Zone and Other Stories, edited by Bill Pronzini, Crippen & Landru, (Norfolk, VA), 2004.

The Casebook of Sidney Zoom, 2006.

OMNIBUS VOLUMES

Erle Stanley Gardner: Seven Complete Novels (contains *The Case of the Glamorous Ghost, The Case of the Terrified Typist, The Case of the Lucky Loser, The Case of the Screaming Woman, The Case of the Long-Legged Models Foot-Loose Doll,* and *The Case of the Waylaid Wolf*), Crown, 1979.

NONFICTION

The Land of Shorter Shadows, Morrow (New York, NY), 1948.

The Court of Last Resort, Morrow (New York, NY), 1952.

Neighborhood Frontiers, Morrow (New York, NY), 1954.

The Case of the Boy Who Wrote "The Case of the Missing Clue" with Perry Mason, Morrow (New York, NY), 1959.

Hunting the Desert Whale, Morrow (New York, NY), 1960.

Hovering over Baja, Morrow (New York, NY), 1961.

The Hidden Heart of Baja, Morrow (New York, NY), 1962.

The Desert Is Yours, Morrow (New York, NY), 1963.

The World of Water: Exploring the Sacramento Delta, Morrow (New York, NY), 1964.

Hunting Lost Mines by Helicopter, Morrow (New York, NY), 1965.

Off the Beaten Track in Baja, Morrow (New York, NY), 1967.

Gypsy Days on the Delta, Morrow (New York, NY), 1967.

Mexico's Magic Square, Morrow (New York, NY), 1968.

Drifting Down the Delta, Morrow (New York, NY), 1969.

Host with the Big Hat, Morrow (New York, NY), 1970.

Cops on Campus and Crime in the Streets, Morrow (New York, NY), 1970.

"COOL AND LAM" MYSTERY SERIES; UNDER PSEUDONYM A.A. FAIR

The Bigger They Come, Morrow (New York, NY), 1939, reprinted, Pocket Books (New York, NY), 1971 (published in England as *Lam to the Slaughter,* Hamish Hamilton, 1939).

Turn on the Heat, Morrow (New York, NY), 1940.

Gold Comes in Bricks, Morrow (New York, NY), 1940, reprinted, Ulverscroft, 1987.

Spill the Jackpot, Morrow (New York, NY), 1941, reprinted, Dell (New York, NY), 1971.

Double or Quits, Morrow (New York, NY), 1941, reprinted, HarperCollins (New York, NY), 1991.

Owls Don't Blink, Morrow (New York, NY), 1942.

Bats Fly at Dusk, Morrow (New York, NY), 1942, reprinted, Random House (New York, NY), 1986.

Cats Prowl at Night, Morrow (New York, NY), 1943, reprinted, HarperCollins (New York, NY), 1991.

Give 'em the Ax, Morrow (New York, NY), 1944, reprinted, Dell (New York, NY), 1974 (published in England as *An Axe to Grind,* Heinemann, 1951).

Crows Can't Count, Morrow (New York, NY), 1946.

Fools Die on Friday, Morrow (New York, NY), 1947, reprinted, Dell (New York, NY), 1971.

Bedrooms Have Windows, Morrow (New York, NY), 1949, reprinted, HarperCollins (New York, NY), 1990.

Top of the Heap, Morrow (New York, NY), 1952, Hard Case Crime, 2004.

Some Women Won't Wait, Morrow (New York, NY), 1953, reprinted, Dell (New York, NY), 1972.

Beware the Curves, Morrow (New York, NY), 1956, reprinted, Pocket Books (New York, NY), 1971.

You Can Die Laughing, Morrow (New York, NY), 1957, reprinted, Pocket Books (New York, NY), 1975.

Some Slips Don't Show, Morrow (New York, NY), 1957.

The Count of Nine, Morrow (New York, NY), 1958.

Pass the Gravy, Morrow (New York, NY), 1959.

Kept Women Can't Wait, Morrow (New York, NY), 1960.

Bachelors Get Lonely, Morrow (New York, NY), 1961.

Shills Can't Cash Chips, Morrow (New York, NY), 1961 (published in England as *Stop at the Red Light,* Heinemann, 1962).

Try Anything Once, Morrow (New York, NY), 1962.

Fish or Cut Bait, Morrow (New York, NY), 1963, reprinted, Simon & Schuster (New York, NY), 1975.

Up for Grabs, Morrow (New York, NY), 1964.

Cut Thin to Win, Morrow (New York, NY), 1965.

Widows Wear Weeds, Morrow (New York, NY), 1966, reprinted, Chivers, 1997.

Traps Need Fresh Bait, Morrow (New York, NY), 1967.

All Grass Isn't Green, Morrow (New York, NY), 1970.

OTHER

The Adventures of Paul Pry, G.K. Hall (Boston, MA), 1991.

Also author of radio scripts. Contributor of over 400 stories and articles to periodicals, including *Black Mask, Smart Set, Argosy, Clues, Writer's Digest, Field and Stream, Liberty Magazine, Cosmopolitan, Saturday Evening Post, True, Atlantic Monthly, Holiday, Collier's, Look, Ladies' Home Journal, TV Guide, Yankee, Boys' Life, Breezy Stories, Top Notch, Fighting Romances, Ace High,* and *Popular Science.*

■ **Adaptations**

Warner Bros. filmed *The Case of the Howling Dog* in 1934, *The Case of the Curious Bride* in 1935, *The Case of the Lucky Legs* in 1935, *The Case of the Velvet Claws* in 1936, *The Case of the Black Cat* in 1936, and *The Case of the Stuttering Bishop* in 1937. Columbia Broadcasting System ran a Perry Mason radio series, 1943-55, the television series *Perry Mason,* 1957-66, *The New Adventures of Perry Mason,* 1973-74, and a series of television movies, 1985-93. Perry Mason has also appeared in a comic book, 1947, and as a

newspaper comic strip, 1951-52. The board game *The Perry Mason Game: Case of the Missing Suspect* was released by Transogram in 1959.

■ **Sidelights**

As creator of Perry Mason, one of the most popular and enduring characters in mystery fiction, Erle Stanley Gardner was a phenomenally successful writer who sold a reported half a billion copies of his many novels. "In terms of total readership," Hank Burchard of the *Washington Post* reported, "[Gardner] ranks right up there with Homer, Matthew, Mark, Luke, and John." Perry Mason also appeared in movies, on a radio program and, most successfuly, in a long-running television series. Perry Mason, the hard-fighting lawyer who uses every trick he can to get his client free, and who investigates murders to uncover the real culprit, has inspired a host of lawyer mysteries, including those by John Grisham, Steve Martini, and Scott Thurow, while the long-running television series inspired such later series as *Matlock* and *McBride.* As Thomas Leitch wrote in *Perry Mason:* "The subgenre of stories with a continuing lawyer hero [was] virtually created by Erle Stanley Gardner." Despite his success, Gardner was a modest man when it came to his writing. He "often insisted," Albin Krebs stated in the *New York Times,* "that he was 'not really a writer at all.'" "I don't consider myself a very good writer. I do consider myself a good plotter," Gardner was quoted as saying. Krebs noted: "Millions of readers . . . looked upon Mr. Gardner . . . as a master storyteller." Gardner enjoyed being called a "fiction factory" or "the Henry Ford of detective novelists," references to the assembly-line nature of his prolific literary output. Gardner's fast-paced stories, able to draw the reader in from the first page with a tantalizing puzzle, are still popular some seventy five years after Perry Mason was first introduced to the reading public.

Gardner was born on July 27, 1889, in Malden, Massachusetts. His father, Charles Walter Gardner, was a mining engineer who specialized in gold dredging. His father's career took the family throughout the United States. Gardner attended schools in Massachusetts, Mississippi, Oregon, and California. In 1906, he spent several months in the remote Klondike region of Alaska with his father. Expelled from high school in Oroville, California, Gardner took up with "Swede" Meyerhoffer, a local promoter of amateur boxing matches. The boxing ring appealed to Gardner's energetic approach to life in a way that sitting in a classroom could not. When a particularly rough bout left Gardner with

In his office decorated with hunting rifles and mementos, Gardner relaxes with a book. (Copyright © Bettmann/Corbis.)

two black eyes and a cut-up face, he began to rethink his career as a boxer. When the local district attorney brought Gardner and Meyerhoffer in to discuss the legal standing of their amateur boxing fights, Gardner decided to drop boxing and give law a try.

Gardner's father put him in the Palo Alto High School. To guarantee that the restless boy would not get bored, he placed him to live in the principal's house. Principal J.C. Templeton diagnosed Gardner's academic problem as not having enough to do. He put the boy on a busy schedule: three hours of reading law, then a full schedule at high school, then a job typing papers for a law office until 9:30, then his homework. The heavy schedule worked. Gardner graduated from high school and took a full-time job at a law firm. In 1911 he passed the California bar examination and became a lawyer.

From Lawyer to Writer

Because he wanted to spend more time hunting and camping, Gardner began to look around for a source of income that would not tie him down to regular business hours. In the 1920s, Gardner decided that writing fiction might be a way to achieve the independence he wanted. He began to write stories at night while working by day as a lawyer. As David Hansard explained in *Mystery Scene*, Gardner "dissected and analyzed stacks of short stories and novels that were regarded as 'well-plotted' and as an aid developed his famous 'plot wheel,' a cardboard circle with moveable arms to aid him in constructing and following his own plot lines." His hectic schedule at the time included a full day of court appearances, several hours of researching points of law at the library, and then writing a self-imposed quota of 4,000 words of fiction when he returned home in the evening. His determination soon paid off. In 1921, the pulp magazine *Breezy Stories* published "Nellie's Naughty Nightie," Gardner's first published work. Despite the title, the story is quite mild. It concerns a misplaced negligee being put into the wrong suitcase by mistake, leading to some comic misunderstandings. Paid fifteen dollars for this story, Gardner sent the check along to his mother, knowing that the good Methodist church-goer would find the money earned for such a "racy" story to be sinful. She at first refused to cash the check but, in the end, decided that wasting the money was more sinful. Gardner was soon selling his stories to a wide variety of pulp magazines at such a steady rate that he cut back his legal practice to two days a week to devote more time to writing. At its peak, Gardner's output reached some one million words of published fiction per year, with his stories appearing in the pulp magazines at a rate of better than one per week. He used at least eleven pseudonyms during this time.

Enter Perry Mason

In these early days Gardner experimented with a variety of story genres, including westerns, confession stories, science fiction, and mysteries. Out of these writing experiments came the publication in 1933 of *The Case of the Velvet Claws*, the first Perry Mason novel. With the publication of this book Gardner's writing career took a new turn. Thayer Hobson, the president of Gardner's publishing house, suggested that Gardner concentrate his efforts on his new character, turning Perry Mason into a series character. Gardner took the advice. Although he would later write mysteries featuring other characters, and some nonfiction books, the bulk of Gardner's later writing concerned Perry Mason. "It is a matter of loyalty to the characters one has created," *Newsweek* quoted Gardner as explaining, "and loyalty to one's associates."

The hard-hitting defense lawyer Perry Mason was easily Gardner's most popular character, appearing in some eighty of his novels. Mason, Otto Penzler stated in *The Private Lives of Private Eyes, Spies, Crimefighters, and Other Good Guys*, "is the most famous lawyer in fiction." "Perry Mason," Isaac Anderson of the *New York Times* believed, "is not only a shrewd lawyer and a brilliant detective, he is a master of stage-craft, who knows how to stage dramatic climaxes in the courtroom when they will do the most good for his client."

The Mason books are based on Gardner's own years as a lawyer in rural California, with each novel being a composite of several actual cases. Many of the techniques employed by Mason were first used by Gardner himself who was, Burchard stated, "noted for his deft use of little-known statutes, penetrating cross-examination and colorful courtroom demeanor." On one occasion Gardner defended a group of Chinese Americans accused of illegal gambling by filling the courtroom with Asian Americans and daring the prosecuting attorney to match the indictments with the accused men. The charges were dropped. On another occasion, Gardner's client was accused of causing a woman's nervous breakdown with his loose talk about her. A small earthquake shook the California courthouse during the proceedings and Gardner quickly used the unexpected event to his advantage, pointing out to the jury that the plaintiff had been the only person in the courthouse to stay calm during the quake. His client was acquitted. Gardner's clients were usually poor, members of minority groups, or those whom Gardner considered unjustly accused. *Time* quoted him as saying that he defended "vagrants, peeping Toms and chicken thieves as if they were statesmen."

In 1948, Gardner founded the Court of Last Resort, an organization of lawyers who took on seemingly

Raymond Burr and Barbara Hale starred in the long-running television series *Perry Mason*. (Copyright © Bettmann/Corbis.)

hopeless cases from across the country. In the twelve years of its existence, the Court of Last Resort was responsible for saving a number of defendants from prison terms. His 1952 title, *The Court of Last Resort*, in which Gardner recounted the most impressive of the organization's cases, won him an Edgar Award from the Mystery Writers of America.

The Perry Mason books, Burchard explained, "are formula books." In each one Mason defended a client charged with murder. The client is always entangled in a set of suspicious circumstances which makes him look guilty. When it seems as if all is lost and his client will be convicted, Mason risks everything—his life, disbarment, and/or a jail sentence—on a desperate last bid, confident that he can win acquittal. In a surprise ending, Mason's desperate bid pays off and he saves his client in a climatic courtroom scene, producing evidence at the last moment which not only clears the defendant but reveals the real murderer as well. "Defying all odds," Penzler observed, "Mason never loses a case." This despite Mason's own admission in *The Case of the Counterfeit Eye:* "I don't ask a client if he's guilty or innocent. Either way he's entitled to a day in court." Cyril Ray of *Spectator* described the Mason books as coming "off a conveyor-belt, of course, but with all the neatness and finish of the machine-made article."

The typical Perry Mason book, Burchard believed, "isn't great, but it isn't bad, either. The prose is mostly workmanlike, with a clinker here and there, the plot turns are less outrageous than many that can be found on any bookstand. . . . Gardner always put in interesting and often informative factual detail . . . , and the legal details are always scrupulously accurate." John C. Arnold, a former vice president of the Pennsylvania Bar, wrote in the *Pennsylvania Bar Association Quarterly* that Gardner's "court scenes are authentic." This attention to detail was noted by several critics, including James Sandoe of the *New York Herald Tribune Book Review.* Sandoe wrote that Gardner's "real assurance lies in the tricks of plotting and the accurate language of trial law." O.L. Bailey of the *Saturday Review of the Arts* stated that Gardner "never pretended to be anything but a commercial writer. His stock in trade was the great care he took to make sure that all the details of his complex plots were right." Gardner went so far as to purchase a new gun for each murder mystery he wrote. During a court trial, he said, the murder weapon's serial number must be entered into the court record. "If I give a phony one [in a Perry Mason book]," Gardner told *Newsweek,* "people write in and say there isn't any such serial number. If I give a real serial number, I face a

lawsuit. So every time I commit a murder, I have to buy the gun." At the time of his death, Gardner was reported to have had a large gun collection.

Gardner ran his business affairs in an eccentric manner. In the early 1940s, his agent was trying to interest the radio networks in a Perry Mason show. Despite his best efforts, the agent could not get anyone in the business interested in the idea. Gardner, however, was impressed with the man's persistence and routinely praised him for his continuing efforts. When Gardner did sell the radio rights to Perry Mason, after the agent had left the business to serve in the U.S. Army during World War II, he sent the agent a commission check. When the agent said he had not earned the money, Gardner told him to shut up and cash the check. Another example of Gardner's business approach came to light when his contract with the publisher William Morrow needed to be renewed. Morrow expected that Gardner would ask for a larger royalty on book sales. But Gardner refused, arguing that he wanted the royalty kept at the same level. Morrow's sales team would then have an incentive to sell more of his books, ultimately earning Gardner more money on the increased sales.

By the mid-1960s, Gardner books were selling some 26,000 copies a day. Seventy-five Gardner novels sold over a million copies each. Krebs reported that Gardner once complained about his phenomenal success: "I have become chained to my fiction factory because my audience can't get enough of my stories, no matter how fast I write them." And Gardner wrote them fast. To help him prepare his usual production of four or five new books a year, he hired a staff of six secretaries to type manuscripts from his recorded dictation. Because he worked on several books at the same time, and because his prolific production was backlogged by his publisher, Gardner was reported to have never been sure which was his most recently published book.

In the 1940s, a Perry Mason radio show was broadcast five days a week in soap opera fashion. This show was superceded in 1957 by *Perry Mason,* a television series starring Raymond Burr. Gardner served as consultant and editor to the series, which used many of his original Perry Mason novels as sources for its episodes. The show was a tremendous success, running nine seasons in prime time and becoming the most popular lawyer series in television history. Because Gardner was the majority owner of Paisano Productions, the packagers of *Perry Mason* for the Columbia Broadcasting System, he was said to have earned some fifteen million dollars from the show. *Perry Mason* is still broadcast in reruns in nearly every major American city, and

Raymond Burr, Barbara Hale, and David Ogden Stiers in a scene from a *Perry Mason* television movie. (Everett Collection.)

broadcast overseas in sixteen different languages. After the original series ended, Raymond Burr made a series of television films as Perry Mason until his death in 1993. In 1973, CBS revived the series as *The New Adventures of Perry Mason* with Monte Markham as Mason. The show lasted one season.

If you enjoy the works of Erle Stanley Gardner, you may also want to check out the following books:

Raymond Chandler, *The Big Sleep*, 1939.
Scott Thurow, *Presumed Innocent*, 1987.
John Grisham, *The Pelican Brief*, 1992.

Although Gardner's popularity with readers was always much greater than his popularity with critics, J. Kenneth Van Dover thought highly of Gardner's work. Writing in his study *Murder in the Millions: Erle Stanley Gardner, Mickey Spillane, Ian Fleming,* Van Dover compared Gardner to Jack London. "Gardner was, in several ways, the heir of his fellow Californian," Van Dover argued. "Both engaged in the mass production of short and long fictions, both developed a fast, efficient prose style, both enjoyed travel and travel writing, both loved the terrain of California and both operated ranches there, [and] both championed—from quite different perspectives—the lower classes."

The continuing popularity of Gardner's work was evidenced in 1973 when the country of Nicaragua issued a series of postage stamps honoring the great detectives of literature. One of the twelve postage stamps featured Gardner's character Perry Mason.

The University of Texas at Austin, which owns a collection of Gardner's manuscripts, letters, and papers, announced in 1970 that it would build a replica of Gardner's study, where most of his many books were written.

"I write to make money," Krebs quoted Gardner as once saying, "and I write to give the reader sheer fun." Burchard quoted Gardner explaining his popularity this way: "Ordinary readers see in me somebody they can identify with. I'm for the underdog. Justice is done in my books. The average man is always in a state of supreme suspense because his life is all complications with no conclusions. In my books, he sees people in trouble get out of trouble."

■ Biographical and Critical Sources

BOOKS

Fugate, Francis L. and Roberta B. Frugate, *Secrets of the World's Best-Selling Writer: The Story-telling Techniques of Erle Stanley Gardner*, Morrow, 1980.

Gardner, Erle Stanley, *The Case of the Counterfeit Eye*, Morrow, 1935.

Gardner, Erle Stanley, *Host with the Big Hat*, Morrow, 1969.

Hirth, Mary, *Erle Stanley Gardner: An Exhibit*, Harry Ransom Humanities Research Center, 1972.

Hughes, Dorothy B., *Erle Stanley Gardner: The Case of the Real Perry Mason*, Morrow, 1978.

Johnson, Alva, *The Case of Erle Stanley Gardner*, Morrow, 1947.

Kelleher, Brian, and Diana Merrill, *The Perry Mason TV Show Book: The Complete Story of America's Favorite Television Lawyer, by Two of His Greatest Fans*, St. Martin's (New York, NY), 1987.

Leitch, Thomas, *Perry Mason*, Wayne State University Press (Detroit, MI), 2005.

Martindale, David, *The Perry Mason Case Book*.

Mott, Frank Luther, *Golden Multitudes*, Macmillan, 1947.

Mundell, E.H., *Erle Stanley Gardner: A Checklist*, Kent State University Press, 1969.

Penzler, Otto, *The Private Lives of Private Eyes, Spies, Crimefighters, and Other Good Guys*, Grosset, 1977.

Pepper, Choral, *Back to Baja: Retracing the Erle Stanley Gardner Expeditions*, Seabar Publishing, 1992.

Senate, Richard L., *Erle Stanley Gardner's Ventura: The Birthplace of Perry Mason*, Charon Press, 1996.

Van Dover, J. Kenneth, *Murder in the Millions: Erle Stanley Gardner, Mickey Spillane, Ian Fleming*, Frederick Ungar (New York, NY), 1984.

PERIODICALS

Armchair Detective, summer, 1992, review of *The Case of the Haunted Husband* audiobook, p. 357.

Atlantic, January, 1967.

Booklist, June 1, 2004, Frank Sennett, review of *The Danger Zone and Other Stories*, p. 1707.

Books and Bookmen, March, 1971.

Christian Science Monitor, January 17, 1973.

Coronet, February, 1956.

Kirkus Reviews, May 15, 2004, review of *The Danger Zone and Other Stories*, p. 474; June 1, 2006, review of *The Casebook of Sidney Zoom*, p. 549.

Kliatt, November, 2000, review of *The Case of the Reluctant Model* audiobook, p. 39.

Mystery Scene, Number 102, 2007, David Hansard, "Erle Stanley Gardner: The Case of the Forgotten Mystery Writer," pp. 32-35.

Newsweek, October 25, 1943; October 7, 1957; January 18, 1960.

New Yorker, November 11, 1950.

New York Herald Tribune Book Review, November 16, 1952; May 25, 1958.

New York Times, June 24, 1934; November 18, 1934; January 6, 1957; May 11, 1958.

New York Times Book Review, September 13, 1959; February 4, 1973.

New York Times Magazine, March 21, 1965.

Publishers Weekly, January 27, 1958; August 11, 1958.

Reader's Digest, August, 1963.

Saturday Evening Post, May 30, 1942; September 1, 1956; January 30, 1960.

Saturday Review of Literature, July 16, 1938.

Saturday Review of the Arts, February, 1973.

Spectator, March 28, 1970.

Syracuse Herald Journal, April 1, 1981, Jennifer Howland, "Author's Idea of Mystique," p. B5.

Time, May 9, 1949.

Variety, April 1, 1970.

■ Obituaries

PERIODICALS

American Bookman, March 23, 1970.

L'Express, March 16-22, 1970.

National Observer, March 23, 1970.

New York Times, March 12, 1970.

Newsweek, March 23, 1970.

Publishers Weekly, March 23, 1970.

Time, March 23, 1970.

Variety, March 18, 1970.

Washington Post, March 12, 1970.*

(Courtesy of Mary Downing Hahn.)

Mary Downing Hahn

■ Personal

Born December 9, 1937, in Washington, DC; daughter of Kenneth Ernest (an automobile mechanic) and Anna Elisabeth (a teacher) Downing; married William E. Hahn, October 7, 1961 (divorced, 1977); married Norman Pearce Jacob (a librarian), April 23, 1982; children: (first marriage) Katherine Sherwood, Margaret Elizabeth. *Education:* University of Maryland at College Park, B.A., 1960, M.A., 1969, doctoral study, 1970-74. *Politics:* Democrat. *Hobbies and other interests:* Reading, walking, photography, and riding trains.

■ Addresses

Home—Columbia, MD. *E-mail*—mdh12937@aol.com.

■ Career

Novelist and artist. Art teacher at junior high school in Greenbelt, MD, 1960-61; Hutzler's Department Store, Baltimore, MD, clerk, 1963; correspondence clerk for Navy Federal Credit Union, 1963-65; homemaker and writer, 1965-70; Prince George's County Memorial Library System, Laurel Branch, Laurel, MD, children's librarian associate, 1975-91; full-time writer, 1991—. Freelance artist for *Cover to Cover*, WETA-TV, 1973-75.

■ Member

Society of Children's Book Writers and Illustrators, PEN, Authors Guild, Washington Children's Book Guild.

■ Awards, Honors

American Library Association (ALA) Reviewer's Choice, Library of Congress Children's Books, and *School Library Journal*'s Best Book citations, all 1983, Child Study Association of America Children's Books of the Year and National Council of Teachers of English Teacher's Choice citations, both 1984, and William Allen White Children's Choice Award, William Allen White Library, 1986, all for *Daphne's Book*; Dorothy Canfield Fisher Award, 1988, and children's choice awards from ten other states, all for *Wait Till Helen Comes: A Ghost Story*; Child Study Association Book Award, 1989, Jane Addams Children's Book Award Honor Book, 1990, and California Young Reader's Medal, 1991, all for *December Stillness*; ALA

Books for Reluctant Reader citation, 1990, and children's choice awards from five states, all for *The Dead Man in Indian Creek*; children's choice awards from seven states, all for *The Doll in the Garden*; ALA Notable Book Citation, Scott O'Dell Award for Historical Fiction, and Joan G. Sugarman Award, all 1992, Hedda Seisler Mason Award, 1993, and children's choice awards from three states, all for *Stepping on the Cracks*; Best Books for Young Adults citation, Young Adult Library Services Association, 1993, and New York Public Library Books for the Teen Age citation, 1994, both for *The Wind Blows Backward*; William Allen White Children's Book Award, 1997, for *Time for Andrew: A Ghost Story*; Edgar Award nomination for best juvenile mystery, Mystery Writers of America, 2008, for *Deep and Dark and Dangerous*.

■ **Writings**

The Sara Summer, Clarion (Boston, MA), 1979.

The Time of the Witch, Clarion (New York, NY), 1982.

Daphne's Book, Clarion (New York, NY), 1983.

The Jellyfish Season, Clarion (New York, NY), 1985.

Wait till Helen Comes: A Ghost Story, Clarion (New York, NY), 1986.

Tallahassee Higgins, Clarion (New York, NY), 1987.

December Stillness, Clarion (New York, NY), 1988.

Following the Mystery Man, Clarion (New York, NY), 1988.

The Doll in the Garden, Clarion (New York, NY), 1989.

The Dead Man in Indian Creek, Clarion (New York, NY), 1990.

The Spanish Kidnapping Disaster, Clarion (New York, NY), 1991.

Stepping on the Cracks, Clarion (New York, NY), 1991.

The Wind Blows Backward, Clarion (New York, NY), 1993.

Time for Andrew: A Ghost Story, Clarion (New York, NY), 1994.

Look for Me by Moonlight, Clarion (New York, NY), 1995.

The Gentleman Outlaw and Me—Eli: A Story of the Old West, Clarion (New York, NY), 1996.

Following My Own Footsteps, Clarion (New York, NY), 1996.

As Ever, Gordy, Clarion (New York, NY), 1998.

Anna All Year Round, illustrated by Diane de Groat, Clarion (New York, NY), 1999.

Promises to the Dead, Clarion (New York, NY), 2000.

Anna on the Farm, illustrated by Diane de Groat, Clarion (New York, NY), 2001.

Hear the Wind Blow: A Novel of the Civil War, Clarion (New York, NY), 2003.

The Old Willis Place: A Ghost Story, Clarion (New York, NY), 2004.

Janey and the Famous Author, Clarion (New York, NY), 2005.

Witch Catcher, Clarion (New York, NY), 2006.

Deep and Dark and Dangerous, Clarion (New York, NY), 2007.

All the Lovely Bad Ones, Clarion (New York, NY), 2008.

Hahn's books have been translated into Danish, Swedish, Italian, German, Japanese, and French. Contributor to anthologies, including *Don't Give up the Ghost*, 1993, *Bruce Coville's Book of Ghost Stories*, 1994, and *Bruce Coville's Book of Nightmares*, 1995.

■ **Sidelights**

Mining her own childhood as well as that of her parents and children, Mary Downing Hahn writes closely detailed stories that explore family issues such as loss of a parent or loved one, the struggle for identity and acceptance, and the blending of families. While her stories are based on real life, they are often concerned with the supernatural. A contributor to the *Children's Bookwatch* noted that "Hahn is noted for her fine ghost stories with their unpredictable twists of plot." In such novels as *Wait till Helen Comes: A Ghost Story*, *Time for Andrew: A Ghost Story*, *The Old Willis Place: A Ghost Story*, *Witch Catcher*, and *Deep and Dark and Dangerous*, Hahn presents ghostly tales filled with an eerie atmosphere and plenty of chills. Her characters are often young people realistically caught in strange situations. Hahn once remarked: "Like the people I know, I want my characters to be a mixture of strengths and weaknesses, to have good and bad qualities, to be a little confused and unsure of themselves." Neither are happy endings always a guarantee in a Hahn novel, for life does not always provide such endings. "At the same time, however," Hahn remarked, "I try to leave room for hope."

A Childhood in Maryland

Hahn was born on December 9, 1937, in Washington, DC, the first child of Anna Elisabeth Sherwood Downing and Kenneth Ernest Downing. She spent most of her childhood in College Park, Maryland, "a wonderful place to grow up," as she typified it in an interview with *Authors and Artists for Young*

Adults (*AAYA*). "The University of Maryland is located there, so the town was a mix of working class people and professionals. It was the sort of place where kids could go off on their own in complete safety. There were few cars then, especially during and just after the Second World War. The only worry for us kids then was wondering if your mother's friends would see you doing things you didn't want your mother to know about. Since my mother was a local teacher, I was well known. It was hard for me to get in trouble."

Hahn stated in an article posted at the *Children's Book Guild of Washington DC Web site:* "Our block was loaded with kids my age. We spent hours outdoors playing 'Kick the Can' and 'Mother, May I' as well as cowboy and outlaw games that usually ended in quarrels about who shot whom. In the summer, we went on day long expeditions into forbidden territory—the woods on the other side of the train tracks, the creek that wound its way through College Park, and the experimental farm run by the University of Maryland. In elementary school, I was known as the class artist. I loved to read and draw but I hated writing reports. Requirements such as outlines, perfect penmanship, and following directions killed my interest in putting words on paper. All those facts—who cared what the principal products of Chile were? To me, writing reports was almost as boring as math. Despite my dislike of writing, I loved to make up stories. Instead of telling them in words, I told them in pictures. My stories were usually about orphans who ran away and had the sort of exciting adventures I would have enjoyed if my mother hadn't always interfered. When I was in junior high school, I developed an interest in more complex stories. I wanted to show how people felt, what they thought, what they said. For this, I needed words. Although I wasn't sure I was smart enough, I decided to write and illustrate children's books when I grew up. Consequently, at the age of thirteen, I began my first book. *Small Town Life* was about a girl named Susan, as tall and skinny and freckle faced as I was. Unlike her shy, self conscious creator, however, Susan was a leader who lived the life I wanted to live—my ideal self, in other words. Although I never finished *Small Town Life*, it marked the start of a lifelong interest in writing."

Hahn's parents both had childhoods marred by loss. In her mother's case, it was the beloved father—Hahn's maternal grandfather—who died when his daughter was thirteen. His death left his family "almost penniless," as she noted in an essay for *Something about the Author Autobiography Series* (*SAAS*). "Her father's death ended my mother's childhood and her happiness. . . . She was left in the hands of a cold and unloving mother who claimed she could not support a daughter." Hahn's mother grew up with relatives, graduated from high school, took a teacher's training course, and began teaching at College Park Elementary School when she was nineteen. Later she met Kenneth Downing, whose early life was also marked by loss, of nationality and family wealth. "My father was first and foremost an English citizen," Hahn recalled in *SAAS*. At age ten, his family left a comfortable life in England to seek their fortune in America, whereupon they lost all their money in a failed farming venture. "Thanks to my grandfather's neglect, my father's life in America was full of hardship," Hahn wrote in *SAAS*. "Looking back, he must have seen England as the lost Eden of his childhood, a place to which he longed to return but could not." Hahn's father kept both his accent and his English citizenship until his death in 1963, working as an auto mechanic all the while. Hahn's parents met at a dance and were married in 1935. The honeymoon was barely over when the mother's mother moved in with the couple. "Unfortunately," Hahn recalled, "my grandmother's presence did not contribute to the happiness of my parents' marriage. She disliked my father." Hahn was born two years later, and the following year, her mother returned to teaching, leaving her daughter in the care of the grandmother. It was an arrangement born out of financial necessity, but not an optimum situation. "Already suffering from arteriosclerosis, Nanny was a strange and frightening person," Hahn noted in *SAAS*. "Given to morbid ramblings about sin and death, she made my early childhood less than happy." By the time she was three, Hahn was already spending as much time as possible out of doors, away from her grandmother.

Growing up during World War II, Hahn was also influenced by the flavor of those times, of the blackout laws and the possibility of air raids and the sounds of sirens. She began her education at a Catholic school, but soon transferred to the public school. Yet her months at Catholic school had gotten her on the way to reading; she now could entertain herself with her favorite tales: *The Little Engine That Could,* the Raggedy Ann and Andy books, and above all, A.A. Milne's Pooh stories. One of Hahn's first artistic efforts, in fact, involved the enhancement of Ernest Shepherd's black-and-white illustrations for Pooh: One rainy day she colored in all the line drawings. Discovering the book, Hahn's mother thenceforth made sure her daughter had plenty of drawing paper to work on.

A sister was born in 1943, but once again Hahn's grandmother tainted the event, convincing Hahn that both her mother and the newborn were dead. The following year, Hahn's favorite uncle, Dudley, her father's brother, was killed in the war, an event

Hahn's 1983 novel *Daphne's Book* is about a secret that may tear a new friendship apart. (Bantam Skylark Books, 1985. Used by permission of Bantam Books, a division of Random House, Inc.)

that stayed with her, only to be purged years later in her novel, *Stepping on the Cracks*. A self-proclaimed "fearful child," such a loss did nothing to make Hahn feel more secure in her early years. Life in College Park, however, did. There were friends on the block, and an understanding teacher at school, Mrs. Schindler, who initiated a book club for some of her precocious first graders. There were also the tracks of the Baltimore and Ohio Railroads only a block from Hahn's house, and the lonely sound of the trains at night that beckoned her to the romance of travel and adventure. Encouraged at school to draw and read—two of her favorite activities—Hahn began to find a place in her childhood world, and she was even able to finally read all the way through the events in the tale of Hansel and Gretel, a story that had frightened her for years.

The eventual death of her grandmother came as a relief to the young Hahn. "My tormentor was gone for good,"she wrote in *SAAS*, but then guilt feelings arose at such a reaction and when only a week later her beloved paternal grandmother died, it was like a punishment. But such events were quickly forgotten with the birth of a baby brother not long after. The postwar world sent the family on a further roller coaster ride when they had to vacate their rented house so that the owner's son, a returning veteran, could take it. Hahn and her family were forced for a time to share the small house belonging to her father's family. Squeezed into insufficient space, there were animosities and rivalries. Hahn's cousin did not want to share her space with her relatives, and squabbles ensued. Hahn was sent off to summer camps, and when she returned, her family had finally been able to buy a house in College Park in her old neighborhood and just next door to her best friend.

Books and friends informed Hahn's world for the next years. During the days she played games with her friends, and at night she read into the late hours. Nancy Drew and the Hardy Boys set her and her friends up in business as self-appointed spy chasers in the early years of the Cold War. Dog books soon replaced mysteries, with *Lassie Come Home*, *Call of the Wild*, and *Greyfriar's Bobby* topping that list. Hahn was also addicted to stories about orphans: *The Secret Garden*, *Anne of Green Gables*, *Oliver Twist*, and *Kidnapped* being early favorites. "Obviously books played an important part in my life," she recalled in *SAAS*. "I didn't just read them, I *lived* them." Radio shows were also an important influence in Hahn's budding sense of storytelling, and soon she was busy writing stories and illustrating them. In the seventh grade she began keeping a diary, and one of her first entries foretold a future career: "What I want to be when I grow up—a writer and illustrator." She began work on her first book, "Small Town Life," about the daily adventures of an awkward twelve-year-old who vaguely resembled the author: self-conscious and different from everyone else. Yet by high school, Hahn had determined to turn her life around, to leave behind her tomboy stage and conform. She became, along with other bobby-soxers of her generation, boy crazy. She was, as she described it in *SAAS*, "a teenager, fifties style." Throughout high school she was friends with a clique of seven or eight girls, and had adventures at the local drugstore and at the seashore—where Hahn fell in love, from a distance, with a sailor.

From Mother to Author

Upon graduation from high school, Hahn attended the University of Maryland, just a mile from her family house in College Park. She majored in studio art and English, two subjects she dearly loved. By the time she was a senior she had met and fallen in love with the man whom she would marry, though no date had been set. After college, Hahn took an art position at a junior high school, but left after a year, despising the role of authority figure she was cast in. After a summer in Europe, Hahn married and started graduate school in English. When her husband decided upon law school, she left her own studies behind to support the family with a variety of low-paying jobs. Her first daughter was born in 1965, and then a second in 1967. Living in College Park, Hahn was a full-time mom for some time, loving the task of reading to her children. It was then she rediscovered her own dream of writing and illustrating books, but her children's tastes were not the same as the publishers, it seemed. She sent off several manuscripts only to have them rejected.

In 1971, as her first marriage began to fall apart, Hahn returned to school to try for a Ph.D in English, a single mother at age thirty-four. Toward the end of the four-year program, Hahn became a freelance illustrator for a children's reading series on PBS, *Cover to Cover.* Through this work her knowledge of children's literature broadened, and eventually she took a job as a children's librarian. Her intention was to continue writing her dissertation in her spare time, but in the event what she wrote was her first novel, *The Sara Summer.* Begun in 1975, that first novel was finally published in 1979. The initial writing took a year, but it was not until a friendly editor at Clarion Books, James Giblin, sent back a rejection with some suggestions for revision that Hahn began her real apprenticeship in children's writing. What ensued were two years and seven revisions until finally in 1978 Giblin took the book on. Hahn has been with Clarion and her editor, Giblin, ever since. "I can't believe how lucky I have been to have the same editor all these years," Hahn said in her interview with *AAYA.* "When I hear the horror stories of other writers, how their editors leave or their publishing houses die, I realize how fortunate I have been."

Similar to her first efforts at juvenile writing with "Small Town Life," *The Sara Summer* takes place in a suburb of Washington, DC, and draws on Hahn's memories of what it is like to be a twelve-year-old, the tallest in school and unsure of oneself. Coltish Emily Sherwood, deserted by her only friend, happily takes on the newcomer in town, Sara Slater, a rough-hewn gem of a girl whose mouth manages to make adults uneasy. Sara is even taller than Emily and exhibits the same disinterest in boys and clothes—the perfect friend, it seems. But Emily must learn to find herself in the relationship, and this is partly accomplished by her saving Sara's little sister from almost certain death on the train tracks. Emily

must learn to speak up for herself, to call her new friend on the cruel manner in which she treats her little sister whom she dubs "Hairball." Most critics commented on the episodic quality of the book, a hazard of first novels. Richard Ashford, writing in *Horn Book,* noted that despite some sketchy characterization of minor characters, "the vivid characterizations of the two girls make the author's first novel a worthwhile venture." Cyrisse Jaffee in the *School Library Journal* also commented on some "one-dimensional characters (especially the adults)," but concluded that Hahn "convincingly portrays the ups and downs of a friendship that kids will find easy to read and relate to." *Publishers Weekly*'s Jean F. Mercier also noted that Hahn exhibited an "intimate knowledge of subteens and a well-tuned ear." It was these qualities which distinguished Hahn's work from the outset and has kept readers coming back for more.

Hahn's second book, *The Time of the Witch,* opened the door to fantasy, with a blending of both a realistic domestic situation and an element of magic. The first of her "entertainments," *The Time of the Witch* tells the story of sulky young Laura who tries to stop her parents' impending divorce. The story was partly inspired by Hahn's own daughters who had trouble accepting Hahn's divorce. But Laura, in her quest, seeks help from the local witch in the mountains of West Virginia where she lives. The witch, however, has a separate agenda: She wants to get even with Laura's family for an old grudge. "One editor at Clarion actually wanted the witch to turn out to be just a regular person, misunderstood by the local children," Hahn told *AAYA.* "But Jim wouldn't go along with that. He didn't want her to be just an old lady with problems. I'm grateful we made that decision, as I was always disappointed in stories that explained away the magic when I was a kid." Critics concurred, including Karen Stang Hanley in *School Library Journal* who noted that "elements of suspense and the occult are expertly balanced against the realistic dimensions" of the story. Such fantasy stories involving witches and ghosts are among Hahn's most popular with children. "People are always asking me when I'm going to write another ghost story," she told *AAYA,* "and I can only tell them I'll write one when it comes to me. I cannot write to order, even if I know sales are assured."

Hahn's third novel, *Daphne's Book,* returned to the serious theme of the outsider and also won awards on both the state and national level. Jessica is none too happy about being stuck with "Daffy" Daphne as a partner on a class project, yet eventually the two girls form a friendship. Jessica, however, soon discovers a secret about Daphne that challenges their friendship. Daphne and her small sister are living with a senile grandparent after the death of their parents. When Jessica discovers this secret, Daphne swears her to silence, but ultimately Jessica feels she must tell the authorities to save her friend. In the construction of this third novel, Hahn had learned her lessons. According to Audrey B. Eaglen in *School Library Journal,* the characters, "even secondary ones, are completely believable and very likable." Nancy C. Hammond, writing in *Horn Book,* while noting that Hahn was "perceptive" in her depiction of preadolescents, commented that each girl "learns that the issues of betrayal and loyalty, hurting and helping, can be perplexingly unclear; the ending . . . is hopeful rather than happy." Writing in the *New York Times Book Review,* Barbara Cutler Helfgott noted that the book's vitality

"derives from a convincing respect for hopeful beginnings and hard choices—two conditions for growth, no matter what your age." *Publishers Weekly*'s Mercier summed up the book by calling it a "gently humorous novel about characters the author endows with humanity."

The realistic approach was also employed in Hahn's fourth book, *The Jellyfish Season,* "a sensitive, moving story that focuses on a family in crisis," according to a critic in *Kirkus Reviews.* Using personal material from the uncomfortable summer when her family had to share housing with her father's relatives, Hahn tells the story of Kathleen, whose family is forced into similar circumstances when the father loses his job at a steel mill. The family must leave Baltimore and move in with an uncle and a spoiled cousin on Chesapeake Bay. Kathleen is on the outs at the new house, a sworn enemy of her cousin Fay until she discovers her cousin's secret—a sailor-boyfriend who thinks Fay is eighteen. Kathleen develops a crush on the sailor herself, and ultimately the two cousins call a truce, though Kathleen's relationship with her mother—pregnant again—takes more work to reestablish their former intimacy. Some family order is restored when the father finds another job, but their former life in Baltimore is gone forever. A contributor in *Kirkus Reviews* noted that Hahn "has drawn an evocative portrait of the struggling American family of our times," and concluded that "readers who come from similar backgrounds will find it easy to identify with" the characters. Nelda Mohr in *Children's Book Review Service* felt that the book was a "very realistic story of a young teen who has all the usual problems of growing up with the additional burden of her parents' economic and marital problems," and observed that the book "should be popular." Marjorie Lewis in the *School Library Journal* echoed this sentiment, concluding in her review that *The Jellyfish Season* "should be a favorite among young teens." Zena Sutherland in *Bulletin of the Center for Children's Books* noted that though she felt the pacing was off, the "characters, dialogue, and interpersonal dynamics are extremely well handled . . . and there's plenty for early adolescents to identify with here. Above all, it's honest." *Horn Book*'s Mary M. Burns also commented on a typical Hahn quality—"the frequently humorous touch" which does not, however, diminish "the difficulties."

Hahn's 1988 novel *December Stillness* concerns a homeless Vietnam veteran and the girl who interviews him for a class project. (Avon Books, 1990. Used by permission of HarperCollins Children's Books, a division of HarperCollins Publishers.)

Blending the Supernatural with the Realistic

Hahn typically does not work from a plot outline; rather she begins with a character and situation and writes until the voice of that character—or others in the story—begin to take over. "Sometimes my characters are reticent," Hahn told *AAYA*. "Then I find other things to do, go for a walk, do the laundry, talk on the phone, doodle. Anything to let the book simmer on the unconscious level. Sometimes I work on more than one project at a time, especially when I've just sent a book off to my editor and am waiting for revisions. I have to admit that I have had the most fun writing my entertainments, involving elements of fantasy in the brew. The serious books take much longer to develop. Not only does the action have to be more consistent, but the resolutions need to be worked out in a realistic manner. Also, since I write in the first person, characterization can be tricky. I need to show the real character behind the facade not by simply telling, but by showing in their actions and interactions with other characters."

Hahn blended supernatural and realistic elements once again in her popular work *Wait Till Helen Comes,* the story of Molly and her brother Michael, who move into a converted church with their mother and new stepfather and his daughter, Heather. This daughter makes life miserable for the family, especially Molly and Michael, but soon there is more in the air than just whining. Heather, Molly comes to understand, has been possessed by a ghost named Helen, buried in the graveyard attached to the converted church. *Wait Till Helen Comes* was widely praised for its effective pacing, realistic characterizations, and convincing supernatural elements. Elizabeth S. Watson in Horn Book observed that Hahn "has written a gripping and scary ghost story that develops hauntingly." Cynthia Dobrez described the story in the Chicago Tribune Books as "suspenseful and often terrifying." As Roger Sutton noted in *Bulletin of the Center for Children's Books:* "This junior gothic is genuinely scary, complete with dark secrets from the past, unsettled graves, and a very real ghost. "Sutton commented also that the realistic portion of the book, the strained family relations, were "heightened and intensified by the supernatural goings-on." Judy Greenfield, writing in the *School Library Journal,* concluded that *Wait Till Helen Comes* "is a powerful, convincing, and frightening tale," and should create "a heavy demand from readers who are not 'faint at heart.'" Hahn herself is one of those faint at heart. "The book is scary," she told *AAYA*. "I don't think I would have been able to read it when I was ten. It has remained one of my most popular titles and was one of the quickest and easiest I've written. I have no idea why some books are so hard and some so easy."

The Doll in the Garden is a supernatural tale. After the death of her father, Ashley and her mother move into a flat rented out by a hostile woman. Ashley and a new friend discover a doll buried in the

Hahn wearing a sandwich board to advertise one of her book signings in Twin Falls, Idaho, in 1989. (Courtesy of Mary Downing Hahn.)

garden and encounter the ghost of a dying child, which leads them back in time to discover the landlady's old secret. Comforting the child in her time travels, Ashley also helps to heal her own pain at her father's death. Ethel Twichell, writing in *Horn Book*, noted that Hahn's "story line is well worked out, and the shift from past to present offers its own enchantment." Other reviewers noted that the book was not as scary as *Wait Till Helen Comes*, and Sutton in *Bulletin of the Center for Children's Books* felt that the book benefited from a "direct style and smooth storytelling."

Hahn further explored the possibilities of time travel with *Time for Andrew*, which features a young male protagonist in 1910 who is dying of diphtheria. He falls through a hole in time into the room now occupied by his great-great nephew, Drew. By changing places, Drew is able to save his relative with modern medicine, and then the two try to switch roles—with less than perfect results. Noting the humorous sections in the book, Virginia Golodetz concluded in the *School Library Journal* that "there is enough tension to keep readers engaged." *Booklist*'s Stephanie Zvirin observed that "there's plenty to enjoy in this delightful time-slip fantasy: a fascinating premise, a dastardly cousin, some good suspense, and a roundup of characters to care about." Sutton, in *Bulletin of the Center for Children's Books*, summed up the book neatly, calling it "an assured work from a deservedly popular writer, who, while gifted with the instincts of a storyteller, doesn't let her narrative get away from her characters."

Quite different in tone is another novel involving the supernatural, this time for older readers and involving a vampire. Set at an inn in a remote part of Maine, *Look for Me by Moonlight* involves the usual Hahn mix of family relations—this time a new stepmother for the sixteen-year-old protagonist, Cynda, to get used to. Cynda soon finds some solace in her new friend, Vincent Morthanos. Vincent has more on his mind than friendship, however, and naive Cynda only slowly realizes that he is a vampire. While Ilene Cooper noted in *Booklist* that the story "both terrorizes and tantalizes," Hahn herself was less pleased with the book. "Of all my books it's my least favorite," she told *AAYA* in her interview. "It has always made me uncomfortable; there is little light in that book. It makes me wonder what part of me that story came from."

A Full-Time Writer

Hahn remarried in 1982, and by 1991 her writing and publishing were steady enough that she could leave her library work and devote herself full time to her novels. "Now that I have all this time, I find lots of ways to use it up," Hahn told *AAYA*. "In ways I was more disciplined when I had to squeeze my writing in between my job and my house." But Hahn has continued to publish a new title almost yearly. Other popular works in her serious vein include *Tallahassee Higgins* and *December Stillness*. With the former title, Hahn revisited the time her family had to share housing with relatives, but in this treatment she has the female protagonist face the situation alone. When Tally's flighty mother takes off to become a star in Hollywood, she parks her daughter with an aunt and uncle. *December Stillness* looks at the Vietnam war and its effects on one veteran. Kelly interviews the homeless vet for a school project. Inspired by a man who used to spend long hours at the library where Hahn worked, *December Stillness* is, according to several reviewers, more didactic in tone than other Hahn titles. Sutton, in *Bulletin of the Center for Children's Books*, while commenting on the "message-driven" nature of the book, also remarked that "Hahn's practiced handling of suspense serves her well here."

Quite different in theme and style are adventure stories Hahn has written for young readers, including *The Dead Man in Indian Creek, The Spanish Kidnapping Disaster*, and *The Gentleman Outlaw and Me—Eli*. Hahn branched out into adventure fiction with *The Dead Man in Indian Creek*, the story of two boys who suspect a local antique dealer of being behind the murder of the man they find in a nearby creek. Reviewers praised the fast-paced action and high suspense of this novel. Although Carolyn Noah in the *School Library Journal* found several "illogical gaps" in the plot, other critics agreed with Diane Roback's assertion in *Publishers Weekly* that the "combination of crackling language and plenty of suspense" found here makes *The Dead Man in Indian Creek* "likely to appeal to even the most reluctant readers." Similarly, in *The Spanish Kidnapping Disaster*, three children are thrown together by the marriage of their parents, whom they are unexpectedly forced to join on their honeymoon in Spain. When one of them lies to the wrong person about their wealth, the three are kidnapped, which "creates action, danger, and suspense," commented Sutherland. The critic nevertheless faulted the book for "an undue amount of structural contrivance." Other reviewers, however, focused on Hahn's superb characterizations, including what Roback and Richard Donohue described in *Publishers Weekly* as "a surprisingly understanding look at what impels people to terrorist activity." With *The Gentleman Outlaw and Me—Eli*, Hahn was able to indulge a childhood fantasy of running off with cowboys. "Growing up in College Park, there was not much opportunity for such high adventure," she told *AAYA*. Orphaned Eliza cuts off her hair and passes as a boy in a grab-bag of adventures. Susan Dove Lempke noted in *Booklist* that "Hahn's writing crackles like gunshot in the Ol' West."

New Literary Territory

Hahn also broke new ground with her young adult novel, *The Wind Blows Backward,* a romantic novel about Lauren and Spencer, who revive a junior high crush during their senior year in high school. But Spencer is haunted now by his father's suicide, and it seems to Lauren that he may be preparing to follow his father's example. Diane Roback commented in *Publishers Weekly* that the novel was a "taut and emotionally driven story that manages to be romantic without romanticizing the fierceness of teenage love," while *Booklist*'s Zvirin noted the "sensitively drawn" characters and concluded that "Hahn evokes a fantasy love gone awry and shows clearly that while loving deeply and truly may be wonderful, it's not always enough."

Hahn returned to the more familiar audience of young teen readers with a trio of books set during and after the Second World War. The first book, *Stepping on the Cracks,* is set during World War II in a small Maryland town, where two patriotic sixth-grade girls get a lesson in compassion when they discover that Gordy, the class bully, is hiding his brother from the authorities. Despite knowing he is a deserter, the girls decide to help Gordy's brother, risking their parents' disapproval. "Hahn's story recreates the tensions and moral climate of its period in authentic detail," wrote a critic in Kirkus Reviews. *Horn Book* contributor Maeve Visser Knoth made a similar comment, adding, "the characters ring true, including the girls' vehement patriotism and initial reluctance to accept a broader view." Critics praised Hahn for effectively handling a number of compelling themes, including pacifism, and the need to defy one's parents in order to do what is right. "Potent stuff," observed Zena Sutherland in the *Bulletin of the Center for Children's Books,* who singled out "the integrity of the plot and the consistency of the characterization"as the elements that make the book "outstanding."

With the war over in *Following My Own Footsteps,* Gordy goes to North Carolina to escape his abusive father in a story that provides a "terrific rendering of day-to-day life in the mid-1940s," according to *Booklist*'s Lempke. *Horn Book*'s Knoth concurred, adding that Hahn "brings many issues, including alcoholism, abuse, and definitions of courage, into her story and handles them deftly." Gordy makes a further appearance in *As Ever, Gordy,* when he returns to College Hill where the action in *Stepping on the Cracks* began. In the eighth grade now, he has learned some lessons from his time in North Carolina. "This book had a very complex structure," Hahn reported in her *AAYA* interview, "and took me a couple of years to write."

The effects of slavery and the Civil War became Hahn's focus when she created *Promises to the Dead,* in which Jesse, a young white boy, promises a dying slave that he will take her newborn son out of slavery and to the sister of her dead master. The boys encounter many obstacles along their way, including slave catchers and the Yankee Army's invasion of Baltimore. Ilene Cooper, writing in *Booklist,* noted that "Hahn has a marvelous touch when it comes to manipulating her story and heightening the tension in a way that keeps readers on the edge of their seats."

In *Hear the Wind Blow: A Novel of the Civil War,* Hahn tells the story of Haswell Magruder, a Southern boy who hides a wounded Confederate soldier at the end of the war. When the Yankees discover the soldier, they burn down Haswell's family farm in retaliation. Soon he and his younger sister are on the road, travelling to the home of relatives amid the chaos and destruction of a devastated country. The critic for *Kirkus Reviews* dubbed it "a memorable journey in the voice of a young boy whom readers will care about [and] a first-rate story." Writing in *Horn Book,* Betty Carter believed that Hahn "gives readers an entertaining and thought-provoking combination: a strong adventure inextricably bound to a specific time and place, but one that resonates with universal themes." Claire Rosser in *Kliatt* concluded: "This is an ideal novel to complement Civil War studies."

The Old Willis Place is the story of Diana and her younger brother, Georgie, who live on the grounds of the old Willis place. When a new caretaker comes to watch over the decayed and abandoned building, Diana, who has no friends, is curious to meet the man's daughter, Lissa. But Georgie reminds her that it is "against the rules" to have friends. Part of the story is narrated by Diana and another part is seen through Lissa's diary entries. Many of the same events are seen from both perspectives. "The story is taut, spooky, and fast-paced with amazingly credible, memorable characters," according to Maria B. Salvadore in the *School Library Journal.* "More than just a ghost story, this riveting novel is a mystery and a story of friendship and of redemption." The critic for *Kirkus Reviews* dubbed the story "spooky, but with an underlying sweetness."

Hahn's *Witch Catcher* tells the story of young Jen, whose father has just inherited a mansion in rural West Virginia. When the two of them move to the mansion, Jen's father comes under the spell of a local antiques dealer, Moura. Jen eventually comes to realize that a fairy has been caught within a glass witch catcher and Moura wants the helpless fairy for herself. Holly Koelling in *Booklist* called the novel "a fast-paced, suspenseful fantasy in which an appealing heroine stands against forces seemingly beyond her control." According to Nicki Clausen-Grace in the *School Library Journal*, "Hahn weaves an engaging story."

If you enjoy the works of Mary Downing Hahn, you may also want to check out the following books:

Ruby Edmond MacDonald, *The Ghosts of Austwick Manor*, 1982.
John Bellairs, *The Ghost in the Mirror*, 1993.
Robert Westall, *The Stones of Muncaster Cathedral*, 1993.

In *Deep and Dark and Dangerous*, "Hahn offers another eerie, suspenseful ghost story filled with family secrets," according to Gillian Engberg in *Booklist*. Ali is invited to spend the summer at her Aunt Dulcie's cottage in Maine. But when she gets there, Ali meets the mysterious Sissie and begins to hear rumors about a family secret invovling her mother and Aunt Dulcie. A torn photograph and an empty grave move her to believe in a hidden tragedy long ago. Marie Orlando in the *School Library Journal* noted that "the well-plotted story [moves] along to a satisfying conclusion." Writing in *Mystery Scene*, Roberta Rogow found that "the shattering conclusion explains the secret that has haunted this family for years." Lyn Seippel, writing for *Bookloons*, claimed: "This chilling ghost story is one of Hahn's best. The suspense never lets up as Ali searches for answers to the questions the adults won't even discuss." *Deep and Dark and Dangerous* was nominated for an Edgar Award by the Mystery Writers of America.

All the Lovely Bad Ones is another ghost story, this time set in a haunted bed and breakfast in Vermont. Corey and Travis have been having some fun by faking a haunting at the inn. But their prank seems to have stirred up the real ghosts of the place, children who died when the building was a poorhouse in the nineteenth century. The ghosts need the children's help to resolve their lingering prob-

lems and achieve a final rest. The critic for *Publishers Weekly* found that Hahn offers "some genuinely spine-chilling moments."

Speaking with Annette Curtis Klause on the *Montgomery Country Public Libraries Web site*, Hahn explained how she works: "My cats seem to think they're helping. They sit on my lap and shed on the keyboard. They chase the cursor as it moves around the screen. When they're hungry, they knock the mouse on the floor. One of them has rodent-like tendencies and loves to chew on small cords. So far he has killed one mouse, bitten through a computer speaker cord, two power cords for my laptop, and at least one telephone cord. Other than that, they're great company—I love to look up and see them sleeping nearby. Writing would be a lonely occupation without the two of them!"

Throughout all of her books, Hahn manages to cast a spell of verisimilitude with her attention to detail and use of personal experience. Her goal in writing is straightforward, as she concluded in her interview with *AAYA*: "I want to tell a good story, first and foremost. I don't think about theme. If it comes, great. But that is not my focus. I want readers to come away from my books feeling that they have read a story that sticks with them, with characters that linger on the mind. They might also gain a bit more understanding about people and realize that everyone has a story inside of them."

■ Biographical and Critical Sources

BOOKS

Something about the Author Autobiography Series, Volume 12, Gale (Detroit, MI), 1991.

PERIODICALS

Book Links, September, 1994, pp. 53-58.
Booklist, October 15, 1982, Barbara Elleman, review of *The Time of the Witch*, p. 311; May 1, 1993, Stephanie Zvirin, review of *The Wind Blows Backward*, pp. 1580, 1582; March 15, 1999, review of *Anna All Year Round*, p. 1329; April 1, 1999, Hazel Rochman, review of *Stepping on the Cracks*, p. 1429; April 1, 2000, Ilene Cooper, review of *Promises to the Dead*, p. 1473; February 15, 2001, Kay Weisman, review of *Anna on the Farm*, p. 1136; May 1, 2001, Stephanie Zvirin, review of *Look for Me by Moonlight*, p. 1610; June 1, 2006, Holly Koel-

ling, review of *Witch Catcher* p. 70; March 15, 2007, Gillian Engberg, review of *Deep and Dark and Dangerous*, p. 47.

Bulletin of the Center for Children's Books, February, 1980, pp. 109-110; January, 1984, pp. 87-88; February, 1986, review of *The Jellyfish Season*, p. 108; April, 1987, Zena Sutherland, review of *Tallahassee Higgins*, p. 146; April, 1988, p. 156; September, 1988, Roger Sutton, review of *December Stillness*, p. 9; March, 1989, Roger Sutton, review of *The Doll in the Garden*, p. 171; May, 1991, Zena Sutherland, review of *The Spanish Kidnapping Disaster*, p. 218; December, 1991, Zena Sutherland, review of *Stepping on the Cracks*, p. 91; May, 1993, Roger Sutton, review of *The Wind Blows Backward*, pp. 281-282; April, 1994, Roger Sutton, review of *Time for Andrew: A Ghost Story*, pp. 259-260.

Children's Bookwatch, July, 2007, review of *Deep and Dark and Dangerous*.

Horn Book, October, 1979, Richard Ashford, review of *The Sara Summer*, p. 534; February, 1983, Ann A. Flowers, review of *The Time of the Witch*, p. 44; December, 1983, p. 708; March-April, 1986, Mary M. Burns, review of *The Jellyfish Season*, p. 201; November-December, 1986, Elizabeth S. Watson, review of *Wait Till Helen Comes*, pp. 744-745; May-June, 1987, pp. 341-342; July-August, 1988, Elizabeth S. Watson, review of *Following the Mystery Man*, p. 493; November-December, 1988, Nancy Vasilakis, review of *December Stillness*, pp. 786-787; May-June, 1989, Ethel R. Twichell, review of *The Doll in the Garden*, p. 370; May-June, 1990, pp. 334-335; July, 1990, review of *Anna All Year Round*, p. 465; November, 1991, Maeve Visser Knoth, review of *Stepping on the Cracks*, p. 736; May, 2001, review of *Anna on the Farm*, p. 324; May-June, 2003, Betty Carter, review of *Hear the Wind Blow: A Novel of the Civil War*, p. 346.

Kirkus Reviews, October 16, 1991, review of *Stepping on the Cracks*, p. 1343; May 15, 2003, review of *Hear the Wind Blow*, p. 751; September 1, 2004, review of *The Old Willis Place: A Ghost Story*, p. 866.

Kliatt, July, 2003, Claire Rosser, review of *Hear the Wind Blow*, p. 12.

Mystery Scene, winter, 2008, Roberta Rogow, review of review of *Deep and Dark and Dangerous*, p. 61.

New York Times, October 23, 1983.

New York Times Book Review, October 23, 1983, Barbara Cutler Helfgott, review of *Daphne's Book*, p. 34.

Publishers Weekly, November 19, 1979, Jean F. Mercier, review of *The Sara Summer*, p. 79; August 5, 1983, Jean F. Mercier, review of *Daphne's Book*, p. 92; December 6, 1985, Jean F. Mercier, review of

The Jellyfish Season, p. 75; July 25, 1986, p. 190; January 29, 1988, p. 431; July 8, 1988, p. 57; February 9, 1990, Diane Roback, review of *The Dead Man in Indian Creek*, p. 62; March 1, 1991, Diane Roback and Richard Donohue, review of *The Spanish Kidnapping Disaster*, p. 73; April 26, 1993, Diane Roback and Richard Donohue, review of *The Wind Blows Backward*, pp. 80-81; April 19, 1999, review of *Anna All Year Round*, p. 74; April 17, 2000, review of *Promises to the Dead*, p. 81; March 10, 2008, review of *All the Lovely Bad Ones*, p. 82.

School Library Journal, December, 1979, Cyrisse Jaffee, review of *The Sara Summer*, p. 86; November, 1982, Karen Stang Hanley, review of *The Time of the Witch*, p. 84; October, 1983, Audrey B. Eaglen, review of *Daphne's Book*, p. 168; October, 1985, Marjorie Lewis, review of *The Jellyfish Season*, p. 172; October, 1986, Judy Greenfield, review of *Wait Till Helen Comes*, p. 176; April, 1988, Elizabeth Mellett, review of *Following the Mystery Man*, p. 100; October, 1988, p. 161; April, 1990, Carolyn Noah, review of *The Dead Man in Indian Creek*, p. 118; December, 1991, p. 114; May, 1993, Gerry Larson, review of *The Wind Blows Backward*, p. 124; May, 1994, Virginia Golodetz, review of *Time for Andrew*, p. 114; May, 1999, Linda Bindner, review of *Anna All Year Round*, p. 90; June, 2000, Cyrisse Jaffee, review of *Promises to the Dead*, p. 146; March, 2001, Debbie Whitbeck, review of *Anna on the Farm*, p. 209; December, 2004, Maria B. Salvadore, review of *The Old Willis Place*, p. 146; August, 2006, Nicki Clausen-Grace, review of *Witch Catcher* p. 121; May, 2007, Marie Orlando, review of *Deep and Dark and Dangerous*, p. 134.

Stone Soup, July, 2001, Reed Gochberg, review of *Promises to the Dead*, p. 32.

Tribune Books (Chicago, IL), April 5, 1987, Cynthia Dobrez, review of *Wait Till Helen Comes*, p. 4.

Voice of Youth Advocates, June, 1987, Dolores Maminski, review of *Tallahassee Higgins*, p. 78; August, 1990, p. 160; August, 1993, Marilyn Bannon, review of *The Wind Blows Backward*, p. 152.

ONLINE

Bookloons, http://www.bookloons.com/ (February 11, 2008), Lyn Seippel, review of *Deep and Dark and Dangerous*.

OTHER

A Visit with Mary Downing Hahn (video), Kit Morse Productions, Houghton Mifflin, 1994.*

Paul Hornschemeier

◼ Personal

Born 1977 in Cincinnati, OH; son of a lawyer father and a judge mother. *Education:* Ohio State University, earned degree in philosophy.

◼ Addresses

Office—Forlorn Funnies, 2324 West Walton, 3F, Chicago, IL 60622. *E-mail*—feedback@sequential comics.com.

◼ Career

Graphic novelist.

◼ Writings

Stand on a Mountain, Look Back: Sequential Book Seven, Last Gasp (San Francisco, CA), 2001.

Mother, Come Home, introduction by Thomas Tennant, Dark Horse Comics, (Milwaukie, OR) 2003.

The Collected Sequential, AdHouse Books (Richmond, VA), 2004.

Return of the Elephant, AdHouse Books (Richmond, VA), 2004.

Let Us Be Perfectly Clear, Fantagraphics (Seattle, WA), 2006.

The Three Paradoxes, Fantagraphics (Seattle, WA), 2007.

Contributor to books, including *Autobiographix,* Dark Horse Comics (Milwaukie, OR), 2003. Writer and illustrator of *Forlorn Funnies* and *Sequential Comics* series.

◼ Sidelights

Graphic novelist Paul Hornschemeier is the creator of *Mother, Come Home, Let Us Be Perfectly Clear,* and *The Three Paradoxes.* In these books, he confronts the painful moments in every life in a thoughtful and measured way. Eric Reynolds of the *Comics Reporter* Web site found that "Hornschemeier's work is defined by its formal experimentation and emotional tone, weaving interconnected visual styles, playing with traditional comic book tropes, and using color as a crucial narrative tool. All of these devices are used to bolster his emotional and philosophical concerns in a fairly direct, though subtle, manner." According to Scott Rosenberg, writing in the *Express,* Hornschemeier turns "out important graphic novels that are intelligent and beautifully rendered—the kind of work that makes you think about life and how to live it."

Hornschemeier was born in Cincinnati, Ohio, in 1977. He was raised in the nearby farming community of Georgetown, Ohio. Although both his parents were lawyers, Hornschemeier explained that the family had little money when he was growing up. "As far as money, my parents are just two of the most, selfless, nice people you could ever hope to meet," he explained to Gary Groth in *MOME*, "and they just, honestly when it comes down to it, my father particularly, has never charged anyone what he ought to."

Hornschemeier began drawing at an early age, mostly comic book superheroes. He soon began drawing his own comic books; the early ones featured popular characters from television, but by the age of eight or nine, they featured his own characters. "It's really interesting if you look at the books, I just went through one of them when I was at my parents' house, just a few weeks ago," Hornschemeier told Groth. "It's just amazing, because it starts off—and, you know, they're fairly decent drawings for somebody at that age and then it just completely degrades to just ciphers and symbols. I actually can still understand the story because I wrote it, but it's so obvious that the only thing that was important to me was getting to the end of the story, like I just wanted to tell the story. The drawings just fell away to nothing, and there were just these completely abstract symbols for things."

Discovers Graphic Novels

It was while attending Ohio State University, where he earned a degree in philosophy, that Hornschemeier first became aware of the possibilities of making his own comic books again. A girlfriend gave him a copy of Dan Clowes's book *Ghost World* for Christmas. The graphic novel impressed him. He told Groth: "I read it and I remember I was just sitting by myself in my apartment, my little crappy basement apartment, and reading this thing through and 'Wow, I can't even believe this exists.'" Soon Hornschemeier had read every other graphic novel he could find. More than that, he got a job at a local comic shop.

Hornschemeier's first published comics work was a strip called "Squares" for the university newspaper *The Lantern*. Some of these original cartoons were gathered together and published in the self-published *Sequential* comic book series. "*Sequential* was Hornschemeier's first, self-published attempt at a regular comic book series," noted Alan David Doane on the *Comic Book Galaxy* Web site. Doane added: "Over the course of its seven issues, *Sequen-*

Let Us Be Perfectly Clear, a 2006 collection of stories and one-panel gags, demonstrates Paul Hornschemeier's range of talents. (Fantagraphics Books, 2006. Courtesy of Fantagraphics Books.)

tial demonstrated an emerging talent eager to assay the parameters and possibilities of his chosen art form." *Forlorn Funnies*, a later, "and artistically more mature work," is a series that "stuns with its sheer dedication to its creator's joy of cartooning," Doane stated. *Stand on a Mountain, Look Back: Sequential Book Seven* and *The Collected Sequential*, gather much of the work first published in these early comics.

A Tale of Grieving

Forlorn Funnies first published the original story that became Hornschemeier's first graphic novel, *Mother, Come Home*. As the story opens, seven-year-old Thomas Tennant has lost his mother to cancer.

His father, a professor, retains a tenuous grip on his emotions and struggles to cope with his own loss while providing as well as he can for Thomas. Gradually, the pair's roles reverse, with Thomas becoming more of the caretaker and caregiver, cleaning up the house, taking care of his mother's garden and grave, and making excuses to his father's colleagues when he misses classes or appointments. Thomas finds his strength in a lion mask and superhero cape he wears to symbolically transform himself into a powerful individual with the ability to cope with his problems and his father's as well. Eventually, Thomas loses his father, too, when the grief-crippled man checks himself into a residential-care center for psychiatric treatment. While living with an aunt and uncle, Thomas retreats into a cheerful cartoonish fantasy world where everything is perfect and just the way he wants it. Thomas's fantasies remain at the forefront as he "rescues" his father in the story's emotional climax.

In *Mother, Come Home*, "Hornschemeier shows the utmost compassion for both father and son, who react to their grief the only way they know how," wrote *Library Journal* reviewer Khadija Caturani. The "book's greatest strength is the story itself and the lessons it offers for life, loss, and, most importantly, how to move on," commented *School Library Journal* reviewer Matthew L. Moffett. "The plot is a real three-hanky weeper, but Hornschemeier leverages some of the heaviness into bittersweet absurdity," observed a *Publishers Weekly* reviewer. Ray Olson, in a review for *Booklist*, called the book "exceptionally powerful work." *Entertainment Weekly* reviewer Jeff Jensen declared that *Mother, Come Home*, "is deserving of the word masterpiece without reservation." Similarly, John Parker, in a review for *Ninth Art*, concluded that "*Mother, Come Home*, is a book unlike most others. It manages to impress visually, technically, and emotionally without being self-conscious or pretentious. It's a good book for its creator's audacity alone, in attempting something that has never quite been done before, in so unique and unconventional a fashion. What makes it a great book is Hornschemeier's success."

Let Us Be Perfectly Clear, Hornschemeier's 2006 book, turns away from the graphic novel. It instead gathers a number of shorter stories and one-panel gags that Hornschemeier first published in various magazines and newspapers. The collection "displays the artist's enormous visual range—'60s-style gag cartooning, gritty caricature, spacey surrealism and a marvelous command of muted, flat-tone colors—as well as his consistently bitter, deadpan writing," according to a critic for *Publishers Weekly*. Olson, writing in *Booklist*, found that the book is "wickedly funny."

A Paradoxical, Personal Story

Hornschemeier's graphic novel *The Three Paradoxes* is, on the surface, an autobiographical story about the artist himself visiting his parents in their small Ohio town. During the visit, Paul takes an evening walk to the store with his father. Along the way, he also snaps photographs of local landmarks to show a girl he has just met. The walk triggers memories for Paul, and those memories become side stories. He also discusses with his father the three paradoxes of the ancient Greek philosopher Zeno. Zeno argued that nothing ever changed, and his paradoxes were stories meant to prove that point. Each side story is done in a different comics style: a story about a childhood fight with a bully is done in a newspaper comic strip style; Paul's attempts to finish a comics story he is working on is done in blue pencil; a story about how a local resident got a scar is done in a 1960s comic book style; and the story of Zeno and his paradoxes is done as if the pages had been torn from an old comic book, complete with ragged page edges. Meanwhile, the walk that Paul and his father are taking through town is done in a realistic, muted-tone style. Zeno's idea that there is no such thing as change is reflected in the multiple stories

The 2007 autobiographical graphic novel *The Three Paradoxes* concerns Hornschemeier's visit to his parents in Ohio. (Fantagraphics Books, 2007. Courtesy of Fantagraphics Books.)

of the book. Paul's life—the present, his memories of the past, and his hopes for the future—are all present at the same time. "Hornschemeier reminds us that we live simultaneously, and paradoxically, in the past, present and future," as Steve Duin put it in a review for *OregonLive.com.*

Calling Hornschemeier "a young luminary of experimental comics," a critic for *Publishers Weekly* concluded that *The Three Paradoxes* "is formally brilliant." Paul Semel of *Geek Monthly.com* judged the book to be "a really great read that's as visually stimulating as it is thought provoking." "It's rare to read a graphic novel with this sort of abstract philosophical depth," Ben Pogany wrote in the *Daily Cross Hatch.* "Hornschemeier's *The Three Paradoxes,*" wrote Danny Graydon in *First Post,* "is a marvellous thing: a striking exploitation of colour and stylistic shifts that's also an impressively avant-garde, yet very readable, autobiographical graphic novel."

If you enjoy the works of Paul Hornschemeier, you may also want to check out the following books:

Daniel Clowes, *Ghost World,* 1999.
Chris Ward, *Jimmy Corrigan: The Smartest Kid on Earth,* 2000.
Adrian Tomine, *Shortcomings,* 2007.

Having finished *The Three Paradoxes,* a project that took some two years to complete, Hornschemeier plans to devote some time to smaller projects for a while. "I want to be able to test ideas, or to just do a single page experiment or gag here or there," he told Will Moss of *Publishers Weekly.* "Having no outlet for that is simply depressing. I want to play: books carry a finality and seriousness to them."

Speaking to Steven Russell in *Rolling Stone Online,* Hornschemeier claimed that his book signings were different from those of other graphic novelists: "Everybody else has girls lining up. I get professors, grad students and fifty-year-old gay men. On the other hand, they are a dedicated lot. When I think about it too much, I get freaked out."

■ Biographical and Critical Sources

PERIODICALS

Booklist, February 1, 2004, Ray Olson, review of *Mother, Come Home,* p. 964; March 15, 2005, review of *Mother, Come Home,* p. 1278; November 1, 2006, Ray Olson, review of *Let Us Be Perfectly Clear,* p. 37; June 1, 2007, Ray Olson, review of *The Three Paradoxes,* p. 54.

Bookwatch, January, 2007, review of *Let Us Be Perfectly Clear.*

Entertainment Weekly, February 13, 2004, Jeff Jensen, review of *Mother, Come Home,* p. L2T20.

Library Journal, March 1, 2004, Khadijah Caturani, review of *Mother, Come Home,* p. 62.

MOME, summer, 2005, Gary Groth, interview with Hornschemeier.

Publishers Weekly, February 16, 2004, review of *Mother, Come Home,* p. 154; October 30, 2006, review of *Let Us Be Perfectly Clear,* p. 43; January 30, 2007, Will Moss, "Paul's Paradoxes"; June 18, 2007, review of *The Three Paradoxes,* p. 42.

School Library Journal, June, 2004, Matthew L. Moffett, review of *Mother, Come Home,* p. 182.

ONLINE

BookMunch, http://www.bookmunch.co.uk/ (August 16, 2007), Peter Wild, review of *The Three Paradoxes.*

Book Slut, http://www.bookslut.com/ (July, 2007), John Zuarino, review of *The Three Paradoxes.*

Comic Book Galaxy Web site, http://www.comicbook galaxy.com/ (August 30, 2004), Alan David Doane, "Floating with Paul."

Comics Reporter, http://www.comicsreporter.com/ (July 17, 2007), Eric Reynolds, "Eric Reynolds on Paul Hornschemeier Show at Fantagraphics Book Store."

Daily Cross Hatch, http://thedailycrosshatch.com/ (October 3, 2007), Ben Pogany, review of *The Three Paradoxes.*

Express, http://www.readexpress.com/ (June 21, 2007), Scott Rosenberg, "Intelligent Designer: Paul Hornschemeier."

Fantagraphics Books Web site, http://www.fantagraph ics.com/ (October 3, 2007), Gary Groth, interview with Hornschemeier.

First Post, http://www.thefirstpost.co.uk/ (September 7, 2007), Danny Graydon, review of *The Three Paradoxes.*

Geek Monthly.com, http://www.geekmonthly.com/ (July 19, 2007), Paul Semel, review of *The Three Paradoxes.*

Loyola Phoenix Online, http://www.loyolaphoenix. com/ (March 17, 2004), Julie Lain, "Hornschemeier Draws on Tragedy for *Funnies,*" interview.

Margo Mitchell Media Web site, http://www.margo mitchell.com/ (August 30, 2004), review of *Sequential.*

Ninth Art, http://www.ninthart.com/ (July 12, 2004), John Parker, review of *Mother, Come Home.*

OregonLive.com, http://blog.oregonlive.com/ (July 10, 2007), Steve Duin, review of *The Three Paradoxes.*

Paul Hornschemeier's Blog, http://newsandheadlice. blogspot.com (February 14, 2008).

Paul Hornschemeier My Space Page, http://www.my space.com/paulhornschemeier (August 16, 2007).

Rolling Stone Online, http://www.rollingstone.com/ (March 24, 2005), Steven Russell, "Paul Hornschemeier, the Existential Cartoonist."*

Maureen Johnson

■ Personal

Born in Philadelphia, PA. *Education:* Graduated from the University of Delaware; Columbia University, M.F.A.

■ Addresses

Home—New York, NY. *E-mail*—maureen@maureen johnsonbooks.com.

■ Career

Has worked in a restaurant, with a stage show in Las Vegas, and as an editor.

■ Awards, Honors

Best Young-Adult Books selection, American Library Association, and Books for the Teen Age selection, New York Public Library, both 2005, both for *The Key to the Golden Firebird; Booksense* selection, 2005, for *Thirteen Little Blue Envelopes.*

■ Writings

YOUNG-ADULT FICTION

The Bermudez Triangle, Razorbill (New York, NY), 2004.

The Key to the Golden Firebird, HarperCollins (New York, NY), 2004.
Thirteen Little Blue Envelopes, HarperCollins (New York, NY), 2005.
Devilish, Razorbill (New York, NY), 2006.
Girl at Sea, HarperCollins (New York, NY), 2007.

■ Sidelights

Maureen Johnson has written a string of young adult novels in which teenaged girls face unexpected circumstances and come through with humor and love. Her stories are sometimes realistic and sometimes filled with humor, but critics consistently praise her ability to create believable characters with whom the reader can identify.

Born in Philadelphia, Pennsylvania, during a massive snowstorm, Johnson was an only child. She claimed in a statement on her Home Page: "I am an only child, which means that I know how to play Candyland by myself." She knew early on that she wanted to become a writer. Although her family is not Catholic, Johnson attended a Catholic girls' school, an experience she claimed "caused me to develop a lifelong aversion to polyester and knee socks." After graduating from the University of Delaware and Columbia University, she began writing in earnest.

In her first novel, *The Bermudez Triangle,* Johnson tells the story of Nina Bermudez's last year in high school. Sent off to summer camp prior to her senior

In the 2004 novel *The Bermudez Triangle,* **Maureen Johnson tells of Nina Bermudez's last year of high school.** (Razorbill, 2007. Reproduced by permission of Razorbill, a division of Penguin Putnam Books for Young Readers.)

year, Nina returns to find that her two best friends, Avery and Mel, have begun a homosexual romance. While at camp Nina had started her own relationship with a boy named Steve, whom she still keeps in contact with via e-mail and phone. The novel follows Nina and her friends through the school year as they make plans for college and try to deal with the fact that the relationship between Avery and Mel has strained the friendship of all three. Writing in the *Bulletin of the Center for Children's Books,* Deborah Stevenson commented that "the omniscient narration slips easily from viewpoint to viewpoint, which helps keep the girls sympathetic through good behavior and bad . . . and makes credible the final restoration and affirmation of friendship." A *Kirkus Reviews* contributor called the book a "warm, humorous, and smoothly readable story" and also noted that "the characterizations of love . . . are

tender even when painful." Susan Riley, writing in the *School Library Journal,* thought the novel "exceptional" and commented that it "perceptively reflects the real-life ambiguities and shades of gray faced by contemporary adolescents."

Confronting a Father's Death

The Key to the Golden Firebird is the story of teenaged May and her strained family, which appears to be falling apart after the death of May's father. May's mother must work even harder to make money, leaving her children alone when they need her. May's teenage sisters, Brooks and Palmer, deal with the death badly; Brooks turns to alcohol and hanging out with a bad crowd while Palmer incessantly watches television to escape from the fear and anxiety she faces. May deals with the situation better than anybody and even debates turning her relationship with her longtime friend and next-door neighbor Peter into something more. Much of the story involves baseball, a favorite pastime of the girls' late father and his Pontiac Firebird. The girls make a road trip in their father's car, which plays an integral role in how all three deal with his death.

Miranda Doyle, writing in the *School Library Journal,* called *The Key to the Golden Firebird* "poignant and laced with wry humor." Doyle went on to note that "this is a wonderfully moving and entertaining novel full of authentic characters and emotions." In a review for *Booklist,* Frances Bradburn called the book "a very special, unexpected coming-of-age novel," while a *Kirkus Reviews* contributor commented that "the story's realism lends credibility to the emotional struggles of a courageous family." *Kliatt* contributor Claire Rosser wrote: "The dynamics of the relationships among the sisters, and with Peter and their other friends, are believable and honest, ringing absolutely true." Writing in the *Bulletin of the Center for Children's Books,* Deborah Stevenson called the book "an honest yet highly reassuring account of surviving loss."

Thirteen Little Blue Envelopes begins when Ginny's eccentric Aunt Peg has just passed away, leaving seventeen-year-old Ginny with a puzzle. Aunt Peg has left her with a list of several European destinations to visit, and envelopes she must open when she reaches each destination. Along the way, she not only uncovers much about her aunt's life that she did not know, but she also learns self-reliance. "As she comes to the last of the letters," wrote Janis Flint-Ferguson in *Kliatt,* "Ginny has grown from the shy teenager she was to one who is more independent, more invested in the life around her." Gillian

Engberg in *Booklist* believed that "readers will probably overlook any improbabilities and willingly accompany Ginny through her sensitive, authentically portrayed experiences—uncomfortable, lonely; giddy, and life changing—as she pieces together family mysteries and discovers herself." Emily Garrett in the *School Library Journal* concluded that "the novel drives home the importance of family, love, and the value of connections that you make with people."

A School Plagued by Demons

Devilish, according to Johnson in a statement posted on her Home Page, is "very loosely based on my Catholic high school experiences. Sadly, there were no demons, angelic creatures, or walking beds in my high school. We did, however, have some scary statues and a marriage class taught by a nun, so it all balances out." Jane Jarvis and Allison ("Ally") Concord attend St. Teresa's Preparatory School for Girls in Providence, Rhode Island. Ally is a little lost at the school, and naive about how things work, so Jane tries to watch out for her. But Jane is surprised when actual demons begin to plague the school, and Ally seems somehow oddly changed. "Well-developed characters are Johnson's forte," Susan Riley noted in the *School Library Journal*, "and readers will delight in meeting the heroine's friends and, especially, her family." The critic for *Kirkus Reviews* wrote: "Johnson writes with flair, intelligence and humor. Her characters are well-realized as she builds suspense as deftly as Stephen King." Ilene Cooper, writing in *Booklist*, called the novel "Fast paced and very funny," concluding that "Johnson does a very clever thing here. She takes a typical high-school story about popularity (amusing enough in Jane's snarky voice) and turns it on its head when evil comes on the scene."

Johnson's 2005 novel *Thirteen Little Blue Envelopes* follows teenaged Ginny on an international trip that uncovers much about her late aunt's life. (HarperCollins, 2005. Jacket photograph © 2005 by Hubie Frowein. Used by permission of HarperCollins Children's Books, a division of HarperCollins Publishers.)

If you enjoy the works of Maureen Johnson, you may also want to check out the following books:

Melissa Kantor, *If I Have a Wicked Stepmother, Where's My Prince?*, 2005.
Sarah Dessen, *Just Listen*, 2006.
Catherine Murdock, *The Off Season*, 2007.

Speaking of the plot for *Girl at Sea*, Johnson explained: "I will not say too much about it, but it does have the three P's: pyramids, pirates, and pizza. Also, a fancy tattoo, two handsome guys, one Swedish-English girl, an awesome bathtub, jellyfish, an exciting historical backstory in London, tiny paper hats, and DANGER!" The story concerns 17-year-old Clio Ford, who has to live with her drifter father in Italy while her professor mother is off on a fellowship. Clio and her father created a popular computer game years before, and the family became quite wealthy. But her father wasted most of that money. Now he is hoping to recoup his fortune, and regain the faith of his daughter, with a mysterious search for a treasure at the bottom of the Mediterranean Sea. But Claire finds that the treasure they are searching for is only part of the mystery. She must cope with her father's archeologist girlfriend, decipher clues as to the whereabouts of a

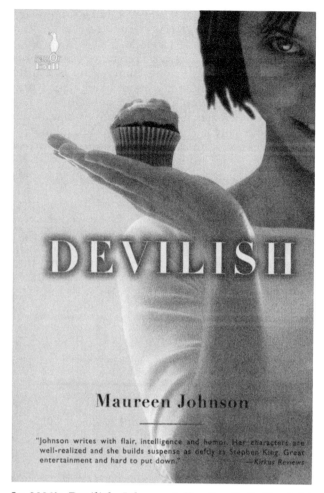

DEVILISH

Maureen Johnson

"Johnson writes with flair, intelligence and humor. Her characters are well-realized and she builds suspense as deftly as Stephen King. Great entertainment and hard to put down."
—Kirkus Reviews

In 2006's *Devilish,* Johnson tells of a Catholic girls' school overrun by demons. (Razorbill, 2006. Photo of girl © Dimitri Vervits/Getty Images. Photo of cupcake © Royalty-Free/Corbis. Reproduced by permission of Razorbill, a division of Penguin Putnam Books for Young Readers.)

shipwreck, and wonder if crewmate Aidan is really interested in her. The critic for *Kirkus Reviews* found the novel to be "full of unforgettable moments and much more complicated than readers may grasp as they turn the pages." Claire Rosser in *Kliatt* stated that "there is diving, excitement, adventure, romance—all in a beautiful setting. And the young people are intelligent, skilled, and responsible." Emily Garrett in the *School Library Journal* wrote: "Johnson does a great job of peppering enough interesting information and planting enough clues to keep the story moving along." The critic for *Publishers Weekly* wrote: "Spirited Clio is immensely personable and witty and Johnson . . . paints her

summer at sea vividly." Heather Booth of *Booklist* concluded that *Girl at Sea* is a "whirlwind of mystery and action, friendship and romance."

■ **Biographical and Critical Sources**

PERIODICALS

Booklist, September 1, 2004, Frances Bradburn, review of *The Key to the Golden Firebird,* p. 122; November 1, 2004, Frances Bradburn, review of *The Bermudez Triangle,* p. 475; September 15, 2005, Gillian Engberg, review of *Thirteen Little Blue Envelopes,* p. 57; October 15, 2006, Ilene Cooper, review of *Devilish,* p. 40.

Bulletin of the Center for Children's Books, July-August, 2004, Deborah Stevenson, review of *The Key to the Golden Firebird,* p. 471; November, 2004, Deborah Stevenson, review of *The Bermudez Triangle,* p. 128.

Kirkus Reviews, May 1, 2004, review of *The Key to the Golden Firebird,* p. 443; October 1, 2004, review of *The Bermudez Triangle,* p. 962; August 1, 2005, review of *Thirteen Little Blue Envelopes,* p. 851; July 15, 2006, review of *Devilish,* p. 724; May 1, 2007, review of *Girl at Sea.*

Kliatt, May, 2004, Claire Rosser, review of *The Key to the Golden Firebird,* p. 10; September, 2004, Janis Flint-Ferguson, review of *The Bermudez Triangle,* p. 12; September, 2005, Janis Flint-Ferguson, review of *Thirteen Little Blue Envelopes,* p. 9; May, 2007, review of *Girl at Sea,* p. 14.

Publishers Weekly, December 6, 2004, review of *The Bermudez Triangle,* p. 61; September 5, 2005, review of *Thirteen Little Blue Envelopes,* p. 63; June 4, 2007, review of *Girl at Sea,* p. 50.

School Library Journal, June, 2004, Miranda Doyle, review of *The Key to the Golden Firebird,* p. 143; November, 2004, Susan Riley, review of *The Bermudez Triangle,* p. 146; October, 2005, Emily Garrett, review of *Thirteen Little Blue Envelopes,* p. 163; October, 2006, Susan Riley, review of *Devilish,* p. 158; June, 2007, Emily Garrett, review of *Girl at Sea,* p. 148.

ONLINE

Bookshelves of Doom, http://bookshelvesofdoom. blogs.com/ (August 16, 2006), "SDQ Interview with Maureen Johnson."

Key to the Golden Firebird Web site, http://www.key tothegoldenfirebird.com/ (March 11, 2008).

Maureen Johnson Home Page, http://www.maureen johnsonbooks.com (March 11, 2008).*

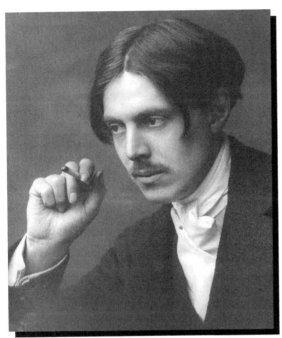

(George C. Beresford/Hulton Archive/Getty Images.)

Wyndham Lewis

■ Personal

Born November 18, 1882, on a ship anchored at Amherst, Nova Scotia, Canada; emigrated to England, 1888; died of a brain tumor, March 7, 1957, in London, England; son of Charles (a former American army officer) and Anne Lewis; married Gladys Anne Hoskyns, 1930; children: five. *Education:* Attended the Slade School of Art, 1898-1901.

■ Career

Artist, poet, literary critic, and novelist. Assumption College, Windsor, Ontario, Canada, lecturer, 1943-44; *Listener,* London, England, art critic, 1946-51. *Military service:* British Army, second lieutenant with artillery battery, World War I.

■ Awards, Honors

Awarded a Civil List Pension by the British government, 1952; received honorary doctorate from Leeds University, 1952.

■ Writings

NOVELS

Tarr, Knopf (New York, NY), 1918, reprinted, Penguin (New York, NY), 1990.
The Childermass, Covici Friede (New York, NY), 1928.
The Apes of God, Arthur Press (London, England), 1930, Robert McBride (New York, NY), 1932, reprinted, Black Sparrow Press (Boston, MA), 1981.
Snooty Baronet, Cassell (London, England), 1932, Haskell House (New York, NY), 1971, reprinted, Black Sparrow Press (Boston, MA), 1984.
The Revenge for Love, Cassell (London, England), 1937, Regnery (Chicago, IL), 1952, reprinted, Penguin (New York, NY), 2004.
The Vulgar Streak, R. Hale (London, England), 1941, Jubilee (New York, NY), 1973, reprinted, Black Sparrow Press (Boston, MA), 1985.
Self Condemned, Methuen (London, England), 1954, Regnery (Chicago, IL), 1955, reprinted, Black Sparrow Press (Boston, MA), 1983.
Monstre Gai, Methuen (London, England), 1956.
Malign Fiesta, Methuen (London, England), 1956.
The Red Priest, Methuen (London, England), 1956.
The Roaring Queen, Liveright (New York, NY), 1973.
Mrs. Dukes' Million, Coach House Press (Toronto, Ontario, Canada), 1977.

NONFICTION

The Ideal Giant, Little Review (London, England), 1917.

The Caliph's Design: Architects! Where Is Your Vortex?, Egoist (London, England), 1919, reprinted, Black Sparrow Press (Boston, MA), 1986.

Harold Gilman, Chatto & Windus (London, England), 1919.

The Art of Being Ruled, Chatto & Windus (London, England), 1926, Harper (New York, NY), 1927, reprinted, Black Sparrow Press (Boston, MA), 1989.

The Lion and the Fox: The Role of the Hero in the Plays of Shakespeare, Harper (New York, NY), 1927.

Time and Western Man, Harcourt, Brace (New York, NY), 1927, reprinted, Black Sparrow Press (Boston, MA), 1993.

Paleface: The Philosophy of the "Melting Pot," Chatto & Windus (London, England), 1929, Haskell House (New York, NY), 1969.

Hitler, Chatto & Windus (London, England), 1931, Gordon (New York, NY), 1972.

The Diabolical Principle and the Dithyrambic Spectator, Chatto & Windus (London, England), 1931, Haskell House (New York, NY), 1971.

The Doom of Youth, Robert McBride (New York, NY), 1932.

Filibusters in Barbary (Record of a Visit to the Sous) (travelogue), National Travel Club (New York, NY), 1932.

The Old Gang and the New Gang, Harmsworth (London, England), 1933, Haskell House (New York, NY), 1969.

Men without Art, Cassell (London, England), 1934, Russell & Russell (New York, NY), 1964.

Left Wings Over Europe: or, How to Make a War about Nothing (essay), Jonathan Cape (London, England), 1936, Gordon Press (New York, NY), 1972.

Count Your Dead: They Are Alive!; or, A New War in the Making (essay), Dickson (London, England), 1937, Gordon Press (New York, NY), 1972.

Blasting and Bombardiering, Eyre & Spottiswoode (London, England), 1937, University of California Press (Berkeley, CA), 1967, reprinted, Calder & Boyers (London, England), 1982.

The Mysterious Mr. Bull, R. Hale (London, England), 1938.

The Jews, Are They Human?, Allen & Unwin (London, England), 1939, Gordon Press (New York, NY), 1972.

Wyndham Lewis the Artist, from "Blast" to Burlington House, Laidlaw & Laidlaw (London, England), 1939, Haskell House (New York, NY), 1971.

The Hitler Cult, Dent (London, England), 1939, Gordon Press (New York, NY), 1972.

America, I Presume, Howell, Soskin (New York, NY), 1940.

Anglosaxony: The League That Works, Ryerson (Toronto, Ontario, Canada), 1941.

America and Cosmic Man, Nicholson & Watson (London, England), 1948, Doubleday (Garden City, NY), 1949.

Rude Assignment: A Narrative of My Career Up-to-Date, Hutchinson (London, England), 1950, published as *Rude Assignment: An Intellectual Autobiography*, Black Sparrow Press (Boston, MA), 1984.

The Writer and the Absolute, Methuen (London, England), 1952, Greenwood (Westport, CT), 1975.

The Demon of Progress in the Arts, Methuen (London, England), 1954, Regnery (Chicago, IL), 1955.

The Letters of Wyndham Lewis, edited by W.K. Rose, Methuen (London, England), 1963, New Directions (Norfolk, CT), 1964.

Wyndham Lewis on Art: Collected Writings, 1913-1956, edited with an introduction by Walter Michel and C.J. Fox, Funk & Wagnalls (New York, NY), 1969.

Wyndham Lewis: An Anthology of His Prose, edited with an introduction by E.W.F. Tomlin, Methuen (London, England), 1969.

Enemy Salvoes: Selected Literary Criticism, edited with an introduction by C.J. Fox, general introduction by C.H. Sisson, Barnes & Noble (New York, NY), 1976.

Blast I, Black Sparrow Press (Boston, MA), 1982.

Blast II, Black Sparrow Press (Boston, MA), 1982.

Creatures of Habit and Creatures of Change: Essays on Art, Literature and Society, 1914-1956, Black Sparrow Press (Boston, MA), 1989.

Wyndham Lewis the Radical: Essays on Literature and Modernity, edited by Carmelo Cunchillos Jamie, Peter Lang (New York, NY), 2007.

OTHER

The Wild Body: A Soldier of Humour and Other Stories, Chatto & Windus (London, England), 1927, Harcourt, Brace (New York, NY), 1928.

Satire and Fiction, Chatto & Windus (London, England), 1930, Folcroft Library (Folcroft, PA), 1975.

Enemy of the Stars (play), Harmsworth (London, England), 1932.

One-Way Song (poetry), Faber & Faber (London, England), 1933.

(Illustrator) Naomi Mitchison, *Beyond This Limit*, Jonathan Cape (London, England), 1935.

Rotting Hill (short stories), Methuen (London, England), 1951, Regnery (Chicago, IL), 1952, reprinted, Black Sparrow Press (Boston, MA), 1985.

A Soldier of Humor, edited and with an introduction by Raymond Rosenthal, New American Library (New York, NY), 1966.

Unlucky for Pringle: Unpublished and Other Stories, edited and with an introduction by C.J. Fox and Robert Chapman, David Lewis (New York, NY), 1973.

Imaginary Letters, edited by Alan Munton, Wyndham Lewis Society (Glasgow, Scotland), 1977.

Collected Poems and Plays, edited by Alan Munton, introduction by C.H. Sisson, Carcanet (Manchester, England), 1979.

A.J.A. Symons to Wyndham Lewis: Twenty-four Letters, Tragara Press (Edinburgh, Scotland), 1982.

Pound/Lewis: The Letters of Ezra Pound and Wyndham Lewis, edited by Timothy Materer, New Directions (New York, NY), 1985.

The Essential Wyndham Lewis: An Introduction to His Work, edited by Julian Symons, A. Deutsch (London, England), 1989.

The Bone beneath the Pulp: Drawings by Wyndham Lewis, Paul Holberton, 2005.

Editor, *Blast,* 1914-15, *Tyro: A Review of the Arts of Painting, Sculpture, and Design,* 1921-22, and *The Enemy,* 1927-29.

■ Sidelights

Called by T.S. Eliot "the most fascinating personality of our time," Wyndham Lewis was a man who was prominent in a number of different fields. He was a renowned painter, art critic, novelist, poet, editor, and social commentator. Lewis was called "one of the great painters of the twentieth century," by Hugh Kenner in his study *Wyndham Lewis.* Kenner also described Lewis's novel *The Revenge for Love* as "a twentieth-century classic" and Lewis's philosophical work, *Time and Western Man,* "one of the key books for the student of modern thought." "Lewis was an *avant garde* by himself," according to Marshall McLuhan, writing in *Wyndham Lewis: A Revaluation: New Essays,* "the greatest pictorial draughtsman of his time, the most controversial prose stylist of our day." Marvin Mudrick, writing in *Shenandoah,* claimed that Lewis possessed "the most expressively original style in English fiction."

Despite this variety of accomplishments, Lewis remains a relatively obscure figure in twentieth-century intellectual history. The sheer variety of his accomplishments is one reason for his neglect. "Wyndham Lewis was one of those originals whose genius as a filibuster in paint and prose is dispersed over so wide a ground that one does not know where to have him," wrote V.S. Pritchett in the *New Statesman.* His political views placed him at odds with the more liberal arts establishment, which hurt his reputation in some circles. Moreover, Lewis's difficult temperament, aggressive nature, and cutthroat talent for mercilessly satirizing fellow writers and artists earned him few friends. For many years,

in fact, Lewis enjoyed calling himself "the Enemy" who attacked the falsities of his time. "Lewis's provocative and even insulting attacks established his ferocious public image, antagonized his enemies, and alienated nearly everyone who was in a position to help him," wrote Jeffrey Meyers in the *Dictionary of Literary Biography.* As a result, he toiled in poverty for long stretches of his career, and often found himself in court as the defendant in libel suits.

Lewis began life in an unusual way. He was born in 1882 on his father's yacht in Canadian waters off the coast of Nova Scotia, which gave Lewis a Canadian passport that he was compelled to use somewhat reluctantly later in life. His mother was English and his father an American Civil War veteran. His parents' marriage ended when he was eleven years old, and he grew up in England with his mother. As a young man, Lewis attended London's Slade School of Art before visiting the continent to experience life in various European capitals. In 1909 Lewis returned to England and began a career in earnest as a painter, becoming a leading proponent of what would become known as Vorticism, England's first abstract art movement.

The cover of the War Number of Wyndham Lewis's *Blast* magazine from 1915. (Digital Image © The Museum of Modern Art. Licensed by SCALA Art Resource, NY. Digital Image © by kind permission of the Wyndham Lewis Memorial Trust (a registered charity).)

It was inspired by the art movements Cubism and Futurism, which Lewis had experienced firsthand on the continent. In the *Dictionary of Literary Biography,* Meyers offered a definition of Vorticism: "It emphasized the importance of African and Polynesian sculpture; employed hard geometrical lines; represented machinery and the city; used iron control and underlying explosiveness, classical detachment and strident dynamics."

Publishes a Radical Arts Journal

While gaining a reputation as a young, challenging artist of his day, Lewis also developed friendships among the literary figures of the time. He counted Rebecca West, Ford Madox Ford, and Ezra Pound as friends. With Pound, Lewis began a collaboration in 1914 on a literary review they called *Blast.* The radical, disjointed look of its typography and layout mirrored its content. Sharon Stockton, writing in *Twentieth Century Literature,* noted that Lewis vented his "righteous anger against a variety of species of decay—materialism, philistinism, chaos, and especially democracy—which he perceives to threaten all that is or could be 'worthwhile' in Western culture." Lewis's writing for the journal attempted to render in prose what he had been creating in his paintings. Descriptions of objects were its primary focus, with Lewis using few verbs while melding words together until they formed their own sense. "It is a style composed of phrases, not actions," Kenner explained. One example from *Blast:* "Throats iron eternities, drinking heavy radiance, limbs towers of blatant light, the stars poised, immensely distant, with their metal sides, pantheistic machines." "If anything extended could be done with it," Kenner believed, "this early style would be one of the most impressive inventions in the history of English literature. It remains one of the most fascinating." An essayist for the *St. James Guide to Fantasy Writers* particularly admired Lewis's play *Enemy of the Stars,* which was first published in *Blast* and employed his early style of Vorticist writing. The play was, the essayist noted, "a fantastic extravaganza whose surreally impractical stage-directions provide a context for the conflict between Hanp—symbolic of violent and dull-witted Mankind—and Arghol, the wise and rational spirit of intellectualism whose adventures can never quite escape the constraints imposed by his adversary. Arghol's refusal to be manifest in a false and debased self ultimately results in his murder by Hanp, but the murder is quickly followed by Hanp's suicide." Lewis modified this style in his later writings, although his work was always rich in quirky imagery.

Blast made Lewis a feted figure on the London intellectual scene. "Very suddenly, from a position of relative obscurity, I became extremely well-known,"

Lewis seated in his art studio with his paintings in the background. (Alvin Langdon Coburn/George Eastman House/Getty Images.)

Lewis wrote in *Blasting and Bombardiering.* "Roughly this coincided with the publication of *Blast.* I can remember no specific morning upon which I woke and found that this had happened. But by August 1914 no newspaper was complete without news about 'vorticism' and its arch-exponent Mr. Lewis."

Years at War

Unfortunately, this sudden fame as an artist and writer would not last long. With the outbreak of World War I, Lewis enlisted in the British Army and served as a second lieutenant with the Royal Artillery. He was stationed in France, where he took part in several horrific battles that would color his political thinking for the remainder of his life. "On the Battlefields of France and Flanders I became curious . . . about how and why these bloodbaths occurred—the political mechanics of war," Lewis later wrote in *Rude Assignment: A Narrative of My Career Up-to-Date.* "I acquired a knowledge of some of the intricacies of the power-game, and the usurious economics associated with war-making." "After the war," Timothy Materer wrote in his book *Wyndham Lewis, the Novelist,* "Lewis could sympathize with any man or program that seemed to offer hope of avoiding a second world war." This sympathy would land Lewis into political trouble during the 1930s.

In January of 1918 Lewis was named an official war artist. His role was to capture images of the battlefield for posterity. For the painting "A Canadian Gun Pit," he modified his earlier Vorticist style to depict an artillery unit in action. William Feaver in the *New Statesman* described the work as "a zigzagging composition of a robotic gun crew, readying shells for loading." But beginning with "A Battery Shelled," he rendered images of battle in his distinctive manner. His "drawings and water-colours depicted soldiers as being as machine-like as their artillery pieces," wrote an essayist for *FluxEuropa*. "Although this illustrated the de-humanising nature of modern war, it is also another manifestation of Lewis' lifelong preoccupation with the image of men as automata." Upon returning to England following the war, Lewis held an exhibition of his wartime paintings and drawings. For the next few years, he essentially abandoned art in favor of writing.

First Novel Appears

In 1918 Lewis published his first novel, *Tarr*. Set in Paris's bohemian Montparnasse quarter, it drew heavily upon Lewis's own somewhat romantic days as a young man there in its tale of the parallel lives of two artists. The Englishman "Tarr" enjoys success in his career and dallies with German and Russian mistresses; the German Otto Kreisler "represents a recurring Lewis theme: the difficult life of the would-be artist, without sufficient talent or money, living under the strain of poverty and fear of failure," opined Meyers in the *Dictionary of Literary Biography*. In its rejection of equality between the sexes, *Tarr*'s themes mirrored Lewis's own turbulent personality; he had numerous affairs throughout his life and fathered, then abandoned, at least five children outside of his childless marriage to Gladys Anne Hoskyns, whom he met in 1918 and wed in 1930. Furthermore, with its neat themes of English-vs.-German dominance, it would appear that Lewis wrote *Tarr* as a timely reflection of the conflicts of World War I, although he claimed to have begun the novel much earlier.

Lewis painted a series of portraits in the early 1920s depicting what he called Tyros. A "tyro" means a novice or beginner, but Lewis used the term to mean, as he wrote, "a new type of human animal like Harlequin or Punchinello. . . . The Tyro is raw and underdeveloped; his vitality is immense, but purposeless, and hence sometimes malignant."

These Tyro portraits are often malignant themselves, with angular-faced creatures smiling in a menacing fashion. (Lewis even did a self-portrait in this style.) The Tyros were Lewis's satirical idea of the kind of hollow, one-dimensional men who ran England following World War I. At this time he also published a new magazine, *Tyro: A Review of the Arts of Painting, Sculpture, and Design,* which lasted two issues.

When Lewis's father died, he was cheated out of an inheritance. This, combined with his devastating combat experiences, left him embittered. He came to see the war as a disastrous event for civilization, and took a hiatus from writing for a time. He read extensively, kept painting, and continued to socialize with the era's best-known literary figures, including James Joyce and Ernest Hemingway. By 1926 Lewis's ruminations on civilization and politics came to the fore in his nonfiction treatise *The Art of Being Ruled*. In this work, he postulates that an authoritarian society, one in which artists are allowed an exalted and compensated status, is the antidote for the disjointedness and dysfunction of modern times. He draws from the writings of Friedrich Nietzsche and Bertrand Russell, excoriates Marxism, parliamentary politics, jazz, post-impressionist art, and feminism. Lewis argued that world peace could only be brought about by a world government, whether that government was capitalist, communist, or fascist made little difference to him. "It is a plea for sanity in the ordering of world affairs," wrote D.G. Bridson in *The Filibuster: A Study of the Political Ideas of Wyndham Lewis*, "and one which is made above all to the rulers of the immediate future." Though *New York Times Book Review* critic William MacDonald called the book "formless and inconclusive," he granted that "Lewis perceives certain trends and has the courage to speak his mind about them, and courageous writing, even when it is irritating, is always to be praised." In 1989, *The Art of Being Ruled* was reissued and *Times Literary Supplement* critic Julian Symons found Lewis's theories surprisingly enduring. "After reading the chapters here about feminism and homosexuality, the cult of youth and the opposition between races, one may look disbelievingly at the publication year of the book, for these are 'wars' going on today in full force," declared Symons, who concluded: "More than sixty years after its publication, this book remains the most valuable guide available to the cant and absurdities of the attitudes about sex, race, 'elitism' and 'prejudice' prevalent in liberal Western society, and to their basic meanings."

An Attack on Time

The second of Lewis's magnum opuses of the 1920s was *Time and Western Man*, published in 1927. It marked the beginning of Lewis's no-holds-barred criticism of his contemporaries; he lambasted both Joyce and Pound in this book, calling the latter an "intellectual eunuch." The book's primary theme, however, was the denunciation of what Lewis called the "cult of time," and, relatedly, the unfavorable changes wrought upon civilization by the advent of mass advertising and motion pictures. These new advances, Lewis argued, created what he called the "time-mind," which he believed changed the way one saw the world, replacing the real, outside world with an interior world. As William H. Pritchard explained it in his study *Wyndham Lewis:* "For Lewis, the 'time-mind' is the twentieth-century mind, spellbound before 'the flux.' Imaginative and

Lewis's painting "A Reading of Ovid (Tyros)" from 1920-21, depicting two of his Tyro characters. (National Gallery of Modern Art, Edinbourgh, UK. The Bridgeman Art Library.)

expository works are alike engaged in redefining 'reality' as wholly temporal; in turning the self into a packet of selves, endlessly replacing one another; and in translating all spatial 'physical' characteristics into temporal 'mental' ones." A *Times Literary Supplement* contributor found the book to be provocative and asserted that the book's "merit is to have singled out a vital idea and presented it with that kind of power which makes you wonder why no one has seen it so before."

Lewis's last significant title of the 1920s was the novel *The Childermass,* published in 1928. It was to be part of trilogy entitled *The Human Age,* and its plot follows two men "who welter in imbecility and drivel," as a *Times Literary Supplement* critic explained. At the gates of heaven, they set off on a walk to pass the time before judging is to commence; along the way they meet fearsome dragons and queer embryonic life forms who jeer at them, while landmarks mysteriously vanish upon approach. The farcical mood also introduces characters who represent leading figures both past and present, including Marcel Proust and Albert Einstein. At their judging, their trial is interrupted by a raucous chorus of elitists, who despise the "common" man represented by the duo. Lawrence S. Morris, reviewing *The Childermass* in the *New Republic,* faulted what he called Lewis's "mannered, self-conscious style," but commended the novel and the way in which its author "leaps from metaphysics to politics to literature, so full of combativeness that he has not yet had time to think any one of his thoughts through. And, in a pinch, he will sacrifice all of them for a slashing phrase." From 1927 to 1929 Lewis edited and wrote much of the literary review *The Enemy.* The "enemy" was a literary persona he "found particularly congenial to his irascible temperament," noted an essayist for the *Encyclopedia of World Literature in the 20th Century.*

Political Trouble

Some of Lewis's writings at this time were perceived to be sympathetic to Fascism, which by then was well-established in Benito Mussolini's Italy and gaining ground in Spain and Germany as well. These sympathies came to the fore in 1930 when Lewis was sent to Berlin on a magazine assignment. The decadent nightlife in the German city stunned him with its sex clubs, flagrant homosexuality, and open prostitution. That so many Germans indulged themselves in this manner during a time of pervasive unemployment and crippling inflation upset Lewis. Nazi leader Adolf Hitler, not yet in power, seemed to want to restore order to his country and talked of maintaining peace in Europe. When Lewis returned to England, he wrote *Hitler,* a book meant to explain this new political movement in Germany that seemed to offer some hope. Lewis described Hitler as a soft-spoken vegetarian and a "Man of Peace." He predicted that the anti-Semitic rhetoric of the Nazis would eventually fade away. Lewis would later regret having been taken in. His dream of avoiding another war on the scale of World War I had led him to believe that Hitler—who had also served as a soldier in the war—shared his honest desire for peace. Observers point out that Lewis was not alone in his mistaken support for a dictator. H.G. Wells expressed admiration for Soviet dictator Vladimir Lenin; George Bernard Shaw praised Joseph Stalin. In 1939 Lewis published *The Hitler Cult,* in which he warned of the dangers of Nazism. The ironically-titled *The Jews, Are They Human?* is another blast at German Fascism.

Throughout the 1930s, Lewis worked to alert his countrymen to the dangers of a coming war that he believed could be avoided. In *Left Wings Over Europe: or, How to Make a War about Nothing* and *Count Your Dead: They Are Alive!; or, A New War in the Making* he warned that, although Europeans did not want a war, their leaders were planning one. *Left Wings Over Europe,* according to Bridson, was "motivated by nothing so much as a passionate desire for peace, and utter horror at the idea of Britain's becoming involved in another European war. Put at its simplest, the book was intended as an appeal to common sense."

Satire of the Artistic

Despite the controversy his writings on peace and politics had brought him, perhaps Lewis met with the most opposition for publishing his 1930 novel *The Apes of God.* The 625-page self-illustrated work chronicles the exploits of an eager young man in his introduction to the bohemian life. Lewis managed to skewer an array of acquaintances, from his patrons to T.S. Eliot to Gertrude Stein to the entire Bloomsbury group. Only thinly disguised by aliases, their foibles and pretensions were savagely illuminated by Lewis's sharp pen. "It is a farcical magnification of inanity that employs linguistic virtuosity and the technique of overkill to demolish its victims," noted Meyers in the *Dictionary of Literary Biography.* "It is also a bitter comedy, a deliberately cruel personal attack, and a savage roman a clef. The satire expresses Lewis's moral and aesthetic values as well as his caustic character, records his friendships and feuds, and gives a lively if biased account of the literary history of the 1920s."

Lewis in 1938 standing next to his portrait of his friend, poet T.S. Eliot. (Fred Ramage/Hulton Archive/Getty Images.)

Not surprisingly, *The Apes of God* caused a stir. Fred T. Marsh, critiquing it for the *New York Times Book Review,* noted that "Lewis applies his lash fiercely for hours upon end" but called the book "a satire of unusual originality and power." Most reviewers concurred that the novel was overwritten, with Henry Bamford Parkes of the *New Republic* terming it "unbearably monotonous." Yet Parkes, like the other critics, found some passages marvelous, and noted that "parts of the book have an originality of observation and a power of expression unequaled by any other English writer of the twentieth century. . . . If it is not a genuine masterpiece, it is from a lack of discipline." Lewis also ventured into poetry. *One Way Song,* published in 1933, poked fun at the new breed of society poets of the 1930s. *Spectator* critic and literary figure Stephen Spender, himself skewered mercilessly as the character Dan Boleyn in *The Apes of God,* claimed that Lewis's poetry was "full of dislike for democracy and democratic ideals."

Misfortune plagued Lewis through the 1930s. He suffered from an array of health problems, some of them the result of venereal disease. Libel suits were filed, and Chatto & Windus recalled his books *The Doom of Youth* and *Filibusters in Barbary,* both published in 1932; later, the house sued Lewis for breach of contract after he tried to sell works to other publishers before completing the other two novels in *The Human Age* cycle. His 1934 work *Men without Art* contained an essay deriding Hemingway entitled "The Dumb Ox"; in it, Lewis compared the writer with "a dull-witted, bovine, monosyllabic simpleton, a lethargic and stuttering dummy." In response, Hemingway pilloried Lewis in *The Movable Feast*, opining that he "had the eyes of an unsuccessful rapist," according to Meyers in the *Dictionary of Literary Biography*. The Royal Academy rejected Lewis's portrait in 1938, an unambiguous snub.

Lewis managed to reverse the backslide of his reputation with his 1937 memoir, *Blasting and Bombardiering*. Set in the years from 1914 to 1926, the work covers his wartime experiences and political evolution and treats his former targets more gently, even commenting favorably upon Joyce and Pound. It was written in Lewis's typical, adjective-laden exhausting prose, prompting *Spectator* reviewer and acclaimed novelist Anthony Burgess to fault its author's powers of over-observation: "Seeing a sardine on toast, he acts as though commissioned to paint its portrait," remarked Burgess.

The 1937 novel *The Revenge for Love* is set in Spain during the Civil War of the 1930s. Victor Stamp, an unsuccessful artist, and his devoted wife Margot are involved in running guns for the Communists. They are betrayed by their comrades for political reasons and left to die in the Pyrenees Mountains. Meyers in the *Dictionary of Literary Biography* wrote of the novel: "Lewis's frustration at his failure to achieve success as an artist is expressed in Victor's struggle to paint, realization that his work has no economic value, and desperate submission to forgery (salable art). Victor also expresses the themes of love and betrayal and relates them to the human factor—so rare in Lewis's novels—and to the social commitment that transcends revolutionary agitation." Steven Marcus in *Commentary* noted that "Lewis shows a remarkably clear grasp of the consequences of the Communist ideology, its appeal, the personal motives that press for its embrace, the pretentious stupidity, neurotic extravagances, and the ideological viciousness it fosters." Mudrick concluded that *The Revenge for Love* was "the most humane and the most comprehensive political novel of our time."

War Years in Canada

The year 1939 marked the onset of World War II with Hitler's surprise invasion of Poland on September 1. The next day, Lewis and his wife sailed for the United States, where he was to execute a portrait

commission; a day later, war was declared and they were unable to return home. Low on funds, his political reputation tarnished, Lewis wound up waiting out the war in a run-down hotel in Toronto, then a far cry from the cosmopolitan hub into which it would later evolve. His hatred of these years and of the provincial-minded city would surface in later novels. The only respite Lewis seemed to have enjoyed during these years was from a teaching stint at Assumption College in Windsor, Ontario, where he engaged in intellectual repartee with its Roman Catholic priests. It was here Lewis also came to know a young Marshall McLuhan, and the elder's theories of humankind and its relationship to time, advertising, and the mass media—as expounded upon in Lewis's 1927 work *Time and Western Man*—had an unquestionable impact on McLuhan.

After the war, Lewis and his wife were on the first passenger ship sailing to England in August of 1945. He resumed his career as a painter and writer, achieving some restoration of his former status. He became the art critic for the *Listener* in 1946, but five years later his increasing loss of vision caused him to resign. "My articles on contemporary art exhibitions necessarily end," he told his readers, "for I can no longer see a picture." With complete blindness inevitable, Lewis defiantly contemplated his future: "Pushed into an unlighted room, the door banged and locked for ever, I shall then have to light a lamp of aggressive voltage in my mind to keep at bay the night." In a private letter to a friend, Lewis enjoyed a moment of humor about his condition: "Loathsome as the world is," he commented, "I do like to *see* it." The following year, some of his financial burdens were eased when the British government awarded him a Civil List Pension, commonly given to artists and writers who have made significant cultural contributions during their career. He continued to write books despite his disability, at first writing his drafts on a board that rested on his knees by means of a pen attached to a wire; his wife and a former mistress, who now helped take care of him, transcribed his longhand; he later used a Dictaphone recorder.

If you enjoy the works of Wyndham Lewis, you may also want to check out the following books:

Christopher Isherwood, *The Berlin Stories: The Last of Mr. Norris and Goodbye to Berlin*, 1963.
Ezra Pound, *The Cantos of Ezra Pound*, 1996.
Marshall McLuhan, *The Essential McLuhan*, 1996.
George Orwell, *Homage to Catalonia*, 1999.

In 1954 his novel *Self Condemned* was published, a work some scholars consider to be Lewis's most outstanding. It follows the travails of an English couple in their self-imposed exile in the claustrophobic "Momaco," a disguised version of Toronto, Canada. A man who could have been great but was ruined by his own egotism, history professor René Harding only appreciates the love that his wife Hester gave him after her death by suicide. Writing in *Encounter,* Walter Allen described the novel as "the most sustained and the most deeply felt effort of self-controntation in the fiction of our time. . . . Lewis is here presenting a full-length portrait of a character very obviously based on aspects of himself, a portrait firmly and classicly controlled and rendered with complete objectivity." Rowland Smith, writing in the *Dalhousie Review,* concluded that *Self Condemned* had a "shattering impact." Materer called it Lewis's "greatest novel."

Lewis was felled by the brain tumor that had brought on his blindness, and died in March of 1957. While he always had admirers of his work, Lewis's reputation was in limbo for some years. Phil Baker in the *Guardian* commented: "Of all the great modernists, Lewis is the one who has stayed out in the cold, despite his double genius as both painter and writer." His political opinions, although modified over the years, were a lingering problem for some observers. But in the 1990s, Lewis began to enjoy a comeback of sorts and a number of appreciative evaluations of his writings were published. Katharine B. Hoskins in her *Today the Struggle* explained his continuing appeal by noting that, while "Lewis was fiercely combative, fully convinced of the unique rightness of his position on any given subject at any given time . . . he was still capable of recognizing when he was wrong, and he repudiated former opinions as unreservedly as he propounded new ones. It is probably this integrity of character, as much as his independence of intellect and his very remarkable talents as writer and artist, that explains the respect in which he has been held even by those who have rarely been able to agree with him."

■ Biographical and Critical Sources

BOOKS

Ayers, David, *Wyndham Lewis and Western Man,* St. Martin's Press (New York, NY), 1992.

Bridson, D.G., *The Filibuster: A Study of the Political Ideas of Wyndham Lewis,* Cassell, 1972.

Campbell, SueEllen, *The Enemy Opposite: The Outlaw Criticism of Wyndham Lewis,* Ohio University Press (Athens, OH), 1988.

Constable, John, and S.J.M. Watson, editors, *Wyndham Lewis & I.A. Richards: A Friendship Documented, 1928-57,* Skate Press (Cambridge, England), 1989.

Dictionary of Literary Biography, Volume 15: *British Novelists, 1930-1959,* edited by Bernard Olsey, Gale (Detroit, MI), 1983.

Edwards, Paul, editor, *Volcanic Heaven: Essays on Wyndham Lewis's Painting and Writing,* Black Sparrow Press (Boston, MA), 1996.

Edwards, Paul, *Wyndham Lewis: Painter and Writer,* Paul Mellon Centre for Studies in British Art/Yale University Press, 2000.

Encyclopedia of World Literature in the 20th Century, revised edition, edited by Leonard S. Klein, Continuum Publishing (New York, NY), 1993.

Farrington, Jane, *Wyndham Lewis,* Lund Humphries, 1986.

Foshay, Toby, *Wyndham Lewis and the Avant-garde: The Politics of the Intellect,* McGill-Queen's University Press, 1992.

Fox, C.J., *Wyndham Lewis and E.J. Pratt: A Convergence of Strangers,* Memorial University (St. John's, Newfoundland, Canada), 1983.

Gasiorek, Andrzej, *Wyndham Lewis and Modernism,* Northcote House/British Council, 2004.

Grigson, Geoffrey, *A Master of Our Time: A Study of Wyndham Lewis,* Gordon Press (New York, NY), 1972.

Hoskins, Katharine B., *Today the Struggle,* University of Texas Press (Austin, TX), 1969.

Houen, Alex, *Terrorism and Modern Literature,* Oxford University Press (New York, NY), 2002.

Humphries, Richard, *Wyndham Lewis,* Harry N. Abrams (New York, NY), 2004.

Kenner, Hugh, *Wyndham Lewis,* New Directions (New York, NY), 1954.

Klein, Scott, *The Fictions of James Joyce and Wyndham Lewis: Monsters of Nature and Design,* Cambridge University Press (New York, NY), 1994.

Kush, Thomas, *Wyndham Lewis's Pictorial Integer,* UMI Research Press (Ann Arbor, MI), 1981.

Materer, Timothy, *Wyndham Lewis, the Novelist,* Wayne State University Press (Detroit, MI), 1976.

Meyers, Jeffrey, editor, *Wyndham Lewis: A Revaluation: New Essays,* McGill-Queen's University Press, 1980.

Michel, Walter, *Wyndham Lewis: Paintings and Drawings,* University of California Press, 1971.

Morrow, Bradford, and Bernard Lafourcade, *A Bibliography of the Writings of Wyndham Lewis,* with introduction by Hugh Kenner, Black Sparrow Press (Santa Barbara, CA), 1978.

Normand, Tom, *Wyndham Lewis the Artist: Holding the Mirror up to Politics,* Cambridge University Press (New York, NY), 1992.

O'Keefe, Paul, *Some Sort of Genius: A Life of Wyndham Lewis,* Jonathan Cape (London, England), 2001.

Perrino, Mark, *The Poetics of Mockery: Wyndham Lewis's 'The Apes of God' and the Popularization of Modernism,* W.S. Maney (London, England), 1998.

Peters-Corbett, David, editor, *Wyndham Lewis and the Art of Modern War,* Cambridge University Press (New York, NY), 1998.

Porteus, Hugh Gordon, *Wyndham Lewis, a Discursive Exposition,* D. Harmsworth, 1932.

Pound, Omar S., *Wyndham Lewis: A Descriptive Bibliography,* Dawson, 1978.

Pritchard, William H., *Wyndham Lewis,* Twayne (New York, NY), 1968.

St. James Guide to Fantasy Writers, St. James Press (Detroit, MI), 1996.

Schenker, Daniel, *Wyndham Lewis, Religion and Modernism,* University of Alabama Press, 1992.

Short Story Criticism, Volume 34, Gale (Detroit, MI), 2000.

Sherry, Vincent, *Ezra Pound, Wyndham Lewis, and Radical Modernism,* Oxford University Press (New York, NY), 1993.

Tomlin, E.W.F., *Wyndham Lewis,* Longmans, Green, 1955.

Twentieth-Century Literary Criticism, Gale (Detroit, MI), Volume 2, 1979, Volume 9, 1983, Volume 104, 2001.

Wagner, Geoffrey Atheling, *Wyndham Lewis: A Portrait of the Artist as the Enemy,* Yale University Press, 1957.

Woodcock, George, editor, *Wyndham Lewis in Canada,* University of British Columbia, Publications Centre, 1971.

Wragg, David A., *Wyndham Lewis and the Philosophy of Art in Early Modernist Britain: Creating a Political Aesthetic,* Edwin Mellen Press, 2005.

PERIODICALS

Agenda, autumn-winter, 1969-70, Wyndham Lewis special issue.

Canadian Literature, winter, 1992, p. 154.

Christian Century, November 30, 1955, pp. 1400-1401.

Commentary, February, 1953, Steven Marcus, "The Highbrow Know-Nothings," pp. 189-191.

Commonweal, July 13, 1932, pp. 294-295; January 6, 1956, p. 356.

Dalhousie Review, summer, 1972, Rowland Smith, "Wyndham Lewis and the Sanctimonious Ice-Box," pp. 302-308.

Encounter, September, 1963, Walter Allen, "Lonely Old Volcano: The Achievement of Wyndham Lewis," pp. 63-70.

Guardian, November 18, 2000, Phil Baker, "Was He Human?: Phil Baker Explores the Weird World of Wyndham Lewis."

London Review of Books, June 22, 1989, pp. 19-20.

Modern Fiction Studies, summer, 1983, p. 237; winter, 1992, pp. 845-869.

Nation, April 20, 1927, p. 446; December 21, 1932, p. 623; September 3, 1949, p. 234; March 27, 1974.

New Republic, September 22, 1926, p. 124; March 7, 1928, p. 102; December 12, 1928, p. 111; June 8, 1932, p. 105; August 22, 1934.

New Statesman, December 24, 1927, pp. 358-359; July 7, 1928, p. 426-427; January 5, 1952, pp. 18-19; January 8, 1955, pp. 48-49; July 28, 1967, pp. 119-120; April 14, 1972, p. 498; February 20, 1976, p. 234; April 27, 1979, p. 598; November 27, 2000, William Feaver, "War Paint," p. 38.

New York Times Book Review, October 10, 1926; November 20, 1927, p. 9; July 15, 1928, p. 2; April 17, 1932, p. 2; June 12, 1932, p. 11; September 25, 1932, p. 12; June 19, 1949, p. 8; August 9, 1964, p. 5; February 10, 1985, p. 29.

New Yorker, June 4, 1955.

Observer, November 14, 1993, p. 22.

Saturday Review, June 18, 1955, p. 16; April 4, 1964, p. 29.

Shenandoah, spring, 1953, Marvin Mudrick, "The Double-Artist and the Injured Party," pp. 54-64.

Spectator, August 13, 1932, pp. 210-211; December 1, 1933, p. 812; December 14, 1951, p. 832; May 20, 1966, pp. 640-642; July 7, 1967, pp. 15-16; January 31, 1976, p. 14; October 21, 1989, p. 39.

Time, September 2, 1940, p. 64; July 4, 1949, p. 70; May 23, 1955, p. 102.

Times Literary Supplement, April 8, 1926, p. 258; February 10, 1927, p. 89; October 27, 1927, p. 760; December 8, 1927, p. 930; July 19, 1928, p. 531; July 7, 1932, p. 490; August 4, 1932, p. 553; March 15, 1934, p. 185; December 7, 1951, p. 777; April 5, 1963, p. 232; August 3, 1973, p. 893; February 6, 1976, p. 128; June 30, 1978, p. 726; December 3, 1982, p. 1934; November 8, 1985, p. 1259; April 10, 1987, p. 381; May 12, 1989, p. 517; September 22, 1989, p. 1024; June 15, 1990, p. 628.

Twentieth Century Literature, fall, 1994, Kelly Anspaugh, "Blasting the Bombardier: Another Look at Lewis, Joyce, and Woolf," p. 365; spring, 1995, Mark Perrino, "Marketing Insults: Wyndham Lewis and the Arthur Press," p. 54; winter, 1996, Sharon Stockton, "Aesthetics, Politics and the Staging of the World: Wyndham Lewis and the Renaissance," p. 494; summer, 2000, Paige Reynolds, "'Chaos Invading Concept': Blast as a Native Theory of Promotional Culture," p. 238; summer, 2001, Paul Scott Stanfield, "'This Implacable Doctrine': Behaviorism in Wyndham Lewis's 'Snooty Baronet,'" p. 241.

Voice Literary Supplement, December, 1983, p. 13.

Washington Post Book World, September 30, 1973, p. 15; September 27, 1981, p. 12; May 29, 1983, p. 12; November 12, 1989, p. 16.

World & I, June, 1988, Jeffrey Meyers, "Wyndham Lewis: Vorticism and Beyond," p. 609.

ONLINE

FluxEuropa, http://www.fluxeuropa.com/ (January 7, 1999), "The Art and Ideas of Wyndham Lewis."

Wyndham Lewis Society Web site, http://www.time -space.net/wynlewis/wynlewis.html/ (April 3, 2008).*

Anita Loos

(Copyright © Hulton-Deutsch Collection/Corbis.)

■ Personal

Born April 26, 1893, in Sisson, CA; died August 18, 1981, of a heart attack, in New York, NY; daughter of Richard Beers (a theatrical producer and newspaper editor) and Minnie Ellen Loos; married Frank Palma, Jr., June, 1915 (marriage annulled one day later); married John Emerson (an actor, director, and playwright), 1919 (died March 8, 1956); children: one adopted daughter. *Education:* Attended high school in San Francisco, CA.

■ Career

Writer, 1912-81.

■ Member

Dramatists Guild.

■ Awards, Honors

Vanity Fair magazine award for *Red-Headed Woman*.

■ Writings

SCENARIOS FOR SILENT FILMS

The New York Hat, American Biograph, 1913.
The Power of the Camera, American Biograph, 1913.
A Horse on Bill, American Biograph, 1913.
A Hicksville Epicure, American Biograph, 1913.
Highbrow Love, American Biograph, 1913.
A Hicksville Romance, American Biograph, 1913.
A Fallen Hero, American Biograph, 1913.
A Fireman's Love, American Biograph, 1913.
A Cure for Suffragettes, American Biograph, 1913.
The Suicide Pact, American Biograph, 1913.
Bink's Vacation, American Biograph, 1913.
How the Day Was Saved, American Biograph, 1913.
Fall of Hicksville's Finest, American Biograph, 1913.
The Wedding Gown, American Biograph, 1913.
Yiddish Love, American Biograph, 1913.
Gentlemen and Thieves, American Biograph, 1913.
Pa Says, American Biograph, 1913.
The Widow's Kids, American Biograph, 1913.
The Lady in Black, American Biograph, 1913.
His Hoodoo, American Biograph, 1913.
The Deacon's Whiskers, Reliance Mutual, 1913.
His Awful Vengeance, Reliance Mutual, 1913.
All for Mabel, Reliance Mutual, 1913.
The Fatal Deception, Reliance Mutual, 1913.
For Her Father's Sins, Reliance Mutual, 1913.
Unlucky Jim, Kornick, 1913.
All on Account of a Cold, Kornick, 1913.

The Saving Grace, Cinemacolor, 1913.

A Narrow Escape, Cinemacolor, 1913.

Two Women, Cinemacolor, 1913.

The Wall Flower, Lubin, 1913.

A Bunch of Flowers, American Biograph, 1914.

When a Woman Guides, American Biograph, 1914.

The Road to Plaindale, American Biograph, 1914.

The Meal Ticket, American Biograph, 1914.

The Saving Presence, American Biograph, 1914.

The Suffering of Susan, American Biograph, 1914.

Where the Roads Part, American Film Manufacturing, 1914.

His Rival, American Film Manufacturing, 1914.

The Chieftain's Daughter (Some Bull's Daughter), Reliance Mutual, 1914.

The Fatal Dress Suit, Reliance Mutual, 1914.

The Girl in the Shack, Reliance Mutual, 1914.

His Hated Rival, Reliance Mutual, 1914.

A Corner in Hats, Reliance Mutual, 1914.

Nearly a Burglar's Bride, Reliance Mutual, 1914.

The Fatal Curve, Reliance Mutual, 1914.

The Million-Dollar Bride, Reliance Mutual, 1914.

A Flurry in Art, Reliance Mutual, 1914.

Nellie, the Female Villain, Reliance Mutual, 1914.

The Gangsters of New York, Reliance Mutual, 1914.

The Tear on the Page, American Biograph, 1915.

The Cost of a Bargain, American Biograph, 1915.

Pennington's Choice, Metro Pictures, 1915.

Sympathy Sal, Reliance Mutual, 1915.

Mixed Values, Reliance Mutual, 1915.

A Corner in Cotton, Quality Pictures, 1916.

Wild Girl of the Sierras, Fine Arts-Triangle, 1916.

Calico Vampire, Fine Arts-Triangle, 1916.

Laundry Liz, Fine Arts-Triangle, 1916.

French Milliner, Fine Arts-Triangle, 1916.

The Wharf Rat, Fine Arts-Triangle, 1916.

The Little Liar, Fine Arts-Triangle, 1916.

Stranded, Fine Arts-Triangle, 1916, also released by Sterling Pictures, 1927.

The Social Secretary, Fine Arts-Triangle, 1916, also released by Tri-Stone Pictures, 1924.

His Picture in the Papers, Fine Arts-Triangle, 1916.

The Half-Breed, Fine Arts-Triangle, 1916.

American Aristocracy, Fine Arts-Triangle, 1916.

Manhattan Madness, Fine Arts-Triangle, 1916.

The Matrimaniac, Fine Arts-Triangle, 1916.

The Americano, Fine Arts-Triangle, 1917.

In Again, Out Again, Artcraft Pictures, 1917.

Wild and Wooly (based on a story by H.B. Carpenter), Artcraft Pictures, 1917.

Down to Earth (based on a story by Douglas Fairbanks), Artcraft Pictures, 1917.

(With John Emerson) *Reaching for the Moon*, Artcraft Pictures, 1917.

(With John Emerson) *Let's Get a Divorce* (based on the play *Divorcons* by Victorien Sardou), Famous Players-Lasky, 1918.

(With John Emerson) *Hit-the-Trail Holiday* (based on the play by George M. Cohan), Famous Players-Lasky, 1918.

(With John Emerson) *Come On In*, Famous Players-Lasky, 1918.

(With John Emerson) *Good-Bye, Bill*, Famous Players-Lasky, 1918.

(With John Emerson) *Oh, You Women!*, Famous Players-Lasky, 1919.

(With John Emerson) *Getting Mary Married*, Marion Davis Film Co., 1919.

(With John Emerson) *A Temperamental Wife*, Constance Talmadge Film Co., 1919.

(With John Emerson) *A Virtuous Vamp* (based on the play *The Bachelor* by Clyde Fitch), Joseph M. Schenck, 1919.

(With John Emerson) *Isle of Conquest* (based on the novel *By Right of Conquest* by Arthur Hornblow), Select Pictures, 1919.

(With John Emerson) *In Search of a Sinner*, Joseph M. Schenck, 1920.

(With John Emerson) *The Love Expert*, Joseph M. Schenck, 1920.

(With John Emerson) *The Branded Woman* (based on the play *Branded* by Oliver D. Bailey), Joseph M. Schenck, 1920.

(With John Emerson) *The Perfect Woman*, First National, 1920.

(With John Emerson) *Two Weeks* (based on the play *At the Barn* by Anthony Wharton), First National, 1920.

(With John Emerson) *Dangerous Business*, First National, 1921.

(With John Emerson) *Mama's Affair* (based on the play by Rachel Barton Butler), First National, 1921.

(With John Emerson) *Woman's Place*, Joseph M. Schenck, 1921.

(With John Emerson) *Red Hot Romance*, Joseph M. Schenck, 1922.

(With John Emerson) *Polly of the Follies*, First National, 1922.

(With John Emerson) *Dulcy* (based on the play by George S. Kaufman and Marc Connelly), Joseph M. Schenck, 1923.

(With John Emerson) *Three Miles Out* (based on a story by Neysa McMein), Kenma, 1924.

(With John Emerson) *Learning to Love*, First National, 1925.

Publicity Madness, Fox Film, 1927.

Author of unproduced scenarios for silent films, including *He Was a College Boy, Queen of the Carnival, The Mayor-Elect, The Making of a Masher, Path of True Love, A Girl like Mother, The Mother, The Great Motor Race, A No Bull Spy, A Balked Heredity, A Blasted Romance, Mortimer's Millions, A Life and Death Affair, The Sensible Girl, At the Tunnel's End,* and *How to Keep a Husband,* all for American Biograph; *The Deadly Glass of Beer, The Stolen Masterpiece, The Last Drink of Whisky, Nell's Eugenic Wedding, The School of Acting, A Hicksville Reformer, The White Slave Catchers, The Style Accustomed, The Deceiver, How They Met, The Burlesque, The Fatal Fourth, The Fatal Fingerprints,* and *Wards of Fate,* all for Reliance Mutual; *The Earl and the Tomboy,* for Lubin; *Heart that Truly Loved,* for Pictorial Review; and *Mountain Bred,* for Mabel Normand.

Also author of *The Telephone Girl and the Lady.* Also author of title cards for the silent films *Macbeth,* Lucky Film Producers, 1916, and *Intolerance,* D.W. Griffith, 1916.

SCREENPLAYS

(With Herman J. Mankiewicz) *Gentlemen Prefer Blondes* (based on her play), 1928.

(With John Emerson) *The Struggle,* United Artists, 1931.

Red-Headed Woman (based on the novel by Katherine Brush), Metro-Goldwyn-Mayer, 1932.

(With Elmer Harris) *The Barbarian* (based on the story by Edgar Selwyn), Metro-Goldwyn-Mayer, 1933.

(With Howard Emmett Rogers) *Hold Your Man,* Metro-Goldwyn-Mayer, 1933.

(With John Emerson) *The Girl from Missouri,* Metro-Goldwyn-Mayer, 1934, released in England as *100 Per Cent Pure.*

Biography of a Bachelor Girl, Metro-Goldwyn-Mayer, 1935.

(With Frances Marion and H.W. Haneman) *Riffraff,* Metro-Goldwyn-Mayer, 1935.

San Francisco (based on a story by Robert Hopkins), Metro-Goldwyn-Mayer, 1936.

Mama Steps Out, Metro-Goldwyn-Mayer, 1937.

(With Robert Hopkins) *Saratoga,* Metro-Goldwyn-Mayer, 1937.

(With Jane Murfin) *The Women* (based on the play by Clare Booth), Metro-Goldwyn-Mayer, 1939.

Susan and God (based on the play by Rachel Crothers), Metro-Goldwyn-Mayer, 1940, released in England as *The Gay Mrs. Trexel.*

(With Edwin Justin Mayer and Leon Gordon) *They Met in Bombay* (based on a story by Franz Kafka), Metro-Goldwyn-Mayer, 1941.

Blossoms in the Dust (based on a story by Ralph Wheelwright), Metro-Goldwyn-Mayer, 1941.

(With S.K. Lauren) *When Ladies Meet* (based on the play by R. Crothers), Metro-Goldwyn-Mayer, 1941.

I Married an Angel (based on the musical by Vaszary Janos, Lorenz Hart, and Richard Rodgers), Metro-Goldwyn-Mayer, 1942.

(With others) *The Pirate,* Metro-Goldwyn-Mayer, 1948.

Also author of unproduced screenplays, *The Great Canadian* and *Alaska,* for Metro-Goldwyn-Mayer; also author of dialogue for *Blondie of the Follies,* Metro-Goldwyn-Mayer, 1932, and contributing writer for *Another Thin Man,* 1939.

PLAYS

(With John Emerson) *The Whole Town's Talking,* produced on Broadway at Bijou Theatre, 1923.

(With John Emerson) *The Fall of Eve,* produced on Broadway at Booth Theatre, 1925.

(With John Emerson) *Gentlemen Prefer Blondes* (based on their book of the same title), produced in New York, NY, at Times Square Theatre, 1926, musical adaptation (with Joseph Fields), produced on Broadway at Ziegfield Theatre, 1949.

(With John Emerson) *The Social Register,* produced in New York, NY, at Fulton Theatre, 1931.

Happy Birthday (produced on Broadway at Broadhurst Theatre, 1946), Samuel French (New York, NY), 1948.

Gigi (based on the novel by Colette; produced in New York, NY, at Fulton Theatre, 1951), Random House (New York, NY), 1952, revised edition, 1956.

Cheri (based on the novels *Cheri* and *The End of Cheri* by Colette), produced on Broadway at Morosco Theatre, 1959.

LIBRETTOS

The Amazing Adele (based on the play by Pierre Barrillet and Jean-Pierre Gredy), produced in Philadelphia, PA, at Shubert Theatre, 1955.

Gogo Loves You, produced in New York, NY, at Theatre de Lys, 1964.

Something about Anne (based on the play *The King's Mare* by Jean Canolle), produced in London, England, 1966.

OTHER

(With John Emerson) *How to Write Photoplays,* McCann (New York, NY), 1920.

(With John Emerson) *Breaking into the Movies*, Mc-Cann (New York, NY), 1921.

"Gentlemen Prefer Blondes": The Illuminating Diary of a Professional Lady (also see below; story collection), Boni & Liveright (New York, NY), 1925.

"But Gentlemen Marry Brunettes" (story collection), Boni & Liveright (New York, NY), 1928.

A Mouse Is Born (novel), Doubleday (New York, NY), 1951.

No Mother to Guide Her (novel), McGraw (New York, NY), 1961, new edition, Prion, 2000.

A Girl Like I (autobiography), Viking (New York, NY), 1966.

(Author of foreword) Dody Goodman, *Women, Women, Women*, Dutton (New York, NY), 1966.

(Translator and adaptor) Jean Canolle, *The King's Mare* (also see below), Evans Brothers (London, England), 1967.

(With Helen Hayes) *Twice Over Lightly: New York Then and Now*, Harcourt (New York, NY), 1972.

Kiss Hollywood Good-by (autobiography), Viking (New York, NY), 1974.

Cast of Thousands (autobiography), Grosset & Dunlap (New York, NY), 1977.

The Talmadge Girls: A Memoir, Viking (New York, NY), 1978.

San Francisco: A Screenplay (also see below), edited by Matthew J. Bruccoli, Southern Illinois University Press (Carbondale, IL), 1979.

Fate Keeps On Happening: Adventures of Lorelei Lee and Other Writings, Dodd (New York, NY), 1984.

Anita Loos Rediscovered: Film Treatments and Fiction by Anita Loos, edited by Cari Beauchamp and Mary Anita Loos, University of California Press (Berkeley, CA), 2003.

Contributor to *Reader's Digest*, *New York Times Magazine*, *Woman's Home Companion*, *Saturday Review*, and *Harper's*. A collection of Loos's letters are housed at the University of Delaware Library.

■ **Adaptations**

Gentlemen Prefer Blondes was filmed by Twentieth Century-Fox in 1953 and was adapted as a musical entitled *Lorelei* in 1974; *But Gentlemen Marry Brunettes* was filmed as *Gentlemen Marry Brunettes* by United Artists in 1955; *Happy Birthday* was adapted for television in Italy and the United States.

■ **Sidelights**

"I really never consider myself as a writer," Anita Loos once commented to Matthew J. Bruccoli in *Conversations with Writers II*. "I'm just a girl out there

trying to get a fast buck." In a career spanning some six decades, Loos wrote over 150 screenplays and scenarios, as well as popular Broadway plays and books of memoirs. But she was always "indissolubly linked" with her bestselling story collection *"Gentlemen Prefer Blondes": The Illuminating Diary of a Professional Lady*, as Alden Whitman noted in the *New York Times*. Adapted as a play, two musicals, and two movies, and translated into fourteen languages, *Gentlemen Prefer Blondes* established Loos's reputation as a writer of sparkling satire. Asked by Roy Newquist of *Palm Springs Life* whether she minded "being so closely identified" with the one book, Loos replied: "Heavens no, not as long as those lovely royalty checks keep coming in."

Loos was born in 1888 in the small town of Etna in northern California. Her father, Richard Beers Loos, known to friends and family as R. Beers, was an entrepeneur who engaged in a series of businesses hoping to make a fast fortune. Her mother, Minnie Ellen Loos, came from a wealthy cattle ranching family. After an unsuccessful attempt at editing tabloid newspapers, R. Beers moved on to managing vaudeville theatres. This last venture took the Loos family to San Francisco, which Anita always considered her hometown. Loos began her career as a child actress in her father's theatrical company in San Francisco. By the time she was ten years old, her stage earnings were a vital cash source for her financially unstable family. As a young girl, Loos enjoyed tagging along with her father as he visited the town's saloons. His various business ventures, even when failures, seemed to her to be adventures that made life interesting. Loos admitted on several occasions that her father's business often kept him away from home for long periods, usually in the company of other women. His "weekend fishing trips," too, involved more women than fish. John Fitzgerald of the *Detroit News* quoted Loos explaining: "My mother was refined . . . my father was a charming tramp." Loos "continued to worship her father in spite of or because of the fact that he was a scalawag," Cari Beauchamp wrote in *Anita Loos Rediscovered: Film Treatments and Fiction by Anita Loos*, "and all her life she would find herself attracted to scoundrels."

Silent Film Star

While still in her teens Loos became interested in the then-new medium of silent films, which were at first shown in-between live acts at local theatres. Believing that she could write a silent film as good as the ones shown in her father's theatre, Loos in 1912 submitted the scenario for *The New York Hat* to D.W. Griffith's American Biograph Company, copying the company's address from a film canister. Griffith accepted the scenario and Loos received twenty-five dollars for her work. The resulting film featured prominent stars Lillian Gish, Dorothy Gish, Mary Pickford, and Lionel Barrymore.

Between 1912 and 1916 Loos wrote at least one hundred scenarios for the silent films, usually for American Biograph but, when a particular idea did not seem strong enough to Griffith, for other film companies as well. The exact number of Loos' silent films, the years they were released, and the production companies that made them, are questions that will never be answered definitively. Few records were kept by those in the business, many films, particularly the very short films, were never registered for copyright, and others were later lost either through haphazard storage or deliberate destruction for the silver nitrate content in the film itself. To many people in the silent film world, the business was nothing but a transitory craze not to be taken too seriously. "We . . . looked on them as a fad that would soon lose public interest," Alden Whitman quoted Loos explaining.

Specializing in writing "slapstick comedies and romantic melodramas," as Thomas Grant noted in the *Dictionary of Literary Biography*, Loos emerged as one of the luminaries of the silent film world. She wrote for such stars as Mabel Normand, Mae Marsh, Marian Davies, Francis X. Bushman, Constance Talmadge, Norma Talmadge, and Douglas Fairbanks, and worked with the legendary director D.W. Griffith. She also wrote the title cards for Griffith's *Intolerance,* one of the silent screen's classic films. Griffith later claimed that Loos was "one of the brainiest young women alive." Yet, despite her position in the industry, Loos never went to see any of her films. She told Bruccoli: "I never paid any attention to any of them. They were a job and I'd get them done." In 1916 Loos became the sole writer for Douglas Fairbanks after the success of the satirical film *His Picture in the Papers.* The film introduced a new element to the silent film genre: satirical title cards which were meant to contrast ironically with the action on the screen. Together with her future husband, director John Emerson, Loos and Fairbanks shaped the Fairbanks screen persona into one of the most popular and lucrative characters in the cinema industry. Speaking of Loos's writing for these early films, Joanne Yeck of the *Dictionary of Literary Biography* reported that she "introduced satire to the silent film. Her dialogue cards were bright with sharp wit, exposing her real talent for verbal comedy."

Marries a Director

In 1919 Loos married Emerson and the two went on to collaborate on a number of films and plays. It was only years later, in her autobiography *Kiss*

Anita Loos with her husband, the director John Emerson.
(Copyright © Bettmann Corbis.)

Hollywood Good-by, that Loos confessed that her husband's "'collaboration' consisted of glancing over my morning's work while he was eating breakfast in bed." The couple's marital problems eventually led to a separation, although they never got divorced. Leah Lowe in the *Dictionary of Literary Biography* explained: "Emerson was a hypochondriac, chronically unfaithful, and demanded joint-authorship credit for stage and screen projects to which, Loos later revealed, his contributions were minimal. As Loos's success and celebrity increased, her relationship with Emerson became more difficult. Frequently, when Loos took jobs at Hollywood studios, she was forced to ask them to create positions for Emerson. Through most of their marriage, Loos made the money, while Emerson mismanaged their financial affairs. In 1937 Emerson was diagnosed as a schizophrenic and confined to a sanatorium. Although they remained married until Emerson's death in 1956, they never lived together for any substantial period of time again."

In 1923 the couple's first stage play, *The Whole Town's Talking,* opened on Broadway with Emerson directing. It ran for 173 performances. Lowe noted: "The play, typical of the Loos-Emerson stage collaborations of the 1920s, is a frothy comedy, reminiscent of French farce. It takes place in Sandusky, Ohio, where successful manufacturer Henry Simmons wants his daughter, Ethel, to marry his business partner, Chester Binney. Ethel, however, is infatuated with a wild young man from Chicago and finds Chester extremely dull in comparison. Simmons persuades Chester to claim that he once had an affair with glamorous Hollywood movie star Letty Lythe. As news of Chester's romantic exploits travels, all the young women of Sandusky, including Ethel, look at him in a new and far more appreciative light. Inevitably, Letty Lythe arrives in town to promote her new movie, accompanied by her extremely jealous fiancé. The play concludes with a knockabout fight between Chester, the fiancé, and Ethel's Chicago beau, from which Chester emerges the victor, winning Ethel's heart and hand."

While her work for the stage in the 1920s was successful, Loos did not think highly of it and, with the higher earnings possible from writing screenplays, focused most of her efforts on filmscripts. By the late 1920s Loos and Emerson had done well enough to leave screenwriting and move to Europe. Loos's movie fame allowed her entrance to European high society, and she was soon a regular at the country houses of royalty. Numbered among her friends were Ernest Hemingway, Gertrude Stein, Aldous Huxley, H.G. Wells, and F. Scott Fitzgerald. But Loos's European lifestyle came to an abrupt end with the stock market crash of 1929; Emerson had invested the couple's money in the market and lost it all. In 1931 Loos returned to the United States to become a screenwriter with Metro-Goldwyn-Mayer at a salary of 3,500 dollars a week. The films had changed and Loos, a prominent figure from the silent screen days, would now have to prove herself in the world of the "talkies."

Enters the Era of the Talkies

Unlike some leading figures of the silent film community, Loos made a successful transition to talking films. Her natural talent for humorous, sometimes racy, dialogue served her well. During the 1930s Loos worked with Irving Thalberg, the head of MGM studios and the man Loos later claimed taught her all about the "talkies." She was to write several of the classic films of the 1930s for Thalberg. Her first film for the studio was *Red-Headed Woman*, the story of a young vamp, Lillian Andrews (played by Jean Harlow), who breaks up a marriage. Harlow played the character as a working-class woman who was unconcerned about the niceties of morals. She thinks only of herself and how she can get ahead in life. "One can't help but be a little repelled by her character even as one laughs," Chris Dashiell

admitted in *CineScene*. "And I believe this is just what the script, by the legendary Anita Loos, intends us to feel." Thalberg had already had several writers try their hand at the script, including F. Scott Fitzgerald, but not one had been able to render the story in the ironic manner Thalberg wanted. He thought that Loos might be able to treat the story's sexual slant humorously. Loos did. The resulting script catapulted lead actress Harlow to instant fame. But the film, because of "its light-hearted view of sex," as Yeck reported, also ran afoul of the religious community. *Red-Headed Woman*, Yeck wrote, "started the national protest of women's clubs and church groups that eventually culminated in the formation of the Breen Office," a censorship group that was to set the "acceptable" standards for the film industry for years to come. Writing in *Kiss Hollywood Good-by*, Loos noted that the film outraged many people because "our heroine, the bad girl of whom all good husbands dream, ended her career as many such scalawags do, rich, happy, and respected, without ever having paid for her sins."

In 1936 Loos wrote *San Francisco* for MGM, a film inspired by her close friend Wilson Mizner. Loos and Robert Hopkins, who wrote the original story for the film, had known Mizner for many years. Mizner had worked in gambling houses, sold nonexistent Florida real estate, and engaged in a score of other fraudulent operations before finally opening a legitimate business: the Brown Derby Restaurant in Hollywood. His notorious past, colorful anecdotes, off-color remarks, and unfailing charm made Mizner a favorite with many among the Hollywood set, including W.C. Fields. After Mizner's death in 1933, Loos and Hopkins wrote *San Francisco*, as Loos explained in *Kiss Hollywood Good-by*, "to the glory of Wilson Mizner and the Frisco all three of us knew when we were kids." In the film, Blackie Norton, played by Clark Gable, is a Barbary Coast gambler in the San Francisco of the turn of the century who is inspired to go straight following the great earthquake of 1906. The story is partly based on Mizner's own career as a gambling house operator, while Gable's cynical yet charming manner is based on Mizner's own personality. In a review for *Reel.com*, Tim Knight called the film a "colorful and entertaining disaster yarn [and] a sterling example of old-fashioned, studio craftsmanship that holds up incredibly well, give or take a few of its hokier elements." The film earned six Oscar nominations. *San Francisco*, Yeck reported, was "by far the most commercially successful film Thalberg ever produced." Loos noted in *Kiss Hollywood Good-by* that "it became one of MGM's most durable hits."

In 1939, Loos cowrote with Jane Murfin *The Women,* a film in which no man appears. The film stars many of the leading actresses of the time, including Norma Shearer, Joan Crawford, Rosiland Russell, Mary Boland, Paulette Goddard, and Joan Fontaine. Revolving around Norma Shearer's character getting a Reno divorce from her unfaithful husband, the film looks at high society of the time and the catty antagonisms between rival women. The censors cut out over eighty racy lines from the original script. Since there was no time for a rewrite, Loos was obliged to be on the set each day, rewriting the script as it was shot. "If you're up for two-hours-plus of coded female innuendo and colorfully veiled insults . . . , your jollies will be tickled," according to Jeremiah Kipp in *Slant Magazine.* Danny Carr, in a review for the *Edinburgh University Film Society Web site,* called *The Women* "the ultimate women's movie of the 1930s and a treat from start to finish (for men also)."

Creates Lorelei Lee

Although she enjoyed great success as a writer for Hollywood films, Loos is best known for *Gentlemen Prefer Blondes,* a book she later adapted as a play, a musical, and for the screen. The story of an uneducated and naive young flapper who uses her charms to coax expensive gifts from her "gentlemen friends," the idea for *Gentlemen Prefer Blondes* apparently came to Loos during a cross-country train ride in the early 1920s. One of her fellow passengers was a blond Broadway actress on her way to Holly-

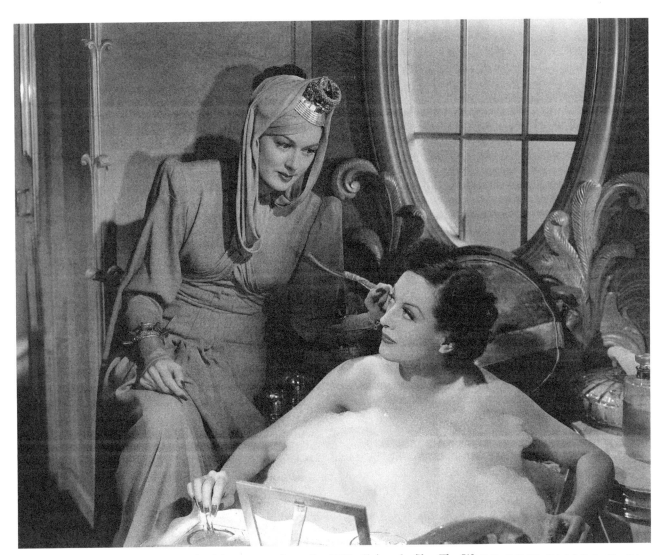

Rosalind Russell and Joan Crawford in a scene from the 1939 all-female film *The Women.* (MGM/The Kobal Collection/The Picture Desk, Inc.)

The film poster for the 1953 film adaptation of Loos's *Gentlemen Prefer Blondes,* **starring Jane Russell and Marilyn Monroe.** (20th Century Fox/The Kobal Collection/The Picture Desk, Inc.)

wood for a screen test. Over the course of the journey, the men on the train fawned over her while Loos, a brunette, steamed. Her resentment took shape as a series of loosely linked satirical short stories written in diary form. But on other occasions Loos claimed that she wrote *Gentlemen Prefer Blondes* because her friend H.L. Mencken had been infatuated with a particularly brainless blond and she wanted to show him his mistake.

Whatever the source of *Gentlemen Prefer Blondes*— Alden Whitman maintained that "Loos seldom permitted precise facts to spoil a good story, so the true origins of her book are in doubt"—the stories were first published in *Harper's Bazaar* and immediately caused sales of the magazine to quadruple. The story proved popular when published in book form in 1925; since its first appearance there have been some eighty-five editions of *Gentlemen Prefer Blondes* and the book has even been translated into Chinese.

The book follows beautiful Lorelei Lee on a tour of Europe with her friend Dorothy. Lorelei's inane observations about European society and culture, and her frankly materialistic attitude toward sexual relations, form the basis of the comedy. "As a fictional character," Grant wrote, "Lorelei harks back to an earlier comic stereotype, the malaprop-inclined, misspelling rustic busybody." Fitzgerald noted that Loos "gave the world neither blonds nor gentlemen but managed to make both shimmer through the eyes of one diamond-loving Lorelei Lee." Perhaps the book's most famous line is Lorelei's observation that "kissing your hand may make you feel very good but a diamond lasts forever." In the course of her European tour Lorelei acquires a number of both kisses and diamonds, including a 7,500 dollar tiara from an English nobleman. She ends the book safely ensconced on Park Avenue, the wife of a wealthy man. "Lorelei's stunning progress from small-town girl to metropolitan socialite," Grant remarked, "makes her story seem like an urban version of the familiar American tall tale, a delightfully improbable yarn perfectly suited to the 1920s era of excess."

Critical response to *Gentlemen Prefer Blondes* was enormously favorable. George Santayana, William Faulkner, James Joyce, Edith Wharton, H.L. Mencken, and Aldous Huxley were among those who recommended it. Years later, Peter S. Prescott of *Newsweek* could still note that *Gentlemen Prefer Blondes* "remains one of the great American comic novels."

The adaptations of the book also proved successful. Loos's stage version of 1926 ran on Broadway for 201 performances. A 1949 musical version enjoyed a run of 740 performances and launched the career of actress Carol Channing. The popular song "Diamonds Are a Girl's Best Friend" is from this play. In 1974 yet another Broadway adaptation appeared under the title of *Lorelei.* Loos also wrote a silent film version of *Gentlemen Prefer Blondes* which was produced in 1928; a later film, featuring Marilyn Monroe as Lorelei, appeared in 1953.

Loos followed *Gentlemen Prefer Blondes* with a sequel, *But Gentlemen Marry Brunettes,* recounting the romantic misadventures of Lorelei's girlfriend Dorothy. Lorelei, who has married successfully, assists Dorothy in her quest to enter Manhattan society. But Dorothy's eventual marriage to a rich polo player comes only after a series of trials, including a marriage to a cocaine addict who is killed by mobsters. One of the novel's high points, according to Grant, is a scene in which the two women visit the Algonquin Hotel and acidly comment on the circle of writers and journalists who frequented the hotel bar in the early 1920s. "Loos's portrayal of the Algonquin wits," Grant wrote, "has become established wisdom. She was one of their first critics, and one of the most accurate." Other reviewers, such as the *New Republic* critic, found that, like its predecessor, *But Gentlemen Marry Brunettes* contains "that wonderful mixture of canned, naive sentiment and equally naive, but extremely business-like gold-digging."

In 1946 Loos returned to the Broadway stage with *Happy Birthday,* a comedy set in a Newark saloon and starring her old friend Helen Hayes. Revolving around an inhibited librarian who finally opens up after a few drinks at the local tavern, *Happy Birthday* ran for 564 performances on Broadway. Hayes won a Tony Award for her role. Speaking to Bruccoli about the play, Loos explained the basis of its plot: "I had this old maid go into a bar and get tight, and in the process of getting tight she regenerates her whole life."

In the late 1940s and early 1950s, Loos began an association with French writer Colette that would result in two successful plays and launch the career of yet another actress. Loos was hired to adapt Colette's book *Gigi* for the Broadway stage, another job that had been unsuccessfully attempted by other writers before Loos came along. The two writers got along famously, and Colette herself chose the actress she wanted to play Gigi when she spotted a striking woman among the extras of a movie being filmed in Monte Carlo. The new actress—Audrey Hepburn—premiered *Gigi* at New York City's Fulton Theater in 1951. It ran for 219 performances. Loos also penned a script based on Colette's *Cheri* in 1959 which ran for fifty six performances.

Publishes Memoirs

Beginning in the 1960s Loos began to publish a series of memoirs about her long career as a writer for Hollywood and Broadway. Written in a chatty, informal style, these books are peppered with lively anecdotes and reminiscences about the many famous people she knew. Grant explained that

A 1978 photograph of Loos holding an early portrait of herself. (Copyright © Bettmann Corbis.)

Loos's memoirs chronicled "her own long, lucrative career and the dazzling times in which she worked." In her review of *A Girl Like I*, Sister M. Gregory of *Best Sellers* found that the "book is more than an autobiography; it is an intriguing bit of Americana that mirrors the brash confidence, rugged independence and changing mores of a rapidly growing, prosperous country." Speaking of *Kiss Hollywood Good-by*, Joel Sayre of the *New York Times Book Review* remarked that if the book reached the best-seller lists, it would be because of Loos's "marvelous, casual putting forth of bizarre doings and sayings." Writing in the *Christian Science Monitor*, Guernsey Le Pelley called the same book "a jolly adventure in trivia. . . . But along with all the flotsam are many delectable and interesting tidbits, which make the book bouncy and largely enjoyable. Also [the book] holds up a mirror of unintended satire to that demi-Disneyland called Hollywood." In similar terms, Richard Lingeman of the *New York Times*, reviewing *Cast of Thousands*, warned that "one should not regard [Loos's] witty, determinedly surface view of life as the sign of a superficial mind. Actually, Miss Loos is a sharp-eyed chatterbox, who lets fly some quick cynical shafts."

If you enjoy the works of Anita Loos, you may also want to check out the following books:

Patrick Dennis, *Auntie Mame*, 1955.
Dorothy Parker, *The Portable Dorothy Parker*, 2006.
Stella Gibbons, *Cold Comfort Farm*, 2006.

Loos died of a heart attack on August 18, 1981, in New York City. Despite the many successes of her long career, she always maintained a cavalier attitude towards her work. Though *Gentlemen Prefer Blondes* firmly established her, she said of the story, "I had no thought of its ever being printed. My only purpose was to make Henry Mencken laugh, which it did." Speaking of her career to Fitzgerald, she said: "I did it for the money and it was the easiest money I ever made." When questioned by Bruccoli about whether *Gentlemen Prefer Blondes* had obscured "the range of your other work," Loos replied: "I think *Gentlemen Prefer Blondes* is the range of my work. I think everything else I do is just earning a living." Perhaps one reason for her adamant refusal to place much value on her writings is revealed in a remark Loos made to Fitzgerald in the last interview she gave. "It was all so easy," she said. "It didn't seem to mean anything."

Faye Hammill, writing in *Critical Survey*, believed that Loos's career was a balancing act between the popular and the intellectual: "Loos works the border between high and popular culture, never fully identifying herself with either. Her books are apparently aimed at a fairly educated audience, since their primary satiric target is a semiliterate, philistine lowbrow, but they also satirize the pretensions of highbrow culture." But critical evaluations of Loos's career usually stress the impressive range of genres in which she excelled and her ability to successfully adapt her writing to new mediums. Her silent film work includes some of that genre's finest examples and introduced depth and subtlety to the medium. Her later films and plays feature sparkling, witty dialogue that ensures their lasting humor and audience appeal. Whether she was writing for film, stage, or the printed page, Loos always entertained her audience. And her character Lorelei Lee is, Grant believed, "a true American original. . . . So memorable [that she] ought to earn her inventor a place as one of the important minor figures among twentieth-century American humorists." Enid Nemy of the *New York Times Book Review* summed up Loos in this way: "The keenness of her eye never faltered, and for something like six decades she sliced neatly through the gauze that surrounds glamour and fame."

■ Biographical and Critical Sources

BOOKS

Acker, Ally, *Reel Women: Pioneers of the Cinema, 1896 to the Present*, [New York], 1991.

Authors in the News, Gale (Detroit, MI), Volume 1, 1976.

Beauchamp, Cari, and Mary Anita Loos, editors, *Anita Loos Rediscovered: Film Treatments and Fiction by Anita Loos*, University of California Press (Berkeley, CA), 2003.

Brown, Karl, *Adventures with D.W. Griffith*, Farrar, Straus (New York, NY), 1973.

Carey, Gary, *Anita Loos: A Biography*, Knopf (New York, NY), 1988.

Conversations with Writers II, Gale (Detroit, MI), 1978.

Dictionary of Literary Biography, Gale (Detroit, MI), Volume 11: *American Humorists, 1800-1950*, 1982, Volume 26: *American Screenwriters*, 1984, Volume 228: *Twentieth-Century American Dramatists, Second Series*, 2000.

Dictionary of Literary Biography Yearbook, 1981, Gale (Detroit, MI), 1982.

International Dictionary of Films and Filmmakers, Volume 4: *Writers and Production Artists*, 4th edition, St. James Press (Detroit, MI), 2000.

Loos, Anita, *A Girl Like I,* Viking (New York, NY), 1966.

Loos, Anita, *Kiss Hollywood Good-by,* Viking (New York, NY), 1974.

Loos, Anita, *Cast of Thousands,* Grosset & Dunlap (New York, NY), 1977.

Women Filmmakers & Their Films, St. James Press (Detroit, MI), 1998.

PERIODICALS

AB Bookman's Weekly, September 5, 1966, review of *A Girl Like I,* p. 885; September 14, 1981.

Akron Beacon Journal, September 8, 1974.

Atlantic, October, 1960; October, 1966, review of *A Girl Like I,* p. 138.

Best Sellers, October 1, 1966, Sister M. Gregory, review of *A Girl Like I;* September 15, 1974, review of *Kiss Hollywood Good-by,* p. 270; April, 1979, review of *The Talmadge Girls: A Memoir,* p. 20.

Booklist, October 15, 1966, review of *A Girl Like I,* p. 222; October 1, 1974, review of *Kiss Hollywood Good-by,* p. 134; April 15, 1977, review of *Cast of Thousands* p. 1233.

Books & Bookman, October, 1985, review of *Fate Keeps On Happening: Adventures of Lorelei Lee and Other Writings,* p. 39.

Boston Transcript, November 25, 1925.

Canadian Review of American Studies, spring, 1976.

Chicago Tribune, August 2, 1961; August 20, 1981.

Christian Science Monitor, September 18, 1974, Guernsey Le Pelley, review of *Kiss Hollywood Good-by.*

Critical Survey, September, 2005, Faye Hammill, "'One of the Few Books That Doesn't Stink': The Intellectuals, the Masses and *Gentlemen Prefer Blondes,*" p. 27.

Detroit News, August 30, 1981.

Harper's Magazine, September, 1966, review of *A Girl Like I,* p. 114.

Kirkus Reviews, July 15, 1966, review of *A Girl Like I,* p. 731.

Library Journal, August, 1966, review of *A Girl Like I,* p. 3709; August, 1974, review of *Kiss Hollywood Good-by,* p. 1978; April 1, 1977, review of *Cast of Thousands* p. 830; October 1, 1978, review of *The Talmadge Girls,* p. 2004; December, 1984, review of *Fate Keeps On Happening,* p. 2280.

Literary Review, November 21, 1925.

Los Angeles Times, January 20, 1985, review of *Fate Keeps On Happening,* p. 8.

New Republic, June 13, 1928; August 10, 1974.

New Statesman, May 19, 1928.

Newsweek, October 17, 1966, review of *A Girl Like I,* p. 112; August 31, 1981; December 17, 1984.

New Yorker, October 15, 1966, review of *A Girl Like I,* p. 243; December 24, 1984, review of *Fate Keeps On Happening,* p. 89.

New York Times, April 29, 1918; September 23, 1918; October 27, 1919; January 23, 1922; February 23, 1925; December 27, 1925; January 16, 1928; May 20, 1928; December 11, 1935; March 2, 1935; January 13, 1936; June 27, 1936; July 23, 1937; September 22, 1939; July 12, 1940; June 27, 1941; July 4, 1941; September 5, 1941; July 10, 1942; August 31, 1974, review of *Kiss Hollywood Good-by,* p. 17; March 23, 1977, Richard Lingeman, review of *Cast of Thousands* p. 29; August 19, 1981.

New York Times Book Review, May 6, 1951; October 2, 1966, review of *A Girl Like I,* p. 6; August 18, 1974, Joel Sayre, review of *Kiss Hollywood Good-by;* March 23, 1977; November 27, 1984; December 30, 1984, review of *Fate Keeps On Happening.*

New York Tribune, December 27, 1925.

Palm Springs Life, October, 1974.

Publishers Weekly, July 11, 1966, review of *A Girl Like I;* May 20, 1974, review of *Kiss Hollywood Good-by,* p. 63; February 24, 1975, p. 118; August 28, 1978, review of *The Talmadge Girls,* p. 379; September 4, 1981.

Saturday Review, June 9, 1928; September 24, 1966; September 21, 1974, review of *Kiss Hollywood Good-by,* p. 26.

Time, August 31, 1981.

Times Literary Supplement, February 23, 1967; December 6, 1974, review of *Kiss Hollywood Good-by,* p. 1368.

Tribune Books (Chicago, IL), November 26, 1978.

West Coast Review of Books, May, 1979, review of *The Talmadge Girls,* p. 14; January, 1985, review of *Fate Keeps On Happening,* p. 40.

ONLINE

CineScene, http://www.cinescene.com/ (December, 2001), Chris Dashiell, review of *Red-Headed Woman.*

Edinburgh University Film Society Web site, http://www.eufs.org.uk/ (October 5, 2007), Danny Carr, review of *The Women.*

Reel.com, http://www.reel.com/ (October 5, 2007), Tim Knight, review of *San Francisco.*

Slant Magazine, http://www.slantmagazine.com/ (October 5, 2007), Jeremiah Kipp, review of *The Women.**

(Amy Sussman/Getty Images Entertainment/Getty Images.)

Mike Lupica

■ Personal

Born May 11, 1952, in Oneida, NY; son of Benedict (a personal manager) and Lee Lupica; married; children: three sons. *Education:* Boston College, B.A., 1974.

■ Addresses

Office—New York Daily News, 220 E. 42nd St., New York, NY 10017. *Agent*—Esther Newberg, International Creative Management, 40 West 57th St., New York, NY 10019.

■ Career

Boston Globe, Boston, MA, correspondent, 1970-74; *Boston Phoenix,* Boston, columnist, 1971-75; *Boston* magazine, Boston, columnist, 1974-75; *Washington Star,* Washington, DC, feature writer, 1974-75; *New York Post,* New York City, basketball writer and columnist, 1975-76; *New York News,* New York City, columnist, 1977-81; *New York Daily News,* New York City, columnist, 1980—. Writer for *World Tennis,* 1974-81, and columnist for *Esquire.* Broadcast sports journalist for Columbia Broadcasting System (CBS) Morning News, 1982-84; Entertainment and Sports Programming Network (ESPN), 1982-83, and as a panelist for *The Sports Reporters;* WCBS-TV, 1983; and WNBC Radio.

■ Member

Newspaper Guild of America.

■ Writings

YOUNG-ADULT NOVELS

Travel Team, Philomel Books (New York, NY), 2004.
Heat, Philomel Books (New York, NY), 2006.
Miracle on 49th Street, Philomel Books (New York, NY), 2006.
Summer Ball, Philomel Books (New York, NY), 2007.
Hot Hand, Philomel Books (New York, NY), 2007.
Two-Minute Drill, Philomel Books (New York, NY), 2007.
The Big Field, Philomel Books (New York, NY), 2008.
Safe at Home, Philomel Books (New York, NY), 2008.

NONFICTION

(With Reggie Jackson) *Reggie: The Autobiography,* Villard Books (New York, NY), 1984.

(With Bill Parcells) *Parcells: Autobiography of the Biggest Giant of Them All,* Bonus Books (Chicago, IL), 1987.

Shooting from the Lip: Essays, Columns, Quips, and Gripes in the Grand Tradition of Dyspeptic Sports Writing, Bonus Books (Chicago, IL), 1988.

(With William Goldman) *Wait Till Next Year: The Story of a Season When What Should've Happened Didn't and What Could've Gone Wrong Did,* Bantam (New York, NY), 1988.

Mad as Hell: How Sports Got Away from the Fans—and How We Get It Back, Putnam (New York, NY), 1996.

(With Fred Imus) *The Fred Book,* Doubleday (New York, NY), 1998.

Summer of '98: When Homers Flew, Records Fell, and Baseball Reclaimed America, Putnam (New York, NY), 1999.

"PETER FINLEY" MYSTERY SERIES

Dead Air, Villard Books (New York, NY), 1986.
Extra Credits, Villard Books (New York, NY), 1988.
Limited Partner, Villard Books (New York, NY), 1990.

NOVELS

Jump, Villard Books (New York, NY), 1995.
Bump and Run, Putnam (New York, NY), 2000.
Full Court Press, Putnam (New York, NY), 2001.
Wild Pitch, Putnam (New York, NY), 2002.
Red Zone, Putnam (New York, NY), 2003.
Too Far, Putnam (New York, NY), 2004.

■ Sidelights

Prominent sportswriter Mike Lupica is known for his syndicated sports column, television and radio appearances, as well as for his sports novels for both adults and young adults. *Booklist* correspondent Wes Lukowsky called Lupica "one of the nation's most visible sports columnists," adding that the writer is also "not a bad novelist."

Lupica began his sports writing career in Boston but assumed national prominence when he joined the staff of the *New York Daily News* in 1980. His reputation as a straight-talking columnist was enhanced by his presence on television shows such as *The Sports Reporters* on ESPN and *The MacNeil-Lehrer NewsHour* on the Public Broadcasting System (PBS). His first two books are "as-told-to" autobiographies, one on baseball legend Reggie Jackson and the other on former New York Giants head coach Bill Parcells. Inevitably, reviewers' attention focused less on the books themselves than on the personalities of their high-profile subjects: Jackson, often seen as arrogant and boastful, and Parcells, known for his single-minded dedication to the sport. In Chicago's *Tribune Books,* however, Robert Cromie found *Reggie: The Autobiography* "highly readable," while Michael Wilbon in the *Washington Post Book World* called *Parcells: Autobiography of the Biggest Giant of Them All* "deftly crafted, as one expects from Lupica."

Shooting from the Lip: Essays, Columns, Quips, and Gripes in the Grand Tradition of Dyspeptic Sports Writing is a collection of Lupica's essays and newspaper columns. Diane Cole in the *New York Times Book Review* found the pieces "engaging and often exhilarating" in their reliance on a single mood or moment to capture the essence of a season or an athlete's career. *Mad as Hell: How Sports Got Away from the Fans—and How We Get It Back* summarizes the complaints of many sports enthusiasts, namely, that the players are overpaid, the owners too greedy, and the ordinary fans priced out of the ballparks. In *Booklist,* Lukowsky maintained that those who share Lupica's concerns "will enjoy sputtering angrily as they read this litany of wrongdoing." The columnist strikes a much more optimistic tone in *Summer of '98: When Homers Flew, Records Fell, and Baseball Reclaimed America.* Taking as its subject the eventful 1998 professional baseball season, Lupica weaves together tales of Mark McGwire and Sammy Sosa battling for the home run record with poignant asides on the ability of baseball to unite fathers and sons. A *Publishers Weekly* reviewer deemed *Summer of '98* a "feel-great book" in which Lupica "gives himself completely over to the beauty of baseball as . . . a game."

Creates Mysteries

In the mid-1980s Lupica tried his hand at fiction, turning out three genre thrillers, all of which feature the same protagonist. Readers were first introduced to the character Peter Finley, an investigative reporter for a New York City cable-TV station, in *Dead Air.* The book's plot is set in motion when a former Miss America, now the host of a late-night talk show, disappears and is presumed dead. When Finley is asked by the victim's husband to look into her disappearance, corpses start turning up, all of

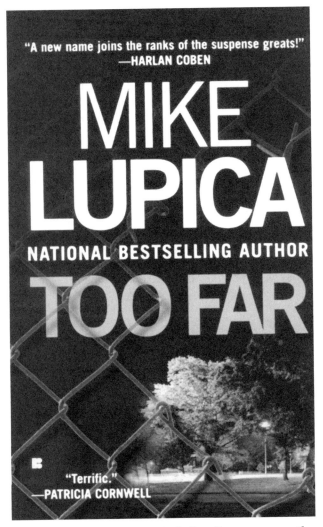

"A new name joins the ranks of the suspense greats!"
—HARLAN COBEN

MIKE LUPICA

NATIONAL BESTSELLING AUTHOR

TOO FAR

"Terrific."
—PATRICIA CORNWELL

Lupica's 2004 mystery novel *Too Far* concerns the murder of a high school basketball coach. (Berkley Publishing Group, 2004. Cover art: Football Pitch at Night, Digital Vision/Getty Images; Hole in Wire Fence, Iconica/Getty Images. All rights reserved. Used by permission of Penguin Group (USA) Inc.)

them connected with the show's network, which is about to be taken over by a Christian broadcasting network. In *Extra Credits,* the next book in the series, Finley is approached by a college student who persuades him to investigate the mysterious suicide of her wealthy and attractive friend. *Limited Partner* finds Finley probing the death by drug overdose of a friend, a recovering addict who is also part owner of a trendy Manhattan night spot. When the victim's girlfriend dies just a few days later, also of an overdose, Finley is convinced of foul play.

At the center of each of these books is the island of Manhattan, its bars and bistros, and its dark side of drug-dealing and amoral wealth. Jean M. White, writing in the *Washington Post Book World,* criticized

Extra Credits for overemphasizing the details of its setting, complaining that the book reads like a "what's-in list for *New York* magazine." In Chicago's *Tribune Books,* however, Alice Cromie found similar details in *Dead Air* "amusingly depicted." Reviewers were similarly divided over Finley, the novels' wisecracking, fast-talking hero. In the *New York Times Book Review,* Michael Lichtenstein wrote that *Limited Partner* is marred by Finley's flip "one-liners." Yet Newgate Callendar, also in the *New York Times Book Review,* admired the "street-smart" hero and concluded of *Extra Credits:* "The writing is sophisticated, the dialogue bright."

Turns to Sports Fiction

Other Lupica novels include *Jump* and *Bump and Run,* both of which draw upon his insider's knowledge of high-profile athletics. In *Jump,* two pro basketball teammates stand accused of rape by a New York City actress. The players call upon investigative attorney Mike DiMaggio to piece together the truth about the assault and to explore the actress's motivations for waiting a year before she lodged the charges. A *Publishers Weekly* reviewer felt that *Jump* "crackles with tension, excitement and hip authenticity." The reviewer concluded that Lupica's "amalgam of tightly written sports story and crime fiction sinks a winning basket." *Bump and Run* takes a more comic tone, as a Las Vegas casino employee inherits his billionaire father's pro football team and applies his casino expertise to the task of constructing a winning franchise. A *Publishers Weekly* contributor found this work "hilarious but slightly disturbing," feeling that Lupica's satire of corporate greed and shady dealing in football holds more than a grain of truth. The reviewer styled *Bump and Run* "a deliciously wicked tale of contemporary professional sports and the people who . . . run the game." In *Booklist,* Lukowsky likewise praised Lupica for "getting fresh laughs from a classic premise—the streetwise kid beating a bunch of snotty rich guys at their own game."

Full Court Press is, according to a reviewer for *Publishers Weekly,* "another irreverent, behind-the-scenes peek into the world of sports." This time Lupica tells the tale of Delilah "Dee" Gerard, a former woman basketball star in Europe who is coaxed out of retirement to play for the New York Knights. The first woman player in the National Basketball Association, she finds herself the center of unwanted abuse and jealousy, despite her outstanding play on the court. Don McLeese in *Book* called the novel "a story with plenty of laughs, but even more heart."

In *Wild Pitch,* washed-up pitcher Charlie Stoddard is given one last chance at redemption in the big leagues. Following Charlie's stint with a physical therapist who works wonders with his pained throwing arm, the Boston Red Sox are willing to hire him. The pennant race brings Charlie into conflict with his son, also a Red Sox pitcher and resentful of his father. "Charlie's likable, and the baseball set pieces are beyond reproach," wrote a critic for *Kirkus Reviews*. Wes Lukowsky, writing for *Booklist*, found that Lupica "captures both the insanity that passes for sport these days and the appeal that baseball still has for the eternal child who lives within every fan."

Lupica's *Red Zone* is a sequel to *Bump and Run*. Jack Molloy, billionaire owner of the New York Hawks football team, loses control of his team to a rival, thanks to the greedy machinations of his twin sons. When the new owner fires the coach and general manager, replacing them with inexperienced men, Molloy must scheme to regain control of the Hawks and bring them back around. Lukowsky found that "Lupica propels the plot at breakneck speed with

sitcom-like zingers, nifty Big Apple atmosphere, and an insider's knowledge of professional sports." David Wright in the Library Journal predicted that "Lupica fans will love it."

The 2004 novel *Too Far* concerns a high school basketball team whose coach, Bobby Ferraro, has been murdered in the middle of a winning season. Former sportswriter Ben Mitchell links up with high schooler Sam Perry to investigate the mysterious death. They uncover what may be evidence of violent hazing activities. But their sleuthing gets in the way of townspeople who want nothing to interfere with their basketball team winning a state championship. "This is a fairly predictable story," Alan Moores wrote in *Booklist*, "but with dialogue that has some snap and a sports setting that's credible." The critic for *Kirkus Reviews* found that "the story is timely and competently told."

Sports Novels for Young Readers

With the novel *Travel Team*, Lupica turned to writing fiction for young adults. Twelve-year-old Danny Walker plays on a basketball team coached by his father, a former professional player whose career was cut short by an injury. He tries to live through Danny, pushing the boy to excel at basketball. "It's such a relief," Claire Rosser stated in *Kliatt*, "to have a sports tale written by someone who truly understands the game—and Lupica knows how to create believable characters as well." "Lupica creates a sports novel that is rich in details," according to Todd Morning in *Booklist*.

Heat finds Michael and Carlos Arroyo in a desperate situation. Their father has died and, if they let anyone know, the two boys will be split apart and put into foster homes. An elderly neighbor helps out, but the boys must fool child services in order to stay together. Meanwhile, Michael wants to pitch for an all-star team but needs to prove his age. Having been born in Cuba, he has a hard time getting a copy of his birth certificate. A critic for *Publishers Weekly* praised the book's "convincing characterization and exciting on-field action." According to Bill Ott in *Booklist:* "The dialogue crackles, and the rich cast of supporting characters . . . nearly steals the show. Top-notch entertainment." "*Heat* is a fast-paced, tightly written novel with believable characters," Renee Kirchner concluded in *TeenReads.com*.

In *Miracle on 49th Street*, Molly Parker confronts Celtics basketball player Josh Cameron with some startling news: she is his daughter. Now that her mother has passed away from cancer, Molly wants

In *Travel Team* Lupica tells of a young basketball player coached by his father. (Philomel Books, 2004. Reproduced by permission of Philomel Books, a division of Penguin Putnam Books for Young Readers.)

Josh to take on his parental responsibilities. "Lupica delivers a winning novel," Morning wrote in *Booklist*, "creating a realistic character in Molly by authentically capturing both her fragility and pluck." "Lupica creates intriguing, complex characters . . . , and he paces his story well, with enough twists and cliff-hangers to keep the pages turning," Jeffrey A. French wrote in the *School Library Journal*.

Danny Walker of *Travel Team* returns in *Summer Ball*. This time he is at a summer basketball camp where the coach will not let him play. The coach says Danny is too short, but the boy suspects that there is an old feud between the coach and his father. He must overcome the bad feelings in order to get on the court and prove himself. Writing in *Booklist*, Morning found that "Lupica is at his best when he puts the reader right in the center of the action on the court. His game descriptions are fast, accurate, and exciting." "Danny is a classic sports-story underdog," admitted Marilyn Taniguchi in the *School Library Journal*, "but he's also sympathetic and engaging. . . . Sports fans will relish the on-court action, expertly rendered in Lupica's taut prose." "Although a sequel to *Travel Team*," Sarah Sawtelle wrote in *TeenReads.com*. "*Summer Ball* is a great stand-alone novel. With humor and fast action both on and off the court, this is a summer read not to be missed."

If you enjoy the works of Mike Lupica, you may also want to check out the following books:

Mark Harris, *Bang the Drum Slowly*, 1956.
Bernard Malamud, *The Natural*, 1980.
David Halberstam, *The Breaks of the Game*, 1981.
Mitch Albom, *Fab Five: Basketball, Trash Talk, the American Dream*, 1993.

Basketball is again the focus in the novel *Hot Hand*, the first in a proposed "Comeback Kids" series of sports novels. Billy finds himself caught between a number of problems. His parents have recently divorced, but his father continues as Billy's basketball coach. His father is easily angered, especially by Billy's play on the court, and criticizes him constantly. His mother is too busy working to have much to do with Billy or his younger brother, Ben. When Ben is picked on by a bully at school, his

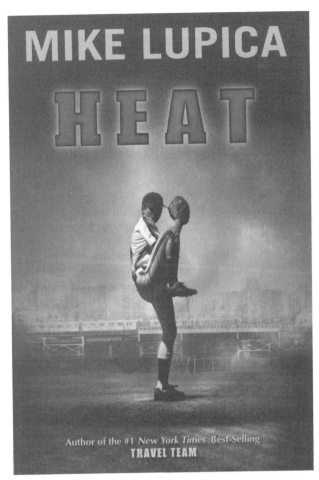

Two brothers must not let anyone know their father has died in Lupica's 2006 novel *Heat*. (Philomel Books, 2006. Jacket illustration © by Cliff Nielsen. Reproduced by permission of Philomel Books, a division of Penguin Putnam Books for Young Readers.)

parents are too busy with their own lives to notice or help, leaving a resentful Billy to come to his brother's rescue. Lupica "again relays fast-paced basketball action . . . ," according to a critic for *Publishers Weekly*. "The narrative moves equally sure-footedly off-court."

Lupica's 2008 title *The Big Field* focuses on a baseball team that makes it to the Florida State Finals. Player Keith Hutchinson can hardly believe it. His father, Carl Hutchinson, played Triple-A ball but was unable to make it to the majors. Maybe Keith can make it. But his father wants Keith to understand that baseball should not be his whole life. Writing in *Booklist*, John Peters found that "Lupica strikes the right balance between personal issues and game action." The critic for *Kirkus Reviews* called the novel "a fast-paced, completely involving story with excellent game sequences." "Lupica," the critic for *Publishers Weekly* concluded, "does not fail to entertain."

■ Biographical and Critical Sources

PERIODICALS

Book, November-December, 2001, Don McLeese, review of *Full Court Press,* p. 66.

Booklist, December 15, 1994, Wes Lukowsky, review of *Jump,* p. 715; October 15, 1996, Wes Lukowsky, review of *Mad as Hell: How Sports Got Away from the Fans—and How We Get It Back,* p. 397; September 1, 2000, Wes Lukowsky, review of *Bump and Run,* p. 7; September 1, 2002, Wes Lukowsky, review of *Wild Pitch,* p. 46; October 15, 2003, Wes Lukowsky, review of *Red Zone,* p. 357; September 1, 2004, Todd Morning, review of *Travel Team,* p. 110; November 15, 2004, Alan Moores, review of *Too Far,* p. 532; September 1, 2006, Todd Morning, review of *Miracle on 49th Street,* p. 116; April 15, 2007, Todd Morning, review of *Summer Ball,* p. 42; December 1, 2007, John Peters, review of *The Big Field,* p. 38.

Kirkus Reviews, August 15, 2000, review of *Bump and Run,* p. 1136; July 15, 2002, review of *Wild Pitch,* p. 983; November 15, 2004, review of *Too Far,* p. 1063; July 15, 2007, review of *Two-Minute Drill;* January 15, 2008, review of *The Big Field.*

Kliatt, September, 2004, Claire Rosser, review of *Travel Team,* p. 13.

Library Journal, November 1, 2003, David Wright, review of *Red Zone,* p. 124.

Los Angeles Times, July 17, 1987.

New York Times Book Review, August 19, 1984, p. 19; May 26, 1986, p. 14; May 29, 1988, p. 15; July 31, 1988, p. 25; October 14, 1990, p. 48; May 30, 1999, George Robinson, "Big Mac, Sammy and the Yanks," p. 16.

Publishers Weekly, February 6, 1995, review of *Jump,* p. 76; August 26, 1996, review of *Mad As Hell: How Sports Got Away from the Fans—and How We Get It Back,* p. 85; February 8, 1999, review of *Summer of '98: When Homers Flew, Records Fell, and Baseball Reclaimed America,* p. 202; October 9, 2000, review of *Bump and Run,* p. 70; September 24, 2001, review of *Full Court Press,* p. 64; November 15, 2004, review of *Too Far,* p. 40; February 20, 2006, review of *Heat,* p. 157; September 3, 2007, review of *Hot Hand,* p. 59; February 25, 2008, review of *The Big Field,* p. 79.

School Library Journal, November, 2006, Jeffrey A. French, review of *Miracle on 49th Street,* p. 141; June, 2007, Marilyn Taniguchi, review of *Summer Ball,* p. 152.

Tribune Books (Chicago, IL), July 1, 1984, p. 28; August 10, 1986, p. 47.

Washington Post Book World, October 2, 1987; June 19, 1988, p. 8.

ONLINE

TeenReads.com, http://www.teenreads.com/ (February 12, 2008), author profile; Sarah Sawtelle, reviews of *Travel Team, Miracle on 49th Street,* and *Summer Ball;* Renee Kirchner, review of *Heat.**

(Copyright © Malcolm Quantrill. Reproduced by permission.)

Brian MacKay-Lyons

■ Personal

Born August 26, 1954, in Arcadia, Nova Scotia, Canada. *Education:* Nova Scotia Technical College (now Dalhousie University), B.S. (environmental design), 1976, B.S. (architecture), 1978; University of California, Los Angeles, M.A. (urban design), 1982.

■ Addresses

Home—Halifax, Nova Scotia, Canada. *Office*—MacKay-Lyons Sweetapple Architects, Ltd., 2188 Gottingen St., Halifax, Nova Scotia B3K 3B4, Canada. *E-mail*—info@mlsarchitects.ca.

■ Career

Architect and educator. Moore, Ruble & Yudell (architectural firm), Santa Monica, CA, member of firm, 1980-82; Emodi & MacKay-Lyons, Halifax, Nova Scotia, Canada, partner, 1983-85; MacKay-Lyons Architecture Urban Design, Halifax, founder, beginning 1985; MacKay-Lyons Sweetapple Archi-

tects, Ltd. (architectural firm), cofounder, 2005—. Dalhousie University (formerly Technical University of Nova Scotia), professor of architecture; holder of endowed academic chairs and visiting professorships at universities, including Harvard University, McGill University, Syracuse University, Tulane University, Auburn University, Texas A & M University, University of Maryland, University of Arkansas, Washington University (St. Louis, MO), and University of Michigan.

■ Member

Royal Architectural Institute of Canada (fellow), Royal Canada Academy of Arts, Nova Scotia Association of Architects, Architects Association of Prince Edward Island.

■ Awards, Honors

Royal Architecture of Canada Medal, 1978; Nova Scotia Association of Architects Award of Merit, 1983; Prix de Rome finalist, 1987; named honorary fellow, American Institute of Architects (AIA), 2001; AIA Honor Award, 2003, for Howard House. MacKay-Lyon's buildings have received over fifty awards for design, including Nova Scotia Home Award, Heritage Canada Restoration Award, Governor General's Medal for Architecture, Royal Society of the Arts award, Nova Scotia Association of Architects honors, Lieutenant Governor's Medal and Award of Merit, Wood Design Merit Award, AIA honors, and Record Houses Award.

■ Writings

(With Charles Moore and others) *A Collective Vision: A Campus Plan for Dalhousie University,* privately published (Halifax, Nova Scotia, Canada), 1991.

Snyder's Shipyard: A Case Study, TUNS Press (Halifax, Nova Scotia, Canada), 1994.

Seven Stories from a Village Architect, MIT Press, 1996.

(Author of foreword) *Casting a Legend: The Story of the Lunenburg Foundry,* privately printed, 2002.

Ghost: Building an Architectural Vision, Princeton Architectural Press (New York, NY), 2008.

Contributor to periodicals, including *Canadian Architect.*

■ Sidelights

Canadian architect Brian MacKay-Lyons has become known world-wide for designing austere structures that evoke the maritime surroundings of his native Nova Scotia. MacKay-Lyons' brand of vernacular architecture—an architecture that reflects the culture, environment, and building traditions of the region in which it exists—utilizes quality materials and imaginative site plans to echo the weatherworn barns, fishing shanties, cape-style homes, and farm outbuildings of coastal Canada. His approach to his art and his clients is equally down to earth: his buildings sometimes feature folk-art-inspired finishes and elements while his relationship with his clients—MacKay-Lyons spends hours conversing with each customer as well as many more hours on the job site with his subcontractors—is almost neighborly. Modern in style, his buildings have also gained an international following, a following he has developed through his work as a college professor. Described by *Residential Architect* writer Vernon Mays as "part mystic, part intellectual, part pragmatist, part master builder," MacKay-Lyons has created a body of work that is unique and yet also integral to its surroundings. Essy Baniassad, writing in *Brian MacKay-Lyons: Selected Projects, 1986-1997,* stated: "The work of Brian MacKay-Lyons is some of the most original work in Canada currently. It is original in that it arises out of a close observation of ordinary buildings in the Maritimes, rather than from conventions of a received vocabulary and aesthetic." "You learn general principles from studying particular things," the architect explained to Mays. "So I'm interested in not being provincial. But I think we all gain strength from where we operate."

Inspired by Childhood in Maritimes

Born in 1954, MacKay-Lyons was raised in Arcadia, a small town in southwestern Nova Scotia where French ancestors on his mother's side of the family settled four centuries before. In addition to farming, the Maritime region bases its economy on fishing, and lobster boats and shanties lined its rugged Atlantic coast. Because his parents enjoyed traveling, as a child he was able to visit cities such as Amsterdam, London, and Rome. In addition to the stark contrast from his quiet home in the Maritimes and the energy and congestion in these large urban centers, he also noted the dramatic differences in the architecture of each city. Analytical by nature, MacKay-Lyons became fascinated with the way these dramatic buildings were made.

Although it has been reported that MacKay-Lyons knew from a young age that he would become an architect, he had a momentary shift during his early teens, when a career as a drummer held more allure.

MacKay-Lyons's 1994 Leahey House is situated on the Atlantic coast near Pugwash, Nova Scotia. (James Steeves/ Atlantic Stock Images.)

Architecture won out, however, and after a program in environmental design at Nova Scotia Technical College (now Dalhousie University), he embarked upon his architecture degree. He incorporated a six-month trip to Asia into his senior-year program, studying the courtyard houses characteristic of Beijing, China, as well as the unique landscape architecture of Kyoto, Japan. Graduating in 1978 with his bachelor's degree in architecture, he was also acknowledged for his superior talent and efforts with the Royal Architectural Institute of Canada Medal. Not one to waste time, MacKay-Lyons immediately joined with one of his professors, architect Larry Richards, and set up an architectural practice in Halifax.

There was still much to learn, however. Within only a few years, MacKay-Lyons relocated to southern California to obtain his master's in architecture and Urban Design at the University of California, Los Angeles (UCLA). As he had at Nova Scotia Technical College, he excelled at his studies and earned the Dean's Award for Design. He also affiliated himself with a professor, in this case architect Charles Moore. Fascinated with Moore's ideas about indigenous building and the evolution of local construction methods, he joined Moore's collaborative Urban Innovations Group. He also attended the International Laboratory for Architecture and Urban Design, located in Siena, Italy, where he studied the Renaissance influence under Italian architect Giancarlo de Carlo.

After graduating with a master's degree in urban design, MacKay-Lyons returned to Halifax in 1983, his goal was to draw on the building traditions of his native Maritimes and contribute to the culture and economy of the region. Dale Mulfinger and Susan E. Davis noted the importance of MacKay-Lyons' childhood to his adult work as an architect. Writing in their *The Cabin: Inspiration for the Classic American Getaway*, Mulfinger and David noted: "MacKay-Lyons' work is grounded in the maritime and agrarian culture of Nova Scotia. As a young boy he watched the boat-building process and was fascinated as a large steam chest was used to contour wood into desired shapes. . . . He enjoys the workability and lightness of wood and uses it liberally to give his structures form. . . . Curved, laminated posts and beams share structural duty with standard stud framing. . . . Like the efficiency of old wooden rowboat construction . . . , MacKay-Lyons's design gains its elegance from minimalism and utility." In 1985 he established Brian MacKay-Lyons Architecture Urban Design, the firm that would become known world-wide for his many award-winning designs. Working with a ten-person staff, his offices were located in a converted gas station.

MacKay-Lyons's Messenger House is located in a residential neighborhood in Halifax, Nova Scotia. (James Steeves/Atlantic Stock Images.)

Inspired by East-Coast Vernacular

Early in his career, MacKay-Lyons focused primarily on residential structures, creating houses that rise starkly from the ground as geometric sculptures composed of wood, concrete, glass, and sheet metal. His spare aesthetic is rooted in his desire to unclutter the busy lives of modern people, removing layers of anachronistic tradition to reveal function. According to many critics, his spare, elegant aesthetic is modern almost to the point of plainness, unique to the point of being edgy. As the architect explained to Philips, this "meanness and . . . stinginess," drawn from the hardscrabble surroundings of the Maritime setting, combines to "produce . . . an interesting aesthetic." "To apply a regional label to Mackay-Lyons' houses is to give them a specificity they lack," noted Philip Arcidi in *Architecture*. "The architect assimilates the utilitarian esthetic of Nova Scotia's wood-frame structures into his work, but there are few similarities between his houses and their neighbors. His are abstract boxes with expansive glazing, corrugated metal, wood siding, and concrete block. The industrial idiom and maritime dialect, which Mackay-Lyons has absorbed, yield a panmodernism that is geographically interchangeable, and, at best, subtly indigenous."

MacKay-Lyons' designs from the mid-1980s reflect his interest in the relationship between structure and site. Located in Upper Kingsbury, Nova Scotia

MacKay-Lyons's Kutcher House is on a granite outcropping overlooking Halifax harbor. (James Steeves/Atlantic Stock Images.)

and designed in 1986, his "House on the Nova Scotia Coast Number 1" refashions the spatial weight of an existing Cape Cod house in relationship to its chimney, while its relationship to its setting is transformed through the regimented structure of an apple orchard planted on site. This house, winner of the Governor General's Award, was followed by many other award-winning designs, among them a mixed use building in downtown Halifax completed in 1990, the "House on the Nova Scotia Coast Number 12," constructed in South Shore in 1996, and many others.

In 1994 MacKay-Lyons designed the Leahey House, built in Pugwash, Nova Scotia. The 3,400 square foot residence is situated on the coast and has a rolling front lawn that leads down to the sea. The wall facing the sea is tall and vertical. The roof curves downward to a shorter wall on the land side. The main house is separated from a storage shed by a long wooden deck covered by a post-and-beam roof. A bay window provides a view of the ocean. Other features include a library, kitchen island, and stairs.

MacKay-Lyons' work during the later 1990s focused increasingly on innovation within the details of construction. Constructed in 1997 in Oxner's Head and designed as a residence for two, his "The House on the Nova Scotia Coast Number 22" is sur-

rounded on three sides by the Atlantic coast. The residence incorporates two cube-shaped structures, aligned north to south. While the main house is set toward the mainland, and overlooks a tidal marsh and the nearby community, a smaller guest house is positioned overlooking the Atlantic. The main house connects to a freestanding concrete-block fireplace, which connects the living space through the use of transparent glass panels that capture dramatic views. Giant trusses, which span the structure, are sectioned to allow the roof to slope downward, forming a huge catch-basin that drains slowly off the south-facing wall. During the few heavy rains that visit the region, water from the roof empties onto a bench visible from the interior, creating a temporary waterfall.

The 1997 work Messenger House is a residence in a Halifax neighborhood. The building is defined by a large room that takes up half the house, and which contains one wall of glass and an opposing wall that is a bookcase. The Messenger House also has a loft located above the kitchen, laundry, and storage rooms. A protruding bathroom separates the entrance area from the house's private terrace. A second-level balcony provides a view of the neighborhood, including a small church down the street. The 1,200 square-foot house is designed for a couple. The Messenger House won a Wood Design Award of Merit in 2003. The jury noted that "the house has a contemporary design well conceived in the spirit of both the landscape and the traditional indigenous buildings."

Other examples of MacKay-Lyons' work include the 1998 Kutcher House, a residence for a family of five which is located on a granite outcropping overlooking Halifax harbor. Featuring an angular standing-seam metal roof and concrete and wood walls, the long rectangular home features an open floor plan demarcated by two large fireplaces as well as massive vertical I-beams. It reveals its dramatic view of the Atlantic only after passage through an entry and onto the terrace. Cape Breton's Danielson House, which is divided into two independent structures, features an angled corrugated aluminum roof supported by exposed two-by-ten studs in the home's interior. Its efficient kitchen, bathroom, and sleeping quarters, which can be enclosed by sliding panels, are balanced by a spacious, high-ceilinged, and unheated living space, creating an energy-efficient environment.

The 1999 Howard House is "wedged in among the boulders of a hook-shaped peninsula that reaches into the sea," according to Alanna Stang and Christopher Hawthorne in their *The Green House:*

New Directions in Sustainable Architecture. The three-bedroom home in West Pennant, Nova Scotia, is 110 feet long and 12 feet wide with a dramatic roof that rises towards the sea. The exterior is covered with industrial corrugated metal. The interior is one continuous space from the covered breezeway at the back of the house to the balcony overlooking the ocean in front. Similar in appearance to the many cargo containers that have been transformed into boatsheds in the area, the Howard House has "a clean, modern, minimal look," Stang and Hawthorne wrote. The American Insitute of Architects selected Howard House for an Honor Award in 2003, calling it an "enchanting home."

Participatory Design Approach

In designing each of his residences, MacKay-Lyons attempts to reflect contrasts, not only in each unique site, but also in the culture and aesthetic of its surrounding area, where a humble fishing shanty may perch near a more upscale home. In *Plain Modern: The Architecture of Brian MacKay-Lyons,* Malcolm Quantrill dubbed the architect's oeuvre as featuring a "peculiar regionality" that reflect the ship-building and fishing traditions of the Maritimes while also acknowledging the relative affluence of his clients. While creating structures that are "accessible and legible to everyday people," the architect explained to Philips that his goal is to pinpoint "something that connects the sublime simplicity of vernacular architecture with the work of the masters—the same quality that you find in a Tuscan barn or a Baroque cathedral."

When working with clients, MacKay-Lyons joins them at the building site, after which they confer for hours over coffee at the nearest restaurant. "We stay about two hours and then leave with a concept for the house. It's like a participatory design approach, which is what I learned from Charles Moore," the architect explained to Philips. A typical MacKay-Lyons home takes, on average, about two years from conception to completion.

While MacKay-Lyons began his career focusing on privately owned homes, he has increasingly expanded his commissions to include public buildings and structures in urban areas of the Maritimes, such as the 65,000-square-foot computer science building for Dalhousie University, which he completed in 1998. A concrete structure surrounded by a zinc curtain wall that appears to float above a recessed base, the building features interior work spaces divided into alternating 30-foot and ten-foot bays, a

central staircase, and an adjoining five-story atrium. Other projects include the Ship's Company Theatre facility located in Parrsboro, Nova Scotia and completed in 2004; a dormitory at Marlboro College, Vermont; a new student center and dining hall at Southern New Hampshire University; and a new Port Campus for the Nova Scotia College of Art and Design. He has also expanded internationally,

MacKay-Lyons's award-winning Howard House is on a peninsula in West Pennant, Nova Scotia. (James Steeves/Atlantic Stock Images.)

designing a new Canadian embassy and official residence in Dhaka, Bangladesh.

Expansion Prompts New Creative Alliance

The expansion in his design work prompted a 2004 move from the converted gas station to a new 5,000-square-foot, two storey building featuring a vast studio space housing a 40-foot-long drawing table. Two years after the move, in the fall of 2006, MacKay-Lyons partnered with architect and long-time colleague Talbot Sweetapple, forming MacKay-Lyons Sweetapple Architects, Ltd. This partnership reflected the firm's transition from small-scale, residential projects to larger-scaled, public structures. The firm, still located in Halifax, employs several architects as well as interns and the administrative personnel necessary to oversee projects in Canada and the United States, as well as internationally.

If you enjoy the works of Brian MacKay-Lyons, you may also want to check out the following:

Three architects who also design houses for specific environments: Tom Kundig, whose houses are found in the Pacific Northwest, Rick Joy, who designs desert houses in Arizona, and Australian architect Glenn Murcutt.

Stays Connected through Ghost Lab

In addition to his design work, MacKay-Lyons is also a full professor of architecture at Dalhousie University, his alma mater. He has also lectured extensively, both in Canada and abroad, and his works have been published in dozens of architectural journals. Each summer, beginning in 1994, he joins twenty select students, as well as teachers and working architects, for the two-week design/build workshop known as Ghost Lab. Motivated by his belief that the best training comes in the field, and drawing on the apprenticeship tradition of the medieval guilds in which knowledge was passed on through practical experience, Ghost Labs stress a

three-part discipline: landscape, construction, and community. Located in 400-year-old stone ruins on MacKay-Lyons' farm, the workshop offers participants the chance to create such projects as a long platform demonstrating regional settlement patterns and a wind tube designed to teach students about wind shear. The completion of each project is highlighted by a community-wide celebration. *Ghost: Building an Architectural Vision*, MacKay-Lyons's 2008 title, documents the Ghost Lab project as it has developed over some fourteen years.

Writing in *Blueprint*, Oliver Lowenstein summed up: MacKay-Lyons's "visually striking, aesthetically simple, modernist buildings, built in equally striking locations throughout the Canadian Maritime Provinces, have brought attention from many far-flung parts of the world." During his career, MacKay-Lyons has been acknowledged for his innovative design with numerous awards. In addition to Governor General Medals, he has also received awards from the American Institute of Architects, and has been named a fellow of both the Royal Architectural Institute of Canada and the Royal Canadian Academy of Arts. Other awards include Lieutenant Governor's Medals of Excellence, *Canadian Architect* awards, and Wood Design awards. In 2001 MacKay-Lyons was made an honorary fellow of the American Institute of Architects, an honor accorded to only seven architects worldwide each year.

■ Biographical and Critical Sources

BOOKS

Carter, Brian, editor, *Brian MacKay-Lyons: Selected Projects, 1986-1997*, TUNS Press (Halifax, Nova Scotia, Canada), 1998, 2nd edition, 2000.

Kalman, Harold, editor, *The Concise History of Canadian Architecture*, Oxford University Press (Toronto, Ontario, Canada), 2000.

Mulfinger, Dale, and Susan E. Davis, *The Cabin: Inspiration for the Classic American Getaway*, Taunton Press (Newtown, CT), 2001.

Quantrill, Malcolm, *Plain Modern: The Architecture of Brian MacKay-Lyons*, Princeton Architectural Press, 2005.

Slavid, Ruth, *Wood Houses*, Laurence King Publishing, 2006.

Stang, Alanna, and Christopher Hawthorne, *The Green House: New Directions in Sustainable Architecture*, Princeton Architectural Press (New York, NY), 2005.

PERIODICALS

Architectural Research Quarterly, September, 2001, Brian Carter, "Architecture at a Threshold: Three Houses by Brian MacKay-Lyons," pp. 39-52.

Architecture, November, 1999, Philip Arcidi, "2 If by Sea," p. 112.

Architecture Week, January 29, 2003, "AIA Honor Awards 2003"; September 10, 2003, "Wood Design Awards."

Blueprint, December, 2006, Oliver Lowenstein, "Brian MacKay-Lyons: Nova Scotia," pp. 40-44.

Canadian House and Home, October, 1993, Larry Richards, "The Surprising Barns of Brian MacKay-Lyons," pp. 74-80.

Canadian Architect, Volume 31, number 11, 1986, Brian MacKay-Lyons, "A Sense of Place," pp. 20-21.

Globe and Mail (Toronto, Ontario, Canada), April 12, 1997, Rhys Philips, profile of MacKay-Lyons; September 13, 2000, Lisa Rochon, "A Vision Grown from Nova Scotia Roots."

Metropolis, April, 2000, Paul Makovsky, "New Architecture Faces the Future" (interview), pp. 74-75.

Montreal Gazette, July 4, 1997, Rhys Phillips, "Brian MacKay-Lyons' Award-winning Coast Houses," pp. 1, 5.

Progressive Architecture, August, 1995, Thomas Fisher, "Folk Tech: Brian MacKay-Lyons' Vernacular Architecture for Agrarian Areas," p. 62.

Residential Architect, July, 2004, Vernon Mays, "Calm Things in a Cluttered World: Brian MacKay-Lyons' Just Plain Modernism Rises above Arguments of Style," pp. 60-68.

ONLINE

MacKay-Lyons Sweetapple Architects Web site, http://www.mlsarchitects.ca/ (April 1, 2008).*

(Photograph by Karen Shell. Reproduced by permission.)

Stephenie Meyer

■ Personal

Born 1973, in CT; married; husband's name Christiaan "Pancho"; children: Gabe, Seth, Eli. *Education:* Brigham Young University, B.A. *Religion:* Mormon.

■ Addresses

Home—Phoenix, AZ.

■ Career

Writer.

■ Awards, Honors

Top Ten Fantasy Books for YAs, *Booklist,* Editor's Choice, *New York Times,* Best Book of the Year list, *Publishers Weekly,* Top Ten Best Books for Young Adults and Top Ten Books for Reluctant Readers lists, American Library Association, and Hot List pick, *Teen Readers,* all 2005, all for *Twilight.*

■ Writings

"TWILIGHT" SERIES

Twilight, Little, Brown (New York, NY), 2005.
New Moon, Little, Brown (New York, NY), 2006.
Eclipse, Little, Brown (New York, NY), 2007.
Breaking Dawn, Little, Brown (New York, NY), 2008.

OTHER

The Host, Little, Brown (New York, NY), 2007.

Contributor to the anthology *Prom Night from Hell,* HarperCollins (New York, NY), 2007.

■ Adaptations

Twilight has been optioned for a feature film by MTV Films/Maverick Films.

■ Sidelights

Stephenie Meyer is the creator of the phenomenally successful "Twilight" series about a teenaged vampire. The first three books in the series—

Twilight, New Moon, and *Eclipse*—have sold over 2.5 million copies, have found their way onto bestseller lists across America, and had translation rights sold in thirty two foreign countries. Often compared to fellow novelist Anne Rice, and with sales reminiscent of J.K. Rowling, Meyer's romantic vampire novels have attracted millions of teenage girl readers. As Cindy Dobrez noted in *Booklist,* Meyer's "Twilight" books "began as a simple vampire series and quickly became a megaselling publishing phenomenon."

Meyer was born in Connecticut in 1973. Her family moved to Phoenix, Arizona, when she was four years old. Meyer told Cynthia Leitich Smith for *Cynsations:* "I am the second of six children. I think that coming from such a large family has given me a lot of insight into different personality types—my siblings sometimes crop up as characters in my stories." "I went to high school," Meyer related in an article posted on her Home Page, "in Scottsdale,

In Meyer's 2006 novel *New Moon,* **Bella's boyfriend is found to be a werewolf.** (Little, Brown, 2006. Jacket photo © John Grant/ Getty Images. Reproduced by permission.)

Arizona, the kind of place where every fall a few girls would come back to school with new noses and there were Porsches in the student lot (for the record, I have my original nose, and never had a car until after I was in my twenties)." After winning a National Merit Scholarship, she attended Brigham Young University in Provo, Utah. "On the list of the biggest party schools in the country," Meyer stated, "BYU consistently and proudly finishes dead last."

A Dreamy Beginning

Meyer got married and gave birth to three sons before she embarked on a writing career. Meyer told Smith: "I have a husband and three young sons who all are slightly bewildered with my sudden career shift from mommy to writer. A lifelong reader, I didn't start writing until I was twenty-nine, but once I began typing I've never been able to stop." The whole thing happened as the result of a dream. In the dream, a young girl was talking with a handsome young vampire. Meyer explained to William Morris of *A Motley Vistion:* "I know the exact date of my dream—it was June 2, 2003. . . . I woke up that morning with a dream fresh in my head. The dream was vivid, strong, colorful. . . . It was a conversation between a boy and a girl which took place in a beautiful, sunny meadow in the middle of a dark forest. The boy and the girl were in love with each other, and they were discussing the problems involved with that love, seeing that she was human and he was a vampire. The boy was more beautiful than the meadow, and his skin sparkled like diamonds in the sun. He was so gentle and polite, and yet the potential for violence was very strong, inherent to the scene. I delayed getting out of bed for a while, just thinking through the dream and imagining what might happen next. Finally, I had to get up, but the dream stayed in my head all through my morning obligations. As soon as I had a free moment, I sat down at the computer and started writing it out so I wouldn't forget it. I wrote ten pages that day—what eventually would be Chapter 13—and that night I started into my imaginings of where the story would have gone if I hadn't woken up. I wrote every single day for the rest of that summer, and finished the book near the end of August."

At first, Meyer told only her sister about the story, letting her read the first few pages. The sister urged her to finish the story and send it to a publisher. As Bob Minzesheimer wrote in *USA Today:* "In one of those rare success stories that inspire unpublished writers, Meyer found an agent via the Web and got a contract." Speaking to Kathy Cano Murillo of the *Arizona Republic,* Meyer explained: "My agent had sent it out to a lot of people on the Wednesday before Thanksgiving. I was not expecting to hear back, but she called Monday morning and said the editor at Little, Brown read it over the weekend on an airplane and wants to make [an] offer." The book sold for 500,000 dollars; film rights were sold as well.

Meyer's *Twilight* propelled her into the ranks of top-selling writers for teenage readers. The novel is a vampire love story featuring the teen narrator Isabella "Bella" Swan and her love interest, Edward Cullen. Bella has just moved from Phoenix to the small town of Forks, Washington, and is now living with her police chief-father. The first day at her new school she is attracted to Edward, who she soon discovers is a vampire, but one who has trained himself to feed only on animal, not human, blood. However, trouble soon arises in the form of another group of vampires who have no such compunctions. While the novel concerns vampires, the story is more romance than horror. Amanda Craig noted on her Web site that *Twilight* is the "chaste yet intensely erotic description of a teenager's love-affair with a vampire." Referring to the novel's romantic story, Meyer told Rick Margolis in the *School Library Journal:* "I do like to say it's a vampire book for people who don't like vampire books."

Twilight won critical praise from many quarters. A *Publishers Weekly* contributor, for example, called it a "riveting first novel, propelled by suspense and romance in equal parts," as well as a "tantalizing debut." Similarly, Hillias J. Martin, writing in the *School Library Journal,* called the book "realistic, subtle, succinct, and easy to follow, [a novel that] will have readers dying to sink their teeth into it." "*Twilight* builds to a dramatic and suspenseful second half, not to mention a nail-biting conclusion," according to Linda M. Castellitto in *BookPage.* For *Booklist* contributor Ilene Cooper, *Twilight* is a "dark romance [that] seeps into the soul."

In Meyer's 2006 sequel, *New Moon,* Bella loses her vampire lover only to be courted by a teen who is an incipient werewolf. The Cullens move from town, fearful that they cannot control themselves and that they may do harm to Bella. Months later she comes out of her depression and strikes up a friendship with a Native American named Jacob. Meanwhile, she is also pursued by an evil vampire whose presence triggers the lycanthropy in Jacob's genes. While all this is happening, Edward is seemingly determined to die at the hands of an Italian vampire cult. *Booklist* contributor Cindy Dobrez predicted that "teens will relish this new adventure and hunger for more," while *Kliatt* reviewer Claire Rosser similarly concluded that young readers "will be eager to share [Bella's] passion and her adventures."

Eclipse finds Bella faced with a difficult choice. She must decide whether to become, like Edward, a vampire or to stay human. Bella knows that her choice will spark a war between the vampires and the werewolves. Meanwhile, Seattle is being terrorized by a serial killer and a female vampire is out for revenge. When Bella is in danger, Edward and Jacob find themselves forging an unlikely alliance to save her. Norah Piehl of *TeenReads.com* noted that, "since Meyer's books have always been more of a love story than a vampire series, . . . many readers will appreciate *Eclipse's* more firm grounding in reality, largely focusing on character realization rather than on melodramatic, metaphysical conflicts." "The supernatural elements," wrote a critic for *Publishers Weekly,* "accentuate the ordinary human dramas of growing up." "Just like the first two novels," Janis Flint-Ferguson wrote in *Kliatt,* "this one is hard to put down as it draws the reader into heart pounding gothic romance tinged with mythic horror." In its first day on sale, *Eclipse* sold some 150,000 copies. Meyer is expected to bring her "Twilight" series to a conclusion with the fourth novel in the series, *Breaking Dawn.*

Fans Reenact a Vampire Prom

Meyer's books have attracted a great number of devoted fans. According to Megan Tingley, Meyer's editor at Little, Brown: "Stephenie has tapped into something very deep in her readers, and they respond on an emotional level. She really understands the hopes and fears of teenage girls." In Pasadena, California, a "vampire prom" was held, just like the prom that Bella and Edward go to in *Twilight.* Tickets for the event sold out in seven hours, so a second prom, later the same day, was added. Hundreds of fans, mostly girls, showed up at both events and, over the course of several hours, Meyer autographed some 1,000 copies of her books.

If you enjoy the works of Stephenie Meyer, you may also want to check out the following books:

Patricia Briggs, *Moon Called,* 2006.
Rachel Caine, *Glass Houses,* 2006.
Lewis Aleman, *Cold Streak,* 2007.

Success has not drastically changed Meyer's life. "In my everyday, normal life, it's just something I don't think about very much," Meyer told Cecelia Good-

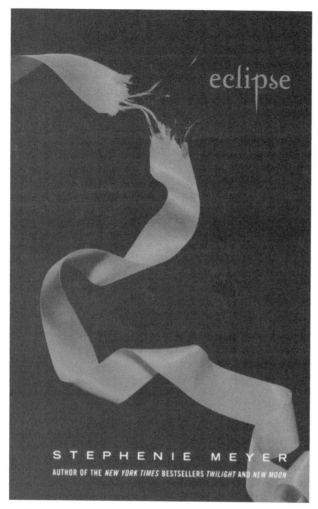

Bella must decide whether to become a vampire in Meyer's 2007 novel *Eclipse*. (Little, Brown, 2007. Jacket photo © Roger Hagadone. Reproduced by permission.)

now in the *Seattle Post-Intelligencer.* "She still manages to stay home with the kids," Megan Irwin wrote in the *Phoenix New Times.* "During the day, she works on editing her novels—a task she can leave to intervene in a snack-time crisis—and does her fresh writing at night after the kids are in bed." Speaking with Gregory Kirschling in *Entertainment Weekly,* Meyer explained the appeal of her books: "I didn't realize the books would appeal to people so broadly. I think some of it's because Bella is an everygirl. She's not a hero, and she doesn't know the difference between Prada and whatever else is out there. She doesn't always have to be cool, or wear the coolest clothes ever. She's normal. And there aren't a lot of girls in literature that are normal. Another thing is that Bella's a good girl, which is just sort of how I imagine teenagers, because that's how my teenage years were."

Speaking to Smith about what young writers should do, Meyer explained: "If you love to write, then write. Don't let your goal be having a novel published, let your goal be enjoying your stories. However, if you finish your story and you want to share it, be brave about it. Don't doubt your story's appeal. If you are a good reader, and you know what is interesting, and your story is interesting to you, then trust in that. If I would have realized that the stories in my head would be as intriguing to others as they were to me, I would probably have started writing sooner. Believe in your own taste."

■ Biographical and Critical Sources

PERIODICALS

Arizona Republic, October 17, 2005, Kathy Cano Murillo, "A Vampire Bit Her with Writing Bug."

Booklist, November 15, 2005, Ilene Cooper, review of *Twilight,* p. 58; March 1, 2006, Karen Cruze, review of *Twilight* audiobook edition, p. 105; July 1, 2006, Cindy Dobrez, review of *New Moon,* p. 51; December 1, 2006, Karen Cruze, review of *New Moon* audiobook edition, p. 71; September 15, 2007, Michael Cart, "Everlasting Love," p. 58, and Cindy Dobrez, review of *Eclipse,* p. 74; March 1, 2008, Jennifer Mattson, review of *The Host,* p. 29.

BookPage, October, 2005, Linda M. Castellitto, "Dreams of High School Vampires Inspire a Toothsome Debut."

Entertainment Weekly, August 10, 2007, Gregory Kirschling, "The Q&A: Stephenie Meyer's 'Twilight' Zone."

Globe & Mail (Toronto, Ontario, Canada), September 8, 2007, review of *Eclipse,* p. D18.

Journal of Adolescent & Adult Literacy, April, 2006, James Blasingame, review of *Twilight,* p. 628.

Kirkus Reviews, September 15, 2005, review of *Twilight,* p. 1031; May 15, 2006, review of *New Moon,* p. S22; July 15, 2006, review of *New Moon,* p. 727; March 1, 2008, review of *The Host.*

Kliatt, September, 2005, Michele Winship, review of *Twilight,* p. 11; May, 2006, Jodi L. Israel, review of *Twilight* audiobook edition, p. 51; September, 2006, Claire Rosser, review of *New Moon,* p. 15; November, 2006, Michele Winship, review of *Twilight,* p. 29; March, 2007, Jodi L. Israel, review of *New Moon* audiobook edition, p. 52; November, 2007, Janis Flint-Ferguson, review of *Eclipse,* p. 12.

Miami Herald, September 8, 2007, Sue Corbett, "The Hero's Tall, Dark and Toothsome."

New York Times Book Review, February 12, 2006, Elizabeth Spires, review of *Twilight,* p. 17; August 12, 2007, Liesl Schillinger, review of *Eclipse,* p. 19.

Phoenix New Times, July 12, 2007, Megan Irwin, "Charmed: Stephenie Meyer's Vampire Romance Novels Made a Mormon Mom an International Sensation."

Publishers Weekly, December 8, 2003, John F. Baker, "LB Preempts 'Anne Rice for Teens,'" p. 12; July 18, 2005, review of *Twilight,* p. 207; October 31, 2005, Jennifer M. Brown, "*Twilight* in Translation," p. 28; November 14, 2005, review of *Twilight* audiobook edition, p. 72; July 17, 2006, review of *New Moon,* p. 159; December 11, 2006, review of *New Moon* audiobook edition, p. 73; July 23, 2007, Rachel Deahl, "Little, Brown Has Big Plans for Meyer"; August 20, 2007, review of *Eclipse,* p. 69; March 31, 2008, review of *The Host,* p. 42.

School Library Journal, October, 2005, Rick Margolis, "Love at First Bite," p. 37, Hillias J. Martin, review of *Twilight,* p. 166; February, 2006, Charli Osborne, review of *Twilight* audiobook edition, p. 76; August, 2006, Hillias J. Martin, review of *New Moon,* p. 125; March, 2007, Francisca Goldsmith, review of *New Moon* audiobook edition, p. 80.

Seattle Post-Intelligencer, August 6, 2007, Cecelia Goodnow, "Stephenie Meyer's Forks-based Saga of Teen Vampire Love Is Now a Global Hit."

USA Today, August 16, 2007, Bob Minzesheimer, "Vampire Tale Takes Bite Out of 'Potter,'" p. 1D.

Virginian Pilot, August 12, 2007, Edward Nowatka, "Teen Series on Vampires Eclipses Rivals," p. E5.

Voice of Youth Advocates, October, 2005, Angelica Delgado, review of *New Moon.*

Wall Street Journal, August 10, 2007, Jeffrey A. Trachtenberg, "Booksellers Find Life after Harry In a Vampire Novel," p. B1.

ONLINE

Amanda Craig Web site, http://www.amandacraig.com/ (January, 2006), "A Quick Bite—Vampires Resurgent."

A Motley Vision, http://www.motleyvision.org/ (October 26, 2005), William Morris, "Interview: *Twilight* Author Stephenie Meyer."

Cynsations, http://cynthialeitichsmith.blogspot.com/ (March 27, 2006), Cynthia Leitich Smith, "Author Interview: Stephenie Meyer on *Twilight.*"

Stephenie Meyer Home Page, http://www.stepheniemeyer.com (March 20, 2007).

Stephenie Meyer MySpace Page, http://www.myspace.com/52906350 (March 20, 2008).

TeenReads.com, (March 20, 2008), biography of Meyer and Norah Piehl, reviews of *Twilight, Eclipse,* and *New Moon.*

Sarah Monette

■ Personal

Born in Oak Ridge, TN; married. *Education:* University of Wisconsin—Madison, Ph.D.

■ Addresses

Agent—Jack Byrne, Sternig & Byrne Literary Agency, 2370 S. 107th St., Apt. 4, Milwaukee, WI 53227-2036. *E-mail*—labyrinthine@sarahmonette.com.

■ Career

Writer.

■ Awards, Honors

Spectrum Award for short fiction.

■ Writings

FANTASY NOVELS

Mélusine, Ace Books (New York, NY), 2005.
The Virtu, Ace Books (New York, NY), 2006.

The Mirador, Ace Books (New York, NY), 2007.
(With Elizabeth Bear) *A Companion to Wolves,* Tor (New York, NY), 2007.
Corambis, Ace Books (New York, NY), 2009.

OTHER

The Bone Key (story collection), Prime Books, 2007.

Contributor to books, including *The Queen in Winter,* Berkley Trade (New York, NY), 2002, *The Year's Best Fantasy and Horror XIX,* St. Martin's Griffin (New York, NY), 2006, and *So Fey: Queer Faery Fiction,* Haworth Positronic Press (Binghampton, NY), 2007. Contributor to periodicals, including *Alchemy, Lady Churchill's Rosebud Wristlet, Ideomancer, Lovecraft's Weird Mysteries, Tales of the Unanticipated, All Hallows: The Journal of the Ghost Story Society, Cemetery Dance, Paradox, Magazine of Speculative Poetry, Fantasy Magazine,* and *Strange Horizons.*

■ Sidelights

In her novels, Sarah Monette has created and explored the fantastical city of Mélusine, "a city both sordid and splendid, rich in history and layered with corruption," as Susan Salpini described it in the *School Library Journal.* Monette has earned praise for the beauty of the setting and for the believability of her characters. According to Romie Stott in a review for *Reflection's Edge,* "the things she does well, she does better than anyone."

Monette was born in Oak Ridge, Tennessee, where much of the work on the first atomic bomb was done. "I've loved fantasy since my father read me L. Frank Baum's Oz books, which he started doing when I was very very small," Monette said in an interview with the *Writer Unboxed* Web site. "There's never been any doubt in my mind that that's what I wanted to write." She wrote her first story at the age of eleven. "The first story I ever wrote was a ghost story," she told *Writer Unboxed*. "The second story I ever wrote was an Epic Fantasy Quest." Speaking of that first work, Monette explained: "In the beginning the only thing I wanted to accomplish was to have fun, and I'm still trying to hold onto that."

A Burglar and an Aristocrat

Monette's debut book, *Mélusine,* is an "extraordinary first fantasy novel" that tells the story of two radi-

In the 2006 novel *The Virtu,* Sarah Monette tells of a quest to locate a powerful magical artifact. (Ace Books, 2006. Jacket illustration © Judy York. Used by permission of Penguin Group (USA) Inc., and the illustrator.)

cally different characters from opposite ends of the social and political spectrum in the city of Mélusine, according to a *Publishers Weekly* reviewer. Mildmay the Fox is a citizen of the city's lower regions, a burglar and professional assassin who survives in a rough, impoverished world deep within the city. Though Mildmay sometimes kills for a living, he still tries to live an honorable life. One of his past targets, however, may have been a mistake: a wizard, or hocus, whose death has made Mildmay hated by magic-users in the city. He is now outcast by a death curse that would activate if he ever again comes near Mirador, the city's fort and area of concentrated magical power.

In counterpoint to Mildmay is the aristocratic Felix Harrowgate, an elegant, well-known Mirador resident who associates with the nobility and with those who hold extravagant wealth and power. The schemer behind Felix's stylish and powerful exterior is Malkar, who raised Felix from his lower-class beginnings to his upper-crust celebrity status. Felix's training was brutal, however, and he still feels the effects of his past when he occasionally falls uncontrollably into a bout of madness. When Felix is exposed by the scheming Robert of Hermione as being a former slave and prostitute, his status is shattered. Remarkably, he simply walks away from the life he once knew. Meanwhile, Mildmay commits a burglary-for-hire, but he cannot escape the feeling that he has been caught within a wizard's spell.

Brought together while fleeing from their respective ill-fortunes, Felix and Mildmay join forces in order to survive the downturn in their luck. As they travel together, they learn that their pasts are unexpectedly interwoven, and that they have more in common than either suspected. They encounter the strange magic that has recently infiltrated the city, and come to suspect Robert of Hermione of plotting to destroy Mélusine. A rugged journey far from the familiar confines of the city brings them both into confrontation with a mutual enemy.

The story's narrative shifts between Felix and Mildmay, until the two main characters meet in the later part of the book. A reviewer on the *GLBT Fantasy Fiction* Web site noted that the "two protagonists are built up in our minds with painstaking care." The reviewer continued: "The texture of the narrative itself, no matter whose head we were in, was lush and mesmerizing, so carefully constructed that I often found myself rereading passages as if letting the smoky flavors of a good red wine roll over my tongue." Paula Luedtke, writing in *Booklist,* commented that, "while Monette's story engages, her characters deserve a standing ovation." A reviewer

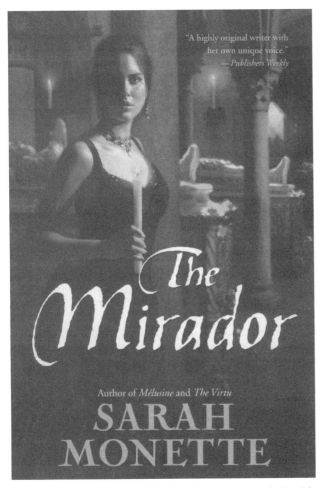

Monette's *The Mirador* is set in a fortress crowded with spies and magicians. (Ace Books, 2007. Jacket illustration © Judy York. Used by permission of Penguin Group (USA) Inc., and the illustrator.)

in *Library Bookwatch* called the novel an "outstanding story which focuses on close ties and alienation alike."

The Virtu, Monette's 2006 novel, continues the story of Felix and Mildmay. Still recovering from the effects of having his magical power stripped by his sadistic master, Felix enlists Mildmay into trying to locate and repair the Virtu, a magical artifact that protects the city of Mélusine. Jackie Cassada in the *Library Journal* dubbed the book "an engagingly intelligent fantasy." "The magic is delightfully inventive, and the world Monette creates includes some truly intriguing aspects . . . ," Paul Luedtke wrote in *Booklist*. "Perhaps best of all is Monette's authorial voice, abundantly blessed with originality, sophistication, and artistry."

In *The Mirador*, Felix has found a new place at the court of the city of Mélusine. The city's fort, Mira-

dor, is the only bulwark standing against an invasion by a neighboring country. Mélusine has become crowded with spies and magicians, all seeking to gain an advantage during the troubled times. When Mildmay's lover, the actress Mehitabel, is forced into spying for a band of wizards, Felix finds himself drawn into dangerous intrigue. "I'm not sure that I really like either Felix or Mildmay," Don D'Ammassa admitted in a review for *Critical Mass*, "but I like reading about them. They're far more credible and vivid than most of the high minded nobles, dedicated or evil wizards, and lovable but roguish thieves that populate most fictional fantasy worlds." Cassada praised Monette's ability to "evoke the wonders of an ancient and mysterious city and its memorable inhabitants."

A Collaboration

Monette teamed with Elizabeth Bear to write the 2007 title *A Companion to Wolves*. In a world based on Norse and German mythology, the people rely on certain men, called wolfcarls, who can telepathically bond with wolves. The wolves help to protect the people from violent trolls and other monsters. Isolfr, a young wolfcarl, and a wolf queen find themselves in the forefront of the battle to save their tribe. According to Regina Schroeder in *Booklist*, Monette and Bear "have taken one of the most escapist of fantasy subgenres, in which humans and animals meld, and turned it into something powerful and surprisingly deeply human." A *Publishers Weekly* critic wrote: "The meticulously crafted setting and powerful, often moving rendition of characters and relationships—human and nonhuman alike—result in a brutal and beautiful novel about the meaning of honor." D'Ammassa found the novel to be "extremely well written, and more suspenseful than most contemporary fantasy I've read." Cassada described it as a "well-written and emotionally powerful quasi-Nordic fantasy."

If you enjoy the works of Sarah Monette, you may also want to check out the following books:

Emma Bull, *Territory*, 2007.
Naomi Novik, *Empire of Ivory*, 2007.
Scott Lynch, *Red Seas Under Red Skies*, 2007.

Monette turned to short fiction with her collection *The Bone Key*, which contains a series of stories about Kyle Murchison Booth. Booth is a shy, quiet man who works as the archivist at the Samuel Mather Parrington Museum, and the stories are homages to the works of horror writer H.P. Lovecraft and ghost story master M.R. James. In one story, the helpful Booth attempts to bring a friend's dead wife back to life, with terrible results. In other stories, he investigates a skeleton found sealed within the walls of the museum, looks into a house haunted by the ghost of a little girl, and discovers the truth about his own parents' premature deaths. These are "bizarre, disturbing, wonder-filled tales," Schroeder believed. A reviewer for *OF Blog of the Fallen* called them "memorable and spine-chilling stories." The critic for *Publishers Weekly* concluded: "Cerebral, ethereal and stylishly understated, this entrancing collection will appeal to fans of literary horror, dark fantasy and supernatural mystery."

In an interview for *Fantasy Book Spot*, Monette explained why she writes fantasy: "As a reader, I'm easily bored by realism; given the choice, I will *always* pick the story that promises to explore beyond the limits of the everyday. In that sense, my tastes as a writer merely reflects my tastes as a reader, but I still can't explain why I'm drawn so strongly to that kind of story. Realism—especially realism as it is practiced by contemporary writers—is a box, and a rather small box at that. I don't like confining my imagination in a box. Which is not to say that excellent stories cannot be told in that box, or that there's anything wrong with staying in the box. Just that I'm not comfortable there."

■ Biographical and Critical Sources

PERIODICALS

Booklist, August, 2005, Paula Luedtke, review of *Mélusine*, p. 2009; July 1, 2006, Paul Luedtke, review of *The Virtu*, p. 43; September 1, 2007, Regina Schroeder, review of *A Companion to Wolves*, p. 65; December 15, 2007, Regina Schroeder, review of *The Bone Key*, p. 32.

Library Bookwatch, October, 2005, review of *Mélusine*.

Library Journal, June 15, 2006, Jackie Cassada, review of *The Virtu*, p. 63; July 1, 2007, Jackie Cassada, review of *The Mirador*, p. 82; September 15, 2007, Jackie Cassada, review of *A Companion to Wolves*, p. 54.

Magazine of Fantasy and Science Fiction, March, 2006, Robert K.J. Killheffer, review of *Mélusine*, p. 38.

Publishers Weekly, July 11, 2005, review of *Mélusine*, p. 67; May 15, 2006, review of *The Virtu*, p. 53; June 25, 2007, review of *The Mirador*, p. 39; August 20, 2007, review of *A Companion to Wolves*, p. 52; November 19, 2007, review of *The Bone Key*, p. 42.

School Library Journal, December, 2005, Susan Salpini, review of *Mélusine*, p. 178.

ONLINE

Best Reviews Web site, http://www.thebestreviews.com/ (November 28, 2005), Harriet Klausner, review of *Mélusine*.

BookPage, http://www.bookpage.com/ (August, 2007), Gavin J. Grant, review of *The Mirador*.

Critical Mass, http://www.dondammassa.com/index.htm/ (April 29, 2007), Don D'Ammassa, review of *The Mirador*; (May 30, 2007), Don D'Ammassa, review of *A Companion to Wolves*.

Fantasy Book Spot, http://www.fantasybookspot.com/ (August 26, 2005), interview with Monette.

GLBT Fantasy Fiction Web site, http://www.glbtfantasy.com/ (November 28, 2005), review of *Mélusine*.

OF Blog of the Fallen, http://ofblog.blogspot.com/ (August 3, 2007), "Interview with Sarah Monette, Part I"; (August 7, 2007), "Interview with Sarah Monette, Part II"; (November 13, 2007), review of *The Bone Key*.

Rambles, http://www.rambles.net/ (September 2, 2006), Laurie Thayer, review of *The Virtu*.

Reflection's Edge, http://www.reflectionsedge.com/ (October 3, 2007), Romie Stott, review of *Mélusine*.

Sarah Monette Home Page, http://www.sarahmonette.com (November 28, 2005).

Sarah Monette Web log, http://www.livejournal.com/users/truepenny (November 28, 2005).

SFF Net Web site, http://www.sff.net/ (November 28, 2005), biography of Sarah Monette.

Writer Unboxed, http://writerunboxed.com/ (February 23, 2007), Kathleen Bolton, "Author Interview: Sarah Monette, Part One"; (March 2, 2007), Kathleen Bolton, "Author Interview: Sarah Monette, Part Two."*

(Copyright © Bettmann/Corbis.)

Louise Nevelson

■ Personal

Born September 23, 1900 (some sources cite 1899), in Kiev, Russia; immigrated to the United States, 1905; died April 17, 1988, in New York, NY; daughter of Isaac (a real estate entrepreneur, contractor, and lumber merchant) and Minna Sadie Berliawsky; married Charles S. Nevelson (a shipping broker) in 1920 (divorced); children: Myron. *Education:* Studied voice with Estelle Liebling and drawing and painting with Theresa Bernstein and William Meyerowitz, New York City, 1920-28; studied art with Kimon Nicolaides and Kenneth Hayes Miller at Art Students League, New York City, 1928-30, with Hans Hofmann at Hofmann School, Munich, Germany, 1931-32, and with Stanley William and others at Atelier 17, New York City, 1953-55.

■ Career

Sculptor, painter, and printmaker. Sang in cafes and worked as movie extra in Berlin, Germany, and Vienna, Austria, 1931-32; assistant to Diego Rivera in New York City, 1932-33; began exhibiting work in New York City galleries, 1933; art instructor at Education Alliance School of Art, New York City,

1937, New York School for the Deaf, and Great Neck Adult Education Program, Great Neck, NY; traveled to Mexico and Central America, 1946-47 and 1951-52; began selling works to major museums, 1956; printmaker at Tamarind Workshops in Los Angeles, CA, 1963. One-woman and group exhibitions of sculpture, paintings, and prints held in numerous cities around the world, including New York, Paris, France, Toronto, Ontario, Stockholm, Sweden, Brussels, Belgium, Berlin, and Florence, Italy. Commissioned sculptor of works for South Mall, Albany, NY, 1968, World Trade Center, New York City, 1972, and for numerous others. Works represented in permanent collections, including Art Institute of Chicago, Museum of Modern Art, Israel Museum, and Tate Gallery.

■ Member

International Association of Artists (vice president), National Artists Equity (president, 1962-64), American Abstract Artists (member of executive board), National Historic Sites Foundation (head of advisory council on art), National Association of Women Artists, American Academy and Institute of Arts and Letters, Federation of Modern Painters and Sculptors (vice president, 1962-64), New York Artists Equity (president, 1957-59), Sculptors Guild of New York (vice president), Art Students League of New York.

■ Awards, Honors

United Society of Artists Grand Prize, 1959; Mr. and Mrs. Frank G. Logan Prize, Chicago Institute of Art, 1960; Sculpture International Grand Prize, Tarcuato Di Tella Institute's Center of Visual Arts, Buenos Aires, 1962; Tamarind fellowship, 1963; Citizens Achievement Award, city of New York, 1966; D.F.A. from Western College for Women, 1966, Art Institute of Boston, 1971, Minneapolis Society of Fine Arts, 1971, and Smith College, 1973; MacDowell Colony Gold Medal, 1969; Skowhegan School of Painting and Sculpture Prize, 1971; creative arts award for sculpture, Brandeis University, 1971; D.H. from Hobart and William Smith Colleges, 1971, and Hamline University, 1971; received National Medal of Arts from President Ronald Reagan; a series of five postage stamps depicting Nevelson's artworks were issued by the United States Post Office in 2000; Louise Nevelson Plaza in New York City, which contains seven of her sculptures, is named in her honor.

■ Writings

CATALOGS

Nevelson, Pace Gallery (New York, NY), 1964.
Louise Nevelson, Galerie Daniel Gervis (Paris, France), 1967.
Nevelson: Wood Sculptures, Dutton (New York, NY), 1973.
(And author of text) *Louise Nevelson: Centre national d'art contemporain,* preface by Frances Beatty and Gilbert Brownstone, Weber (Paris, France), 1974.
Louise Nevelson: Graphica, Napoli, Villa Pignatelli, introduction by Raffaello Causa and Gene Baro, Societa Editrice Napoletana, 1976.
Louise Nevelson: A Loan Exhibition, text by Jan Ernst Adlmann, William A. Farnsworth Library and Art Museum (Rockland, ME), 1979.
Louise Nevelson: The Fourth Dimension, Phoenix Art Museum (Phoenix, AZ), 1980.
Louise Nevelson: Atmospheres and Environments, introduction by Edward Albee, C.N. Potter (New York, NY), 1980.
Louise Nevelson: Silent Music, Galerie Gmurzynska (Koln, Germany), 1995.
Louise Nevelson: Sculpture, 1957-1987, Pace Wildenstein (New York, NY), 1997.
Louise Nevelson: Sculpture & Collage: October 1-October 30, 1999, Locks Gallery (Philadelphia, PA), 1999.
Louise Nevelson: Sculpture of the '50s and '60s: March 18-April 27, 2002, Pace Wildenstein (New York, NY), 2002.

OTHER

Louise Nevelson: Prints and Drawings, 1953-1966 (monograph), text by Una E. Johnson, Brooklyn Museum, 1967.
Nevelson: The Prints, introduction and commentary by Gene Baro, Pace Editions, 1974.
(With Diana MacKown) *Dawns and Dusks: Taped Conversations with Diana MacKown,* Scribner (New York, NY), 1976.

■ Sidelights

After a long struggle to get her sculpture noticed by the art world, Louise Nevelson finally won recognition for her work in 1959, at the age of 60, when she was invited to participate in a group exhibition at New York's Museum of Modern Art. "By the time she died in 1988 at the age of 89," Carol Diehl wrote in *Art in America,* "her public sculptures dotted the American landscape, and, honored by presidents and universities, she was hailed as a national treasure." Cassandra Langer, writing in *Gay & Lesbian Review Worldwide,* explained that Nevelson "was considered a towering figure in postwar American art. Her monumental installations and innovative sculptures made from found objects and wood greatly influenced the creation of many celebrated works of art and public site pieces."

Once she had won the art world's attention, Nevelson relished publicity and behaved the way the public wants an artist to behave—with style and vivacity. "Nevelson made old age the stage for a fashion revolution," Leslie Camhi wrote in the *New York Times.* "Gradually, her full-blown style emerged, an immense collage whose elements were subject to miraculous transformations—the head scarves and multiple pairs of false eyelashes, the ethnographic jewels and enormous furs, the couture garments layered under and over peasant clothing." "With her Tiparillo cigars, false eyelashes, crazy hats and the unconventional fashions she . . . designed for herself," Roberta Brandes Gratz elaborated in the *New York Post,* "Louise Nevelson . . . clearly established that she [was] one of those marvelous, off-beat characters who know they are characters, enjoy the image and never fail to live up to it."

The traditional problem with maintaining a dramatic persona, Robert Hughes noted in *Time,* is that it often leaves little time for work. Yet this was not true for Nevelson, the critic asserted—in her early eighties, the artist continued to produce prodigious

Nevelson surrounded by her sculptures at a Venice exhibit of her work. (Loomis Dean/Time Life Pictures/Getty Images.)

amounts of work, inventing new modes of expression. Nevelson completed a total of forty or fifty pieces a year. "She [was] so entirely involved in *doing* that she [didn't] pause long enough to let us see her as monumental," said *Ms.* contributor Ruth Adams Bronz. Nevelson's creations have met with high praise, but the sculptor's obsession for work characterized her entire artistic life, including many years of little public recognition and not a single sale.

"It's a miracle that I survived and rose above it," Nevelson told Leslie Bennetts of the *New York Times* about those lean years. "It's like a horse that has these blinders on. I didn't know that I could do anything else; I felt art and I were one. No sacrifice was too much; it was just more important than whether or not I was sleeping on the floor or getting a good meal." After two decades of enduring success, little bitterness remained from that time; Nevelson told Ray Bongartz of the *New York Times* that one of her happiest moments came late in life, when she gave work valued at 350,000 dollars to

the Whitney Museum. "I was high . . . and joyous, because I had never given anything of this size. I thought, a millionaire can give only one little piece, but I, as an artist, can give much more, and it was very satisfying. I hope I live long enough to make that look small."

Nevelson and her Russian-Jewish family immigrated to Rockland, Maine, in 1905. Although her father would later become a successful lumber merchant, he began as a scavenger who searched through the town dump for useable objects to resell. "It's interesting to note," wrote Diehl, "that his means of survival ultimately became a component of his daughter's as well." Louise was ambitious and headstrong even as a child, feeling her artistic calling early. "I had a blueprint all my life from childhood and I knew exactly what I demanded of this world," Nevelson explained in her memoir *Dawns and Dusks: Taped Conversations with Diana MacKown.* "Now, some people may not demand of life as much as I did. But I wanted one thing that I thought belonged to me. I wanted the whole show. To me, that is living." The sculptor often told the story of how, as a small girl visiting the library, she was asked by the librarian what she wanted to be when she grew up. "An artist," she replied immediately. "No—a sculptor; I don't want color to help me." And then Louise ran home frightened and crying, overwhelmed by what she had just said.

Nevelson's tenacious pursuit of artistic realization prompted her to leave her provincial home town as soon as she could, marrying Charles Nevelson, a New York shipping broker, in 1920. Once in New York City, Louise plunged into dance, voice, and art studies, enjoying the freedom and cultural activities that the city had to offer. In 1922 the couple had a son, Myron. "When the marriage ended in divorce and Mrs. Nevelson began to pursue her artistic career in New York and Europe in the early 1930s," Andrew L. Yarrow wrote in the *New York Times,* "the son was reared by various family members in her home state of Maine. Until the last few decades of her life, contact between the two was relatively limited and their relationship was often strained."

In 1931 Nevelson traveled to Germany to study art with Hans Hofmann for a year; on her return she became an assistant to Mexican muralist Diego Rivera. Nevelson showed her first sculpture in 1933 at the Brooklyn Museum, and she continued to work non-stop for the next twenty-five years without commercial success, sometimes burning whole collections of sculptures because she had no room for them in her studio, sometimes scavenging from finished works parts for new ones.

By the mid-1950s, Nevelson had emerged as a significant force in American sculpture. She was

Nevelson's 1958 wall-sized assemblage "Sky Cathedral."
("Sky Cathedral," 1958, wood construction, painted black, 11' 3 1/2" x 10' 1/4", assemblage by Louise Nevelson. The Museum of Modern Art, New York; gift of Mr. and Mrs. Ben Medwoff. Photo © 1999 The Museum of Modern Art, New York. Reproduced by permission.)

constructing freestanding, wall-sized assemblages consisting of boxes, shelves, found wood scraps and furniture parts, all painted black. Douglas C. Mcgill in the *New York Times* described these works as "the walls of black wood collage that, when first shown to the world, did not look like sculpture at all, but something like environments or stage sets or grandly cluttered closets or tool sheds." An essayist for *Contemporary Women Artists* described Nevelson's work of the time: "Large low relief panels in boxwood, some more than eight feet tall, offered their black presences with mystery and an aura of religious solemnity not denied by the evidence of their source materials—cheap boxes with fitted ingredients of newel posts, chair legs and bevelled shelf edgings and, now and then, a rude hunk of unplaned wood. This compartmentalization of the relief wall emphasized the multiplicity of the contained detail so that on each shelf appeared what seemed the miniature furnishings of a chapel in an overcrowded baroque cathedral." Diehl described Nevelson's wall-sized assemblage works in this way: "When many elements are packed together, the impact of each is diminished, and we're left

with an 'overall' composition, so that the eye is rapidly drawn from one thing to the next, so that it's almost impossible to take everything in at once. The three-dimensionality of Nevelson's work, plus her use of familiar, everyday objects, further increases the effect. What catches one person's eye is not necessarily what will catch another's, nor is the pattern that seems so evident today going to be the same one you see tomorrow, with the result that the sculpture never devolves into a unitary 'thing' to be completely grasped."

It was not until 1959 that Nevelson's first official recognition came in a Museum of Modern Art show. Ironically, after creating so many black sculptures, she was chosen to exhibit her gleaming white sculpture series "Dawn's Wedding Feast." The scale of this exhibition seemed to foreshadow her large single wall reliefs "Homage to 6,000,000 I" (1964) and "Homage to the World" (1966). Her works began selling consistently, and her reputation grew steadily thereafter. "One can think of no other . . . sculptor who seems within reach of her eminence in the field," observed *Art International*'s James R. Mellow.

Assemblage Technique

The artist created environments by "assemblage," arranging bits of wood in boxes and stacking these shapes into wall-like ensembles meant to be seen frontally. Through subtle organization, Nevelson created varied relationships among the components, frequently executing a series of sculptures with similar themes that interact both with space and with one another. Because her compositions and their components can be moved and rearranged at will, the sculptor's art has been called "environmental," an art concept she helped pioneer.

Hughes described Nevelson's sculpture: "There is no apparent limit to the richness of her patterning. The objects are disciplined by a vertical-horizontal grid, or held like parts of a collage in shallow framing boxes; those formal devices, along with the shapes themselves . . . allude to cubism." Bongartz reiterated that the cubism of the early 1920s did influence Nevelson's art strongly, and that she never abandoned the cube as the basic form of her work, even in her painting, drawing, and printmaking. Nevelson said in the *New York Times,* "I was born with that objective form in me, and I never wanted to try to improve it"; and again, in *Newsweek:* "Metaphysicians say that while all *thinking* is circular, *wisdom* is squaring off your corners."

Produces Monumental Works

Nevelson used "found objects" in her sculptures—discarded bits of furniture, pieces of architectural ornamentation, old wheels, driftwood—infusing the common and the cast-off with new life. "I like it that life twisted those old nails and wood," Nevelson told Stevens. "I also like it that in back of them you see a human hand." Although the artist exhibited a similarity to the Dadaists, pop artists, and junk artists in her use of discarded objects, she insisted: "One reason for my use of 'found' materials is that I never could afford much else. But now that I'm economically free—my God! There's nothing I can't use. Plastic, plexiglas, metal." During the 1960s Nevelson did turn to other materials and simpler, more open forms to produce architectural works of monumental scale. She subsequently enjoyed numerous public and private commissions. The most impressive of these is New York's Louise Nevelson Plaza, a huge outdoor environment of her black sculptures, located on Maiden Lane in lower Manhattan. Another highly visible example of her work was in the lobby of the World Trade Center, which featured one of her massive black wall sculptures.

The artist frequently painted her groups of sculptures a uniform color: gold, white—most often—black. This has prompted several critics to call Nevelson's art "black magic," suggesting silence, mysteriousness, and dreams. According to John Russell in the *New York Times*, Nevelson "brought mystery back into sculpture. . . . Her black walls lived in shadow and drew sustenance from it, and a large public found in her work a satisfaction that it found nowhere else in modern art." Nevelson claimed that shadow and space are the most important elements of her work, that she was a sculptor of shadow and light. Bongartz summarized the evocative presence of her work: "Nevelson's great, labyrinthine walls of mystery boxes represent her spirit marvelously: the restless experimenting in shape, size and positioning of the infinite varieties of parts, and the eerie sense that the collected whole is somehow always alive and growing combine to trouble a viewer deeply, as well as surround him with a deep peacefulness at the same time."

Experts have likened a Nevelson sculpture to a musical composition, for both take form from the accumulation of their parts. One critic wrote of her works: "There is something medieval in their somber fortitude and absolute straightforwardness.

President Ronald Reagan presenting Nevelson with the National Medal of Arts. (Diana Walker/Time and Life Pictures/Getty Images.)

If they were instruments they would play Bach." A second critic called one work "a beautiful piece of nightmusic." And still another assessed that the disorder in Nevelson's creations "suddenly acquires genuine meaning, like some wild music."

Publishes Memoirs

In 1976's *Dawns and Dusks* Nevelson related her memoirs to Diana MacKown, her assistant and companion for twelve years. It is a book about an artist-celebrity and, according to Hilton Kramer in the *New York Times Book Review,* it shares both the interest and the limitations of that genre. He noted: "[It] is a book very much in the operatic mode, with the artist herself cast in the role of a triumphant heroine who overcomes all obstacles to achieve artistic success and worldly fame. . . . It is at its best, as such books usually are, in dealing with the artist's early years—the years before fame and the company of name-dropping, ceremonial events, and 'philosophical reflection.'"

Bronz commented that the artist's unedited recollections seemed so rambling and discursive at first that the book was almost irritating to read. "Gradually, though, I realized that Louise Nevelson is always in control of her monologues. . . . It is entirely commanding, and mostly charming, and it is an impertinence to have wanted to change it." And Kramer agreed, acknowledging some difficulty with Nevelson's "high-spirited. . . somewhat shapeless account," but concluding that *"Dawns and Dusks* is a vivacious book, and everyone interested in the art of Nevelson will want to read it. . . . It is a fascinating story."

If you enjoy the works of Louise Nevelson, you may also want to check out the following:

The sculptors Richard Serra and Robert Rauschenberg, and the collagists Kurt Schwitters and Joseph Cornell.

Nevelson passed away in 1988 at the age of 87. Following her death, her son Myron and her long-time companion Diana MacKown had a legal disagreement over her estate. Although MacKown had not been mentioned in Nevelson's will, she claimed that some valuable sculptures had been given to her. She also lived in an apartment in a building owned by Nevelson. When Myron Nevelson wanted to sell the property, she refused to leave. The matter was taken to the courts for settlement.

"Nothing has been able to shake me," Nevelson once said about the course of her life. "I don't think anyone could have stopped me from doing my art." She continued: "I really don't regret too much. I've been too busy. It's been constructive so how can I regret anything? I give myself a 100-plus for the way I've lived my life, the choices I've made, what has come out of it. Every day I've lived I wanted to flower more and more."

In 2005, the Louise Nevelson Foundation was founded in Philadelphia by Maria Nevelson, Louise's granddaughter. The organization seeks to educate the American public about the life and career of Louise Nevelson. They have recorded and archived oral interviews with those people who knew and worked with Nevelson, including her friends and family members, and sponsor lectures and workshops.

■ Biographical and Critical Sources

BOOKS

Bober, Natalie S., *Breaking Tradition: The Story of Louise Nevelson,* Atheneum (New York, NY), 1984.

Cain, Michael, *Louise Nevelson,* Chelsea House (New York, NY), 1989.

Contemporary Artists, 5th edition, St. James Press (Detroit, MI), 2001.

Contemporary Women Artists, St. James Press (Detroit, MI), 1999.

Danto, Arthur Coleman, *The Sculpture of Louise Nevelson: Constructing a Legend,* Yale University Press, 2007.

Glimcher, Arnold B., *Louise Nevelson,* Praeger, 1972.

Guerrero, Pedro E., *Pedro E. Guerrero: A Photographer's Journey with Frank Lloyd Wright, Alexander Calder, and Louise Nevelson,* Princeton Architectural Press, 2007.

Lipman, Jean, *Nevelson's World,* introduction by Hilton Kramer, Hudson Hills Press in association with the Whitney Museum of American Art (New York, NY), 1983.

Lisle, Laurie, *Louise Nevelson: A Passionate Life,* Washington Square Press (New York, NY), 1990.

Nevelson, Louise, and Diana MacKown, *Dawns and Dusks: Taped Conversations with Diana MacKown,* Scribner (New York, NY), 1976.

Schwartz, Constance, *Nevelson and O'Keeffe: Independents of the Twentieth Century,* The Museum (Roslyn Harbor, NY), 1983.

PERIODICALS

Art in America, July 1, 2000, "Nevelson Goes Postal"; January 1, 2008, Carol Diehl, "The World of Mrs. N," p. 106.

ARTnews, May, 1979.

Forward, August 3, 2007, Elissa Strauss, "Louise Nevelson: Constructing a Legend."

Gay & Lesbian Review Worldwide, January-February, 2008, Cassandra Langer, "A Tribute to Louise Nevelson, 20 Years Gone," p. 50.

Newsweek, March 8, 1967.

New York Post, March 8, 1967.

New York Times, March 12, 1967; April 28, 1967; July 16, 1979; January 11, 1987, Douglas C. Mcgill, "The Sculptor Louise Nevelson's Life Is Told in a 3-Dimensional Biography"; June 10, 1989, Andrew L. Yarrow, "Nevelson Estate Is the Focus of a Battle"; April 15, 2007, Leslie Camhi, "Designed for Living."

New York Times Book Review, February 6, 1977.

New York Times Magazine, January 28, 1971; April 27, 1980.

Saturday Review, August, 1980.

Time, March 31, 1967; December 12, 1977; June 19, 1978; June 16, 1980.

Time Out Chicago, June 1-7, 2006, Philip Berger, "The Urban Landscape: Meet the Nevelson."

ONLINE

Louise Nevelson Foundation, http://www.louisenevelsonfoundation.org/ (April 3, 2008).

OTHER

Nevelson: Awareness in the Fourth Dimension (film), Acadia Moving Pictures.

■ Obituaries

PERIODICALS

Chicago Tribune, April 19, 1988.

Los Angeles Times, April 19, 1988.

New York Times, April 19, 1988.

Times (London, England), April 19, 1988.

Washington Post, April 19, 1988.*

Willis O'Brien

■ Personal

Born March 2, 1886, in Oakland, CA; died of cancer, November 8, 1962, in Los Angeles, CA; son of William Henry (an attorney) and Minnie Gregg O'Brien; married Hazel Ruth Colette, 1917 (died, 1934); married Darlyne Prenett, November 16, 1934; children: (first marriage) William, Willis, Jr.

■ Career

Film director, special-effects technician, and writer. Worked variously as a ranch hand, trapper, wilderness guide, bartender, draftsman, professional boxer, and fireplace modeler. *San Francisco Daily News,* San Francisco, CA, cartoonist; commercial sculptor Conquest Programs, New York, NY, stop-motion animator and founder of Manikin Films, 1916-17. Director of films, including (and cinematographer) *The Dinosaur and the Missing Link,* 1915; *The Birth of a Flivver,* 1916; *R.F.D. 10,000 B.C.,* 1917; *Morpheus Mike,* 1917; *Prehistoric Poultry,* 1917; *Curious Pets of Our Ancestors,* 1917; *Nippy's Nightmare,* 1917; *Sam Lloyd's Famous Puzzles,* 1917; *Mickey and His Goat,* 1917; *In the Villain's Power,* 1917; (uncredited; and cinematographer) *The Ghost of Slumber Mountain,* 1918; *Along the Moonbeam Trail,* 1920; and *Creation* (not produced), 1931. Special effects techician for films *The Lost World,* 1925; *King Kong,* 1933; *Son of Kong,* 1933; *The Last Days of Pompeii,* 1935; *The Dancing Pirate,* 1936; *Mighty Joe Young,* 1949; *This Animal World,* 1955; *The Black Scorpion,* 1957; *The Giant Behe-moth,* 1959; (uncredited) *The Lost World* (remake), 1960; and (uncredited) *It's a Mad Mad Mad Mad World,* 1963. *Exhibitions:* Sculptures exhibited at San Francisco World's Fair, 1913.

■ Awards, Honors

Academy Award for special effects, c. 1949, for work on *Mighty Joe Young;* Winsor McCay Award for lifetime achievement (posthumous), Association internationale du film d'animation, 1997.

■ Writings

SCREENPLAYS

(Uncredited) *The Ghost of Slumber Mountain,* Cinema Distributing, 1918.

(Author of story) *The Beast of Hollow Mountain,* United Artists, 1956.

(Author of story) *Kingu Kongu tai Gojira* (also released as *King Kong vs. Godzilla*), Toho Studios/ Universal, 1962.

(Author of story; uncredited) *The Valley of Gwangi,* Warner Bros., 1969.

■ Sidelights

Known to his friends and colleagues as O'Bie, Willis O'Brien was a pioneer in the cinematic field now known as special effects. His work developing and perfecting stop-motion animation, which involves photographing clay models a frame at a time, pausing after each shot to move the model slightly so that they seem to move on their own, was fundamental in creating all later film effects. "Overall, O'Brien's career boasts a dual triumph," according to Paul M. Jensen in his *The Men Who Made the Monsters.* "First, . . . O'Brien . . . blended subject matter with technology to define and perfect a new type of motion picture. In this way, he established precedents for generations of future filmmakers. He was not, however, only a pioneer, for he also created three enduring films: *The Lost World* (1925) and *Mighty Joe Young* (1949) continue to amuse and fascinate viewers, while *King Kong* (1933) remains an unmatched work of adventure and imagination." "O'Brien was the greatest of all stop-motion artists because he had the ability to really invest his

creations with sympathy and personality," wrote Richard Scheib in *Moria: The Science Fiction, Horror, and Fantasy Film Review.* Sadly, O'Brien's long career in film yielded little financial success, and instead played a part in the man's personal tragedy. Although O'Brien never saw many of his ideas reach film audiences, he did receive recognition for his work during his lifetime, when he received a special Academy Award—the first-ever awarded for special effects—for his animation work on *Mighty Joe Young.*

Finds Creative Outlet

Born in northern California in 1886, O'Brien grew up in a well-off family, thanks to his father's job as assistant district attorney in the city of Oakland.

Willis O'Brien, seated in white suit, with actress Faye Wray and others on the set of the 1933 film *King Kong.* (RKO/The Kobal Collection/The Picture Desk, Inc.)

However, the family's fortunes had changed by the time O'Brien was a teen, and at age thirteen he quit school and struck out on his own. While work as a ranch hand, a trapper, and a wilderness guide for a group of paleontologists working in the Crater Lake region drew on O'Brien's love of physical activity, at age seventeen he found an outlet for his analytical side by working as a draftsman. From drafting, he moved to a job as sports cartoonist at the *San Francisco Daily News,* where he was introduced to boxing. Characteristically impulsive, O'Brien left the *Daily News* in favor of the boxing ring, but an early loss as a professional boxer convinced him to find another vocation. After a short stint with the Southern Pacific Railroad, he found work as a fireplace modeler for a San Francisco stonecutter who used the clay models O'Brien crafted to create cut-marble fireplaces.

O'Brien's job as a modeller coincided with his growing interest in the new art of cinematography. As a former cartoonist, he was fascinated by cartoon animation: the drawing of a series of almost-identical frames in such a way that projected images appear to move. O'Brien realized that the medium of clay could be used to make three-dimensional animated objects if the camera could be stopped after each frame and the clay image readjusted slightly through each range of motion to create movement. Sculpting a small clay dinosaur figurine as well as a clay caveman, he began to experiment with this technique—called stop-motion photography—and produced a one-minute film. Although pioneering photographer George Melies had already experimented with stop-motion photography, O'Brien perfected the technique and linked it with the images—dinosaurs and other prehistoric creatures—that would make it so appealing to Hollywood.

Catches Eye of Thomas Edison

With his one-minute black-and-white film "in the can," O'Brien gained backing for a longer work from San Francisco film producer Herman Wobber. Bankrolled by Wobber's five-thousand-dollar advance, O'Brien devoted two months in the summer of 1915 to creating *The Dinosaur and the Missing Link: A Prehistoric Tragedy,* which featured a full five minutes of stop-motion action. Based on O'Brien's earlier test footage, the proto-claymation short focuses on a romantic showdown between two caveman vying for the love of Miss Araminta Rockface.

When *The Dinosaur and the Missing Link* found its way to Thomas Edison, the inventor quickly picked it up for distribution by his Edison Company. He also hired its creator to produce more cinematic novelties. Moving to New York City, O'Brien formed Manikin Films and spent 1916 and 1917 honing the art of stop-motion animation as an employee of Edison's Conquest Programs film unit. In his three-minute silent film *Morpheus Mike,* a hungry hobo is outsmarted by a clever goat, then daydreams about what the menu would be like in a prehistoric restaurant, where the food supply is literally supersized. Another short produced for Conquest Programs, *R.F.D. 10,000 B.C.* combines live action and clay animation to bring to life the courtship woes of a mailman whose cart is pulled by a dinosaur. In this film O'Brien outfitted his dinosaur character with tiny air bladders which, when filled, then emptied, made the creature appear to be breathing. Other 1917 releases included *Prehistoric Poultry* and *Curious Pets of Our Ancestors.*

Directs First Full-length Feature

After the Edison Company was sold in 1917, O'Brien returned to California, where he was hired by producer Herbert Dawley to create animation

The original film poster for *King Kong.* (Copyright © Bettmann/ Corbis.)

for *The Ghost of Slumber Mountain*. Based on a story by O'Brien and released in 1918, the nineteen-minute-long feature focuses on Uncle Jack as he entertains his young nephews with a story about a ghostly paleontologist. Coming across the apparition's cabin, Jack discovers a haunted spyglass that reveals scenes from the age of the dinosaurs to anyone who peers through its lens. Originally forty five minutes in length, *The Ghost of Slumber Mountain* took O'Brien three months to film. Although the film netted Dawley a handsome profit—his three-thousand-dollar investment netted him back one hundred thousand dollars—O'Brien was given no cut of the profits. In addition, Dawley attempted to take full credit for the stop-action animation in the film.

Ending his relationship with Dawley, O'Brien worked on the animated film *Along the Moonbeam Trail*. Despite Dawley's assertions to the contrary, he was soon sought out by producer Watterson R. Rothacker to work with director Harry O. Hoyt and create the animation for Hoyt's film adaptation of Conan Doyle's *The Lost World*. The story tells of an expedition to an isolated South American plateau where dinosaurs are said to be found. After an arduous climb to the location, the scientists find themselves in danger from the prehistoric monsters. After escaping from the plateau, they find a brontosaurus trapped in a mudhole, capture him, and take him back to London. There, the giant creature gets loose and goes on a rampage. Jenn Dlugos, reviewing the film for *Classic Horror,* called it a "unique tale coupled with wonderful special effects." Scheib noted that the realistic dinosaur sequences were "something that had never been seen on the screen before." Considered among the best epic films of the silent-film era, *The Lost World* was the first Hollywood feature film to showcase the combined talents of O'Brien and fellow animators Marcel Delgado, Arthur Edelson, and Ralph Hammeras. Delgado would continue to work under O'Brien's direction on several more films, helping to advance the realism of stop-motion technology by incorporating multi-jointed metal "skeletons" covered by textured rubber skins. Now considered a landmark film, *The Lost World* was released in 1925 and became hugely popular with audiences.

Stress Follows Success

Although *The Lost World* drew thousands to the cinema, the film did not draw any lucrative directing opportunities O'Brian's way. He wasted the next six months on a failed project that was set in the lost kingdom of Atlantis, and a proposed sequel to *The Lost World* also fell through. O'Brien also attempted to realize his dream of creating a film about the Frankenstein monster, but that too failed.

The stress of working on *The Lost World* had by now taken a toll on his marriage to Hazel Ruth Collette, a woman twelve years younger than he. Unhappy in the marriage, he had found a refuge in alcohol, and by the late 1920s he was also gambling and cheating on his wife. Fortunately, O'Brien managed to sustain relationships with his sons, and these got him through the rough times.

Despite the disruption in his personal life, O'Brien was forced by economic necessity to continue working. A new film opportunity, the RKO production *Creation,* surfaced in 1931. Intended to be the first stop-action dinosaur film to feature sound, *Creation* brought together several crew-members from *The Lost World,* among them Hoyt as director. The film had a storyline similar to that of *The Lost World* as well: a small group of bedraggled survivors from a shipwreck make it to a remote volcanic island inhabited by prehistoric beasts. Although bad luck in the form of the Great Depression ultimately derailed the ambitious and costly project, *Creation* allowed O'Brien to experiment with the new Dunning traveling matte system, which allowed live action footage to be inserted directly over an existing frame, eliminating the need for presenting the insertion point during initial filming.

Although *Creation* became another in O'Brien's series of failed projects, the technical director's work on the film caught the attention of RKO producer and director Merian C. Cooper. Together with fellow director Ernest B. Schoedsack, Cooper wanted to wow audiences with a film spectacular about a giant ape. And to accomplish this, it was clear that O'Brien was the man for the job.

Journey to Skull Island

In *King Kong* O'Brien combined stop-motion photography with other innovative technology, and the range of models he created of this famous gorilla incorporated complex mechanisms that allowed Kong to "breathe" and exhibit the variety of facial expressions that made the film such an emotional experience for filmgoers. Directed by Cooper and Schoedsack, the historic film starred Robert Armstrong as Carl Denham, a film director who has heard legends about the remote Skull Island in the South Pacific. A monster is said to live there, and Denham thinks it would make a great movie, just perfect for his new leading lady, starlet Ann Darrow (the role that immortalized actress Faye Wray). He takes his film crew on a voyage to the distant location. Upon arriving at Skull Island, the adventurers find unfriendly natives and a strange, giant wall that cuts off the native village from the island's jungle. The wall is to keep out Kong, a giant gorilla,

The giant gorilla King Kong on stage in chains after being brought back to New York City. (Henry Guttmann/Hulton Archive/Getty Images.)

and other prehistoric creatures who still roam the jungle. The natives routinely offer Kong a female sacrifice and, when they see Ann Darrow, they want her to be the next offering. They kidnap Ann and, before the crew can stop it, she is taken away by Kong. Jack Driscoll (Bruce Cabot) leads a party into the jungle to rescue her, but their efforts enrage Kong, who breaks through the protective wall and runs wild in the village. Only knockout gas can stop him. Denham then comes up with a great idea. Instead of merely filming Kong, he will take him back to New York and display him as "King Kong, the Eighth Wonder of the World." Upon arrival in Manhattan, events play out to the climactic scene in which a panicked and heartbroken Kong clings to the top of the Empire State Building, where he has carried Ann. The giant gorilla is then attacked by Army planes firing machine guns. He vainly swats at them before finally falling to his death. Scheib noted a similarity between *King Kong* and *The Lost*

World. "Both films," wrote Scheib, "feature explorers venturing into a primaeval lost world, encountering prehistoric beasts, and returning to civilization with one of the lost world's greatest creatures, which then gets loose in a major city, causing chaos."

In creating the animation for *King Kong*, O'Brien spent time at zoos observing the way gorillas moved. He also drew on his knowledge of professional boxing and wrestling, giving Kong the ability to make the same aggressive moves in battling his foes. Another lifelike touch came about quite by accident. When reviewing the first takes of his animated sequences, O'Brien realized that the gorilla's fur was ruffled differently in each scene due to his manipulation of the model, and when run in sequence the ruffling gave the appearance of wind blowing through Kong's fur. When *King Kong* had its Hollywood premier at the Chinese Theatre in

1933, O'Brien's life-size model of Kong stood in the lobby, where it towered over appreciative filmgoers. "It is perhaps the greatest of all fantasy films," Scheib wrote about *King Kong*, "it is certainly the greatest monster movie ever made."

Despite the success of *King Kong,* O'Brien saw little change in his fortunes. During his next film, the lighthearted Schoedsack-directed sequel *The Son of Kong,* he made the same three hundred dollars per week that he earned filming *King Kong*. By now O'Brien and his wife had separated, a result of both O'Brien's infidelities and his financial problems, and the couple's two teenaged sons lived with their mother. Hazel had always acted rather oddly, and her behavior became more erratic in 1931, when she was diagnosed with cancer and tuberculosis (TB). When her oldest son, William, became totally blind as a result of contracting TB, Hazel could no longer emotionally cope. In October of 1933, while O'Brien was attempting to wrestle some more money for his work on *Son of Kong,* Hazel shot her two sons, and then unsuccessfully attempted to end her own life. While fourteen-year-old William and thirteen-year-

old Willis, Jr., died at their mother's hand, Hazel survived another year and died in the prison ward at Los Angeles General Hospital in November of 1934. O'Brien married his second wife, Darlyne Prenett, the very next day.

Mentor to Harryhausen

This family tragedy cast a pall over the rest of O'Brien's career, and he struggled to find work during the remainder of his life. He rejoined Schoedsack in 1935 as chief technician for *The Last Days of Pompeii,* an historic epic set in the doomed Mediteranean city, and the following year he worked on *The Dancing Pirate*. A dry spell was relieved by a young man named Ray Harryhausen, who would figure in O'Brien's later career.

Thirteen years old when *King Kong* was released, Harryhausen was captivated by the film, especially by O'Brien's special effects. After studying O'Brien's

Kong atop the Empire State Building, battling airplanes, in the climactic scene in the film *King Kong*. (Hulton Archive/Getty Images.)

stop-motion techniques, he created his own short film and showed it to O'Brien, who decided to mentor the young man. That opportunity came in the mid-1940s, when the two men worked together on the film crew of the Schoedsack-directed *Mighty Joe Young*, about a young Tanzanian girl who is convinced by an unscrupulous promoter to send her pet gorilla, Joe, to America. Joe is unusually large, and when he is mistreated by his American handlers, he escapes with predictably catastrophic results. Unlike his gorilla predecessor, however, Joe exhibits more human traits; he ultimately saves a group of children and is sent home to Tanzania a hero. Although O'Brien was credited as technical director on *Mighty Joe Young*, his responsibilities extended only to producing the animation designs and storyboards, leaving the bulk of the animation to Harryhausen. Nonetheless, when *Mighty Joe Young* won a special Academy award in 1950, O'Brien received the award in honor of his innovation in the field of special effects.

O'Brien's special-effects credits during the 1950s included the films *The Animal World*, *The Black Scorpion*, and *Behemoth the Sea Monster*, all low-budget films that combined O'Brien's stop-action work with high-action romance. In *The Black Scorpion* volcanoes in Mexico release giant insects that ravage the city until an American geologist finds a way to fight them. Ecological upheaval also sparks problems in *Behemoth the Sea Monster*, as oceanic atomic testing unleashes a dormant dinosaur upon London.

If you enjoy the works of Willis O'Brien, you may also want to check out the following:

The films of Ray Harryhausen, who was mentored by O'Brien; Mark Coulier, who did the special effects for the "Harry Potter" films; and Richard Taylor, who did the special effects for the "Lord of the Rings" films.

When director Irwin Allen decided to film a 1960 remake of *The Lost World*, he brought O'Brien on board as a special effects technician. However, when O'Brien learned that Allen intended to use actual live lizards to portray the dinosaurs, adding horns, spikes, and other fake appendages to make them appear realistic, he understood that his name recognition had been all that Allen wanted. His last work was animating a short scene in the madcap all-star comedy *It's a Mad, Mad, Mad, Mad World*. He would not survive to see the film's 1963 release, however, passing away in November of 1962, at the age of seventy-six.

By the mid-1960s Harryhausen had become the reigning master of the special-effects field, in part due to his work on the 1953 film *The Beast from 20,000 Fathoms*. In an homage to his cinematic mentor, seven years after O'Brien's death, Harryhausen directed *The Valley of Gwangi*. The film, a remake of the 1956 Mexican film *The Beast of Hollow Mountain*, was based on O'Brien's short story "El Toro Estrella." Starring James Franciscus, *The Valley of Gwangi* follows an American cowboy who goes on the hunt for a predatory T-Rex that has been snacking on the cattle grazing in Mexico's Forbidden Valley. The 1969 film, which with its "prehistoric creature trapped in an unfamiliar and unfeeling modern world" plot, has all the characteristics of an O'Brien picture, was the last film to feature O'Brien's name in the credits. His work would not be officially acknowledged until 1997, when O'Brien was posthumously awarded the Winsor McCay Award by the U.S. chapter of the Association internationale du film d'animation.

"He may not have amassed a fortune," Jensen wrote, "but Willis O'Brien left much behind at his passing. He created one motion picture destined to endure as an unmatched masterpiece, and others that still offer distinctive rewards. In the process, he originated and perfected a new type of adventure film, one that continues to fill viewers with excitement and awe."

■ Biographical and Critical Sources

BOOKS

Archer, Steve, *Willis O'Brien: Special Effects Genius*, McFarland (Jefferson, NC), 1993.

Brosnan, John, *Movie Magic: The Story of Special Effects in the Cinema*, St. Martin's Press (New York, NY), 1974.

Fry, Ron, and Pamela Fourzon, *The Saga of Special Effects*, Prentice Hall (Englewood Cliffs, NJ), 1977.

Goldner, Orville, and George E. Turner, *The Making of King Kong*, A.S. Barnes (New York, NY), 1975.

Gottesman, Ronald, and Harry Geduld, editors, *The Girl in the Hairy Paw*, Avon (New York, NY), 1976.

Jensen, Paul M., *The Men Who Made the Monsters*, Twayne (New York, NY), 1996.

Kinnard, Roy, editor, *The Lost World of Willis O'Brien: The Original Shooting Script of the 1925 Landmark Special Effects Dinosaur Film*, McFarland (Jefferson, NC), 1993.

Morton, Ray, *King Kong: The History of a Movie Icon from Fay Wray to Peter Jackson*, Applause Theatre & Cinema Books (New York, NY), 2005.

Rickitt, Richard, *Special Effects: The History and Technique*, Watson-Guptill Publications (New York, NY), 2007.

Rovin, Jeff, *From the Land Beyond: The Films of Willis O'Brien and Ray Harryhausen*, Berkley (New York, NY), 1977.

Wray, Fay, *On the Other Hand: A Life Story*, St. Martin's Press (New York, NY), 1989.

PERIODICALS

American Cinematographer, August, 1992, George Turner, "Sailing Back to Skull Island: *The Son of Kong*," pp. 67-71.

Boxoffice, June, 1997.

Cahiers du Cinema, November, 1980, "Willis O'Brien."

Chicago Sun-Times, February 3, 2002, Roger Ebert, review of *King Kong*.

Cinefantastique, Volume 27, number 2, 1993.

Cinefex, January, 1982, special O'Brien issue.

Classic Film Collector, summer, 1974, E.K. Everett, "Willis O'Brien, the Man Who Loved Dinosaurs."

Classic Images, May, 1986, "Interview with Darlyne O'Brien," pp. 10-11; May, 1988, Tony Crnkovich, "King Kong's Hidden Appeal," pp. C20-21.

Entertainment Weekly, November 18, 2005, Steve Daly, review of *King Kong* DVD.

Focus on Film, autumn, 1973, Don Shay, "Willis O'Brien: Creator of the Impossible."

New York Times, June 3, 1922, "Dinosaurs Cavort in Film for Doyle," pp. 1, 4; June 25, 1950, Ezra Goodman, "Master Monster Maker: Willis O'Brien," Section 2, p. 4; June 26, 1955, Vance King, "From a 'Missing Link' to Tyrannosaurus Rex," Section 2, p. 5; September 21, 1969, Fay Wray, "How Fay Met Kong, or The Scream That Shook the World," Section 2, p. 17.

ONLINE

Classic Horror, http://classic-horror.com/ (January 10, 2003), Jenn Dlugos, review of *The Lost World*; (October 23, 2006), Robert Ring, review of *King Kong*.

FilmReference.com, http://www.filmreference.com/ (October 8, 2007).

Mania.com, http://www.mania.com/ (November 29, 2005), Brian Thomas, review of *King Kong* (DVD).

Moria: The Science Fiction, Horror, and Fantasy Film Review, http://www.moria.co.nz/ (March 26, 2008), Richard Scheib, reviews of *The Lost World*, *King Kong*, and *Mighty Joe Young*.

Sci Fi Weekly, http://www.scifi.com/sfw/ (March 26, 2008), Tamara Hladik, review of *The Lost World*.

Senses of Cinema, http://www.sensesofcinema.com/ (November, 2003), John McGowan-Hartmann, review of *King Kong*.

■ Obituaries

PERIODICALS

New York Times, November 12, 1962.*

Steven Pressfield

(Copyright © Jerry Bauer. Reproduced by permission.)

■ Personal

Born in September, 1943, in Port of Spain, Trinidad; divorced. *Education:* Duke University, B.A., 1965. *Hobbies and other interests:* Golf.

■ Addresses

Agent—Sterling Lord Literistic, Inc., 65 Bleecker St., 12th Floor, New York, NY 10012.

■ Career

Novelist and screenwriter. Former copywriter for Benton & Bowles. *Military service:* United States Marine Corp., 1965-71.

■ Awards, Honors

In September, 2003, the city of Sparta, Greece, made Pressfield an honorary citizen.

■ Writings

NOVELS

The Legend of Bagger Vance: Golf and the Game of Life, William Morrow (New York, NY), 1995.
Gates of Fire: An Epic Novel of the Battle of Thermopylae, Doubleday (New York, NY), 1998.
Tides of War: A Novel of Alcibiades and the Peloponnesian War, Doubleday, 2000.
Last of the Amazons, Doubleday (New York, NY), 2002.
The Virtues of War: A Novel of Alexander the Great, Doubleday (New York, NY), 2004.
The Afghan Campaign, Doubleday (New York, NY), 2006.
Killing Rommel, Doubleday (New York, NY), 2008.

SCREENPLAYS

King Kong Lives, DEG, 1986.
Above the Law (also known as *Nico*), Warner Bros., 1988.
(With Ronald Shusett and Dan Gilroy; and author of story) *Freejack,* Warner Bros., 1992.
Separate Lives, Trimark Pictures, 1995.

OTHER

The War of Art: Winning the Inner Creative Battle, foreword by Robert McKee, Rugged Land (New York, NY), 2002.

■ Adaptations

The Legend of Bagger Vance: Golf and the Game of Life was adapted as the film *The Legend of Bagger Vance* and released by DreamWorks SKG, 2000. Several of Pressfield's books have been released on audiocassette.

■ Sidelights

While Steven Pressfield's novel *The Legend of Bagger Vance: Golf and the Game of Life* was made into a popular movie, he is perhaps best known for his historical novels set in the days of ancient Greece. A critic for *Publishers Weekly* called Pressfield an "esteemed historical novelist." According to William Dietrich in the *Seattle Times,* Pressfield presents "a personal, vividly imagined, and singular world: that of the Greek warrior. His era is simpler, more brutal, more personal, and more heroic than ours,

and so carefully researched that the reader is never sure where fact leaves off and fiction begins." David Walton in the *St. Petersburg Times* believed that, "like the sea novels of Patrick O'Brian, Pressfield's historical novels . . . are popular for their richness and authenticity of period detail."

Born in 1943, in Port of Spain, Trinidad, Pressfield earned a degree from Duke University in 1965 before serving six years in the U.S. Marines. After his military service, he worked as a copywriter for an advertising agency. He claimed on his Home Page that it was "while rewriting the just-add-water text for the back label of Gravy Train dog food" that he decided he should be doing something more important with his life. He chose to become a writer, something that resulted in a divorce from his wife and a long period of financial hardship. Over the years he picked fruit, tended bar, drove a cab, and lived in a van. He wrote three novels, but not one was published. In 1980 he headed for Hollywood, intent on trying his hand at screenwriting. The move worked. Over the next few years, he wrote thirty four screenplays and saw several of them made into

Will Smith and Matt Damon star in the 2000 film adaptation *The Legend of Bagger Vance.* (Wildwood/Allied Filmmakers/The Kobal Collection/The Picture Desk, Inc.)

films. His success moved Pressfield to write another novel. Inspired by a classic of Eastern mysticism, the *Bhagavad-Gita*, Pressfield wrote the novel *The Legend of Bagger Vance.*

Creates A Mystical Golfer

An avid golfer, Pressfield explores the psychological and spiritual facets of golf in *The Legend of Bagger Vance.* Unlike other sports in which a team of athletes compete against another team, golf is an individual game in which a golfer must compete against himself or herself. Golfers having trouble with their games can have psychological as well as physical problems preventing them from playing well. Elderly Hardison L. Greaves narrates the novel. When Greaves was a young boy in the 1930s, he attended a golf tournament in Georgia that featured the notable professional golfers Bobby Jones and Walter Hagen. The novel also features Georgian World War I hero Rannulph Junah. The story centers on the relationship between Junah and his caddie, the mysterious Bagger Vance. The reclusive Junah initially declined a chance to join the tournament, but Vance finally encourages Junah to play. As the novel progresses, Vance emerges as much more than Junah's golfing tutor. He teaches Junah a great deal about life. *The Legend of Bagger Vance*'s "mysticism promotes thought, and golf references are simple enough for nonplayers," wrote Diane Goheen in the *School Library Journal.* In a review of the audio cassette version of *The Legend of Bagger Vance,* a *Publishers Weekly* reviewer noted that "Pressfield manages to make this unlikely golf-as-metaphysics hybrid come across as engrossing good fun." The novel was adapted as a film starring Will Smith as Bagger Vance and Matt Damon as Rannulph Junah.

Pressfield turned to the world of ancient Greece for his next novel, *Gates of Fire: An Epic Novel of the Battle of Thermopylae.* He had been reading books on ancient Greek history for a number of years, just for enjoyment, but unexpectedly found himself drawn to writing about the period. The novel recounts the famous Battle of Thermopylae in 480 B.C. in which a few hundred Greeks, mostly Spartans, held off a much larger force of Persians at a narrow pass. Though the Greeks knew they could not triumph, the delay they caused the Persians allowed their fellow Greeks to prepare themselves for invasion. The Greeks managed to fend off the invaders for three days and might have lasted longer had they not been betrayed by a traitor who showed the Persians a way to get behind the defending Greeks. Caught between two Persian forces, the Greeks fought to the last man. In addition to its depiction of courage,

Pressfield's 1998 novel *Gates of Fire: An Epic Novel of the Battle of Thermopylae* is a fictional recounting of the pivotal ancient battle. (Doubleday, 1998. Used by permission of Doubleday, a division of Random House, Inc.)

Gates of Fire offers readers insight into the lives of Greek soldiers, from their intense training to their sense of loyalty and honor as they defend their families and homes. Reviewing the book in the *Library Journal,* Jane Baird stated that "this work portrays the men and women of ancient Sparta in intimate, dynamic detail." According to *New York Times Book Review* contributor and classicist Mary Lefkowitz, "in *Gates of Fire,* Steven Pressfield gives the reader a perspective no ancient historian offers, a soldier's-eye view." Lefkowitz concluded: "Reading this fine novel, it is not hard to understand why warfare has proved to be one of the most enduring subjects of literature." In a review for *Infantry Magazine,* Kenny Toole wrote: "This is an extraordinary book on so many different levels. Pressfield does a tremendous job of recreating the Greek society from 2,500 years ago. . . . *Gates of Fire* is a tremendously entertaining and magnificent work for soldiers and civilians alike."

In *Tides of War: A Novel of Alcibiades and the Peloponnesian War*, Pressfield creates a fictional account of the thirty-year war between Athens and Sparta for dominance of Greece. The general Alcibiades provoked a war between the rival city-states and was assassinated. Despite the violence of the period, it was also the time of the statesman Pericles, the playwright Sophocles, and the philosopher Socrates—prominent Greeks whose influence on later Western Civilization is still felt today. "Pressfield's historic fiction has the ability to captivate readers," Eric Robbins claimed in *Booklist*, "letting them feel as if they have intimate knowledge of the times and people." Baird concluded: "Pressfield's attention to historic detail is exquisite, but he shines brightest in his graphic and brutal descriptions of battle and its horrific affects on soldier and civilian alike. This novel will remain with the reader long after the final chapter is finished." "Pressfield," wrote a critic for *Publishers Weekly*, "is a masterful storyteller,

especially adept in his graphic and embracing descriptions of the land and naval battles, political intrigues and colorful personalities, which come together in an intense and credible portrait of war-torn ancient Greece."

For his third novel set in ancient Greece, *Last of the Amazons,* Pressfield went further back in time, to 1250 B.C., when Athens was at war with the barbaric Amazons, whose female warriors were known for their ferocity in battle. When Amazon queen Antiope falls in love with the Greek king Theseus, who has led a band of his troops into the Amazon territory, her subjects revolt, sparking a war between the two peoples. Partly based on mythology and partly on historical research, "Pressfield's splendid tale of valor, honor, and comradeship memorializes those women whose lives and deeds have faded into the mists of legend," Baird concluded. The battle scenes, according to a *Publishers Weekly* critic, ring "with the clamor and horror of close combat, sword on shield, battle-ax on helmet and javelins thudding into armor." Bob Gross, in a review for *Minerva: Quarterly Report on Women and the Military,* admitted: "I was engrossed from cover to cover."

Depicts History's Greatest Warrior

In *The Virtues of War: A Novel of Alexander the Great,* Pressfield creates a fictional account of the great Greek leader's life. A critic for *Kirkus Reviews* believed that "Pressfield, deft and graceful as always in his historical authenticity, creates an Alexander so understandable, personable, and psychologically almost modern that, for the only very occasionally doubting reader, the pleasure of sitting back and letting the tale go by is as great as usual in the company of this author." The story follows Alexander's ascent from son of the leader of Macedonia, to his conquest of all of Greece, and then to his conquests of Persia, Egypt, and India. Along the way, Pressfield provides "a firsthand look inside Alexander's mind," according to Margaret Flanagan in *Booklist*. Because of this, "the reader is quickly made aware of the multiple contradictions, ambitions, and passions that contributed to the complex sum of the entire man." Susan Kelly in *USA Today* concluded: "Pressfield captures the magnetism that this greatly gifted, greatly flawed man must have had to inspire legions of soldiers to follow him across thousands of miles and into the pages of history."

Pressfield returns again to Alexander the Great in *The Afghan Campaign,* which focuses on Alexander's conquest of the mountainous region. The three-year campaign is seen from a young recruit's perspective as he goes from one of Alexander's eager followers to a jaded veteran fighter. Matthias is a young Mace-

Pressfield's *Last of the Amazons* tells of a war between Amazon women-warriors and the Greek city-state of Athens. (Bantam Dell, 2003. Used by permission of Doubleday, a division of Random House, Inc.)

donian who finds that the guerrilla tactics used by the Afghans are unlike anything Alexander's army has met. The fierceness of their fighting is also new, with even the Afghan women attacking wounded Greeks and mutilating their bodies. Writing in *Armor,* Youssef Enein Aboul found that the novel "gives you the feel of the terrain, the hunger, and the hardships of a place that Alexander could not subdue by force alone." William Dietrich in the *Seattle Times* stated: "Pressfield's portrayal of ancient Afghanistan is fascinating, his details are convincing, and the book's timing is apt."

In a statement posted on his Home Page, Pressfield spoke of his interest in ancient Greece: "Our age has been denatured. The heroic has been bled out of it. The callings of the past—the profession of arms, the priesthood, the medical and legal professions, politics, the arts, journalism, education, even motherhood and fatherhood—every one has been sullied and degraded by scandal after scandal. We're hard up for heroes these days, and even harder up for conceiving ourselves in that light. That's why I'm drawn to the ancient world. It's truer, in my view, to how we really are. The ancient world has not been reductified and deconstructed as ours has; it has not been robbed of all dignity. They had heroes then."

If you enjoy the works of Steven Pressfield, you may also want to check out the following books:

Mark Frost, *The Greatest Game Ever Played: Harry Vardon, Francis Ouimet, and the Birth of Modern Golf,* 2002.
Ernle Bradford, *Thermopylae: The Battle For The West,* 2004.
Nicholas Nicastro, *The Isle of Stone: A Novel of Ancient Sparta,* 2005.
Scott Oden, *Men of Bronze,* 2005.

Pressfield turned to the real-life figures of World War II in his 2008 novel *Killing Rommel.* General Erwin Rommel, nicknamed the "Desert Fox," led the German tank forces in the deserts of North Africa during World War II. Respected on both sides in the conflict for his brilliant tactics and gentlemanly approach to warfare, Rommel has conquered much of North Africa west of Egypt as the novel begins. There is widespread fear that Rommel's forces will conquer Egypt, capture the Suez Canal, and take

the Arab oilfields. This would cut off England from her colonies in the East and give the oil-starved German military a much-needed source of supply. Pressfield's story imagines an assassination team of British soldiers sent behind the lines to find and kill Rommell. Michael Gannon in *Booklist* found that "this gripping novel is chockfull of evocative, historical details that readers of military fiction will voraciously devour." "Pressfield's story, remarkable for its historical accuracy, is dense with detail," wrote Ron Terpening in the *Library Journal.* "At times, like war, this can be a hard slog, but readers will be rewarded with a vivid and gripping recreation of the North African campaign. A signal achievement." The critic for *Publishers Weekly* found that "Pressfield effortlessly gives fresh life to wartime romance and the rigors of combat in a superior WWII thriller."

■ Biographical and Critical Sources

BOOKS

Rosen, Steven J., *Gita on the Green: The Mystical Tradition Behind Bagger Vance,* Continuum, 2000.

PERIODICALS

Armor, September-October, 2007, Youssef Enein Aboul, review of *The Afghan Campaign,* p. 51.
Booklist, September 15, 2004, Margaret Flanagan, review of *The Virtues of War: A Novel of Alexander the Great,* p. 210; February 1, 2008, Michael Gannon, review of *Killing Rommel,* p. 27.
Kirkus Reviews, August 1, 2004, review of *The Virtues of War,* p. 710; February 15, 2008, review of *Killing Rommel.*
Library Journal, September 1, 1998, Jane Baird, review of *Gates of Fire: An Epic Novel of the Battle of Thermopylae,* p. 217; March 15, 2000, Jane Baird, review of *Tides of War,* p. 128; March 15, 2002, Jane Baird, review of *Last of the Amazons,* p. 109; November 1, 2007, Ron Terpening, review of *Killing Rommel,* p. 60.
New York Times Book Review, June 11, 1995, p. 61; November 1, 1998, Mary Lefkowitz, review of *Gates of Fire,* p. 35.
Publishers Weekly, July 3, 1995, p. 26; August 17, 1998, review of *Gates of Fire,* p. 45; March 11, 2002, review of *Last of the Amazons,* p. 50; October 11, 2004, review of *The Virtues of War,* p. 57; February 4, 2008, review of *Killing Rommel,* p. 36.
St. Petersburg Times, November 21, 2004, David Walton, review of *The Virtues of War,* p. 4P.
School Library Journal, December, 1995, p. 142.

Seattle Times, August 13, 2006, William Dietrich, review of *The Afghan Campaign,* p. K8.

USA Today, November 30, 2004, Susan Kelly, review of *The Virtues of War,* p. 4D.

ONLINE

Steven Pressfield Home Page, http://www.stevenpress field.com (March 3, 2008).*

(The Library of Congress.)

Charles Marion Russell

■ Personal

Born March 19, 1865 (some sources say 1864), in St. Louis, MO; died of a heart attack, October 24, 1926; son of Charles Silas (a businessman) Russell; married Nancy Cooper, 1896.

■ Career

Painter, sculptor, illustrator, and writer. Worked sporadically as a cowboy, 1882-93.

■ Awards, Honors

LL.D., Montana State Board of Education, 1925.

■ Writings

Studies of Western Life, Albertype (New York, NY), 1890.

Pen Sketches, W.T. Ridgely (Great Falls, MT), 1899.

Rawhide Rawlins Stories, Montana Newspaper Association (Great Falls, MT), 1921.

Back Trailing on the Old Frontiers, Cheely-Raban Syndicate (Great Falls, MT), 1922.

More Rawhides, Montana Newspaper Association (Great Falls, MT), 1925.

Trails Plowed Under, Doubleday, Page (Garden City, NY), 1927.

Good Medicine: The Illustrated Letters of Charles M. Russell, Doubleday, Doran (Garden City, NY), 1929, published as *Good Medicine: Memories of the Real West*, Garden City Publishing Company (New York, NY), 1936.

Forty Pen and Ink Drawings, Trail's End (Pasadena, CA), 1947.

Rawhide Rawlins Rides Again; or, Behind the Swinging Doors: A Collection of Charlie Russell's Favorite Stories, Trail's End (Pasadena, CA), 1948.

Paper Talk: Illustrated Letters, edited by Frederic G. Renner, Amon Carter Museum of Western Art (Fort Worth, TX), 1962.

The CMR Book, Superior (Seattle, WA), 1970.

Fifty CMR Paintings of the Old American West, Crown (New York, NY), 1978.

Charles M. Russell: Paintings, Drawings, and Sculpture, in the Collection of the R.W. Norton Art Gallery, Shreveport, Louisiana, The Gallery (Shreveport, LA), 1979.

Contributor to periodicals, including *Northwest Magazine, Helena Journal, Great Falls Weekly Tribune, Western Field and Stream, Field and Stream, Rocky Mountain Magazine, Great Falls Tribune, Butte Miner,*

Frank Leslie's Illustrated Newspaper, Outing, Scribner's Magazine, Popular Magazine, McClure's, Great Falls Leader, Treasure State, American Magazine, American Art News, Literary Digest, Saturday Evening Post, St. Nicholas, and *Montana Magazine.* Collections of Russell's papers are located at the Amon Carter Museum, Fort Worth, TX; Buffalo Bill Historical Center, Cody, WY; Colorado Springs Fine Art Center, Colorado Springs, CO; C.M. Russell Museum, Great Falls, MT; and the National Cowboy Hall of Fame and Western Heritage Center, Oklahoma City, OK.

ILLUSTRATOR

John H. Beacom, *How the Buffalo Lost His Crown,* Forest & Stream (New York, NY), 1894.

Charles Wallace, *Cattle Queen of Montana,* C.W. Foote (Saint James, MN), 1894.

E. Hough, *Story of the Cowboy,* Appleton (New York, NY), 1897.

Wallace D. Coburn, *Rhymes from a Round-up Camp,* W.T. Ridgely (Great Falls, MT), 1899.

Robert Vaughn, *Then and Now; or, Thirty-six Years in the Rockies,* Tribune (Minneapolis, MN), 1900.

Harry C. Freeman, *Brief History of Butte, Montana,* Henry O. Shepard (Chicago, IL), 1900.

William A. Allen, *Adventures with Indians and Game; or, Twenty Years in the Rocky Mountains,* A.W. Bowen (Chicago, IL), 1903.

Frances Parker, *Hope Hathaway: A Story of Western Ranch Life,* C.M. Clark (Boston, MA), 1904.

Olin D. Wheeler, *Trail of Lewis and Clark,* Putnam (New York, NY), 1904.

Charles J. Steedman, *Bucking the Sagebrush: or, The Oregon Trail in the Seventies,* Putnam (New York, NY), 1904.

W.T. Hamilton, *My Sixty Years on the Plains Trapping, Trading, and Indian Fighting,* Forest & Stream (New York, NY), 1905.

B.M. Bower, *Chip of the Flying U,* Street & Smith (New York, NY), 1906.

B.M. Bower, *The Range Dwellers,* Street & Smith (New York, NY), 1907.

B.M. Bower, *The Lure of the Dim Trails,* G.W. Dillingham (New York, NY), 1907.

Alice Harriman-Browne, *Chaperoning Adrienne: A Tale of Yellowstone National Park,* Metropolitan (Seattle, WA), 1907.

Carrie Adell Strahorn, *Fifteen Thousand Miles by Stage,* Putnam (New York, NY), 1911.

Owen Wister, *The Virginian,* Macmillan (New York, NY), 1911.

B.M. Bower, *The Uphill Climb,* Little, Brown (Boston, MA), 1913.

Bret Harte, *Trents Trust and Other Tales,* Houghton Mifflin (Boston, MA), 1914.

Frank B. Linderman, *Indian Why Stories,* Scribners (New York, NY), 1915.

Frank B. Linderman, *Indian Lodge-Fire Stories,* Scribners (New York, NY), 1918.

Frank B. Linderman, *Indian Old-Man Stories,* Scribners (New York, NY), 1920.

Agnes C. Laut, *Blazed Trail of the Old Frontier,* McBride (New York, NY), 1926.

John Willard, *The CMR Book,* Superior (Seattle, WA), 1970.

■ Adaptations

Russell's artwork has appeared as posters and on calendars.

■ Sidelights

Charles Marion Russell captured the romance and drama of America's frontier West in both his paintings and his writings. "Russell was a brilliant painter, sculptor, and illustrator . . . ," wrote Robert L. Gale in *Twentieth-Century Western Writers.* "He spent 40 years in the West, as cowboy, itinerant artist, and studio celebrity. His art work depicts most phases of range life and many aspects of Indian life." Michael Kennedy, writing in *Charles Marion Russell: Artist, Illustrator, Writer,* claimed that "no one will ever again recapture the time and the place as graphically, as devotedly, and with such fidelity, as did Charles Marion Russell." Nonetheless, Russell was born and raised in St. Louis, Missouri, and reared in an upper-middle-class, urban environment, far from the cowboy lifestyle he would later adopt.

From childhood, Russell exhibited signs of leading a strikingly different life than his father, Charles Silas Russell, a Yale-educated businessman. Russell was always an avid drawer, taking a particular interest in images of Indians and horses. Though not inclined to study or read much, he did have a penchant for dime novels that told tales about such old West heroes as Buffalo Bill and Kit Carson. His lack of interest in schoolwork led to numerous troubles with teachers and his family. A stint at a New Jersey military academy did little to settle the boy down. Eager to travel west and see the frontier for himself, Russell begged his father for a chance to go. But his father hoped young Charley, as he was called, would join the family's brickmaking business. Finally his father agreed. As a birthday present, he talked a family friend, Pike Miller, into taking sixteen-year-old Charley with him for the summer. Miller was traveling from St. Louis to Montana. Russell's father hoped that the journey would show the boy not only the natural beauty of the West but its hardships as well. He assumed Charley would come back "cured" of his interest in the frontier. However, what was supposed to be just a birthday journey turned out to be a watershed event. Rather than return to St. Louis, Russell took a job as a sheepherder in Montana. He also came to know seasoned local hunter and trapper Jake Hoover, who taught him much about outdoor life. In 1882, at age eighteen, Russell became a real cowboy when he was hired as a night herder for a cattle raiser in Montana.

Becomes a Cowboy

Russell developed his art skills while working as a cowboy. Inspired by the surrounding terrain, he sketched scenes of the countryside and made models of animals, local cowboys, and Native Americans. Though not the best cowboy—he admitted he never fully learned how to ride or rope—Russell's personal experiences allowed him to accurately depict Western scenes, down to the details of dress and setting. He strove for this kind of truth in his artwork, filling his studio with examples of such local objects as guns, Native American costumes, saddles, and Wild West memorabilia.

Despite Russell's drive for accuracy, his paintings and sculptures were nostalgic. During the 1880s, the West was experiencing widespread cultural changes. By 1890 the Indians, no longer riding free, were occupying reservations. The herds of buffalo that used to wander the plains had disappeared by the last decade of the nineteenth century. Donald A. Barclay described the West that Russell experienced in the *Dictionary of Literary Biography*: "Russell himself never witnessed Indian warfare or saw buffalo hunted from horseback though he eventually did become acquainted with several old-timers—Indians as well as whites—who had witnessed or participated in both of these quintessentially western pursuits. . . . Within six years of the start of his cowboy career a combination of shifting economic conditions, summer droughts, and winter blizzards had finished off open-range grazing as surely as the coming of the whites had finished off the buffalo and the free-roaming Indian."

These changes, however, did not deter Russell from depicting the West that had occupied his childhood fantasies. By 1887 he had developed a local reputation as an artist. One of his watercolor pictures, known both as "Waiting for a Chinook" and as "The Last of 5,000," shows a scene of a steer and several

Russell in full cowboy attire, complete with holster and gun. (Corbis-Bettmann.)

wolves suffering during the winter snowstorms of 1886 to 1887. It was widely reproduced and won Russell acclaim. In 1890 Russell published a portfolio of oil works called *Studies of Western Life.*

In 1893 Russell retired from cowboy work to become a full-time artist. Around this time he was commissioned to paint several pieces for the owner of N Bar N ranch, where Russell had done some cowboy work. Three years later Russell married Nancy Cooper, age seventeen, an event that profoundly affected Russell's career. Nancy proved a savvy businesswoman who took a hands-on interest in her husband's career.

If not for his new wife, Russell probably would have failed as an artist without the backup income of his cowboy work. Nancy changed her husband's lifestyle, requiring him to cut down on his drinking and increase his productivity. She also worked as his agent, seeking more money for Russell's paintings. Beginning in 1903 she insisted they regularly visit New York City, where she rightly believed collectors would pay more for her husband's work. During these trips Russell befriended several New York illustrators, and started drawing for such magazines as *Scribner's*, *Leslie's*, *Outing*, and *McClure's*. He also provided illustrations for books.

Russell's paintings and sculptures were well received in New York. In 1911 he had his first solo show at a New York gallery on Fifth Avenue. The show featured a range of his oils, watercolors, and bronzes under the title "The West That Has Passed." Russell himself was also a hit, fitting the Easterner's view of the cowboy in his boots, Stetson hat, and red sash—a costume he adopted soon after moving to Montana. He found that dressing like a cowboy, and playing the part of a soft-spoken, barely-educated rustic, helped sell his Western paintings. "In playing the part of the unlettered, unschooled

cowboy," Barclay explained, "Russell was to an extent pulling a fast one on the public. Though he never studied in any of the great art schools, Russell was a deliberate, purposeful artist who did not spring up full grown from the cattle camps of Montana. Though he refused to talk publicly about the fine points of art, disparaging it as a rather sissified subject, in private he was eager to learn what he could from master artists. Russell's work after his contact with New York illustrators . . . shows improvement in technique when compared to his earlier efforts. Also, the development of his drawing and painting clearly shows that he was a good student who paid careful attention to what other artists were doing." Russell's paintings remain in demand. A 2005 art auction saw Russell's oil painting "Piegans" sold for a world record 5.6 million dollars. At the same auction his watercolor "Crow Scouts in Winter," 18 by 13 inches in size, sold for 962,000 dollars.

The Cowboy Storyteller

While he is held in great esteem as an artist, Russell was also an effective storyteller, entertaining friends

In the 1903 painting "Buffalo Hunt," Russell depicts traditional hunting methods in the Old West. (Hulton Archive/Getty Images.)

Michael A. Stackpole

■ Personal

Born November 27, 1957, in Wausau, WI; son of James Ward (a physician) and Janet (an educator and community volunteer) Stackpole; companion of Elizabeth Turner Danforth (an artist). *Ethnicity:* "Caucasian/Irish-American." *Education:* University of Vermont, B.A., 1979. *Politics:* Democrat. *Religion:* Roman Catholic. *Hobbies and other interests:* Indoor soccer, arena football, gaming, shooting.

■ Addresses

Agent—Ricia Mainhardt, 612 Argyle, No. 5-L, Brooklyn, NY 11230.

■ Career

Flying Buffalo, Inc., Scottsdale, AZ, game designer, 1979-87; writer, 1987—.

■ Member

Game Manufacturers Association (chairperson of Industry Watch Committee), Science Fiction and Fantasy Writers of America, Academy of Gaming Arts and Design, Phoenix Skeptics (executive director, 1988—).

■ Awards, Honors

H.G. Wells Award, for best role playing adventure, 1983, for *Citybook I,* and 1984, for *Stormhaven;* Best Adventure Game, Computer Gaming World, 1988, for *Wasteland,* and 1989, for *Neuromancer; Wasteland* was inducted into the Computer Gaming World's Hall of Fame, 1993; Meritorious Service Award, Game Manufacturers Association, 1993; inducted into Academy of Gaming Arts and Design Hall of Fame, 1994.

■ Writings

NOVELS

Natural Selection, FASA Corp. (Chicago, IL), 1992.
Assumption of Risk, FASA Corp. (Chicago, IL), 1993.
Bred for War, FASA Corp. (Chicago, IL), 1994.
Once a Hero, Bantam (New York, NY), 1994.
Mutant Chronicles: Dementia, FASA Corp. (Chicago, IL), 1994.
Malicious Intent, FASA Corp. (Chicago, IL), 1996.

"WARRIOR" SERIES

Warrior: En Garde, FASA Corp. (Chicago, IL), 1988.
Warrior: Riposte, FASA Corp. (Chicago, IL), 1988.
Warrior: Coupe, FASA Corp. (Chicago, IL), 1989.

"BLOOD OF KERENSKY" SERIES

Lethal Heritage, FASA Corp. (Chicago, IL), 1990.
Blood Legacy, FASA Corp. (Chicago, IL), 1990.
Lost Destiny, FASA Corp. (Chicago, IL), 1991.

"DARK CONSPIRACY" SERIES

A Gathering Evil, Game Designers Workshop (Bloomington, IL), 1991.
Evil Ascending, Game Designers Workshop (Bloomington, IL), 1991.
Evil Triumphant, Game Designers Workshop (Bloomington, IL), 1992.

"BATTLETECH" SERIES

Bred for War, New American Library (New York, NY), 1995.
Malicious Intent, New American Library (New York, NY), 1996.
The Twilight of the Clans II: Grave Covenant, New American Library (New York, NY), 1997.
Prince of Havoc, Roc, 1998.
Warrior: Coupe, Roc, 1998.

"STAR WARS X-WING" SERIES

The Krytos Trap, Bantam (New York, NY), 1996.
Rogue Squadron, Bantam (New York, NY), 1996.
Wedge's Gamble, Bantam (New York, NY), 1996.
The Bacta War, Bantam (New York, NY), 1998.
Battleground: Tatooine, Dark Horse Comics (Milwaukie, OR), 1998.
The Phantom Affair, Dark Horse Comics (Milwaukie, OR), 1998.
The Warrior Princess, Dark Horse Comics (Milwaukie, OR), 1998.
(With Steve Crespo, James W. Hall, and Drew Johnson) *Blood and Honor,* Dark Horse Comics (Milwaukie, OR), 1999.
In the Empire's Service, Dark Horse Comics (Milwaukie, OR), 1999.
Isard's Revenge, Bantam (New York, NY), 1999.
Requiem for a Rogue, Dark Horse Comics (Milwaukie, OR), 1999.
Masquerade, Dark Horse Comics (Milwaukie, OR), 2000.
Mandatory Retirement, Dark Horse Comics (Milwaukie, OR), 2001.

"REALMS OF CHAOS" SERIES

A Hero Born, Harper (New York, NY), 1997.
An Enemy Reborn, Harper (New York, NY), 1998.

"STAR WARS: THE NEW JEDI ORDER" SERIES

Dark Tide I: Onslaught, Del Rey (New York, NY), 2000.
Dark Tide II: Ruin, Del Rey (New York), 2000.

"DRAGONCROWN WAR CYCLE" SERIES

The Dark Glory War: A Prelude to the DragonCrown War Cycle, Bantam Books (New York, NY), 2000.
Fortress Draconis, Bantam Books (New York, NY), 2001.
When Dragons Rage, Bantam Books (New York, NY), 2002.
The Grand Crusade, Bantam Books (New York, NY), 2003.

"MECHWARRIOR: DARK AGE" SERIES

Ghost War, Roc, 2002.
Masters of War, Roc, 2007.

"AGE OF DISCOVERY" SERIES

A Secret Atlas, Bantam Books (New York, NY), 2005.
Cartomancy, Bantam Books (New York, NY), 2006.
The New World, Bantam Books (New York, NY), 2007.

GAMES

Citybook I, Flying Buffalo (Scottsdale, AZ), 1983.
Stormhaven, Flying Buffalo (Scottsdale, AZ), 1984.
Wasteland, Interplay Productions (Los Angeles, CA), 1988.
Neuromancer, Interplay Productions (Los Angeles), 1989.
Wolf and Raven, Roc, 1998.
(Author of foreword) *Core Rulebook (Star Wars Role Playing Game),* Wizards of the Coast (Renton, WA), 2000.

OTHER

(Editor, with Liz Danforth) *Mages, Blood and Old Bones,* Flying Buffalo (Scottsdale, AZ), 1992.
Talion: Revenant, Spectra (New York, NY), 1997.

Eyes of Silver, Spectra (New York, NY), 1998.

I, Jedi, Bantam (New York, NY), 1998.

(With Timothy Zahn and Carlos Ezquerra) *Star Wars—Mara Jade: By the Emperor's Hand,* Dark Horse Comics (Milwaukie, OR), 1999.

Star Wars: Union, Dark Horse Comics (Milwaukie, OR), 2000.

Perchance to Dream and Other Stories, Five Star, 2005.

Also author of nonfiction books on gaming. Work represented in anthologies, including *Shrapnel,* FASA Corp., 1988; *Into the Shadows,* FASA Corp., 1990; *An Armory of Swords,* edited by Fred Saberhagen, Tor Books (New York, NY), 1995; *Warriors of Blood and Dreams,* Avon (New York, NY), 1995; *Superheroes,* Ace (New York, NY), 1995; and *Insufficient Evidence: Distant Planes,* Harper, 1996. Contributor of short stories to magazines, including *Amazing Stories.*

■ **Sidelights**

Best-selling fantasy writer Michael A. Stackpole is "prolific and gifted," according to Roland Green in *Booklist.* In addition to his many novels set in the "Star Wars" universe, including *I, Jedi* and the "Star Wars X-Wing" series, Stackpole has also written novels set in worlds of his own creation, such as the "Dragoncrown War Cycle" and the "Age of Discovery" series.

Stackpole was born in Wassau, Wisconsin, in 1957; his parents moved to Vermont six months later. His father, James Ward Stackpole, is a physician, and his mother, Janet, was a teacher before turning to local politics. "After the return to Vermont," Stackpole noted on his Home Page, "my brother Patrick was born and, four years after that, my sister Kerin was born. Patrick is career military, having graduated from West Point. My sister is a lawyer and quite good at what she does. (I find it rather comforting to know that in my family I can get good medical advice, good legal advice, and good military advice, all of which are vital in my trade.)"

From a young age, Stackpole noted on his Home Page, he wanted to be a writer: "In the sixth grade I realized it was something I was interested in doing. My grandfather, Austin H. Kerin, had written and had published a little book titled *Yankees in Court.* It was a book of legal anecdotes. My mom was very proud of her father's accomplishment, so I grew up in a household where writers were held in high regard. In sixth grade I turned out stories that were a bit longer than those of my classmates and, by the

time I hit college, I started sending stories out to magazines." Stackpole graduated from Rice Memorial High School in 1975, then attended the University of Vermont. He earned a bachelor's degree in history in 1979. Already interested in creating games—he had sold his first game to Flying Buffalo Inc. in 1977—Stackpole moved to Arizona to work for Flying Buffalo Inc. as a game designer. He left that position in 1987 when FASA Corporation hired him to write the Warrior trilogy of BattleTech novels.

Stackpole has gone on to write a number of novels, many of which are set in existing fictional universes such as "Star Wars." He has written a number of books in the "Star Wars X-Wing" series, the "Star Wars: The New Jedi Order" series, and standalone

In the 1998 "Star Wars" novel *I, Jedi,* **Michael A. Stackpole relates the adventures of Corran Horn.** (Bantam Books, 1999. Cover art copyright © 1998 by Lucasfilm Ltd. Used by permission of Bantam Books, a division of Random House, Inc.)

Stackpole's 2002 novel *When Dragons Rage* concerns a battle for the DragonCrown, a magical object of great power. (Bantam Books, 2003. Cover illustration copyright © 2002 by Ciruelo Cabral. Used by permission of Bantam Books, a division of Random House, Inc.)

Creates the "Dragoncrown War Cycle"

Stackpole's "Dragoncrown War Cycle" begins with *Fortress Draconis*, in which the thief known as Will the Nibble steals the priceless living silver leaf. The leaf may be part of the Dragoncrown, the royal crown, so the crime leads to dangerous political intrigue in Fortress Draconis. Evil sorceress Chytrine is plotting to conquer the world by assembling all the pieces in the Dragoncrown and thereby creating an object of great magical power. There are those who believe Will the Nibble has been prophecied to lead an army against her. *Booklist*'s Paula Luedtke declared: "With a deliciously evil antagonist and some truly remarkable supporting characters, this is a terrific read." Jackie Cassada of the *Library Journal* regarded the book as "a solid addition to the epic fantasy genre." A reviewer for *Publishers Weekly* made special mention of the novel's exciting conclusion, commenting that, "as usual, Stackpole provides a compelling and engaging escape."

The story continues in *When Dragons Rage*, in which Chytrine is pitted against Will, the Princess Alexia, and the young sorcerer Kerrigan, who try to prevent the evil sorceress from gaining all the pieces to the DragonCrown, which would give her enormous power. In her review of the novel, Luedtke found that "there is plenty of terrific dragonlore, . . . not to mention enough sex, love, bloody battles, and high adventure to keep reading lamps lit well into the wee hours." "*When Dragons Rage* has some wonderful elements," Cindy Lynn Speer admitted in her review for the *SF Site*, "brought together by a writer who deftly and colorfully manipulates this world, bringing things that are familiar and mixing them in with the new, creating an adventure of quick pace and amazing color."

The story is completed in Stackpole's *The Grand Crusade*, which finds Will dead and his remaining companions battling Chytrine on their own. The evil sorceress threatens to unleash the dreaded Oromise, a race long ago banished from the earth. Sayce, Will's lover, is kidnapped, while Oracle, a blind prophet, believes that there is still a possibility to thwart Chytrine. "This is fantasy on the most epic of scales, with plenty of bloody conflict and treacherous double-dealing," according to a critic for *Publishers Weekly*. Luedtke concluded: "With a plot like a set of Chinese boxes, complex military strategies, horrific undead creatures, a fabulous mage, and a sweet love story to soften it a bit, Stackpole's white-knuckle ride of an epic fantasy continues in fine form."

novels featuring the same characters. In one such standalone, *I, Jedi*, Stackpole tells of Corran Horn, a Jedi Knight who must rescue his girlfriend Mirax, who is being held captive. A critic for *Publishers Weekly* praised the novel as "lavish" and found Corran Horn to be "a more complex protagonist than many, formidably competent but with believable limitations." Roland Green of *Booklist* commented on the secondary characters, noting that it is "unusual and pleasurable to see Luke, Leia, and Han as comparative bit players in the [Star Wars] universe." "*I, Jedi* is smartly executed and fun reading," wrote Thomas F. Cunningham in a review for the *SF Site*, "and that's one of the highest endorsements I can give."

"Age of Discovery" Series

Stackpole began the "Age of Discovery" series in 2005 with *A Secret Atlas*. Set in a fantasy world similar to our own fifteenth century, when European explorers set out to discover new lands, the story tells of the Anturasi family, official mapmakers and explorers for the king of Nalenyr. When Keles and Jorim Anturasi are sent by their grandfather to explore and map an uncharted region, they find secrets that have been hidden for centuries. "Stackpole takes a fresh approach to fantasy adventure with this series launch," wrote Jackie Cassada in the *Library Journal,* "which offers an original premise, intriguing characters, a richly detailed world, and a suitably ambiguous ending." Green found that "Stackpole is, as usual, discursive but also deft and detailed in his worldbuilding."

In *Cartomancy,* political intrigue rages between factions who hope to use the Anturasi family's maps and mapmaking skills to take over the Nine Princi-

palities of the known world. Keles Anturasi has been captured by Prince Pyrust of Deseiron while mapping the unexplored territory of Ixyll. His grandfather, Qiro Anturasi, has been taken prisoner by the Imperial Prince Cyron of Nalenyr. Legendary heroes of the distant past may be summoned by magic to reappear and save the world. A critic for *Publishers Weekly* noted that "there's adventure aplenty for those who like their fantasies big and bloody." Cassada called the novel an "ambitious tale of love in a time of danger and faith in a time of no hope."

The New World, published in 2007, concludes the "Age of Discovery" series. While a ruthless prince seeks to unseat his empress mother, an elder god hopes to destroy all of creation in a vengeful cataclysm. "With its huge cast, numerous byzantine subplots and nonstop action," wrote a critic for *Publishers Weekly,* "Stackpole's ambitious epic is comparable to—if not quite at the level of—sagas by adventure fantasy heavyweights like George R.R. Martin and Robert Jordan." Green believed that, "when the roster of [Stackpole's] work is complete, the 'Age of Discovery' may be deemed his finest fantasy."

Stackpole once remarked: "My motivations for writing are simple. I want to write the kind of story I like to read. I want to create stories that entertain the readers. I want to make readers feel for characters and care about what happens to them because, by involving a reader on an emotional level, a book can allow the reader to experience things that are outside the purview of a normal life. I also write for money, because bills have to be paid.

Stackpole's 2003 novel *The Grand Crusade* finds an evil sorceress threatening to release a deadly prehistoric race. (Bantam Books, 2004. Used by permission of Bantam Books, a division of Random House, Inc.)

If you enjoy the works of Michael A. Stackpole, you may also want to check out the following books:

Dennis L. McKiernan, *The Eye of the Hunter,* 1992.
Scott Lynch, *The Lies of Locke Lamora,* 2006.
Patrick Rothfuss, *The Name of the Wind,* 2007.

"A number of writers have influenced me. From Edgar Rice Burroughs I learned how to structure a plot, and I got a refresher course in that from Frederick Forsyth. Walter Gibson, Lester Dent, and Rex Stout all showed me how to make fascinating characters from individuals who are largely unknowable. J.R.R. Tolkien showed how a contemporary author can tap into the elements of myth, Dennis L. McKiernan and Stephan Donaldson showed how it could be done differently and better, and Roger Zelazny showed how the use of detail can suggest whole universes.

"Much of my work is military in nature. I find warfare fascinating and decidedly terrifying. Except for a natural disaster, war is the most catastrophic thing that can happen to a human being. Despite its horrors, war is a crucible that creates heroes, and it is their stories that I like to tell. My books don't praise war, but they praise the triumph of individuals over war."

■ Biographical and Critical Sources

PERIODICALS

Booklist, March 15, 1997, Roland Green, review of *Talion: Revenant*, p. 1231; April 15, 1998, Roland Green, review of *I, Jedi*, p. 1357; November 15, 2001, Paula Luedtke, review of *Fortress Draconis*, p. 560; October 15, 2002, Paula Luedtke, review of *When Dragons Rage*, p. 396; December 15, 2003, Paula Luedtke, review of *The Grand Crusade*, p. 734; March 1, 2005, Roland Green, review of *A Secret Atlas*, p. 1150; February 1, 2006, Roland Green, review of *Cartomancy*, p. 38; July 1, 2007, Roland Green, review of *The New World*, p. 42.

Kirkus Reviews, October 1, 2001, review of *Fortress Draconis*, p. 1397; October 1, 2002, review of *When Dragons Rage*, p. 1435; December 15, 2004, review of *A Secret Atlas*, p. 1171.

Library Journal, December, 2001, Jackie Cassada, review of *Fortress Draconis*, p. 181; February 15, 2005, Jackie Cassada, review of *A Secret Atlas*, p. 123; February 15, 2006, Jackie Cassada, review of *Cartomancy*, p. 111.

MBR Bookwatch, March, 2005, Harriet Klausner, review of *A Secret Atlas*; April, 2005, review of *Perchance to Dream and Other Stories*.

Publishers Weekly, April 27, 1998, review of *I, Jedi*, pp. 50-51; November 26, 2001, review of *Fortress Draconis*, pp. 44-45; November 11, 2002, review of *When Dragons Rage*, p. 45; December 1, 2003, review of *The Grand Crusade*, p. 45; February 7, 2005, review of *A Secret Atlas*, p. 47; January 16, 2006, review of *Cartomancy*, p. 41; June 11, 2007, review of *The New World*, p. 43.

ONLINE

Game Spy, http://pc.gamespy.com/ (August 17, 2004), Allen Rausch, "Mike Stackpole Interview."

Michael A. Stackpole's Home Page, http://www.stormwolf.com (September 20, 2007).

SFF World, http://www.sffworld.com/ (December 4, 2000), interview with Stackpole.

SF Site, http://www.sfsite.com/ (September 20, 2007), Alma A. Hromic, review of *Cartomancy*, Cindy Lynn Speer, review of *When Dragons Rage*, S. Kay Elmore, review of *Eyes of SIlver*, and Thomas F. Cunningham, review of *I, Jedi*.*

Olen Steinhauer

(Photograph by Slavica Pilic-Steinhauer.)

■ Personal

Born in Baltimore, MD; divorced. *Education:* University of Texas at Austin, undergraduate degree; Emerson College, M.F.A.

■ Addresses

Home—Budapest, Hungary. *Agent*—Stephanie Cabot, The Gernert Company, 136 E. 57th St., New York, NY 10022; email: scabotthegernertco.com.

■ Career

Writer and film producer. Has worked as a librarian, teacher, manual laborer, film producer, and author. Coproducer, with Krista Steinhauer, of film documentary *Central Square,* 1999.

■ Awards, Honors

Fulbright fellowship; production grant, Massachusetts Institute of Technology, for film *Central Square;* Ellis Peters Historical Dagger nomination, Crime Writers' Association, Bouchercon World Mystery's Anthony Award for best historical novel, Macavity Award for best novel from Mystery Readers International, and Edgar Allan Poe Award nomination for best first novel by an American, Mystery Writers of America, all 2004, all for *The Bridge of Sighs;* Edgar Allan Poe Award nomination, 2006, for *Liberation Movements.*

■ Writings

The Bridge of Sighs, St. Martin's Minotaur (New York, NY), 2003.

The Confession, St. Martin's Minotaur (New York, NY), 2004.

36 Yalta Boulevard, St. Martin's Minotaur (New York, NY), 2005, published as *The Vienna Assignment,* HarperCollins (London, England), 2005.

Liberation Movements, St. Martin's Minotaur (New York, NY), 2006, published as *The Istanbul Variations,* HarperCollins (London, England), 2006.

Victory Square, St. Martin's Minotaur (New York, NY), 2007.

Contributor of poems and stories to periodicals, including *Ellery Queen's Mystery Magazine, Manoa, Beacon Street Review,* and *Quarterly West.* Creator of online journal; also author of the *Olen Steinhauer—News* blog. Books have been translated into Swedish, French, and Japanese.

■ Adaptations

Blackstone Audiobooks recorded audio versions of *The Bridge of Sighs,* 2003, and *The Confession,* 2004.

■ Sidelights

Olen Steinhauer's crime novels are set in an imaginary Eastern European country during the Cold War. "I chose a fictional country because what I am doing, in a sense, is a form of Western decadence," Steinhauer told Mark Baker in the *Wall Street Journal.* "I am writing about real people who had bad things happen in their lives. I don't want to be accused of treating something lightly or of getting a particular country's history wrong." Steinhauer's books chronicle the daily life of people under a totalitarian

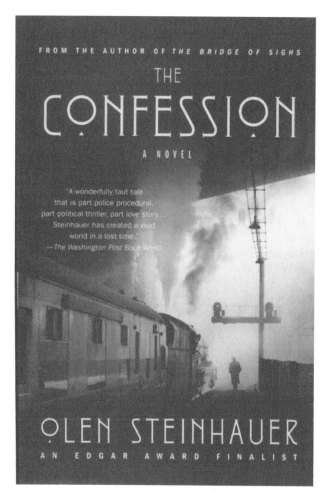

Steinhauer's 2004 novel *The Confession* tells of a homicide inspector in a politically-sensitive investigation. (St. Martin's Minotaur, 2005. Cover photograph © Burt Hardy/Getty Images. Reprinted by permission of St. Martin's Press, LLC.)

regime and trace the events that led to the eventual collapse of communism in Eastern Europe. "The stories are not just about history or politics . . . ; they are about what all good literature is about: human nature," wrote Kevin Holtsberry in a review for *National Review Online.* "Their aesthetic power comes from artfully drawn characters and emotions. The setting may be exotic and the history may be unique, but fundamentally these are human dilemmas that we can all relate to: love and betrayal, conflicting loyalties, career pressures, family dynamics, questions about fate and the future." Steinhauer's mysteries are, according to a critic for *Mystery News,* "one of the most unique and remarkable series of thrillers being written today."

Born in Baltimore, Maryland, Steinhauer grew up in Virginia. He later lived all over the United States, in Georgia, Mississippi, Pennsylvania, Texas, California, Massachusetts, and New York. He earned his undergraduate degree at the University of Texas at Austin and then an M.F.A. in creative writing from Emerson College in Boston. After leaving college, Steinhauer moved to Europe and lived in Croatia, then a part of Yugoslavia. "I was there in the fall of '89, when the Berlin Wall came down," he told Jeff Salamon in the *Austin American-Statesman.* "I was 19, I was just learning to drink and smoke and dance, and this wasn't part of my reality—the whole political situation. And when everything started crumbling in all of the neighboring countries, it was shocking just how little I knew. So I became obsessed with writing about it." He spent a year in Romania on a Fulbright grant and later lived in the Czech Republic and Italy. He now lives in Budapest, Hungary. In an article for the *Daily Telegraph,* Steinhauer wrote: "I arrived here five years ago to research a series of thrillers about communist Eastern Europe. I stayed because of the city. . . . This is a vibrant metropolis, throbbing with culture, history, food and industry."

A Rookie Cop in Eastern Europe

Steinhauer's first book, drawn from his Ph.D. thesis, is *The Bridge of Sighs.* Set in 1948, the year of the Berlin Airlift, the story follows Emil Brod, a young homicide inspector for the People's Militia (the name for the official police force) as he tries to solve two murders in a small Eastern European country. Brod's police colleagues treat him with disdain, thinking that he is a spy, and he is not even given a gun. He encounters many other obstacles as he moves from location to location to solve the murder of a well-known songwriter, Janos Crowder, who has been found beaten to death in his apartment. The fact that the murdered man was politically well connected makes the rookie inspector's job all the more difficult.

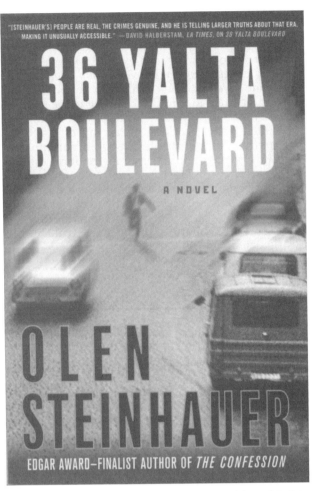

Communist spy Brano Sev is in trouble with his superiors in Steinhauer's 2005 novel *36 Yalta Boulevard*. (St. Martin's Minotaur, 2006. Cover photograph of street scene © Bettmann/Corbis. Cover photograph of man running © Arthur Tress/Getty. Reprinted by permission of St. Martin's Press, LLC.)

Critical response to *The Bridge of Sighs* was positive, and the novel received several awards and nominations. In the *Houston Chronicle*, P.G. Koch wrote that "what [Steinhauer] does best . . . is re-imagine the palpable dangers of that perilously tilted postwar landscape." Edna Boardman, writing in *Kliatt*, called the novel a "richly drawn detective mystery." Ronnie H. Terpening wrote in *Library Journal* that the book is an "intelligent, finely polished debut, loaded with atmospheric detail." A writer for *Kirkus Reviews* maintained: "Time, place, and cast are all richly evoked in a well-written, often gripping debut."

"Originally, when I was writing *The Bridge of Sighs*, I didn't know if it was going to be set in a fictional country or in Romania," Steinhauer told Salamon. "When I was in Romania . . ., I researched the history of the country very intensely, so I had a good picture of 1948 there. But honestly, I didn't want to deal with the tedium of getting every single fact right—like, Do you turn left or right on Boulevard Eminescu? And I was kind of entranced by the idea of creating a fictional country because that meant I could use something from Romania in one book, something from Hungary in another book or Poland in another book—whatever seemed most interesting."

Steinhauer continued his series with *The Confession*. This story, set in 1956, follows an older homicide inspector, Ferenc Kolyeszar, as he investigates a murder and the apparent suicide of a prominent Communist Party member's wife. Kolyeszar has to deal not only with the intricacies of a totalitarian system, but also with his own crumbling marriage and his grisly memories of World War II. David Wright, in a review for *Booklist*, wrote that although the premise of a detective troubled by personal "demons is hardly new . . . seldom is it presented with such depth and personal intensity." Terpening, writing in the *Library Journal*, called the novel "a gripping and fully realized portrayal of a man whose strengths, flaws, struggle, and ultimate fall are emblematic of the fate of Eastern Europe itself." A reviewer for *Publishers Weekly* commented on the "deaths and deceptions snowballing grotesquely" and wrote that "the novel makes readers wonder just what Steinhauer will do for the next book in his series."

A Spy on the Outs

The third book in Steinhauer's series about an un-named Communist-era Eastern European country, *36 Yalta Boulevard,* features communist spy Brano Sev, who finds himself on the outs with his Soviet bloc nation's commanders. Sent to Vienna to find and close a security breach, Sev is instead accused of foiling the mission. He soon finds himself back home, working long hours in a factory. Months later he is offered a chance at redemption: Check out Jan Seroka, a defector to the West who has now unaccountably returned home. Sev suspects his bosses are setting him up and soon finds that he is right. "Brano Sev is Steinhauer's most intriguing hero yet, and that's saying something," wrote David Wright in *Booklist*. Sev drew the praise of P.G. Koch in the *Houston Chronicle*, who noted: "Le Carre's spies look almost floridly sentimental in comparison to this austere man, whose convictions carry him all the way to the subtle full stop of the book's last, quietly appalling moment."

Ronnie H. Terpening, once again writing in the *Library Journal*, referred to *36 Yalta Boulevard* as "an imaginative, brilliantly plotted espionage thriller."

In Steinhauer's 2007 novel *Victory Square*, **a police official investigates the strange death of a general while the Soviet bloc collapses around him.** (St. Martin's Minotaur, 2007. Jacket photograph courtesy of Nailya Alexander Gallery. Reprinted by permission of St. Martin's Press, LLC.)

plane hijacking by Armenian terrorists. *Library Journal* contributor Terpening noted that the author "again displays his masterful manipulation of character, plot, and reader expectations." A *Kirkus Reviews* contributor called *Liberation Movements* a "cool and cerebral crime thriller, full of political nuance and bathed in irony." According to the reviewer for *Publishers Weekly*, the novel was an example of "a skilled writer working at the top of his form." "*Liberation Movements* is first and foremost an elegantly written and entertaining political thriller," wrote a critic for *Mystery News*. "On another and more important level, however, this is a memorable and philosophically profound novel by a writer whose growing body of work seems destined to transcend the limitations of the genre within which it originated."

If you enjoy the works of Olen Steinhauer, you may also want to check out the following books:

Ian Rankin, *Knots and Crosses*, 1987.
Jason Goodwin, *The Janissary Tree*, 2006.
Martin Cruz Smith, *Stalin's Ghost*, 2007.
Tom Rob Smith, *Child 44*, 2008.

Investigating Crime During a Revolution

Another reviewer of *36 Yalta Boulevard* compared Steinhauer to a recognized "master" of the spy genre. Andi Shechter, writing on the *Book Reporter* Web site, noted: "In only his third novel, author Olen Steinhauer brings to mind the baroque, highly complicated and yet spare plots of the master, John le Carre." Shechter went on to write: "My comparison . . . comes from an appreciation of both authors' ability to show a distinctly non-glamorous everyday espionage, devoid of ringing heartfelt flag-waving or patriotism." Jeff Siegel, writing in *Mystery Scene*, believed that "when people wonder, in a generation or two, what the Cold War was like and how we lived with it, especially in Eastern Europe, they can read *36 Yalta Boulevard.*"

Liberation Movements continues the story of Sev, who this time is supervising two younger agents in their investigation of a murder in Prague in 1968. As the story unfolds, the murder becomes linked with a

Victory Square brings back Emil Brod, who has risen up the police ranks to become chief of police. Only days away from retirement, Brod is brought in to investigate the death of Lieutenant General Yuri Kolev. Though his death seems to be from a heart attack, the coroner has discovered traces of heroin and cocaine in the general's blood. Signs point to the involvement of an anti-government underground group. As Brod investigates, the fall of the Berlin Wall marks the beginning of a series of revolutions across Eastern Europe in which Soviet-backed communist regimes begin to fall. The liberatory turmoil soon spreads to Brod's country as well, and he is hard-pressed to finish his investigation amid the celebration and chaos. "Employing an intricate story, characters both sympathetic and despicable as well as a remarkable sense of place," according to the critic for *Publishers Weekly*, "Steinhauer subtly illuminates an unforgettable historical moment." Keir Graff in *Booklist* wrote: "This is remarkable storytelling, exploring the life cycle of a state through the eyes of political idealists, government informants, and good cops like Brod who just want to solve crimes." Holtsberry concluded: "*Victory Square* is an exciting and thought-provoking fictional portrayal of historic events, as well as a meditation on the personal corruption that pervades totalitarianism. It is both a suspenseful espionage thriller with enough twists and turns—and surprises and betrayals—to keep you frantically turning the pages."

Speaking to Barker about how he writes his novels, Steinhauer explained: "I don't plot beforehand. A lot of times I know what's going to happen in the next 30 pages, but I have no idea after that. Writers are often advised to work from an outline, but that's just not interesting for me. As I write, I discover things that I had no idea I was going to write. Themes emerge that I had never planned. This type of organic writing is the only way I can do it . . . the only way I can get results that I really believe."

■ Biographical and Critical Sources

PERIODICALS

Austin American-Statesman (Austin, TX), August 25, 2007, Jeff Salamon, "Writer Seeks Out the Mystery in Eastern Europe Thriller," p. F1.

Booklist, January 1, 2004, David Wright, review of *The Confession*, p. 835; May 1, 2005, David Wright, review of *36 Yalta Boulevard*, p. 1539; July 1, 2007, Keir Graff, review of *Victory Square*, p. 37.

Daily Telegraph, July 20, 2007, Olen Steinhauer, "Budapest: My Kind of Town."

Entertainment Weekly, March 12, 2004, Michelle King, review of *The Confession*, p. 120.

Houston Chronicle, May 4, 2003, P.G. Koch, "Shades of Gray: Nominal Hero Seen in Terrifying Light," p. 19; August 7, 2005, P.G. Koch, review of *36 Yalta Boulevard*, p. 16.

Kirkus Reviews, November 1, 2002, review of *The Bridge of Sighs*, p. 1576; December 1, 2003, review of *The Confession*, p. 1385; May 1, 2005, review of *36 Yalta Boulevard*, p. 505; June 1, 2006, review of *Liberation Movements*, p. 544.

Kliatt, November, 2003, Edna Boardman, review of *The Bridge of Sighs*, p. 44.

Library Journal, December, 2002, Ronnie H. Terpening, review of *The Bridge of Sighs*, p. 184; January, 2004, Ronnie H. Terpening, review of *The Confession*, p. 166, Scott R. DeMarco, review of *The Bridge of Sighs*, p. 183; April 15, 2005, Ronnie H. Terpening, review of *36 Yalta Boulevard*, p. 80; May 15, 2006, Ronnie H. Terpening, review of *Liberation Movements*, p. 95; May 15, 2007, Phillip Oliver, review of *Liberation Movements* audiobook, p. 130; July 1, 2007, review of *Victory Square*, p. 59.

Los Angeles Times, August 20, 2007, David Cotner, review of *Victory Square*.

Mystery News, August/September, 2006, review of *Liberation Movements*.

Mystery Scene, summer, 2005, Jeff Siegel, review of *36 Yalta Boulevard*.

New York Times Book Review, August 12, 2007, Marilyn Stasio, review of *Victory Square*, p. 25.

Publishers Weekly, January 20, 2003, review of *The Bridge of Sighs*, p. 59; December 1, 2003, review of *The Confession*, p. 38; May 15, 2006, review of *Liberation Movements*, p. 51; June 11, 2007, review of *Victory Square*, p. 41.

Sunday Telegraph (London, England), January 1, 2006, Susanna Yager, review of *The Vienna Assignment*, p. 47.

Texas Monthly, June 1, 2005, Mike Shea, review of *36 Yalta Boulevard*, p. 64.

Wall Street Journal, January 25, 2008, Mark Baker, "Backstage with Olen Steinhauer: Reliving the Soviet Era in the Eastern Bloc."

Wisconsin Bookwatch, August, 2005, review of *36 Yalta Boulevard* audiobook.

ONLINE

Armchair Interviews, http://www.armchairinterviews.com/ (June 21, 2007), Sharon Broom, review of *Liberation Movements*.

Bookreporter.com, http://www.bookreporter.com/ (June 21, 2007), Andi Shechter, review of *36 Yalta Boulevard*; Maggie Harding, review of *The Bridge of Sighs*.

National Review Online, http://article.nationalreview.com/ (September 17, 2007), Kevin Holtsberry, "Homicide Behind the Iron Curtain."

Olen Steinhauer Home Page, http://www.olensteinhauer.com (March 3, 2008).*

Bryan Talbot

■ Personal

Born February 24, 1952, in Wigan, Lancashire, England; married; wife's name Mary (a university professor). *Education:* Preston Polytechnic, degree (graphic design).

■ Addresses

Home—Nottingham, England.

■ Career

Author and illustrator of comic books. Longcastle Advertising, former graphic designer; designer for British Aerospace. *Exhibitions:* Work has been exhibited in one-man shows in Lancashire and London, England, Tuscany, Italy, and New York, NY.

■ Member

Comics Creators' Guild of Great Britain.

■ Awards, Honors

Eagle Award for Best Character, 1984, for Torquemada, from *Nemesis the Warlock;* Eagle Award for Favourite Artist, 1987; Eagle Award for Best Artist, Best New Comic, Best Character, and Best Comic Cover, all 1988, and Mekon Award for Best British Work, Society of Strip Illustration, all for *The Adventures of Luther Arkwright;* Eagle Awards, 1993, Eisner Award for Best Graphic Album, 1996, Comic Creators' Guild Award, two Don Thomson Awards, *Comic Buyers' Guide,* Internet Comic Award for Best Graphic Novel, Unghunden award (Sweden), Rueben Award, National Cartoonists' Society of America, Harvey Award, and Haxtur Award (Spain) for Best Long Comic Strip, 1999, all for *The Tale of One Bad Rat;* two Eisner Award nominations, for "MASK"; Inkpot Award, 2000; named Ambassador of Sunderland, Sunderland, England, City Council; *Alice in Sunderland: An Entertainment* was chosen as one of the best books of the year, 2007, by *New Statesman;* Eagle Award nominations, 2008, for Favorite Original Graphic Novel, for *Alice in Sunderland: An Entertainment* and for Comics-related Book Category, for *The Naked Artist: Comic Book Legends;* British Science Fiction Association Award shortlist, 2008, for *Alice in Sunderland: An Entertainment.*

■ Writings

Brainstorm!: The Complete Chester P. Hackenbush and Other Underground Classics, Alchemy (London, England), 1982.

The Adventures of Luther Arkwright (first published in comic-book form), Volumes 1-2, Valkyrie (London, England), 1982–1987, Volume 3, Dark Horse (Milwaukee, OR), 1990.

(Illustrator) Pat Mills, *Nemesis the Warlock, Book 3* (originally published in comic-book form as part of "2000 A.D." series), Titan (London, England), 1985.

(Illustrator, with others) Neil Gaiman, *The Sandman: The Game of You*, Titan (London, England), 1993.

(Illustrator, with others) Neil Gaiman, *The Sandman: Fables and Reflections*, Titan (London, England), 1994.

The Tale of One Bad Rat (originally published in comic-book form), Dark Horse (Milwaukie, OR), 1995.

The Ex-Directory: The Secret Files of Bryan Talbot, Knockabout, 1997.

(With Terry LaBan and Peter Doherty) *The Dreaming: Gates of Horn and Ivory* (originally published in comic-book form), Titan (London, England), 1999.

Heart of Empire; or, The Legacy of Luther Arkwright (originally published in comic-book form), Dark Horse (Milwaukie, OR), 1999.

Alice in Sunderland: An Entertainment (originally published in comic-book format), Dark Horse (Milwaukie, OR), 2007.

The Naked Artist: And Other Comic Book Legends, illustrated by Hunt Emerson, Moonstone, 2007.

The Art of Bryan Talbot, NBM (New York, NY), 2007.

Author of comic-book series "Frank Fazakerley, Space Ace of the Future," 1978; "Graphixus 4," 1978; and "The Dead Boy Detectives," four volumes, Vertigo, 2001. Contributor to comics series, some published as graphic novels, including: (with Alan Moore and Pat Mills) "2000 A.D.," beginning 1982; (with John Wagner and others) "Judge Dredd," 1986-87; (With Jamie Delano) "Hellblazer," 1989; (with Tom Veitch) "The Nazz," 1990; (with Neil Gaiman) "The Sandman Special No. 1: The Song of Orpheus"; (with Glen Fabry and David Pugh) *Sláine: Time Killer*, 1991; (with Rick Veitch) "Neil Gaiman's Teknophage," 1995-96; (with Justin Richards) *Doctor Who*, 2001; (with others) "Batman: Legends of the Dark Night: MASK," Titan, 1996; (with Moore) "Alan Moore's Yuggoth Cultures and Other Growths," 2003; (with Bill Withingham and others) "Fables: Storybook Love," Vertigo, 2004; and "Cherubs!," illustrated by Mark Stafford, Desperado, 2007.

Author's works have been translated into Spanish, Italian, German, French, Danish, and Finnish.

■ Adaptations

The Adventures of Luther Arkwright was adapted for audio CD, Big Finish Productions, 2005, and are under contract to be adapted for film by Benderspink Productions; *Heart of Empire* has been released as a CD-ROM.

■ Sidelights

Known among British comic-book aficionados as the creator of the first "underground" comic in that country, Bryan Talbot has been both writing and illustrating comic books and graphic novels professionally since the mid-1970s. In another first, his nine-volume *The Adventures of Luther Arkwright* series, when published in book format, gained distinction, together with Raymond Briggs' *When the Wind Blows*, as the first home-grown British graphic novel. Talbot's literary sophistication and avant garde approach, as well as his skills as an artist, helped encourage the development of sophisticated indie British comics such as "2000 A.D." He also is credited with providing inspiration for some of the writers and artists who, in the 1980s, would later become known as the British Invasion of American comics, among them Alan Moore, Neil Gaiman, Grant Morrison, Dave Mckean, and Jamie Delano.

During his long career Talbot has worked with some of the top writers and illustrators in his field, producing award-winning original works such as *The Tale of One Bad Rat* in addition to collaborating on Gaiman's historic "The Sandman" series and working on the creative teams that produce the "Batman," "Judge Dredd," and other comic-book series. Talbot's best-known work, *The Tale of One Bad Rat*, was described by George Khoury in *True Brit: Celebrating the Comic Book Artists of England*, as "one of the most emotional works ever created in comics."

Gets Start in Comix

An artist and doodler from an early age, Talbot started his career during the late 1960s, when the U.S. underground comix scene—a publishing phenomenon fueled by small-press books coming out of San Francisco, New York City, and Chicago and featuring artists such as Robert Crumb, Art Spiegelman, Jay Lynch, and Rick Griffin—was approaching its height. In 1969 Talbot's first illustrations appeared in *Mallorn*, a magazine published by the British Tolkien Society. Although Talbot had enrolled at Preston Polytechnic with the intention of pursuing a career in graphic design, cartooning soon began to occupy much of his attention. Joining with a fellow cartoonist, he created a weekly comic strip that was published in the Preston Polytechnic student newspaper in 1972.

After graduation, Talbot linked up with Alchemy Press, a small British comics publisher, and both wrote and illustrated the six-issue "Brainstorm" series. "Brainstorm" mixed elements of science fiction, the drug culture of the 1970s, and rock music into a humorous saga featuring Chester P. Hackenbush, the Psychedelic Alchemist. The first three issues of "Brainstorm," which together numbered sixty-five pages, were collected and published in book format in 1982 as *Brainstorm!: The Chester P. Hackenbush Trilogy.* The Hackenbush character was later Americanized into Chester Williams, the lead protagonist in "Swamp Thing" by DC Comics writer Alan Moore.

Enter Luther Arkwright

Talbot continued his science-fiction bent with "Frank Fazakerley, Space Ace of the Future," a comic-book spoof on the heroic space opera genre inhabited by classic heroes such as Flash Gordon. Published in 1978, "Frank Fazakerley, Space Ace of the Future" was quickly overshadowed by another of its creator's projects: "The Adventures of Luther Arkwright." Arkwright first appeared in the British magazine *Near Myths,* wherein the time traveler helped a gang of biker nuns retrieve some sacred relics from some power-hungry priests. The strip moved to *pssst!* magazine in 1981 and the first issues were collected and published in book form the following year by Never Ltd. Characteristic of the multi-talented—and amazingly industrious—Talbot, further work on "The Adventures of Luther Arkwright" were put on the back burner in late 1981, when he began assisting writer Bob Shaw and director David Richardson on a television program for British television. Talbot would undertake a similar effort a few years later, in 1994, when he created storyboards for the television film *Above the World* directed by John Sorenson.

Geared for adult readers, *The Adventures of Luther Arkwright* focuses on a man whose psychokinetic skill allows him to travel via airship through a series of parallel worlds known as the Multiverse. In Arkwright's future world, the British Empire is still holding sway over the world within its war-ravaged universe, while peaceable universes such as zero-zero are threatened by the predations of evil forces capable of operating across each of these realities. The series features sophisticated political and historical references, archetypes, and mythology, while the inclusion of explicit sex broadened its appeal. Completed from 1987 to 1989, Talbot's saga features fantastic storylines rife with science-fiction and cinematic influences, all set against a well-researched, minutely detailed, and painstakingly rendered Victorian backdrop. Published in England by Valkyrie Press, the series was eventually made available to U.S. readers through Oregon-based Dark Horse Comics.

Bryan Talbot's 1995 graphic novel *The Tale of One Bad Rat* tells of a girl who runs away from an abusive home life. (Dark Horse Books, 1995. Entire contents of "The Tale of One Bad Rat" are copyright © 1995, 2008 Bryan Talbot. All prominent characters and their likenesses are trademarks of Bryan Talbot. All rights reserved. Reproduced by permission.)

While the initial buzz on "The Adventures of Luther Arkwright" series made Talbot increasingly well known in the comic-book community, he focused his energies on an illustration assignment for a series of German-language RPG (role-playing game) books. In 1982 Talbot also created the sci-fi comic strip "Scummworld," which was published in *Sounds,* a weekly rock-music magazine. By the following year, however, "Scummworld" was no more because its creator was asked to join the creative staff behind the influential British comics anthology *2000 A.D.* Working with fellow writer Pat Mills, in 1984 Talbot created the story arc that would be published in book form in 1985 as "Nemesis the Warlock." His work bringing to life the villain of this series, the ruthless Torquemada, earned him three Eagle Awards for favorite villain. From "Nemesis the Warlock," Talbot moved on to other projects, including a stint on popular comic "Judge Dredd" alongside writer John Wagner. Talbot's full-color strip for "Judge Dredd," in which he becomes the first artist to depict the face of Judge Fear, found its way into the *2000 A.D.* annual as well as into the debut issue of England's *Diceman* magazine.

Enters U.S. Comics Mainstream

In the early 1990s, in the wake of the second install-ment of his award-winning opus "The Adventures of Luther Arkwright," Talbot joined forces with well-known writer Gaiman on Gaiman's ongoing "Sandman" series. Their collaborations, the story arcs *Fables and Reflections* and *The Game of You*, were republished in graphic-novel format as part of the long-running "Sandman" series. With Gaiman as consulting editor, he also reentered the Sandman's macabre world as coauthor of *The Dreaming: Gates of Horn and Ivory*.

Because of Gaiman's popularity among American readers, Talbot now caught the eye of U.S. publishers. In 1989 he joined the DC Comics team to produce "Hellblazer" and "The Nazz," the latter a series written by Tom Veitch. He then joined Veitch's brother Rick Veitch to create the "Neil Gaiman's Teknophage" series for Hollywood-based Tekno Comix until that company dissolved in 1997. Working as an illustrator, Talbot created cover art for several issues of the "Raggedy Man" series, and balanced this out with writing duties on "Shad-owdeath," featuring art by David Pugh. Adding his vision to the long-running superhero classic "Bat-man," Talbot also created the two-part story-arc "MASK" for the "Legends of the Dark Knight" strip published in 1996. This work earned him two Eis-ner Award nominations.

Addresses Child Abuse in Comic Serial

One of Talbot's most resonant works has been his graphic novel *The Tale of One Bad Rat*. With its spare white cover clearly imitating the tiny child-sized books of popular nineteenth-century author Beatrix Potter, this compelling story follows a girl named Helen Potter as she decides to run away from her sexually abusive father and her uncaring mother. Lost and homeless on the streets of London, Helen inevitably winds up on the wrong side of the law. Looking for something to establish structure in her life, the teen travels to Potter's native Lake District, finds a job at a local inn where Potter once stayed,

and ultimately creates a surrogate family to support her move into adulthood. With its appeal to even reluctant readers and its focus on a teen's ability to transcend the emotional harm caused by childhood sexual abuse, *The Tale of One Bad Rat* has been used by counselors in schools and child abuse centers in both the United Kingdom and the United States. It also appeared on the recommended reading list of the *New York Times* and has won several major awards. Praising Talbot's art in the work, Gordon Flagg wrote in *Booklist* that the "vivid, realistic full-color illustration" is matched by the story's "com-passionate characterizations" and a heroine whose achievement is "genuinely inspirational."

In 1999 Talbot returned to the time-travel world of Luther Arkwright in *Heart of Empire; or, The Legacy of Luther Arkwright*. First appearing in the pages of nine sequential comic books, *Heart of Empire* won several Eisner Award nominations upon its publica-tion as a 284-page graphic novel. The book was also adapted for CD-ROM and released in a one-volume deluxe limited-edition slipcased hardcover. Featur-ing Talbot's characteristic mix of humor, wit, his-tory, metaphysics, science fiction, and romance, the work extends the Arkwright epic and reintroduces the original sequence to a new generation of fans.

A Nostalgic Story

Inspired by Talbot's love of his former home town in northeastern England, *Alice in Sunderland: An Entertainment* mixes history, myth, and time travel, this time in a story that is grounded in literary history. The graphic novel documents the relation-ship between Lewis Carroll (the pseudonym of Victorian mathematician and author Charles Dodge-son), Carroll's young friend Alice Liddell, and the history of the industrial shipbuilding region of Sun-derland, England, wherein much of the action of Carroll's storybooks *Alice in Wonderland* and *Alice through the Looking Glass* take place. Talbot's story pivots around an imaginary performance taking place at the Sunderland Empire music hall, and he weaves himself into the patchwork of vignettes that emanate from this performance. As Carl Hays explained in *Booklist*, "along with insights into famous battles, bridges, and ghost-infested castles, Talbot provides updates to Carroll's biography via recent information concerning his controversial relationship to the 'real' Alice, Alice Liddell."

Alice in Sunderland, with its nostalgia for the British past, was described by London *Daily Telegraph* contributor Michael Moorcock as a "generous-hearted, ambitious book" that would serve as "a

An interior page from Talbot's graphic novel *The Tale of One Bad Rat.* (Dark Horse Books, 1995. Entire contents of "The Tale of One Bad Rat"
are copyright © 1995, 2008 Bryan Talbot. All prominent characters and their likenesses are trademarks of Bryan Talbot. All rights reserved. Reproduced by permission.)

fine introduction to the graphic novel for anyone yet to sample the pleasures of this peculiarly contemporary art form." Calling it "a detailed exploration of the concordances, coincidences and parallels that tie past to present," James Lovegrove in his *Financial Times* review noted that Talbot's story is "a ravishingly rendered reminder that the world around us is curiouser and curiouser than we can possibly imagine." As the story shifts stylistically, so too does Talbot's art, veering from black-and-white to full color and ranging through media as diverse as pen-and-ink and watercolor, found-image collage, and digitized computer imaging. While somewhat fragmented, Talbot's "freewheeling, metafictional magnum opus is a map of the curious and delightful territory of its cartoonist's mind," noted a *Publishers Weekly* writer. Hailing *Alice in Sunderland* as a "showcase for the explosive verve of Talbot's protean illustrative style," the *Publishers Weekly* critic also dubbed its creator "a remarkable raconteur." Paul Gravett in the London *Independent* found that "*Alice in Sunderland* is a tour de force landmark in graphic literature." Caroline Callaghan, writing for *Pantechnicon*, called *Alice in Sunderland* "a master class in the art of storytelling. In composition and form, it uses diverse styles and methods to weave the many complex threads into a meaningful whole. If you've considered writing a graphic novel yourself, this book has to be an essential read; it's a tutorial in the art of researching and constructing such a novel."

If you enjoy the works of Bryan Talbot, you may also want to check out the following books:

Alan Moore, *The League of Extraordinary Gentlemen*, 2001.
Daniel Clowes, *David Boring*, 2002.
Osamu Tezuka, *Ode To Kirihito*, 2006.
Shaun Tan, *The Arrival*, 2007.

Reflecting in the London *Guardian* on the body of work that extends from "Brainstorm" forward to *Alice in Sunderland*, Michel Faber called Talbot "almost a grand old man of British comics," qualifying his remark with the fact that Talbot, at only fifty-five years of age, was not yet "old." Although Faber contended that *Alice in Sunderland*, with its "gloriously ambitious fusion of myth, history and autobiography, . . . is clearly meant to be [Talbot's] . . .

magnum opus," the author and illustrator continues to expand the possibilities in the comic-book medium. In addition to more recent comic-book mini-series such as "The Dead Boy Detectives," Talbot has turned his attention to his own industry with a collection of anecdotes and stories titled *The Naked Artist: Comic Book Legends*. In 2008, *The Art of Bryan Talbot* appeared, offering a collection of Talbot's illustrative work for CD covers, books, and advertising, as well as examples of his private drawings from the age of twelve years old. According to Gordon Flagg in *Booklist*, this collection highlights "the detailed clarity and exuberant inventiveness of his acclaimed illustrations."

On the *Official Bryan Talbot Fanpage*, Talbot turned to his fans, giving advice to those wishing to join him in the comics business. In addition to attending comic-book conventions and scanning the racks of comic-book stores for editors and publishers to contact, he encouraged young comics artists "to be conversant with the medium. This entails reading all types of comic books and becoming familiar with the visual grammar, the ways used by comics to tell stories," Talbot noted. "To artists, of whatever ability," he added, "I can't stress too strongly the importance of Life Drawing classes. These will help your drawing, no matter what style you work in."

■ Biographical and Critical Sources

BOOKS

Khoury, George, editor, *True Brit: Celebrating the Comic Book Artists of England*, TwoMorrows Publishing (Raleigh, NC), 2004.
Sorensen, Lita, *Bryan Talbot*, Rosen Publishing (New York, NY), 2004.
Talbot, Bryan, *The Art of Bryan Talbot*, NBM (New York, NY), 2007.

PERIODICALS

Booklist, September 15, 1995, Gordon Flagg, review of *The Tale of One Bad Rat*, p. 1511; May 1, 2007, Carl Hays, review of *Alice in Sunderland: An Entertainment*, p. 80; February 1, 2008, Gordon Flagg, review of *The Art of Bryan Talbot*, p. 13.
Daily Telegraph (London, England), May 5, 2007, Michael Moorcock, review of *Alice in Sunderland*.
Financial Times (London, England), May 19, 2007, James Lovegrove, review of *Alice in Sunderland*, p. 35.

Guardian (London, England), June 9, 2007, Michel Faber, review of *Alice in Sunderland*, p. 10.

Independent (London, England), April 27, 2007, Paul Gravett, "An Artistic Wonder from Wearside."

Publishers Weekly, April 12, 2007, review of *Fable: Storybook Love*, p. 41; April 23, 2007, review of *Alice in Sunderland*, p. 36.

ONLINE

Bryan Talbot Official Fan Page, http://www.bryan-talbot.com/ (April 9, 2008).

Pantechnicon, http://pantechnicon.net/ (December 1, 2007), Caroline Callaghan, "Bryan Talbot: Artist Extraordinaire."*

Sigrid Undset

(Reproduced by permission of the Carl Van Vechten Trust.)

■ Personal

Born May 20, 1882, in Kalundborg, Denmark; died after a stroke, June 10, 1949, in Lillehammer, Norway; daughter of Ingvald Martin (an archeologist) and Anna Charlotte Undset; married Anders C. Svarstad (an artist), 1912 (marriage annulled, 1924); children: Anders, Maren Charlotte, Hans. *Education:* Received secretarial certificate from Christiania Commercial College, c. 1898. *Religion:* Roman Catholic.

■ Career

German Electric Company, Christiania (now Oslo), Norway, secretary, c. 1898-1908. Full-time writer, 1908-49.

■ Awards, Honors

Nobel Prize for literature from the Swedish Academy, 1928; Grand Cross of the Order of Saint Olav from King Haakon VII, 1947; Undset's portrait, painted by her husband, appears on a Norwegian postage stamp.

■ Writings

NOVELS

Fru Marta Oulie (title means "Mrs. Marta Oulie"), Aschehoug (Christiania, Norway), 1907, reprinted, 1977.

Jenny, Aschehoug (Christiania, Norway), 1911, reprinted, 1967, translation by W. Emme published under the same title, Knopf (New York, NY), 1921, reprinted, Fertig, 1975.

Vaaren (title means "Spring"), Aschehoug (Christiania, Norway), 1914.

Gymnadenia, Aschehoug (Oslo, Norway), 1929, reprinted, 1973, translation by Arthur G. Chater published as *The Wild Orchid,* Knopf (New York, NY), 1931.

Den brænnende busk, Aschehoug (Oslo, Norway), 1930, reprinted, 1974, translation by Arthur G. Chater published as *The Burning Bush,* Knopf (New York, NY), 1932.

Ida Elisabeth, Aschehoug (Oslo, Norway), 1932, translation by Arthur G. Chater published under the same title, Knopf (New York, NY), 1933.

Den trofaste hustru, Aschehoug (Oslo, Norway), 1936, translation by Arthur G. Chater published as *The Faithful Wife,* Knopf (New York, NY), 1937.

HISTORICAL FICTION

Fortællingen om Viga-Ljot og Vigdis [and] *Sankt Halvards liv, død og jærtgen,* Aschehoug (Christiania,

Norway), 1909, translation of the former by Arthur G. Chater published as *Gunnar's Daughter,* Knopf (New York, NY), 1936, Penguin (New York, NY), 1998.

Kristin Lavransdatter, three volumes, Aschehoug (Christiania, Norway), Volume I: *Kransen,* 1920, translation by Charles Archer and J.S. Scott published as *The Bridal Wreath,* Knopf (New York, NY), 1923, reprinted, Bantam (New York, NY), 1978, translated by Tiina Nunnally and published as *The Wreath,* Penguin (New York, NY), 1997; Volume II: *Husfrue,* 1921, translation by Archer published as *The Mistress of Husaby,* Knopf (New York, NY), 1925, reprinted, Bantam (New York, NY), 1978; Volume III: *Korset,* 1922, translation by Archer published as *The Cross,* Knopf (New York, NY), 1927, reprinted, Bantam (New York, NY), 1978; single volume Nobel Prize edition translated by Archer and Scott published as *Kristin Lavransdatter,* Knopf (New York, NY), 1929, Penguin (New York, NY), 2005.

Olav Audunssøn i Hestviken, two volumes, Aschehoug (Oslo, Norway), 1925, two-volume translation by Arthur G. Chater published as *The Axe,* Knopf (New York, NY), 1928, and *The Snake Pit,* Knopf (New York, NY), 1929 (both volumes included in *The Master of Hestviken* also see below).

Olav Audunssøn og hans børn, two volumes, Aschehoug (Oslo, Norway), 1927, two-volume translation by Arthur G. Chater published as *In the Wilderness,* Knopf (New York, NY), 1929, and *The Son Avenger,* Knopf (New York, NY), 1930 (both volumes included in *The Master of Hestviken;* also see below).

The Master of Hestviken (contains novels *The Axe, The Snake Pit, In the Wilderness,* and *The Son Avenger*), translated by Arthur G. Chater, Nobel Prize edition, Knopf (New York, NY), 1934, reprinted, New American Library (New York, NY), 1978.

Madame Dorthea, Aschehoug (Oslo, Norway), 1939, reprinted, 1968, translation by Arthur G. Chater published under the same title, Knopf (New York, NY), 1940.

The Axe (originally published in Norwegian as part 1 of *Olav Audunssøn i Hestviken*), Vintage Books (New York, NY), 1994.

The Snake Pit (originally published in Norwegian as part 2 of *Olav Audunssøn i Hestviken*), Vintage Books (New York, NY), 1994.

In the Wilderness (originally published in Norwegian as part 1 of *Olav Audunssøn og Hans Børn*), Vintage Books (New York, NY), 1995.

The Son Avenger (originally published in Norwegian as part 2 of *Olav Audunssøn og Hans Børn*), Vintage Books (New York, NY), 1995.

OTHER

Den lykkelige alder (stories; title means "The Happy Age"), Aschehoug (Christiania, Norway), 1908.

Fattige skjebner (stories; title means "Poor Fortunes"); contains "Forste mote," "Simonsen," "Selma Brøter," "Omkring sedelighetaballet," "Frøken Smith Tellefsen," and "Nikkedukken"), Aschehoug (Christiania, Norway), 1912, translations of "Simonsen," "Selma Brøter," and "Frøken Smith Tellefsen" by Naomi Walford published in *Four Stories,* Knopf (New York, NY), 1959.

Fortellinger om Kong Artur og ridderne av det Runde bord (adapted from Thomas Mallory's tales of King Arthur), Aschehoug (Christiania, Norway), 1915.

Splinten av troldspeilet (contains *Fru Hjeld* and *Fru Waage*), Aschehoug (Christiania, Norway), 1917, translation of *Fru Hjeld* by Arthur G. Chater published as *Images in a Mirror,* Knopf (New York, NY), 1938.

De kloge jomfruer (stories; title means "The Wise Virgins"; contains "Smaspiker," "Thjodolf," and "Gunvald og Emma"), Aschehoug (Christiania, Norway), 1918, reprinted, 1968, translation of "Thjodolf" by Walford published in *Four Stories,* Knopf (New York, NY), 1959.

Et kvindesynspunkt (essays), Aschehoug (Christiania, Norway), 1919, reprinted, 1982.

Die saga von Vilmund Vidutan und seinen Gefaehrten (children's story), Hausen Verlagagesellschaft, 1931, translation published as *Sigurd and His Brave Companions: A Tale of Medieval Norway,* illustrations by Gunvor Bull Teilman, Knopf (New York, NY), 1943.

Etapper: Ny række (essays), Aschehoug (Oslo, Norway), 1933, translation by Arthur G. Chater published as *Stages on the Road,* Knopf (New York, NY), 1934, reprinted, Books for Libraries Press (Freeport, NY), 1969.

Elleve aar (autobiography; title means "Eleven Years"), Aschehoug (Oslo, Norway), 1934, reprinted, 1966, translation by Arthur G. Chater published as *The Longest Years,* Knopf (New York, NY), 1935, reprinted, 1971.

Norske helgener (essays), Aschehoug (Oslo, Norway), 1937, translation by E.C. Ramsden published as *Saga of Saints,* Longmans, Green (New York, NY), 1934, reprinted, Books for Libraries Press (Freeport, NY), 1968.

Selvportretter og landskapsbilleder (essays), Aschehoug (Oslo, Norway), 1938, translation by Arthur G. Chater published as *Men, Women, and Places,* Knopf (New York, NY), 1939, reprinted, Books for Libraries Press (Freeport, NY), 1969.

Return to the Future (autobiography), translated by Henrietta C.K. Naeseth, Knopf (New York, NY), 1942.

(Editor) *True and Untrue, and Other Norse Tales* (based on original stories from Asbjoernsen and Moe's *Folkeeventyr*), illustrations by Frederick T. Chapman, Knopf (New York, NY), 1945.

Lykkelige dager (reminiscences), Aschehoug (Oslo, Norway), 1947, reprinted, Aschehoug (Oslo, Norway), 1971, translation by Joran Birkeland published as *Happy Times in Norway*, Knopf (New York, NY), 1948, reprinted, Greenwood Press (Westport, CT), 1979.

Caterina av Siena (biography), Aschehoug (Oslo, Norway), 1951, translation by Kate Austin-Lund published as *Catherine of Siena*, Sheed & Ward (New York), 1954.

Artikler og taler fra krigstiden, edited by A.H. Winsnes, Aschehoug (Oslo, Norway), 1952.

Four Stories (contains "Thjodolf," "Selma Brøter," "Simonsen," and "Miss Smith-Tellefsen"), translated by Naomi Walford, Knopf (New York, NY), 1959, reprinted, 1978.

Kirke og klosterliv: Tre essays fro norsk middelalder, Cappelen (Oslo, Norway), 1963.

Djaere dea (letters), edited with foreword by Christianne Undset Svarstad, Cappelen (Oslo, Norway), 1979.

Kritikk og tro: Tekster (essays), edited by Liv Bliksrud, St. Olav (Oslo, Norway), 1982.

Sigrid Undset skriver hjem: En vandring gjennom enigrantarene i Amerika (letters), edited by Arne Skouen, Aschehoug (Oslo, Norway), 1982.

Also author of the play *In the Gray Light of Dawn* and a verse collection; translator of various Icelandic tales. Work represented in anthologies, including *A Woman's Point of View*, 1919. Contributor to periodicals.

COLLECTED WORKS

Middelalder-romaner (medieval novels), ten volumes, Aschehoug (Oslo, Norway), 1949.

Romaner og fortellinger fra nutiden (contemporary works), ten volumes, Aschehoug (Oslo, Norway), 1964, reprinted as *Natidsverker*, twelve volumes, 1983.

Middelalder-verker (medieval works), eight volumes, Aschehoug (Oslo, Norway), 1982.

The Unknown Sigrid Undset: Jenny and Other Works, edited by Tim Page, translated by Tiina Nunnally, Steerforth Press (South Royalton, VT), 2001.

Works also published in other collections.

■ Adaptations

Kristin Lavransdatter was adapted as a film directed by Liv Ullman in 1995.

■ Sidelights

Sigrid Undset won a secure place in literary history as one of the foremost authors of historical novels and as the most prominent Catholic author Scandinavia has produced. She was also, as Kirsten Wisloff Andresen noted in the study *Sigrid Undset*, "one of the very few women to receive the Nobel Prize for Literature." Carl F. Bayerschmidt, in his critical study *Sigrid Undset*, labeled the Norwegian novelist "one of the greatest realistic writers of the first half of the twentieth century." A.H. Winsnes, in *Sigrid Undset: A Study in Christian Realism*, called the author "the Christian realist *par excellence*." Most of Undset's best known works are set in Norway of the Middle Ages. They are powerful not only because of their moral message but also because of her mastery of technique: few other novelists have so accurately painted background and setting or so completely banned romanticism from their works. As Winsnes pointed out, Undset has been called "the [Emile] Zola of the Middle Ages." Very few other writers have understood so fully the past and its connection with the present. Winsnes noted that "history is Sigrid Undset's muse. No one since [thirteenth-century poet and historian] Snorri Sturluson has presented medieval Norway with such power."

Although Undset's fame was secured by her novels of medieval Norway, she also wrote realistic novels of contemporary life, a play, a collection of poems, many volumes of short stories and essays, and works of literary criticism. She followed the events of her day with attention and made significant contributions in fiction and nonfiction to the awakening movement for women's rights. She protested against the "new paganism" of materialism and was an untiring champion of democracy.

An Archeologist Father

The story of Unset's life is one of self-sacrifice and responsibility. Born in Kalundborg, Denmark, she was the eldest of three daughters of Anna Charlotte Undset and the renowned Norwegian archeologist Ingvald Undset. Ingvald Undset had come from Trondelag, an area of Norway accurately described in his daughter's masterpiece, *Kristin Lavransdatter*. Anna Charlotte Undset, who was a reserved and proud woman, inspired respect in her daughter but not the deep affection that the child felt for her father—in the portrayal of Kristin's father Lavrans in *Kristin Lavransdatter*, Undset paid tribute to her own father. At the age of two, she moved with her family to the city of Christiania (now Oslo), where her father was associated with the archeological section of the University Museum. As Ingvald Undset's health declined (he had caught malaria on an expedition to the Mediterranean), the family moved frequently, and Undset became intimately acquainted with many areas of the city of Oslo. As the daughter of an archeologist, she acquired an acute sense of history; the Undset home was filled with books, and the child was encouraged by her father to read extensively, especially works of history and Old Norse sagas. When Undset was eleven years old, her father died, and the family experienced genuine poverty. Her autobiographical memoir, *Elleve aar* (*The Longest Years*), records memories of the first eleven years of her life. That she gave herself the name "Ingvild" in these memoirs suggests the strength of her attachment to and identification with her father.

Although Undset attended the liberal school of Ragna Nielsen and had the opportunity to enroll in the university, she chose at the age of fifteen to prepare for a secretarial career at the Christiania Commercial College. Her certificate from this school a year later helped her to obtain a position in the local office of the German Electric Company, where she worked for ten years. Undset's intimate acquaintance with young working girls provided the material for many of her earliest works. In her free time from her secretarial job, Undset turned her hand to writing. She submitted a historical novel to the Gyldendal publishing house in Copenhagen only to be told that she should turn to modern themes that seemed more suited to her talents. Undset followed this advice, and her first contemporary social novel, *Fru Marta Oulie* (title means "Mrs. Marta Oulie"), appeared in the fall of 1907. In 1909, her novel *Fortællingen om Viga-Ljot og Vigdis* was published (later translated as *Gunnar's Daughter*). "Though this novel, which is often viewed as a pastiche of the saga, does not measure up in quality to [Undset's] later epics," wrote Claudia Berguson in the *Dictionary of Literary Biography*, "it demonstrates her knowledge of medieval history and literary style, as well as her ability to build an intense narrative around the themes of male-female relationships, violation, and revenge." After the publication of two additional works of moderate success, Undset felt secure enough to quit her job for a full-time career as a writer. In 1909 she received a travel grant from the Norwegian government and went to Rome, where she met her future husband, the painter Anders Svarstad. Married in 1912, the couple lived first in London and later in Norway, where Undset continued to produce fiction, nonfiction, and translations. After the births of three children—Anders, Maren Charlotte, and Hans—

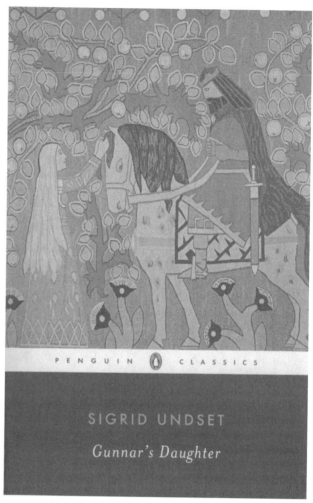

Undset's novel *Gunnar's Daughter* is a tale of youthful violence and longed-for revenge. (Penguin Books, 1998. Cover art: Gerhard Munthe, Bendik and Arolilja, or The Golden Hair, 1903-1908. Nordenfjeldske Kunstindustrimuseum, Trondheim, Norway. Used by permission of Penguin Group (USA) Inc.)

Svarstad and Undset eventually became estranged, and their marriage was annulled when she accepted the Catholic faith on All Saints' Day, November 24, 1924.

Wartime Hardships

Remaining in Lillehammer, Norway, until 1940, Undset devoted herself both to her work, for which she received the Nobel Prize for literature in 1928, and to her children. Maren Charlotte, who was born retarded, lived only to the age of twenty-three; Anders, Undset's eldest son, was killed in 1940 when German armies invaded Norway. With Hans, her only surviving child, Undset then made the long journey through Sweden to Russia, from there to

Japan, and from there to San Francisco. During the war, she channeled her considerable energies into the war effort, giving lectures, writing propaganda, and calling attention to the plight of occupied Norway. In August, 1945, she returned to her homeland, and in 1947 King Haakon VII conferred upon her the Grand Cross of the Order of Saint Olav for service to her country. On June 10, 1949, Undset died in Lillehammer. Her life provided the impetus for her works: her religious faith, her pride in the past of her people, and her assessment of motherhood as woman's most important calling are all mirrored in her imaginative works and clearly stated in her nonfiction.

Although there is no clear chronological division between Undset's novels of contemporary life and her works set in earlier historical periods (in 1909 she published a pastiche of the Icelandic saga, and contemporary social novels reoccur in the 1930s), most of her early writing was inspired by her knowledge of the working class of Oslo. *Fru Marta Oulie* treats infidelity in marriage. The novel, which is written in diary form, begins with the confession, "I have been unfaithful to my husband." Undset's only play, "In the Gray Light of Dawn," is likewise concerned with adultery, and this theme is prominent in Undset's novels of the Middle Ages as well. Two collections of short stories, *Den lykkelige alder* (title means "The Happy Age") and *Fattige skjebner* (title means "Poor Fortunes"), address themselves to problems of adolescence, motherhood, and spinsterhood in the lower economic classes of Norwegian urban society.

Undset's novel *Jenny,* the story of a promising young artist who commits suicide, caused a sensation in Scandinavian feminist circles. "*Jenny* was Undset's breakthrough novel," wrote Berguson. "It is a powerful narrative of the self-destruction of Jenny Winge, an idealistic young woman, inexperienced in love, who is striving to realize her dreams to become an artist." Jenny has had an affair with her fiance's father, borne a child out of wedlock, suffered through the death of that child, and experienced frustration as a creative artist. Whether Jenny's suicide is caused by her failure as an artist or by her failure in erotic and maternal relationships is open to interpretation. Alrik Gustafson, writing in his study *Six Scandinavian Novelists,* found some melodramatic aspects to the story, but noted: "Despite these faults, however, the novel does somehow affect one: we do become intensely concerned about the destiny of Jenny—perhaps so much so that we are to an extent revolted . . . by the severe judgment which Sigrid Undset comes finally to pass upon her heroine." Jenny's "concerns—career, love, family—wouldn't be unfamiliar even to Bridget Jones, but infusing all of them is a

moral seriousness, a desire to live a just and truthful life," according to James Crossley in the *Review of Contemporary Fiction.* "This brooding book," wrote Donna Seaman in *Booklist,* "can stand with the best of the moderns."

Several later works also treat realistically problems of sexual fidelity and parenthood, stressing the importance of forgiveness and presenting the child as the element that can weld the most disparate parents together. *Vaaren* (title means "Spring") describes the marriage of a young couple; *Splinten av troldspeilet* (half of which was later translated as *Images in a Mirror*) contains two short stories that deal with infidelity and a young wife's conflict between family and career; *De kloge jomfruer* (title means "The Wise Virgins") emphasizes the importance of motherhood. Written towards the end of Undset's career, *Ida Elisabeth* presents a wife who sacrifices her personal happiness to remain faithful to her marriage vows, and *Den trofaste hustru* (*The Faithful Wife*) records the disintegration of a childless marriage, though in the latter work a religious element new to the social novels is introduced. Through these novels Undset was placed squarely at the head of the women's movement in Scandinavia, whether she wished to be in that position or not. An intelligent, creative working woman who also experienced marriage and motherhood, she could write eloquently of the problems that beset such women.

Medieval Masterpieces

As controversial as some of her novels of contemporary life may have been, none of them could compare with Undset's masterpieces of medieval life. Critics agree that it is the multi-volume *Kristin Lavransdatter* and the *Olav Audunssøn* series (*The Master of Hestviken*), that have secured her place in literary history. Showing a mastery of style lacking in the novels of contemporary life, these works also reveal an understanding of vanished cultures and love of the past instilled in the writer by her father. Her intimate knowledge of the laws, culture, and history of earlier ages had given her a sense of the continuity of life. Despite the copious and meticulously accurate historical details that embellish these novels, there is nothing strange about the people who inhabit that distant world. Berguson noted that "the trilogy *Kristin Lavransdatter* has been in continuous print since its original publication and has been translated into more than seventy languages." Similarly, a critic for *Publishers Weekly* stated that *Kristin Lavransdatter* "has remained an international classic since its publication."

Kristin Lavransdatter consists of three volumes: *Kransen* (*The Bridal Wreath*), *Husfrue* (*The Mistress of*

Undset's historical trilogy _Kristin Lavransdatter_ is an epic story set in 14th century Sweden. (Penguin Books, 2005. Cover art, trunk painted by Jorund Tallaksen Tjorehom in Setesdal, Norway, dated 1839. Courtesy of Vesterheim Norwegian-American Museum. Used by permission of Penguin Group (USA) Inc. and the photographer.)

Husaby), and _Korset_ (_The Cross_). In the first volume, the affectionate relationship between the upright Lavrans Bjrgulfsson and his beloved daughter Kristin is vividly portrayed; however, when Kristin defies her father to marry the man whom she loves and her father deems unworthy, the relationship is strained. The novel ends with a pregnant Kristin finally joined in wedlock with Erlend Nikulausson, the man of her choice. She has forced her father to acquiesce to her will, but she has used deception and is unaffected by the worst sin: she and Erlend have forced the suicide of Eline Ormsdatter, Erlend's former mistress and mother of his two illegitimate children. The Norwegian title _Kransen_ is significant in more than one way. As a child Kristin had been frightened in the woods by an elf-maiden, who beckoned to her with a garland of flowers; according to Bayerschmidt, the elf-maiden "is a symbol of the beautiful but dangerous world of the senses which makes use of all its snares and temptations to entice people who would put their own desires and gratifications above the higher order of a supernatural will." Furthermore, in the second novel, Kristin must make a pilgrimage to the shrine of St. Olav and offer her golden "krans," symbol of her virginity, to the priests. The meaning in the garland and virginal golden ornament is thus twofold.

The second and third volumes of _Kristin Lavransdatter_ detail further hardships. _The Mistress of Husaby_ documents the unhappy marriage of Erlend and Kristin, whose selfish passion has brought unhappiness to many. Kristin must suffer the infidelity of her husband, his seeming indifference to their seven sons, and the loss of his estate because of his attempted coup against King Magnus. Kristin herself has been petty and vindictive; the thoughtless Erlend is never allowed to forget all the wrongs he has done her, and finally he leaves her to retire to a shack in the mountains—the last bit of property he owns. The third volume, _The Cross,_ relates Kristin's disappointment in her sons after the violent death of Erlend—the oldest two join a monastery (the second of the youths has been afflicted with blindness), the youngest dies of illness, her twins move away to serve Knights in other parts of the country, another of the young men travels to Iceland, and the son who takes over the estate of Kristin's father is revealed as a weakling. In despair, Kristin joins a convent, where she is stricken with the Black Death and dies. In the course of the trilogy Kristin Lavransdatter has to learn to accept whatever destiny God inflicts on her; she has to learn to subjugate her own will to the supernatural will, embodied in the figure of a holy monk, Brother Edvin. Here the work stresses the Medieval belief that the spiritual world has primacy over the material one, a belief with which Undset herself concurred but found lacking in most of her twentieth-century contemporaries.

Undset thoroughly researched the period of Norwegian history treated in her novel, although she deliberately chose for the setting an epoch for which sources are few. While some figures mentioned in the novel are historical (King Magnus, Erling Vidkunsson, Queen Ingibjrg), most of the characters are created; critics maintain that all are credible, and the unfolding of Undset's vast panorama is natural and effortless. The reader senses the religious nature of the fourteenth century but also the newness of Christianity. Superstition is rife: witches, ghosts, and elf-maidens seem to exist, and some of the people revert to heathen sacrifice in desperation when the Black Death devastates the population. *Kristin Lavransdatter* contains realistic, graphic depiction of childbirth and death, of marriage and inheritance laws and customs, of religious practices, and of military and chivalrous codes of conduct. What is most striking in the work, however, is that the individual does not perceive himself as an individual but as a member of a family and a clan. It is in his relationships that he is important; as an individual he does not exist. This mentality seems very foreign to the self-absorbed twentieth century.

Gustafson commented on Undset's writing style in *Kristin Lavransdatter:* "Sigrid Undset's art—such as it is—simply *grows,* naturally, intensely, sometimes with strangely awkward pregnancy of utterance, out of the plentiful resources of a deeply sensitive, a profoundly serious genius. In consequence it has its faults: there are passages which might profit by greater concentration of phrasing; there are episodes which might move more swiftly, more decisively; there are details which at times might better be omitted. But by these we are only momentarily disturbed, if at all; for there is so much else in Sigrid Undset's pages to impress the reader—so much more to make him intensely conscious of the existence in *Kristin Lavransdatter* of a kind of truth in art that is more than art alone."

The Master of Hestviken, which stretches from the second half of the thirteenth century to the early part of the fourteenth century, also pivots around guilt and unconfessed sin. In this work, as in *Kristin Lavransdatter,* two young people who love each other are separated by circumstances. When the young woman Ingunn becomes pregnant by the Icelander Teit, the protagonist Olav kills his rival and disposes of the body. He marries Ingunn and claims the child as his own. Throughout his life he bears the burden of his secret guilt. The book presents a gloomy picture: Olav, who has been moved by love for Ingunn and who cared for her tenderly throughout an extended illness, is unable to win the affection of Ingunn's child and of the daughter they have together. Eventually Olav is wounded and deformed in battle and at the end of the novel is prevented from confessing his crime by a stroke which deprives him of the power of speech. While Winsnes saw the novel's conclusion as pessimistic, Margaret Mary Dunn, in her two *Scandinavian Studies* articles, disagreed, contending that Olav eventually comes to realize that the greatest sin "is to despair of God's mercy." Chosen by God to bear much, the Job-like Olav thus becomes the man who "does full penance." "Throughout a lifetime of purgation," Dunn asserted, "Olav's spirit has been purified like gold in a furnace, and it is thus exult-

ant at the end of the novel." "These two mediaeval novels, *Kristin Lavransdatter* and *The Master of Hestviken,* stand among the great stories of all time," wrote N. Elizabeth Moore in her *The Novel and Society: A Critical Study of the Modern Novel.* "This is in part because they employ great themes and explore them with unparalleled depth and penetration, and in part because Mrs. Undset has the art of telling a story so that what happens next becomes of supreme importance at every turn in the way. This is a remarkable achievement for stories with a slow, leisurely pace and great density of material."

Undset's descriptions of nature in *Kristin Lavransdatter* and *The Master of Hestviken* reveal her appreciation of the land. Moreover, nature is used to suggest the medieval consciousness of the continuity of life. Characters feel themselves links in a chain tied to a single location: ancestors and coming generations thus take precedence over individuals. The emphasis on genealogy, on the extended family, and on topography is reminiscent of the old Icelandic family sagas, by which Undset was heavily influenced. In *The Longest Years,* for instance, she recorded the thematic and stylistic importance of Norse sagas—especially *Nal's Saga*—on her own work.

Undset's last historical novel is *Madame Dorthea,* published in incomplete form in 1939. The writer abandoned the work when she fled Norway at the onset of World War II, and after 1939 she turned her energies to the war effort and to nonfiction. Set in the eighteenth century, the Age of Enlightenment, *Madame Dorthea* charts the title figure's efforts to solve the mystery of her husband's unexplained disappearance. An intelligent and rational woman, she seeks logical explanations to an enigma. Much of the almost plotless novel concerns the contrast between Madame Dorthea's intellectualism and the fervent belief of the Catholic, Scharlach.

Madame Dorthea, the medieval historical novels, and some of the social novels of contemporary times clearly contain religious themes. At least two of the later novels with modern settings may be regarded primarily as Catholic propaganda. *Gymnadenia* (*The Wild Orchid*) and its sequel, *Den Brœnnende busk* (*The Burning Bush*), chart the conversion to Catholicism of Paul Selmer. Bayerschmidt stated that Paul's long struggle for truth "reflects Sigrid Undset's own development from an agnostic or freethinker to a believing Christian, so that the novel [cycle] may be considered the most autobiographical of all her works." Once again in these works the theme of the renunciation of selfish passion in favor of familial responsibility is explored.

Concerned with the Role of Women in Society

In addition to her fictional works, Undset wrote countless essays on issues of the day. Many of these essays deal with the role of the mother in contemporary society and with the question of women's rights. "Some Observations on the Emancipation of Women," published in the journal *Samtiden* and collected in *A Woman's Point of View*, expressed Undset's views on the importance of home and family to women. Other essays were literary criticism, often on the Icelandic sagas but also on other subjects: "On the Ballad" pointed out the relationship between popular didactic literature and religious elements in the ballad form. Many of her articles explained and defended her religious views, criticized Martin Luther and the Reformation, and praised the saints (Undset's biography of St. Catherine of Siena was published posthumously in 1951). And during the war years Undset tirelessly defended democracy.

If you enjoy the works of Sigrid Undset, you may also want to check out the following books:

Margaret Mitchell, *Gone with the Wind*, 1939.
Kathleen Winsor, *Forever Amber*, 1944.
Anya Seton, *Katherine*, 1954.

Whether they are set in modern times or in the Middle Ages, Undset's works explore both the importance of the family and the dangers inherent in selfish physical passion. Undset had an understanding of sensuality and a dislike of prudishness, but she also realized the risks to the psyche passion poses. As Bayerschmidt explained, "Physical love has no rights of its own when it comes into conflict with moral and ethical laws. This is a thought which finds a constant echo in [Undset's] entire literary production." Although an emancipated woman herself, the novelist considered the natural desire of women to be for home and children and felt that a career should not be pursued instead of motherhood but only in addition to it. In "Some Observations on the Emancipation of Women," the writer claimed that "the loneliest and most worn-out worker at a typewriter, in office, shop or factory, or at a sewing machine has the right to hope and wait and dream of a happiness as a lover and wife and mother." The heroine of the early novel *Jenny* longs for family and despairs over the death of her child; art cannot fill the void for her. She realizes, according to Bayerschmidt, that "women can never reach the point where their work means everything to them." Motherhood is, in Undset's view, woman's inescapable destiny.

The question of whether Undset was a feminist or an antifeminist is a thorny one; selective quoting can produce arguments for either side. Bayerschmidt maintained that "Sigrid Undset was not a militant feminist, but neither was she an antifeminist. She believed that every woman should be free to practice an art or a profession or occupy herself in any form of work without losing the right to love and to establish a family." It was after the children were in bed that the author worked on her novels. In her portrait of Kristin Lavransdatter, Undset presents in a negative light Kristin's defiance of her father. On the other hand, Undset shows us a Kristen who lives for her seven sons and who, as mistress of Husaby, efficiently manages an estate and a family. Thus, if Undset's message is conservative in essence, it is also liberal in the respect that it confirms a woman's right to excel in whatever field she might choose.

"Responding to the rapid changes of the first decades of the twentieth century, Undset was a bold skeptic of modernity who regarded industrialization, materialism, and individualism as threats to social stability," according to Berguson. "Many of her early essays were directed against the rhetoric of the feminist movement, which, she believed, overlooked the value of the role of women within the traditional circles of family and kin: Undset argued that the rights to vote, to work, and to decide whether to have children must be considered within the context of the individual's greater responsibility to society as a whole. Her concern for the direction of modern society gradually came to include a contemplation of the role of religion, and in 1924 she converted to Roman Catholicism. . . . Undset's interest was not merely in writing against the current of modern thought; her convictions were rooted in a belief that knowledge of the past should inform the present and the future. Whether she should be labeled a reactionary or an antifeminist has been debated from her own time until the present; one can say for certain, however, that her engagement with the social issues of her day was the wellspring of her fiction."

"Undset's contribution to culture is memorable," Moore concluded. "She is one of the greatest historical novelists of all times. She has succeeded in describing the Middle Ages honestly, without romanticizing the past or concentrating on what is merely picturesque. Even when her stories are not altogether successful as novels, they have the quality of greatness because they enthrall the mind through the moving drama of human life."

■ Biographical and Critical Sources

BOOKS

Bayerschmidt, Carl F., *Sigrid Undset*, Twayne (New York, NY), 1970.

Beach, Joseph Warren, *The Twentieth Century Novel: Studies in Technique*, Appleton-Century-Crofts (New York, NY), 1932.

Dictionary of Literary Biography, Gale (Detroit, MI), Volume 297: *Twentieth-Century Norwegian Writers*, 2004, Volume 332: *Nobel Prize Laureates in Literature*, 2007.

Dunn, Margaret, Sister, *Paradigms and Paradoxes in the Life and Letters of Sigrid Undset*, University Press of America (Washington, DC), 1994.

Feminist Writers, St. James Press (Detroit, MI), 1996.

Garton, Janet, *Norwegian Women Writing, 1850-1990*, Athlone (London, England), 1993.

Grondahl, Carl Henrik, editor, *Sigrid Undset*, DYADE, 1983.

Gustafson, Alrik, *Six Scandinavian Novelists*, Princeton University Press (Princeton, NJ), 1940.

Hudson, Deal W., editor, *Sigrid Undset on Saints and Sinners: New Translations and Studies*, Ignatius Press (San Francisco, CA), 1993.

Maman, Marie, *Sigrid Undset in America: An Annotated Bibliography and Research Guide*, Scarecrow Press (Lanham, MD), 2000.

McFarlane, James Walter, *Ibsen and the Temper of Norwegian Literature*, Oxford University Press (New York, NY), 1960.

Monroe, N. Elizabeth, *The Novel and Society: A Critical Study of the Modern Novel*, University of North Carolina Press (Chapel Hill, NC), 1941.

Reference Guide to World Literature, 3rd edition, St. James Press (Detroit, MI), 2003.

Slochower, Harry, *Three Ways of Modern Man*, International, 1937.

Twentieth-Century Literary Criticism, Volume 3, Gale (Detroit, MI), 1980.

Vinde, Victor, *Sigrid Undset: A Nordic Moralist*, translated by Babette Hughes and Glenn Hughes, University of Washington Book Store (Seattle, WA), 1930.

Winsnes, A.H., *Sigrid Undset: A Study in Christian Realism*, translated by P.G. Foote, Sheed & Ward (New York, NY), 1953.

World Literature Criticism, Gale (Detroit, MI), 1992.

PERIODICALS

American Enterprise, July-August, 1997, Todd R. Flanders, review of *Kristin Lavransdatter*, p. 85.

American-Scandinavian Review, June, 1929; July, 1929.

Booklist, May 15, 2001, Donna Seaman, review of *The Unknown Sigrid Undset: Jenny and Other Works*, p. 1734.

Books Abroad, winter, 1950.

Critic, January-February, 1974.

Library Journal, March 15, 1995, p. 102; May 15, 2001, review of *The Unknown Sigrid Undset*, p. 168.

Literary Review, April, 1923.

Ms., January, 1981.

New Republic, October 5, 1921.

New York Times Book Review, June 3, 2001, Bruce Bawer, review of *The Unknown Sigrid Undset*, p. 42.

Publishers Weekly, April 30, 2001, review of *The Unknown Sigrid Undset*, p. 54.

Review of Contemporary Fiction, fall, 2001, James Crossley, review of *The Unknown Sigrid Undset*, p. 220.

Saturday Review of Literature, June 2, 1928.

Scandinavian Studies, November, 1966; August, 1968; spring, 1999, Otto Reinert, "Unfashionable *Kristin Lavransdatter*," pp. 67-80; spring, 2002, Sherrill Harbison, review of *The Unknown Sigrid Undset*, p. 108; fall, 2003, Ellen Rees, "Dreaming of the Medieval in *Kristin Lavransdatter* and *Troldsyn*," pp. 399-416.

Scandinavica, Volume 45, 2006, Christine Hamm, "The Maiden and the Knight: Gender, Body and Melodrama in Sigrid Undset's *Kristin Lavransdatter*," pp. 5-27.

Thought, spring, 1965.

ONLINE

NobelPrize.org, http://nobelprize.org/ (April 4, 2008), biography of Undset.

OTHER

Sigrid Undset: A Portrait (video), Landmark Media, 1998.*

Mark Waid

(Courtesy of Mark Waid.)

■ Personal

Born March 21, 1962, in Hueytown, AL. *Education:* Attended Virginia Commonwealth University.

■ Addresses

E-mail—mwaid@aol.com.

■ Career

Comic-book writer. Worked variously as a bank teller, legal secretary, waiter, TV repairman, lounge singer, salesman, and accountant. Freelance writer, c. 1980s; *Amazing Heroes*, editor, 1986; DC Comics, New York, NY, editor, 1987-89; freelance writer, 1989-2002; CrossGeneration (comic-book publisher), Oldsmar, FL, senior writer, 2002; freelance writer.

■ Awards, Honors

Eisner Award nominations for best writer, 2002, for *Ruse: Enter the Detective.*

■ Writings

GRAPHIC NOVELS

The Flash: Terminal Velocity (originally published in comic-book form), DC Comics (New York, NY), 1995.

The Flash: The Return of Barry Allen (originally published in comic-book form), DC Comics (New York, NY), 1996.

(With Fabian Nicieza) *Justice League: Midsummer's Nightmare* (originally published in comic-book form), DC Comics (New York, NY), 1996.

(With Alex Ross) *Kingdom Come* (originally published in comic-book form), illustrated by Ross, DC Comics (New York, NY), 1997.

Impulse: Reckless Youth (originally published in comic-book form), DC Comics (New York, NY), 1997.

(With Brian Augustyn) *The Flash—Green Lantern: Faster Friends*, DC Comics (New York, NY), 1997.

(With Brian Augustyn and Mike Wieringo) Iris Allen, *The Life Story of the Flash* (originally published in comic-book form), DC Comics (New York, NY), 1997.

(With Scott Peterson) *Underworld Unleashed*, DC Comics (New York, NY), 1998.

(With Tom Peyer McGraw) *Legion of Super-Heroes: The Beginning of Tomorrow* (originally published in comic-book form), DC Comics (New York, NY), 1999.

The Kingdom (originally published in comic-book form), DC Comics (New York, NY), 1999.

JLA: Heaven's Ladder, (originally published in comic-book form), DC Comics (New York, NY), 2000.

The Flash: Dead Heat, DC Comics (New York, NY), 2000.

JLA: Tower of Babel (originally published in comic-book form), DC Comics (New York, NY), 2001.

Ruse: Inferno of Blue, illustrated by Butch Guice, CrossGeneration (Oldsmar, FL), 2002.

Ruse: Enter the Detective, illustrated by Butch Guice, CrossGeneration (Oldsmar, FL), 2002.

Sigil: The Lizard God, CrossGeneration (Oldsmar, FL), 2002.

Crux: Atlantis Rising, illustrated by Steve Epting and Rick Magyar, CrossGeneraton (Oldsmar, FL), 2002.

Fantastic Four, Volume 1, Marvel Comics (New York, NY), 2004.

Superman: Birthright, DC Comics (New York, NY), 2005.

City of Heroes (originally published in comic-book form), Image Comics, 2005.

(With others) *House of M: Spider-Man*, Marvel Comics (New York, NY), 2006.

(With Alex Ross) *Absolute Kingdom Come*, DC Comics (New York, NY), 2006.

(With others) *52*, Volumes 1-4, DC Comics (New York, NY), 2007.

Supergirl and the Legion of Super-Heros: Dominator War, Volumes 1-3, DC Comics (New York, NY), 2007.

The Lords of Luck: The Brave and the Bold, DC Comics (New York, NY), 2008.

OTHER

The Golden Age of Superman: The Greatest Covers of Action Comics from the '30s to the '50s, Artabras (New York, NY), 1993, published as *Superman in Action Comics*, Abbeville Press (New York, NY), 1993.

The Silver Age of Superman: The Greatest Covers of Action Comics from the '50s to the '70s, Artabras (New York, NY), 1995.

(Author of introduction) *Superman in the Sixties*, created by Jerry Siegel and Joe Shuster, DC Comics (New York, NY), 1999.

Writer for comic book series, including *The Avengers, Captain America, Flash, Impulse, JLA, Kingdom Come, Underworld Unleashed,* and *X-Men.*

■ **Sidelights**

Mark Waid is an Eisner Award-nominated comic-book writer who has penned stories featuring almost every major super hero who ever threw a punch. He has been called in several times to revamp or refresh familiar comic book characters who need to reach a new audience, including the Flash and Superman. Perhaps what makes Waid's comics writing so popular is his approach to the job. Speaking with Robert Taylor in an interview for *Comic Book Resources*, Waid remarked: "A good writer makes these characters real. He sees the world through their point of view. He imagines what it's like to have their powers, what their life is like."

An Early Comics Fan

"The first comic I read as a child was *Batman #180* in 1966, the first issue to come out after the Adam West TV show premiered in the U.S.," Waid told Danilo Guarino on the *Amazing Comics* Web site. "From that moment on, I was hooked—though I'd have to say that the single most influential comic book from my childhood wasn't that one. It was *Adventure Comics #369*, by Jim Shooter and Curt Swan. It's a classic Legion of Super-Heroes tale full of heart and humor and a chilling cliffhanger, and the basic plot structure of that issue is an influence than can still be seen in my work to this day." Speaking with Vaneta Rogers of *Newsarama* Waid recounted: "When I started reading comics, I knew every comic's schedule. I knew exactly. I knew that *Detective Comics* came out every fourth week; I knew that *Superman* comics came out every second week; I knew that the *Hulk* came out every third week of the month. It was part of my genetic coding that I knew this as a teenager."

Waid got involved with the comics fan press in the early 1980s. He wrote articles for such publications as *Amazing Heroes* and the *Comic Buyer's Guide*. While still writing for the fan press, Waid sold a Superman story that was used in *Action Comics*. Waid told Mark Salisbury in *Writers on Comics Scriptwriting*: "I recall it took something like two weeks to write this little eight-page story, which I look back upon now and laugh." In 1986 he became the editor of *Amazing Heroes*, published by Fantagraphics, a job he was to keep for only a year. In 1987, Dick Giordano at DC Comics called Waid and offered him an editor's job. Waid was on the staff of DC Comics from 1987 to 1989 before launching a freelance career that has allowed him to write the adventures of everyone from Marvel's X-Men and Captain America to DC's the Flash and Impulse.

Chronicles the Adventures of the Flash

Salisbury claimed that "Waid first revealed his immense skill for characterization as a writer on *The Flash*." Beginning in the early 1990s Waid was the

In Waid's 1997 graphic novel *Kingdom Come*, an earlier generation of superheroes comes out of retirement to assist in the battle of good versus evil. (DC Comics, 1997. Cover copyright © 1997 DC Comics. Reproduced by permission.)

chief writer on the series, which features a superhero who can move at lightning speed. Waid's version of the character focuses on Wally West, once known as Kid Flash (the original Flash was really Barry Allen) but who now has taken over as the Flash. In his interview with Robert Taylor for *Comic Book Resources,* Waid recalled: "My favorite Flash line that I ever wrote was when Wally got his Flash powers for the first time and said 'The only sound in the world was the rush of the wind and the thunder of my own two feet.'" Other series regulars include the popular Impulse, which became a spinoff series. Waid's *Impulse* comic introduced thirtieth-century teen Bart Allen, who, armed with innumerable futuristic devices and the incredible speed of his ancestor, Barry Allen, comes back in time to the twentieth century to understand his past and becomes a twentieth-century superhero into the

bargain. Speaking to Salisbury about what he considered the highlight of his career, Waid stated that "the highlight is the whole run of *The Flash,* using the character of the Flash to unintentionally learn volumes about myself as a person. In that way it's been a very symbiotic relationship, and that has been the most rewarding thing."

Among Waid's most notable original works has been his project with Marvel artist Alex Ross, *Kingdom Come,* a futuristic comic that was published in graphic-novel format in 1997. Waid recounted: "*Kingdom Come* was probably the single most collaborative project I've ever worked on, because Alex was a co-plotter on the story and very invested in it, more than any other artist I've ever worked with." In *Kingdom Come* the first—and now aging—generation of super heroes returns to the front-lines in the battle against evil in order to teach a newer generation of crime-fighters the moral underpinnings of the battle between good and evil. Once again Superman and Wonder Woman do battle with the likes of Lex Luthor (also newly un-retired as Superman's nemesis) in a "gorgeously illustrated" story that *Washington Post Book World* contributor Mike Musgrove characterized as a "dark vision of the next generation inhabiting the world of Metropolis and Gotham City."

Speaking to Alan Kistler about the popularity of his work in an interview for *Monitor Duty,* Waid noted: "I can't tell you how many meetings I've had out here as a writer with studio heads and execs who want to meet me, partly to talk about things I can do for them, but they also just want to meet me because I wrote *Kingdom Come* or I created *Impulse* or whatever, and they're like, 'I wanna meet that guy, I'm a fan of his work.' Which is very flattering, don't get me wrong, but it seems like a weird *Twilight Zone* moment when I go to these meetings."

As a freelancer during the 1990s Waid gained a reputation as one of the hardest-working comic writers in the United States. In fact, he had his hand in almost all the major action-hero series, from *Superman* and *Batman* to such lower-profile projects as *Legionnaires* and *Ka-Zar.* Popular comic-book series by Waid include *Justice League of America*—or *JLA*—which he took over from writer Grant Morrison and which features the time-honored roster of super heroes as well as crime-fighters like Green Arrow as they organize against dark forces such as the Brotherhood of Evil. Waid's award-winning *Ruse* comic book series is about a Victorian-era detective modeled on Sherlock Holmes. In praise of *Ruse: Enter the Detective,* a *Publishers Weekly* reviewer was laudatory of Waid's skills, noting that despite the

An interior page from Waid's 1997 graphic novel *Kingdom Come.* (DC Comics, 1997. Copyright © 1996 DC Comics. Reproduced by permission.)

"high-end representational illustration . . . the real star here is Waid's droll but exciting scripts." In the graphic novel *Underworld Unleashed,* which Waid coauthored, a horde of DC Comics villains take advantage of a limited-time offer: sell their soul to the demonic Neron, and their powers against the forces of good will double in strength.

In 2002 Waid left freelancing to take a job as senior writer at the Florida-based comic publisher CrossGeneration. There he penned the "Crux" and "Sigil" series, both of which have been re-released in graphic-novel format. The futuristic space saga "Sigil" pits soldiers Sam Rey and Roiya against a lizard-like race of aliens. In *Crux: Atlantis Rising,* readers meet the occupants of Atlantis, guardians of all humanity, whose culture has been fueled by magic and who have evolved from one race into two. Those who have gained in energy are preparing for the Transition, during which they will change form, while others will remain as Earth's guardians. However, something malfunctions and Atlantis is submerged, her people left sleeping in stasis pods from which a small group led by the watcher Capricia are awakened 10,000 years after the Transition to find humanity gone and an evil menace threatening their world. Praising the artwork by Steve Epting and Rick Magyar, *Library Journal* contributor Steve Raiteri heralded *Crux* as a "fine work, full of compelling characters and situations," while in *School Library Journal* reviewer Susan Salpini found Waid's "intriguing" storyline to be "more thoughtful and thought provoking than the usual fare."

Revamps Superman

In 2003 Waid was called in to revamp the Superman character for DC Comics. Over the years, the character and his "universe" had undergone a number of variations and expansions. The various ongoing comic book series featuring Superman had introduced a range of supporting characters, storylines, and background explanations that were not consistent. Characters and storylines were also introduced by the big-screen Superman movies and in such television spinoffs as *Smallville.* The world of Superman simply contained too many contradictions. Waid created the 12-part limited series *Superman: Birthright* to resolve the problem. The book incorporates and reconciles elements from the various versions of the character and became the "bible" for subsequent stories involving the superhero. Speaking of this project, Waid told Daniel Robert Epstein of *Underground Online:* "The job was to reinvent and rethink Superman for a very

City of Heroes, **Waid's 2005 adapation of the popular multiplayer online game, is set in Paragon City.** (Image Comics, 2005. City of Heroes is © 2008 Cryptic Studios, Inc. and NC Interactive, Inc. NCsoft, the interlocking of NC logo, City of Heroes, and all associated NCsoft logos and designs are trademarks or registered trademarks of NCsoft Corporation. City Heroes is a registered trademark of Cryptic Studios, Inc. and NCsoft Corporation, Inc. Cryptic Studios is a trademark of Cryptic Studios, Inc. All other trademarks are the property of their respective owners.)

modern, very contemporary audience. . . . I don't know what's going to appeal to everybody. But I have to have faith that, when you strip away and rebuild from the ground and take the elements of Superman that everyone knows, I think that history has proven that there is a common appeal to all that stuff."

Waid was called in for another project in 2005 when Cryptic Studios wanted their popular multi-player online game "City of Heroes" adapted as a comic book series. Because of the complexity of the game, and the fact that it is constantly evolving as it is played online, Waid faced a great challenge. "While the foundation is laid beforehand," he explained to

Michael Lafferty of *Game Zone*, "it's still up to the artist and I to invent an actual storyline that plays to the comics format rather than the online gaming format—something with a definite beginning, middle and end, and something that turns on emotion as much as action." One problem in the game is that no character ever dies from injuries; they are simply taken out of play for a time for recuperation. Waid changed that. His characters can actually die, which makes the story that much darker and more realistic than the game. While the series was sold to the general public, all 100,000 subscribers to the "City of Heroes" online game received a free copy of the series' first issue.

Waid's 2007 project *52*, on which he served as one of four writers, was a weekly title which played out in real-time over the course of a year. It centered on a number of DC Comics superheroes, although not the top ones, and involved an evolving script that needed to develop and then conclude over the course of the year. Speaking with Vaneta Rogers of *Newsarama* about the difficulty of writing such a project, Waid admitted: "There were no easy weeks. Every week, it seemed like there was something that, like, at the last second, we'd find out these two scenes that Geoff and I wrote separately don't work together, or you know, we're using a character that somebody else has staked out for another series, or any number of things that were always a last minute race to the finish. And as we got closer and closer to the finish, it just got more manic." Speaking to Dan Phillips for *IGN Entertainment*, Waid explained: "There have been little adjustments we've had to make to our series because sometimes, inadvertently other books in the [DC Comics universe] have revealed a little too much about what might happen to the characters in our series. That's really been the only real headache."

If you enjoy the works of Mark Waid, you may also want to check out the following books:

Marv Wolfman, *Crisis on Infinite Earths*, 1998.
Brad Meltzer, *Identity Crisis*, 2005.
Kurt Busiek, *Marvels*, 2008.

In addition to writing his own comic-book stories, Waid has compiled several volumes of classic comic-book art. *The Golden Age of Superman: The Greatest Covers of Action Comics from the '30s to the '50s* and its companion volume, *The Silver Age of Superman: The Greatest Covers of Action Comics from the '50s to the '70s* collects the drawings that caused issues of the comic by Jerry Siegel to be snatched from store shelves with lightning speed. *Superman in the Sixties* contains Waid's introduction to seventeen stories featuring not only the beloved Man of Steel, but also Superboy, Superbaby, Lois Lane, and Jimmy Olsen.

Asked in an interview with Minh Ta for *Comic Fan* online what caused him to devote his career to comic books, Waid was very clear: "A belief that heroic-fiction comics are perhaps the last best place to remind tomorrow's adults that Right Makes Might and that doing good is its own reward. These are philosophies, as simplistic as they sound, that . . . [I] strongly champion."

■ Biographical and Critical Sources

BOOKS

Salisbury, Mark, *Writers on Comics Scriptwriting*, Titan Books (London, England), 1999.

PERIODICALS

Booklist, August, 2002, Carlos Orellana, review of *Ruse: Inferno of Blue*, p. 1944; February 1, 2008, Gordon Flagg, review of *The Lords of Luck: The Brave and the Bold*, p. 37.

Library Journal, September 1, 2002, Steve Raiteri, review of *Ruse: Enter the Detective*, p. 151; November 1, 2002, Steve Raiteri, review of *Crux: Atlantis Rising*, p. 67; November 15, 2006, Steve Raiteri, review of *Absolute Kingdom Come*, p. 50; September 15, 2007, Steve Raiteri, review of *Supergirl and the Legion of Super-Heroes: Dominator War*, p. 41.

Publishers Weekly, August 12, 2002, review of *Ruse: Enter the Detective*, p. 278; August 26, 2002, review of *Sigil: The Lizard God*, p. 46; May 26, 2003, review of *Ruse: The Silent Partner*, p. 51; May 7, 2007, review of *52*, p. 48.

School Library Journal, October, 2002, Susan Salpini, review of *Crux*, p. 198.

Sojourners, July-August, 1997, review of *Kingdom Come*, p. 1997.

Teacher Librarian, February, 2008, Joe Sutliff Sanders, review of *Supergirl and the Legion of Super-Heroes*, p. 57.

Washington Post Book World, January 11, 1998, Mike Musgrove, review of *Kingdom Come,* p. 4.

ONLINE

Amazing Comics, http://www.amazingcomics.it/ (February 11, 2003), Danilo Guarino, interview with Mark Waid.

Comic Book Resources, http://www.comicbook resources.com/ (May 13, 2007), Robert Taylor, "Talking with Mark Waid."

Comic Fan, http:// www.comicfanmag.com/ (January 29, 2003), Minh Ta, interview with Mark Waid.

Dragon*con, http:// www.dragoncon.org/ (July 1, 1999), "Mark Waid."

Game Zone, http://pc.gamezone.com/ (June 21, 2005), Michael Lafferty, "Top Cow's Mark Waid Talks about Creating a Comic Book Based on the Popular NCsoft MMO."

IGN Entertainment, http://comics.ign.com/ (February 9, 2007), Dan Phillips, "Exclusive Interview & Preview: Mark Waid Speaks."

Monitor Duty, http://www.monitorduty.com/ (September 21, 2005), Alan Kistler, "Alan Kistler's Interview with Mark Waid."

Newsarama.com, http://forum.newsarama.com/ (May 2, 2007), Vaneta Rogers, interview with Mark Waid.

Sequential Tart, http: //www.sequentialtart.com/ (June, 1999), Barb Lien, "Comic Books Aren't about Rules, They're about Flying"; (September, 2003), Carrie Landers, "The Crux of the Matter."

Underground Online, http://www.ugo.com/ (February 12, 2008), Daniel Robert Epstein, interview with Mark Waid.*

Nathanael West

■ Personal

Name originally Nathan Weinstein; name legally changed, August 16, 1926; born October 17, 1903, in New York, NY; died following an automobile accident, December 22, 1940, near El Centro, CA; buried in Mount Zion Cemetery, Queens, NY; son of Max (a building contractor) and Anna Weinstein; married Eileen McKenney, April 19, 1940. *Education:* Attended Tufts College (now University), 1921; Brown University, Ph.D., 1924.

■ Career

Writer. Worked for father's construction firm during early 1920s; Kenmore Hall (residence hotel), New York, NY, assistant manager, 1927-30; Sutton Club Hotel, New York, NY, manager, 1930-33; screenwriter for film studios in California, including Columbia, 1933 and 1938, Republic, 1936-38, RKO, 1938 and 1939-40, and Universal, 1938-39.

■ Member

League of American Writers (member of Hollywood committee), Screen Writers Guild (member of executive board, beginning 1939), Motion Picture Guild (member of executive board), Motion Picture Artists Committee (member of executive board), Motion Picture Democratic Committee, Hollywood Anti-Nazi League.

■ Writings

NOVELS

The Dream Life of Balso Snell, Contact Editions, 1931, Dover (New York, NY), 2004.

Miss Lonelyhearts, Liveright, 1933.

A Cool Million: The Dismantling of Lemuel Pitkin, Covici, Friede (New York, NY), 1934.

The Day of the Locust, Random House (New York, NY), 1939, reprinted with an introduction by Budd Schulberg, Time-Life Books (Alexandria, VA), 1982.

The Complete Works of Nathanael West (omnibus volume of four novels), introduction by Alan Ross, Farrar, Straus (New York, NY), 1957.

Miss Lonelyhearts & The Day of the Locust, New Directions (New York, NY), 1962, 13th edition, 1969.

The Collected Works of Nathanael West, Penguin (New York, NY), 1975.

Novels and Other Writings, Library of America (New York, NY), 1997.

A Cool Million; The Dream Life of Balso Snell: Two Novels, Farrar, Straus (New York, NY), 2006.

SCREENPLAYS

(With Jack Natteford) *Ticket to Paradise,* Republic, 1936.

(With Lester Cole) *The President's Mystery*, Republic, 1936.

(With Cole and Samuel Ornitz) *Follow Your Heart*, Republic, 1936.

Rhythm in the Clouds, Republic, 1937.

(With Ornitz) *It Could Happen to You*, Republic, 1937.

Born to Be Wild, Republic, 1938.

I Stole a Million, Universal, 1939.

(With Jerry Cady and Dalton Trumbo) *Five Came Back*, RKO, 1939.

(With Whitney Bolton) *The Spirit of Culver*, Universal, 1939.

Men Against the Sky, RKO, 1940.

Let's Make Music, RKO, 1940.

Also author of unproduced screenplays.

OTHER

(With Joseph Schrank) *Good Hunting* (play), first produced on Broadway, 1938.

(Under name Nathan Weinstein) *My Island of Sonnets* (poems), Exposition, 1974.

Also author, with S.J. Perelman, of the unproduced play *Even Stephen*. Contributor of articles, short stories, and poems, sometimes under name Nathan von Wallenstein Weinstein, to periodicals, including *Casements, Americana, Contact, Contempo,* and *Pacific Weekly*. Associate editor of *Contact*, 1931-32, and *Americana*, 1933.

■ Adaptations

Miss Lonelyhearts was adapted by Leonard Praskins for the film *Advice to the Lovelorn*, Fox/United Artists, 1933; by Howard Teichmann for a play of the original title, 1957; by Dore Schary for the film *Lonelyhearts*, United Artists, 1958; and by Michael Dinner and others for a television play of the original title, Public Broadcasting Service, 1983. *The Day of the Locust* was adapted by Waldo Salt for a film of the same title, Paramount, 1975.

■ Sidelights

An American novelist who wrote primarily during the Great Depression of the 1930s, Nathanael West was called "the chief neglected talent of [his] age" by Leslie Fiedler in *Love and Death in the American Novel*. While many of his contemporaries composed straightforward novels about social and economic injustice, West produced an idiosyncratic blend of pathos and comedy, realism and wild unreality. "He too deplored the emptiness of twentieth-century life in the United States," declared Richard B. Gehman in the *Atlantic Monthly,* "but he chose to depict that life in terms not of people who were consciously involved in a struggle, but of those who were unconsciously trapped—people who were, in their blindness, so tragic as to be comic figures." "West pursued his quest of exposing America's myths relentlessly," wrote Daniel Walden in the *Dictionary of Literary Biography*. "Compelled to do what he had to do, he described the cancers that threatened American society, and in depicting these horrors, he made his readers shudder and laugh." Little-known to the American public for years after his death, West's work maintained a select following in literary circles. As popular tastes in the novel changed, West's fiction gained a broader audience, and he was widely hailed as a precursor of the "black humor" novelists who wrote in the 1950s, 1960s, and beyond. Stanley Edgar Hyman wrote in his book *Nathanael West* that, "in his short tormented life, West achieved one authentically great novel, *Miss Lonelyhearts,* and three others less successful as wholes but full of brilliant and wonderful things."

Early Years in New York

Born in 1903 in New York City, West was the son of Russian-Jewish immigrants Max Weinstein, a prosperous building contractor, and Anna Wallenstein, who fancied herself a descendant of a German nobleman of the same last name. West's parents were more concerned with status and money than art. His father expected him to enter the family business, and he gave West several Horatio Alger novels—highly popular tales in which honest young men work their way to financial success. But West was a high-school dropout whose friends called him "Pep" because he showed so little energy.

To enroll in Tufts College, West lied about his grades, and when Tufts asked him to leave because of laziness, another student's transcript gained him admission to Brown. There West read widely, but he was better known for his enthusiastic socializing and a biting intellectual wit. When classmate and future journalist Quentin Reynolds pressed him for a graduation speech, West created the story of St. Puce, a flea who lives in the armpit of Christ. Unsure of his future after his graduation from Brown in 1924, West convinced relatives to fund a trip to Paris, where he could join other Americans on the city's literary scene. Jay Martin, writing in the *Dictionary of Literary Biography*, recounted: "Before applying for a passport he decided to change his name; and in August 1926 he took the name Nathanael West. In October 1926 he sailed for Paris, where he remained for three months, fully on his own for the first time. Though he wrote relatively little, West's experience in Paris had a permanent influence on his understanding of the writer's life, and it solidified his preferences in fiction." In early 1927, only a few months after he arrived in Europe, the family construction business began to decline—an economic downturn that presaged the Great Depression. West's family recalled him to America, and through their influence he obtained a succession of jobs managing inexpensive residential hotels. Outside the social mainstream West gained an education far different from his college years, and the experience would inspire his most successful novels.

By providing rent-free lodgings to struggling writers, West remained close to the New York literary world. His charity aided the literary critic Edmund Wilson; novelists Robert M. Coates, Erskine Caldwell, and Dashiell Hammett; and playwright Lillian Hellman. West also housed his newlywed sister and her husband, S.J. Perelman, a renowned satirist and a lifelong friend. West became fascinated with the desperate lives of his other tenants: a onetime actress worked as a prostitute; young men headed for work at businesses failing under the impact of the Depression; lonely residents killed time in the lobby reading magazines. At the Sutton Club Hotel six people committed suicide by jumping from the same terrace. When West was especially curious about a lodger, he would steam open the person's mail, sometimes with Hellman's assistance.

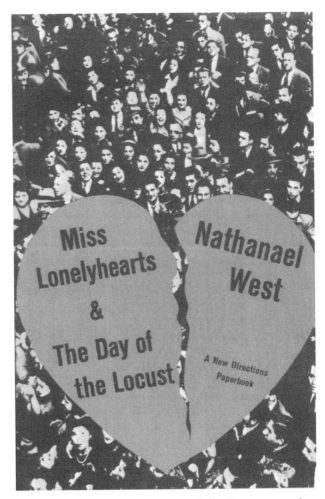

Miss Lonelyhearts & The Day of the Locust **contains both of Nathanael West's most popular novels.** (New Directions, 1969. Cover photo © Culver Pictures. Reproduced by courtesy of New Directions Publishing Corp.)

In 1931 West published his first novel, *The Dream Life of Balso Snell*. As James F. Light noted in *Nathanael West: An Interpretative Study*, if "there is any constant pattern in the novels of West, it is the pilgrimage around which each novel centers." He continued: "In each the hero is in search of something in which he can believe and to which he can belong . . . but the result is always the same: tragic disillusionment." In *The Dream Life of Balso Snell*, the title character pursues cultural enlightenment by journeying to the site of ancient Troy, where Trojans and Greeks had clashed thousands of years earlier in a war that inspired the earliest classic of Western literature, Homer's *Iliad*. Snell finds the wooden horse that the Greeks used to invade and conquer Troy. Entering the horse through its anus, he begins a dreamlike journey through Western culture. The artists and philosophers Snell meets, however, are frauds and fools—one is the devoted chronicler of

St. Puce. West derides the characters by making them blatantly repulsive, often associating them with excrement.

Commentators have generally agreed that West has a serious point to make in *The Dream Life of Balso Snell*—that art and ideas have become too removed from human reality—but they disagreed substantially about the merits of his technique. Admirers observed that West's vivid imagery and his concern with human dreams and delusions anticipate his later works. Detractors, however, found that *The Dream Life of Balso Snell* is overstated and contains too many scholarly allusions—mistakes, some suggested, that a recent college graduate might make. In the *New York Times Book Review*, Malcolm Cowley called the book "an elaborate joke . . . that doesn't quite come off."

Advice Columnist Caught in a Dilemma

But West soon transcended his penchant for "gratuitous and perverse humour," as V.S. Pritchett observed in the *New Statesman.* One evening Perelman introduced West to an advice columnist for the *Brooklyn Eagle.* She showed the two men a sample of her mail, wondering if it might inspire Perelman to write a comedy. West was deeply moved by the pain and helplessness the letters displayed, and he soon began work on his second novel, *Miss Lonelyhearts,* the tale of a young advice columnist who destroys himself by becoming personally involved in the miserable lives of his readers. In this novel, Pritchett noted, West "became [both] comic and humane." The title character, whose real name West never reveals, is a young newspaperman assigned to write an advice column. At first Miss Lonelyhearts agrees with his friends that the job is a joke, but the letters he receives are a wrenching mixture of inane comedy and undeniable sorrow. A teenage girl, for instance, laments that no one will ask her on dates because she "was born without a nose"; at the end of her letter, she asks for advice—"ought I to commit suicide?" Miss Lonelyhearts finds himself tangled in a moral dilemma: how can he reconcile himself to the existence of such meaningless suffering?

West depicts the plight of the columnist with "ironic and bitter humor," as T.C. Wilson wrote in the *Saturday Review.* The characters around Miss Lonelyhearts offer him solutions that are too simple for him to accept. While his girlfriend ignores the world's troubles by remaining silly and naive, his editor, Shrike, presents an air of worldly disillusionment edged with sadism. When Miss Lonelyhearts becomes physically ill with anxiety, Shrike visits his bedside to belittle him. Shrike lists the columnist's hopes of escape—art, a place in the country, suave indifference—and dismisses them all with a sneer. Miss Lonelyhearts, Shrike declares, is a "leper-licker." The columnist becomes convinced that he can heal his readers with Christian love, but his efforts are ludicrous and futile. Visiting one troubled couple, he holds hands with the husband and is seduced by the wife. The husband, in a jealous rage, seizes a gun and kills Miss Lonelyhearts—by accident. As Wilson concluded, "the tragic lives of [West's] characters impress us even more powerfully because they are made to seem stupid and comic."

Miss Lonelyhearts has repeatedly garnered praise for its adept language and its tight dramatic focus. In fifteen short chapters, West chronicles progressive stages of the columnist's emotional disintegration.

Pritchett called the book "a selection of hard, diamond-fine miniatures"and noted the "precision" of the author's "poetic images." As Brad Darrach noted in *Time:* "Nothing else in American fiction radiates the compacted fury of this little parable."

As the 1930s wore on West became increasingly concerned about his failure to gain either artistic recognition or a steady income from his writing. He joined the staffs of two literary magazines—including *Contact,* where he joined poet William Carlos Williams—but the journals soon folded. When Columbia Pictures offered West a screenwriting job, he eagerly accepted, only to be laid off within a year. Supported by friends he wrote a third novel, *A Cool Million: The Dismantling of Lemuel Pitkin,* which vented his bitterness about the Great Depression by satirizing the myth of success portrayed in Horatio Alger novels.

A Cool Million is a political satire directed against America's image as a land of prosperity—a predictable target during the Great Depression. Subtitled "The Dismantling of Lemuel Pitkin," the book chronicles the misadventures of a well-intentioned fool who is physically torn apart as he quests for financial success. As the novel opens, Pitkin gets a loan from Shagpoke Whipple, a dishonest banker who advises him to venture forth from their small town to pursue his fortune. After Pitkin loses his teeth, an eye, his leg, a thumb, and his scalp, he becomes a performing freak in a vaudeville show, entertaining the audience by being beaten on stage. Shot dead by a Communist agent, Pitkin is turned into a martyr by Whipple's Fascist party. Though *A Cool Million* displays West's gift for a colorful plot, most commentators agree that the book is hampered by a heavy-handed use of mock-heroic prose. West seems uninvolved with his characters, biographer Robert Emmet Long averred, and the book "seems surprisingly crude and rambling," especially "in comparison with *Miss Lonelyhearts.*"

Screenwriting in California

A major Hollywood studio bought the rights to *A Cool Million,* however, and the sale encouraged West to move to California in 1935 for a second try at screenwriting. Several months passed and he was unable to find work, even with the aid of an agent. Hammett had become successful in the movie business, and West repeatedly approached him for help with a job but was greeted with taunts. Moreover, at a time when the major studios were trying to keep unions out of the film industry, West's mem-

Film poster for the 1975 adapation of West's tragic Hollywood novel *The Day of the Locust.* (Paramount/The Kobal Collection/The Picture Desk, Inc.)

bership in the Screen Writers Guild hurt his prospects. Depressed and poor, West became desperately afraid that he would always be a failure. Only money sent by Perelman sustained him.

As in New York, West occupied a succession of shabby lodgings, and he began to meet the marginal people of Southern California. He became a confidant of prostitutes and considered compiling their slang into a dictionary. His circle of acquaintances gradually grew to include midgets, petty criminals, and murder investigators. Long before West felt accepted as a Hollywood screenwriter, he was familiar with the industry's stuntmen and laborers.

After a year West found a screenwriting job at Republic, a minor studio known as a factory for formulaic, low-budget films. He adapted readily to this commercial atmosphere, for he saw screenwriting as merely a craft that could support him while he wrote novels and plays. For extra money he

eventually teamed with writer Boris Ingster, developing scripts and script ideas that producers purchased eagerly. As biographer Jay Martin explained, Ingster generated conventional story lines and gave them to West, who contributed his flair for distinctive characters and twists of plot.

Hollywood Madness

Immersed in the unglamorous side of Hollywood, West wrote *The Day of the Locust,* his fourth and final book. Unusual among Hollywood novels, it ignores film stars and financiers to concentrate on the obscure, disheartened people who inhabit the town's social fringes. *The Day of the Locust* centers on Tod Hackett, a recent Yale art-school graduate who designs sets in Hollywood. Lacking funds, awaiting the inspiration for a painting, he haunts the underside of California life much as West had done. Tod meets Homer Simpson, a timid bookkeeper from Iowa; Adore Loomis, a snide child actor; Abe Kusich, an angry dwarf; and Faye Greener, a flirtatious aspiring actress who arouses the unfulfilled desires of many men she meets, including Tod and Homer.

Frustration becomes the motif of the novel, for as many critics note, West sees California as a deceptive land of promise inhabited by Americans whose dreams have failed to come true. Feeling bored and deceived, these masses occupy their time with idle thrill-seeking. In the climactic episode of the novel, which reviewers found particularly compelling, a crowd assembles outside a movie house to see the pageantry of a Hollywood premiere. Taunted once too often by Adore, the long-suffering Homer erupts in anger and kills him. The crowd becomes a lynch mob, tearing Homer to pieces, and Tod—nearly crushed in the riot—envisions his completed painting. It will be a portrait of apocalypse entitled "The Burning of Los Angeles."

The Day of the Locust has repeatedly been called the best Hollywood novel ever written. "Mr. West has caught the emptiness of Hollywood," wrote Edmund Wilson in *New Republic,* "and he is, as far as I know, the first writer to make this emptiness horrible." In the *Hudson Review,* Daniel Aaron praised West for turning the movie capital into a powerful symbol. "Not an isolated piece of dreamland or a national joke," Aaron wrote, West's Hollywood "is America carried out to its logical conclusion." Unfortunately, the novel did not catch on with a Depression-weary audience. The novel sold few copies.

By contrast, the commercial film industry that West scorned in *The Day of the Locust* began to appreciate his screenwriting. He continued to write undistinguished films, but now he worked for the higher-paying major studios, particularly Universal and RKO. While his friend F. Scott Fitzgerald, a highly popular novelist during the 1920s, struggled to survive as a screenwriter, West earned a comfortable income for the first time in his life. He bought a pleasant house in the Hollywood hills and married Eileen McKenney.

Literary critics have generally agreed that West's work is difficult to categorize. Many have linked him to surrealism, a French aesthetic movement of the 1920s and 1930s that stressed the imagery of dreams; others, citing his interest in America's downtrodden, have linked him to naturalism, a more political movement that stressed an individual's helplessness in a hostile society. In an article titled "West's Disease," which appeared in *The Dyer's Hand and Other Essays*, poet W.H. Auden declared that West "is not, strictly speaking, a novelist" because he portrays neither dreams nor society in an accurate fashion. Fiedler praised this characteristic of West's work, calling the author "the inventor of a peculiar kind of book . . . the neo-gothic novel," which derived from West's understanding that "literary truth is not synonymous with fact." Fiedler wrote that such a style, unburdened by the minutiae of factual and psychological detail, "opened up possibilities . . . of capturing the quality of experience in a mass society." He concluded: "Putting down a book by West, a reader is not sure whether he has been presented with a nightmare endowed with the conviction of actuality or with actuality distorted into the semblance of a nightmare; but in either case, he has the sense that he has been presented with a view of a world in which, incredibly, he lives."

As West himself observed, the world he presents is unrelieved by hope. "There is nothing to root for in my books," Martin quotes him as saying. Reviewers have been particularly troubled by West's portrayal of human relationships. In his books friendship and sexual love appear repulsive, inadequate, or ridiculous, for such ideals are overwhelmed by loneliness, despair, and brutality. Some critics call West's world-view a sign of his limitations as a writer, and some suggest that it reflects deep-seated psychological problems. In West's books, wrote biographer Kingsley Widmer: "Female sexuality tends to be fascinatingly horrific, women destructive powers demanding hostile responses. . . . West's sex-violence obsessions in his fiction may suggest erotic difficulties in [his] life."

West, however, found nothing abnormal about centering his fiction on brutality. In an essay titled "Some Notes on Violence," he told readers of *Contact* that manuscripts submitted to the magazine generally had this same obsession. "In America,"he declared, "violence is idiomatic," so much so that only great violence can attract any attention. As Martin observed, "West's notion of how to express the 'American grain' was to 'do it obviously—cruelly, irresponsible torture, simply, obviously, casually told.'" Sexuality in West's novels was a literary device, according to Victor Comerchero in *Nathanael West: The Ironic Prophet*. "The disorder of the individual mirrors the disorder of the society," Comerchero declared. "Sexual inadequacy is ineffectualness at its most primitive biological level. Tied up in one vivid image are man's social, biological, psychological, and 'metaphysical' inadequacies—man's inadequacy before the 'laws of life.'" West remained true to his artistic vision, but the price he paid was unpopularity. Critics speculated that West's pessimism, coming at a time when America faced the twin burdens of the Great Depression and an impending world war, was simply too painful for his audience to bear.

A Tragic End

West was to die tragically with his wife of eight months, Eileen McKenney West. Walden related: "On 22 December 1940, returning from a weekend hunting trip in Mexico, West and his new bride were killed in an automobile accident near El Centro, California. He was thirty-seven years old." West, who was notorious among his friends for his reckless driving, reportedly had said that he would probably die in a car accident. The accident came just days before the opening of the play *My Sister Eileen*, which immortalized Eileen West, written by her older sister, Ruth McKenney. Writing in *Harper's Magazine*, David Gargill noted: "West's obituary in the *New York Times* appeared on the 'Amusements' page and botched his name, the titles of two of his novels, and his age. We'll never know if West was aware of his friend F. Scott Fitzgerald's death from a heart attack in Los Angeles the day before; it's been suggested that West was distraught over the news, and that this may have in some way contributed to the accident, but there's no evidence to support the claim. All we're left with are the decidedly unsentimental particulars of his passing: Eileen's watch stopped at 2:55, they crashed into a 1937 Pontiac sedan, that part of the county had only one ambulance, which was slow in coming, both were thrown from the vehicle, he was thirty-seven, she was twenty-seven."

Near the end of his life West recognized that his writing had always been too unusual to appeal to a broad audience. As Martin quoted him in a letter to Fitzgerald: "Somehow or other I seem to have slipped in between all the 'schools.' My books meet no needs except my own, their circulation is practically private and I'm lucky to be published. And yet I only have a desire to remedy that *before* sitting down to write, once I begin I do it my way. I forget the broad sweep, the big canvas, the shot-gun adjectives, the important people, the significant ideas, the lessons to be taught . . . and go on making what one critic called 'private and unfunny jokes.'"

If you enjoy the works of Nathanael West, you may also want to check out the following books:

William Faulkner, *The Sound and the Fury*, 1929.
Flannery O'Connor, *Wise Blood*, 1952.
Walker Percy, *The Moviegoer*, 1961.
Donna Tartt, *The Secret History*, 1992.

After West's death his literary reputation languished for many years. But prominent old friends such as Coates and Williams continued to praise him, and in 1947 Daniel Aaron helped begin a broad reassessment of West's work when he praised the novelist in the literary magazine *Partisan Review*. The West revival became extensive in 1957, when the four novels were published in one volume for the first time. Known somewhat inaccurately as the *The Complete Works of Nathanael West*, the collection received lengthy positive reviews in a wide variety of publications in the United States and England. The first book-length studies of West appeared in the early 1960s, followed by many more works of literary criticism and biography, including Martin's highly detailed *Nathanael West: The Art of His Life*.

"West wrote, from his mid-twenties to his mid-thirties, a small body of often intense and insightful prose fiction," Widmer concluded. "The four relatively short books—*The Dream Life of Balso Snell*, *Miss Lonelyhearts*, *A Cool Million*, and *The Day of the Locust*—were published during the Great Depression, the 1930s, and often reflect its sour conditions and angers. While his writings received rather limited responses in his lifetime, they became widely recognized as important and influential a generation later. The aesthetic and moral pertinence of his fictions continues and, in spite of the limited quantity and scope of his work, his role in American literary history and modernist sensibility will probably remain intriguing and significant. West stands out."

West also influenced such later novelists as Joseph Heller, Thomas Pynchon, and Flannery O'Connor. His writings, stated Martin in his *Nathanael West*, seem not only to have accurately pictured his time but to be "permanent and true explorations into the Siberia of the human spirit." As Hyman wrote, West "was a true pioneer and culture hero, making it possible for the younger symbolists and fantasists who came after him, and who include our best writers, to do with relative ease what he did in defiance of the temper of his time, for so little reward, in isolation and in pain."

■ Biographical and Critical Sources

BOOKS

Auden, W.H., *The Dyer's Hand and Other Essays*, Random House (New York, NY), 1962.

Barnard, Rita, *The Great Depression and the Culture of Abundance: Kenneth Fearing, Nathanael West, and Mass Culture in the 1930s*, Cambridge University Press (New York, NY), 1995.

Bloom, Harold, editor, *Nathanael West: Modern Critical Views*, Chelsea House, 1986.

Comerchero, Victor, *Nathanael West: The Ironic Prophet*, Syracuse University Press, 1964.

Concise Dictionary of Literary Biography: The Age of Maturity, 1929-1941, Gale (Detroit, MI), 1989.

Dardis, Tom, *Some Time in the Sun: The Hollywood Years of F. Scott Fitzgerald, William Faulkner, Nathanael West, Aldous Huxley and James Agee*, Penguin (New York, NY), 1981, new edition, Limelight Editions, 2004.

Dictionary of Literary Biography, Gale (Detroit, MI), Volume 4: *American Writers in Paris, 1920-1939*, 1980, Volume 9: *American Novelists, 1910-1945*, 1981, Volume 28: *Twentieth-Century American Jewish Fiction Writers*, 1984, Volume 288: *The House of Boni & Liveright, 1917-1933*, 2004.

Fiedler, Leslie A., *Love and Death in the American Novel*, revised edition, Stein & Day (New York, NY), 1966.

Hyman, Stanley Edgar, *Nathanael West*, University of Minnesota Press, 1962.

Light, James F., *Nathanael West: An Interpretive Study*, 2nd edition, Northwestern University Press, 1971.

Long, Robert Emmet, *Nathanael West*, Ungar (New York, NY), 1985.

Madden, David, editor, *Nathanael West; The Cheaters and the Cheated: A Collection of Critical Essays*, Everett/Edwards, 1973.

Malin, Irving, *Nathanael West's Novels*, Southern Illinois University Press (Carbondale, IL), 1972.

Martin, Jay, *Nathanael West: The Art of His Life*, Farrar, Straus (New York, NY), 1970.

Martin, Jay, editor, *Nathanael West: A Collection of Critical Essays*, Prentice-Hall, 1971.

Novels for Students, Volume 16, Gale (Detroit, MI), 2003.

Reference Guide to American Literature, St. James Press (Detroit, MI), 2000.

Reid, Randall, *The Fiction of Nathanael West*, University of Chicago Press (Chicago, IL) 1967.

Short Story Criticism, Gale (Detroit, MI), Volume 16, 1994.

Siegel, Ben, editor, *Critical Essays on Nathanael West*, G.K. Hall (New York, NY), 1994.

Twentieth-Century Literary Criticism, Gale (Detroit, MI), Volume 1, 1978, Volume 14, 1984, Volume 44, 1992.

Veitch, Jonathan, *American Superrealism: Nathanael West and the Politics of Representation in the 1930s*, University of Wisconsin Press, 1997.

West, Nathanael, *Miss Lonelyhearts*, introduction by Robert M. Coates, New Directions (New York, NY), 1946.

West, Nathanael, *The Day of the Locust*, introduction by Richard B. Gehman, New Directions (New York, NY), 1950.

West, Nathanael, *The Complete Works of Nathanael West*, introduction by Alan Ross, Farrar, Straus (New York, NY), 1957.

White, William, *Nathanael West: A Comprehensive Bibliography*, Kent State University Press, 1975.

Widmer, Kingsley, *Nathanael West*, Twayne (New York, NY), 1982.

Wisker, Alistair, *The Writing of Nathanael West*, St. Martin's Press (New York, NY), 1990.

PERIODICALS

Atlantic Monthly, September, 1950; October, 1970.

Canadian Review of American Studies, fall, 1973, John Graham, "Struggling Upward: *The Minister's Charge* and *A Cool Million*," pp. 184-196.

Commentary, November, 1997, Algis Valiunas, review of *Novels and Other Writings*, p. 64.

Commonweal, May 10, 1957; October 23, 1970.

Contact, Volume 1, number 3, 1932.

Entertainment Weekly, December 23, 1994, p. 84.

Harper's Magazine, July, 2006, David Gargill, "Master of the Convincing Lie: Nathanael West's Brilliant Distortions," p. 83.

Hudson Review, winter, 1951, Daniel Aaron, "Writing for Apocalypse," pp. 634-636.

Library Journal, July, 1997, Michael Rogers, review of *Novels and Other Writings*, p. 132; August, 2004, Michael Rogers, review of *The Dream Life of Balso Snell*, p. 131.

Modern Language Quarterly, December, 1993, Richard Keller Simon, "Between Capra and Adorno: West's 'Day of the Locust' and the Movies of the 1930s," p. 513.

Modern Language Review, April, 2007, Doug Haynes, "'Laughing at the Laugh': Unhappy Consciousness in Nathanael West's *The Dream Life of Balso Snell*," p. 341.

Nation, July 25, 1934; July 15, 1939; May 4, 1957; August 17, 1970.

New Republic, July 26, 1939; May 23, 1970.

New Statesman, December 7, 1957; October 11, 1968.

Newsweek, September 4, 1950; May 13, 1957; June 29, 1970.

New York, April 17, 1995, p. 111.

New Yorker, April 15, 1933, Robert M. Coates, "Messiah of the Lonely Hearts," p. 59; May 18, 1957, Norman Podhoretz, "A Particular Kind of Joking," pp. 156-165; October 10, 1970.

New York Times, June 2, 1974; February 2, 1987; February 8, 1987.

New York Times Book Review, April 23, 1933; July 1, 1934, Fred T. Marsh, "*A Cool Million* and Other Recent Works of Fiction," p. 6; May 21, 1939; May 12, 1957; December 23, 1990, p. 3.

Review of Contemporary Fiction, spring, 1998, John Kulka, review of *Novels and Other Writings*, p. 221.

Saturday Review, May 13, 1933; May 20, 1939; May 11, 1957; June 27, 1970.

Spectator, July 19, 1968.

Studies in Short Fiction, spring, 1994, Richard P. Lynch, "Saints and Lovers: 'Miss Lonelyhearts' in the Tradition," p. 225; summer, 1996, Diane Long Hoeveler, "This Cosmic Pawnshop We Call Life: Nathaniel West, Bergson, Capitalism and Schizophrenia," p. 411.

Time, June 17, 1957; August 17, 1970.

Times Literary Supplement, January 24, 1958; April 11, 1958.

Washington Post, January 25, 1983.*

Author/Artist Index

The following index gives the number of the volume in which an author/artist's biographical sketch appears: